Pushing
the Envelope

Pushing the Envelope

Critical Issues in Education

Allan C. Ornstein

St. John's University

Upper Saddle River, New Jersey
Columbus, Ohio

Vice President and Publisher: Jeffery W. Johnston
Executive Editor: Debra A. Stollenwerk
Assistant Editor: Jessica Crouch
Editorial Assistant: Mary Morrill
Production Editor: Kris Robinson
Design Coordinator: Diane C. Lorenzo
Photo Coordinator: Sandy Schaefer
Cover Designer: Rokusek Design
Cover Image: Artville
Production Manager: Susan Hannahs
Director of Marketing: Ann Castel Davis
Marketing Manager: Krista Groshong
Marketing Coordinator: Tyra Cooper

This book was set in Berkeley Old Style (ITC) by Carlisle Communications, Ltd. It was printed and bound by R.R. Donnelley & Sons Company. The cover was printed by Phoenix Color Corp.

Photo Credits: Barbara Schwartz/Merrill, p. 15; Anne Vega/Merrill, pp. 63, 225; Anthony Magnacca/Merrill, p. 125; Ken Karp/PH College, p. 185.

Pearson Education Ltd.
Pearson Education Australia Pty. Limited
Pearson Education Singapore Pte. Ltd.
Pearson Education North Asia Ltd.
Pearson Education Canada, Ltd.
Pearson Educación de Mexico, S.A. de C.V.
Pearson Education–Japan
Pearson Education Malaysia Pte. Ltd.
Pearson Education, *Upper Saddle River, New Jersey*

10 9 8 7 6 5 4 3 2 1
ISBN 0-13-099090-6

Preface

Certain words and phrases used in education seem to creep into our daily professional lives, words such as *lesson plans, goals and objectives, critical thinking, classroom climate, high-stake testing,* and *standard-based education.* These catchwords and phrases take over our patterns of professional speech, as if they were almost indispensable. They invade our textbooks and conversations with colleagues. Indeed, they seem to grow stronger with repetition, making education textbooks and teacher conversation a special kind of ordeal—what some might call trite, pedantic, cliché, or boring.

The Approach of This Text

In writing this book, I have tried to stray from this conventional approach and have introduced a mix of crisp and peppy prose, pop culture, and imaginative and controversial conversation. The intent is to lighten the reading and appeal to the college-aged reader, to stimulate, irritate, and provoke the reader so he or she becomes genuinely engaged in the public debate about schooling.

This book represents a radical abandonment of the traditional text; its deliberate use of words, arguments, and sarcasm may be troublesome for some readers, but it is intended to result in a unique blend of controversial and serious discussions of important educational issues.

The book critiques and analyzes important issues in education. The issues are presented in a sort of pro–con debate style and in a highly descriptive, challenging, and controversial manner that is designed to encourage discussion, free expression, and reflective thought. The treatment of the issues is representative of a continuum of ideas or multiple perspectives—rather than an either/or philosophy or taking-sides type of debate. Sometimes the discussion is presented in a way that may remind some readers of a mix of *Hardball, The O'Reilly Factor,* and *Crossfire*—a back-and-forth chat that's in your face.

The Organization of This Text

Each chapter or issue is introduced with a conventional overview that provides background information and helps put the issues in perspective.

At the end of each chapter, there are seven questions designed to elicit critical thinking, ideas, and opinions. There are no right, wrong, or preferred answers to the questions. The last question in each chapter incorporates a library, Internet, or school-based activity. They are hands-on activities that extend beyond cognitive thought or intellectual speculation. Following these questions is a list of recommended readings, representing a mix of classic and current authors and books.

For readers who would like a research or theoretical base, there is an annotated reference section at the end of the book which locates and describes every educator and reference cited in the case studies. The short descriptions of each reference should be useful to the reader.

Some readers may argue that the book has too many chapters or issues. The idea is for professors and students to pick and choose the most relevant ones, based on their own needs, interests, and perspectives.

The Case Format

The text format is based on case studies and fictitious characters involved in lively dialogue; some of their comments are highly expressive and freewheeling. Remarks are purposely sprinkled throughout the text that go beyond polite and public conversation and represent effrontery and closet conversation. The characters inhabit a mixed world, representing mainstream parents, teachers, administrators, professors, and others. These characters exhibit multifaceted lives and extend their frame of reference beyond the boundaries of professional jargon and popular writing. Some of the characters are humdrum and colorless, others are polite and politically correct, and still others dissect things, raise issues, and exhibit a sharp intelligence.

The Issues

The topics or issues are relevant and represent the current focus of educational controversy. The arguments—and there are plenty of them for all kinds of people with all different types of opinions and positions—represent the entire political/social spectrum. The stories and subjects make us aware of different perspectives and force us to be honest about our own biases.

Nearly every political and social group in education is open to critical analysis in the book; this includes majority groups, disenfranchised groups, and special needs groups; it also includes political categories—conservative, liberal, reform, and radical; academic groups—perrenialists, essentialists, progressivists, reconstructionists, and existentialists; and theorists—scientific, technocratic, humanistic, artistic, and reconceptualist. In short, something is said for and against nearly every argument, position, or group in education.

The Audience

Some readers will be put off by the language, metaphors, and politics of the book. Other readers will be baffled by the double-meaning names and phrases that are possibly too clever, even cute. Still others will find it challenging and rewarding—and appreciate the no-nonsense style of conversations and the deductive constructs of the book. Some readers may find my wit and rhetorical ploys to be tiresome and frustrating, and others will find the approach to be fresh and imaginative. I do not expect to satisfy everyone.

This is not a book for someone who prefers to maintain a simple view of the ideas and issues that affect education. It is certainly not for a student or professor who prefers convention and plays it safe—somewhere in the middle—or prefers facts, routine knowledge, and common ideas.

This book is for the student who can think and make inferences from a combination of premises and perspectives and who is willing to reflect on various ideas and issues regardless of political correctness, personal perspective, or professional advantage. It is a book for someone who is hungry to push the education envelope.

Consider this to be a fun book and a serious book at the same time, written for the nimble and literate mind. Used on its own, the book is a valuable resource for a course on advanced foundations, education issues, curriculum or school reform, school policy, or a seminar for graduate students entering the profession. Used with another book, it can be a valuable supplement to a text in American educational, philosophical, historical, or social foundations.

Finally, if you have found this preface to be too silly, sarcastic, or downright stupid, you need not read any further. The book is not for you. If, however, you found some glimpse of wit or redeeming humor in it, or if you are intrigued by my analysis of the book, I advise you to read on.

Acknowledgments

Professors and authors incur obligations, but I feel my debt is heavier than most. First, I wish to acknowledge my new colleagues at St. John's University who have provided warm greetings and wonderful support and friendship. I am particularly grateful to Dean Jerry Ross, who provides a model for democratic leadership, fiscal integrity, and academic creativity. As my department chair, Dr. Gene Geisert (who is the ex-superintendent of the New Orleans school district) promotes a collegial and cooperative climate, free of bureaucratic restraints and paperwork. Some people call him the "old wise owl." He has been particularly generous in providing ample office space, free time, and secretarial support.

A note of thanks goes to my student typist, Leeanne G-Bowley, who not only had the fortitude and ability to decipher my handwriting (I am still writing the old-fashioned way with legal-size pad), but also displayed a traditional work ethic that is becoming increasingly difficult to find among young college students.

I owe a special debt of gratitude to the editors at Merrill. Allyson Sharp won me over with her blink, which I thought was a wink, as well as her smile at the AERA Convention, and provided prompt feedback and support which convinced me to sign with Merrill. Debra Stollenwerk kept her remarks to a minimum, but provided the necessary knowledge and experience for improving the manuscript. Jessica Crouch, as an assistant editor, had the smarts and faith to give me ample latitude to tweak the manuscript at the final stages. In the same vein, I would like to thank my reviewers, even the one who thought that the manuscript was a piece of sh–t, full of anti "this" and anti "that" and would burn the book before assigning it. Five of the seven reviewers gave it the green light, and two thought the manuscript was the best thing since sliced cheese was invented. The reviewers were Jason Earle, John Carroll University; Jeanne Ellsworth, Plattsburgh State University; Marilyn Howe, Clarion University of Pennsylvania; Kristi Johnson, Marymount University; Bob Krajewski, University of Wisconsin, La Crosse; Gayle Mindes, DePaul University; and Fred Muskal, University of the Pacific.

There is the debt one never manages to acknowledge fully, and no matter what you say, it is rarely enough to capture personal feelings and joy. Esther Miller, my fiancé, provided loving and psychological support, and for a guy at my age, this is an important priority as one ranks life experiences. My daughter Stacey, and my sons Joel and Jason, provided the spark needed to keep their dad's interest and imagination in forward drive. The three of them are characters in the book, with their designated first names.

Finally, after reading the book, if you have some pithy remarks that need saying, you may write to me at St. John's University, 8000 Utopia Parkway, Jamaica, New York, 11439.

About the Author

Allan C. Ornstein received his doctorate at New York University and teaches at St. John's University in New York. He has consulted for more than seventy-five government and educational agencies and published more than four hundred articles and forty books, including *Foundations of Education,* 8th edition, and *Curriculum: Foundations, Principles, and Issues,* 4th edition, which are among the leading books in their respective fields.

Contents

Introduction:
About the
Author's Intent

One of my graduate students, John Dough, came to my office one day and told me he had been given a manuscript by a man who had been my student about twenty years ago. This former student, who wished to remain anonymous, was now teaching at a private college somewhere between Mudd Puddle and Podunk.

Since the mystery author had read a few of my textbooks and felt I had some clout with publishers, Dough was instructed to give me the manuscript. He was convinced that I would enjoy the manuscript, since it was different from typical textbooks in which authors are required to walk the white line, down the middle, to avoid controversy and opinion. Although I was somewhat annoyed by the cloak-and-dagger conversation, I promised to read the manuscript.

The next day, I gave the manuscript to my colleague H. H. Mann, sometimes called H. H. or Herbert, who claimed to be a descendent of Horace Mann. H. H. was a former English teacher and editor, and I knew he would look to each syllable and sentence with great eagerness, that he could distinguish between jargon, hyperbole, and rhetoric. He had experience in dealing with those who pave new trails in print and talk the talk that few people talk. I was convinced he would have a few choice words about the manuscript, since it was experimental in that it toyed with the reader's imagination and intelligence (or lack thereof). Although the author seemed to have depth of knowledge, and mixed philosophy and history with current issues, I was unsure about some words and phrases—and whether something was being pointed out or inferred, or if nothing was being pointed out or inferred. As a person steeped in the English language, I was convinced Mann could add some nuggets of knowledge. He would understand the author's parables and parody and extrapolate beyond the written word.

Afterwards, I called Dough and pressed for the author's name. After much persuasion, he revealed that the author was J. Abner Gadfly, II. Gadfly refused to leave his address and phone number with my graduate student, and insisted that he would learn if the book was published by surfing the Internet, browsing the publishers' catalogs, and reading the reviews.

Gadfly told my graduate student he had written the manuscript during a one and a half year period while flying twice a month from Muddville Airport (which was twenty miles outside of Mudd Puddle) to Gotham City to visit family and friends. As a frequent flyer, Gadfly would upgrade to first class and order two to three drinks, usually cognac or red wine, and write his manuscript.

After about one hour in the friendly skies, he would become inebriated. Since he felt education was one-third babble, one-third gobbledygook, and one-third Mickey Mouse, it didn't really matter if he was a little tipsy—or that his prose, written on a legal-size pad, was slanted and running off the page. When Gadfly was lost for an idea, possibly a word or phrase, or if he just wanted to reflect, he would gaze out the window at the blue sky and moving clouds to help crystallize his thoughts. His purpose was to speak the brutal truth, regardless of political correctness or personal or professional advantage.

Apparently, Gadfly made it clear to Dough that most prominent educators, at the most prestigious colleges and universities, could not agree on philosophical issues, teaching methods, and learning principles. So, it didn't really matter if he introduced his own ideas on the subject—based on little scholarship, a little speculation, and a little wit. Most of the great theories and principles of education, he felt, were based on sketchy evidence or selective evidence advanced as objective evidence. While traditionalists proceeded with the idea that research and science proceeded cautiously from facts to theories, he believed that research and science started with bold speculation and proceeded with experimentation and controversy. Hopefully, people reading his book would understand that his suppositions and hypotheticals were written to stir up controversy and debate among readers. A lack of research or supportive evidence had never served to limit the number or fervor of advocates in any educational discussion, and in this regard he felt his manuscript was not unusual.

To ascertain whether his author was merely a pedagogical flash in the pan or a new bold author with fresh insights into education, I asked Dough to provide me with some more information about Gadfly. I admitted to Dough that I had never read or seen Gadfly's publications in professional journals, and I have never seen his name appear or heard him speak at any professional conference or symposium. I tried tracking the author down on the Internet and was unsuccessful. "He has no e-mail address and is not listed in any telephone book that I was able to find on the Internet," I told Dough. "I have checked with five or six professional friends from Seattle to Savannah and came up empty handed. One friend from Ohio State thought he might have studied with Harold Benjamin, and another friend from Columbia University thought he studied with Lawrence Cremin." Someone suggested I call Stanley Elam, the old editor of *Phi Delta Kappan,* because he knew all the old educational medicine men, charmers, and chieftains who wrote lively prose and could cite the difference between the science and art of teaching.

One of my colleagues thought Gadfly grew up on the shores of Rockaway, New York, or Asbury Park, New Jersey, and was related to Bruce Springsteen. Another colleague thought he met Gadfly in Las Vegas, playing blackjack and drinking chocolate milk, and my dean, Dr. Friendly, thought he met him in a bar in Beloit, WI, listening to country-western music—Johnny Cash, Willie Nelson and Merle Haggard. Even worse, about three days ago, when I was reading the manuscript in Starbucks, someone claimed that Gadfly was a character in *Moby Dick,* and the store manager thought he may have been a character, Nicky Arnstein, in the movie *Funny Girl.* Confused and somewhat bewildered, I pressed my graduate student for more information.

Dough said that the author believes that, since the manuscript is partially satiric and politically incorrect, its publication might be detrimental to his career; even worse, it would upset many readers and reviewers. The narrative relies more on wit than research, more on controversy and opinion than on facts and figures. However, I have been assured by Gadfly that the few facts and figures that are cited are valid. Nonetheless, the book would probably be considered journalistic trifle by many colleagues, since there are no footnotes, no tables or graphs, no tips for teachers, no summaries, and no conclusions. It is doubtful whether some of his colleagues would adopt the book because it would give Gadfly some recognition on his own campus. Moreover, it would validate a new political voice and new storytelling/case study technique that his colleagues might not be ready to accept.

I concluded that Gadfly had problems. "It appears that he works in a small place with small people who are concerned about small potatoes." However, I felt there were a sufficient number of professors across the country who would welcome this new approach—a controversial, freewheeling, honest book about educational issues. Anyone with a sense of humor would also be inclined to read the book.

My colleague H. H. Mann insisted that Gadfly was teaching at Hocus Pocus University and Hocus Pocus had its own limited vision of schooling which corresponded with an outdated bit of philosophical lore. Further, it was a misnomer to use the term *case studies* to describe the book. "What about *hypothetical discussions, reflections on education, hot topics,* or *issues in education*?"

"Frankly, I don't think it matters," I responded.

"I think there is a bigger problem," Mann remarked. "There are too many assertions that are questionable, based on little evidence or facts."

I answered, "It is up to the students to challenge the assertions and extreme opinions. More important, it is the professor's job to facilitate these matters with students, to get them to think about their own 'isms' and the 'isms' of others."

Dr. Mann refused to accept my viewpoint. "This author is too fast and loose with what he has his characters saying and the reader cannot easily discern what is credible or accurate."

"I'm not a Gadfly fan or follower," I responded, "but I get the feeling that the author intentionally makes 'wild and woolly' statements to provoke and annoy the reader. He exhibits a frank style of writing—exhibiting both contempt toward convention and courage to write what others silently think. It's a way of getting the juices flowing and fighting off the dullness and drowsiness that often plague many students who have to sit and listen to long lectures or read blah or boring textbooks."

Mann was also concerned that the book was politically incorrect, there were too many instances of overkill, and that students would be unable to separate reality from fiction, or when the author was serious or joking. "Even worse, the book is sure to offend many professors who believe in one 'ism' or another 'ism.'"

"Listen, professors get into a discussion in which almost every public issue becomes an argument or a war of words and ideas. Although there are a few professors walking around with hobo or Mohawk haircuts and red-band visors, there are a sufficient number of independent thinkers who welcome unusual speculation and enjoy rocking down the river and zigzagging down a different trail."

"I don't fully understand your idea. Are you referring to some new postmodern theory which permits or encourages this type of hoopla."

"Let me move my thoughts to center stage. Gadfly is trying to rattle the reader's mind, just like many professors try to rattle their students' minds—to get them to think."

"But there are no footnotes," asserted Mann, "and no way of proving or disproving the essence of the ideas and theories in the book."

"I do not have this obsessive concern for surface detail; ideas are more important than facts. Frankly I would rather enjoy a book and have a good laugh—and not belabor over names, dates, and places, what some experts might call essential knowledge or functional literacy."

"Anyway," interrupted Dough, "I'm glad you support Gadfly because he has entrusted you with an important responsibility—to see if you can help publish his book. He hopes it will be used in many different courses, especially in introductory and advanced education foundation courses, as well as education issues and curriculum courses. Gadfly envisioned the book as a supplement or main text for the purpose of encouraging discussion and exchange of ideas."

"I'm sick of this Gadfly," asserted Mann. "In fact, I don't believe this is his real name. He is no gadfly! I think he is just trying to be funny and hip with young readers and encourage them to glaze over the real issues in education. There is just not enough factual information to enable the reader to formulate research-based or properly supported opinions. What we need is an in-depth analysis of the issues—not a book that glosses over topics or insults the reader with overgeneralized and politically charged statements."

"There you go again with the need for research and citations. Gadfly has an annotated reference section at the end of the book, which is more helpful than a bunch of footnotes. The point is, Gadfly gets you angry, and that is part of the rationale for the book. Most students are tired of reading so-called in-depth textbooks which often drag on and on and put students asleep. Students count the pages of these books before they start reading each chapter—to discern how much medicine they must endure. The idea is to get their medicine over with as soon as possible, that is, to skim or skip parts of their reading assignment."

I continued, "Perhaps the writing is a little glib and contains too much sarcasm and tongue-and-cheek statements. But I think the book is designed for this purpose: to create controversy and excitement among students and make protagonists of them. The book represents a radical abandonment of the usual textbook."

"Well, I have trouble with the author's sarcasm. It's hard, in some places, to discern just what he is actually trying to accomplish; in fact, I think he has strayed off the maps and charts in places," said Mann.

"H. H., it appears we disagree. I find the author's writing to be clear and crisp, written at a level for all students to easily comprehend, analyze, and discuss in class. The messages are sometimes abstract, sometimes witty, sometimes provocative. But the content and style are designed to provoke, even upset people—in short, to get students involved in dialogue and debate."

"I feel the author should have identified himself as one of the characters in each chapter or in some way deal with his own biases," responded Mann.

"The challenge is for the professors to remind the students that the author is not acting as an authority, rather as a provocateur. The book is designed as a discussion starter and the content provides both historical and current information about each topic," I remarked. "I think his biases change with the topic, and it is very difficult to label Gadfly."

"I still think that Gadfly does not address the key issues," Mann insisted. "There is no attempt to present specific research to support the various opinions and positions. Much of the information is based on polymetrics and political rhetoric—and designed to insult and incite."

"If the material weren't so provocative, no one would care, including you, Herbert."

"Overlooking the author's politics and parodic style, I still find the author's rhetorical ploys and so-called wit to be tiresome, frustrating, and politically charged. Under the guise of pushing the envelope, he veers off the edge. He may think he is cute, but I find some of his statements to be pointless and silly."

"Well, I enjoy the author's parody—as a test of one's intelligence—with its subtle etymons, obvious puns, political statements, self-indulgent digressions, and names that remind me of old-time sports figures, food, and other odd objects. I find myself amused at many points by the author's nimble prose and references to pop culture, what appears to be an attempt to lighten the reading and appeal to the college-aged reader."

"If the author weren't so flippant, I wouldn't be so angry. Even worse, I feel this author is reactionary at times. I wouldn't be surprised if he were some card-carrying member of some paramilitary organization or right-wing club."

"Maybe he owns a pickup truck and maybe he has pinko leanings and Marxist memorabilia in his office. Maybe he is a food junkie and maybe he thinks there is magic or marijuana in the air. Who cares?"

"It's a matter of research, scholarship, and political correctness," answered Mann.

"Gadfly is mocking this type of technocratic talk; therefore, readers may find the book uncomfortable and be unwilling to test its ideas in the public arena. Without supporting documentation, here and there and everywhere, Gadfly may throw some professors into a tizzy.

"Herbert, through your political and social lens, you see his opinions as faulty or unsubstantiated. However, other people might see it as a point/counterpoint or a reflective treatise in education. Gadfly uses, in fact, some of the same narrow stereotypes and inflammatory language as do some political radicals, critical theorists, and postmodernists, but in reverse. Herb, the problem is that you feel uncomfortable with Gadfly's arguments and opinions. You are unwilling but he is willing to discuss ideas in an open forum which sounds mean spirited or politically incorrect."

"You are wrong," responded Mann. "The point is, we don't need anyone mocking the disenfranchised and disadvantaged groups in America, nor do we need people who misconstrue or simplify educational issues so as to increase selfishness and injustices within our community."

"Dr. Mann, as far as I'm concerned, you are one dimensional in your viewpoint, void of humor, perhaps too angry to understand—like so many other cultural warriors. Gadfly is purposely using narrow stereotypes, sarcasm, and simplified statements to discuss issues that are important for teachers but rarely discussed honestly in public. He is relying on dialogue and overstated assertions to make his point, to encourage discussion, to stimulate free expression of ideas. Instead of citing party line or publicly acceptable conversation, he is pushing debate and forcing us to air some of our passionate and strident opinions which characterize our closet conversations. No question he is adding fuel to the political and cultural fires raging among academic critics; some of us might even say that he represents the so-called 'bad guys' or 'ugly guys' in the battle of ideas. But I like what he has to say; it is written with arresting verve and vitality."

At this point Dough interrupted our dialogue. "I apologize for my intrusion but I feel the author is a moderate—merely trying to introduce shades of gray in context with many controversial subjects. He is certainly unapologetic—a free spirit and a person who cannot be bullied or hushed, bought, or persuaded by the political left or right. His specialty, throughout the book, is his willingness to flaunt convention, whether left, right, or even center—to use satirical conversation and to state frankly what others think but rarely say or endorse in public."

"Personally, I think the author, this Gadfly, is a dreamer or some kind of revisionist educator trying to take advantage of the case study approach. I see no need to concoct fictitious characters and silly episodes. Why not have students read about John Dewey or John Goodlad?" commented Mann. "Why read about Dillie Lilly, Harriet Hamburger, Yegor Dubinin, or Abba Dabba-do—and other fictitious names that confuse the reader?"

After Mann finished, I turned to Dough to see if he had any clue as to why Gadfly used so many foreign-sounding, ethnic names in the text. "I don't know," was his response.

Mann, then asserted: "My students will laugh at, even worse, get lost with the various ethnic names; they slow down and confuse the reader. At best, the names sound like a roster in the U.N."

"The rosters in my class coincide, to a large extent, with the names in the text," I responded. "America has always been a nation of many nations, and that appears to be the message. You may find these ethnic names tedious and boring, not funny or relevant; nonetheless, they reflect the new wave of immigration and the subsequent educational landscape that is finding its way into American schools. It may not be happening in Wyoming, Iowa, or South Dakota, but it is a fact within the major metropolitan centers: California, Florida, Texas, New York—where the political and voting power resides."

Dough interrupted, "Can I ask you a question?"

"Of course. The Socratic dialogue is essential in higher education."

"What chance does the text have for success? As an experienced author, you must have some thoughts on the subject."

"Since the textbook market is fickle, many bad books drive out good books. Some publishers go on fishing expeditions, not sure whether they have a winner or loser, so they don't invest too much money in the first edition. One thing is sure, however. As a professor and author, I can say this is a different kind of book—guaranteed to turn off some and turn on others."

"Since Gadfly's text is different, what chance does it have for success? Can you hypothesize with any degree of confidence?"

"Let's be frank. We educators observe, administer tests, and tally scores on hundreds of thousands of subjects. With all the new computer software, we can generate hundreds of correlations about almost any topic, and many at the .01 confidence level. It's all a matter of counting beans and how you want to use the beans to represent the data you are collecting."

"You know," said Dough, "I had a research professor who was convinced that everything related to education could be measured and counted. If it could not, then it had little value. We even learned to separate unknown factors from unknown effects and learned the differences between dependent variables, independent variables, and extraneous variables. The idea was to make the course as difficult as possible to impress the professors of arts and science. Still, his colleagues from other fields attacked the course as 'fluff and bluff.'"

"I feel sorry for this professor. Doesn't he realize that his stress on numbers and statistics is a masculine model and based on 'gendered' metaphors. He should introduce more storytelling and collaborative writing, which is a feminine approach."

"This discussion is leading to gender stereotypes and gender hysteria," claimed Mann. "I prefer that we leave the sexual euphemisms out of professional work; in fact, some of our colleagues may think this conversation borders on a 'thought crime.'"

"H. H., I believe you are becoming a wiser, more intelligent, and sensitive man," I said. "But Dough's original point should be the focus of our intention. There are professors who teach education courses and make them more abstract and theoretical, and less practical, to impress their colleagues or students. They use special terminology like *epistemology* and *axiology* that few people understand and split hairs over special ideologies such as *pragmentation* and *progressivism, conservativism* and *neoconservatism,* or *postmodernism* and *post–postmodernism*. Although there is no agreement or meaning, they fearlessly plunge into classroom discussions and teach those doctrines as guiding principles for school reform."

"Are you criticizing philosophical thought or critical thinking?" asked Mann. "Or are you being cute? Are you really sincere about my intelligence and sensitivity? Personally, I think your glasses are crooked."

"I didn't mean to insult you. Believe me, I think you organize your subject logically, provide a real progressive spirit in the classroom, and make the subject difficult enough to earn the respect of all your colleagues. Most important, the articles you publish are in refereed journals. So long as you are polite and smile at your colleagues you should get a merit raise."

"I resent your attitude," remarked Mann. "It's the same attitude that Gadfly exemplifies: the way he talks about rural America—Muddville, Mudd Puddle, and Podunk; the way he describes education—Mickey Mouse and gobbledygook; his criticism of prestigious colleges and educators; that theories and principles of education are based on sketchy evidence; that the text was written when he was under the influence of alcohol; and that he includes every ethnic name under the sun in an attempt to be cute or relevant."

Mann continued, "You seem to have the same bizarre attitude as the author—what you have mislabeled as humor or wit. From my perspective, the book encourages shallow understanding of educational issues, rather than in-depth understanding of the issues. It fosters tiresome, not provocative, reading; contrived conversations, not engaging dialogue. Finally, the book is offensive and politically insensitive to people who identify themselves as belonging to a political or oppressed minority group. You even make the same flawed assumptions about the book that the author does; that is, the book will stimulate discussion and free expression in class."

"Herbert, let me quickly get to the bottom line. Your opinions reflect your own political biases and lack of humor. Gadfly is attempting to stir the pot and push the envelope for the purpose of discussion and debate. Some of the content may be too abstract for the average freshman or sophomore student, and some of the conversations by the characters may involve mental leaps that will escape unsophisticated readers, but I think we need to give our students the benefit of the doubt. Some students may never have heard of a few terms in the book we professors take for granted, such as *Sputnik* or the War on Poverty, and they may never have seen some of the TV programs mentioned by the author such as *Ozzie and Harriet* and *Father Knows Best*, but all of them have views on issues which deal with vouchers, accountability, sex education, bilingual education, gifted education, global education, inclusion, homogeneous grouping, and tracking. And this is what the book is about—issues that confront American teachers."

Mann responded, "The book merely encourages student glibness. Their personal feelings and attitudes count more than facts or research-based opinions. Anything goes. It is not a matter of perspective or politics, as you infer, rather the content is superficial and simplistic—also inflammatory."

"I understand your concerns, and they represent a legitimate professional voice. However, the book is written so that the content means whatever the reader wants it to mean and supports whatever opinion he or she wants to support: that, I argue, is a strength of the book. The topics are politically charged, but on purpose. The idea of the book is to expose students to various sides of an argument, to have them reflect and make professional choices and decisions."

"The most conservative students and most liberal students, as well as students who seek the middle ground, will find enough statements and opinions to represent their views. The professor doesn't need to change students' opinions, and one course alone is insufficient. The need is for students to learn to use logical and rational reasoning to support their own arguments, to respect competing opinions, and to see the other sides of numerous positions. There are many topics and issues that can be examined and reexamined."

"The goal is to find productive compromises during class discussion, not to wage argumentive warfare or a turn-back-the-clock orthodoxy. This means finding a way to work out differences and build coalitions among those who represent politically different continuums: Those who perceive themselves as radicals, on some mission to dethrone the existing system, and those who are labeled as conservatives, bent on promoting a laissez-faire approach to reinforce life's unfairness."

"I think it's quackery," asserted Mann.

"Come on, Herbert, you need to get with it—lighten up or sow some oats. Don't take me so literally. Remember King Lear who recommended that we kill all the lawyers? He was really talking about doing away with the system of justice; lawyers were secondary."

"Do you think the readers will appreciate the book or make these mental leaps?" asked Dough.

"That's tough to answer. I think the author makes an attempt to reach out to the serious and not so serious minded, to the older, intellectual, hippy, and artsy crowd, as well as the younger, semi-intellectual, straight, and techno generation, to all types, sizes, and shades, to those who enjoy reading Henrik Ibsen or John Grisham or listening to Andrea Bocelli or Eminem."

"Personally, I'm a Marilyn Manson fan," remarked Dough, "and prefer the more juicy stories of Stephen King or Dean Koontz."

Mann responded, "This discussion brings new meaning to the concept of scholarly research and writing in education—the style to which is not witty or urbane but rather silly and somewhat deplorable. It really proves that most of us have done our most serious and best reading by age twenty-five—and maybe our best living, too."

"You don't expect middle-aged teachers and professors, especially with soft and pudgy bellies, to admit to this possibility—do you?"

"You miss the point," asserted Mann. "This discussion has more to do with fantasy than fact. I'd rather be teaching my undergraduate students what should have been learned in high school than listen to this academic dribble."

"I wish you could lighten up and smell the roses. King and Koontz are in, so is Eminem. Once it was 'Elvis the Pelvis,' Jimmy Dean, and Jack Kerouac. If you go back further, it was Humphrey Bogart, the Platters, and Joltin' Joe. Revisionists arguments are both inevitable and constructive, producing endless debates about society's heroes and yearnings for reform."

Commented Mann, "If I can appeal to reason, the book is one big exaggeration, just like the discussion, and you're acting like some old professor trying to hang on to your youth. You're like one of our colleagues down the hall who wears shorts and sandals during summer school and thinks he is cool. I mean the guy is fifty-five or sixty years old, and he should know better. His stomach is too big and his legs are too thin."

"Let me put it in terms you might appreciate," I responded. "The book, I believe, is for the high-minded crowd who grew up on a steady diet of John Dewey, George Counts, and Robert Hutchins, as well as for the quickie-book reader who counts pages and prefers lots of photos and quick-and-easy-to-read prose."

"What about all the tangential remarks that I find meaningless and pointless," Mann responded.

"There are breaks and pauses in the book that are designed to make the reader chuckle. The author expects readers to know that Joltin' Joe is Joe DiMaggio, not some boxer, musical group, or some unknown character in a Stephen King novel; that Sputnik is not some down-home salad dressing or chic downtown café, but part of the Cold War period with the former Soviets that led to the beefing up of the curriculum (Chapter 2); that DNA is not an Irish rock band, but U2 is (Chapter 10); *YM* is not a candy bar or part of the YMCA, but a fashion magazine (Chapter 10), and *Quake* and *Doom* (Chapter 11) are not part of the Junior Great Books program, rather they are video games played by young students at home that compete with homework time. The reader should also know that Machiavelli and Carole King (Chapter 17) are not educators, and that the original Pepsi generation had a few wrinkles and gray hairs but that guppies are graying yuppies (Chapter 21), etc. It is this type of tongue-in-cheek wit that represents the not-so-serious part of the book and creates a very different type of book."

Mann responded: "The book has no scientific or theoretical basis. It's merely a bunch of characters talking gibberish."

"Words that seem to be gibberish for some people may have special meaning to others; smoke signals, algebraic symbols, or Mandarin may be dubious or meaningless for the majority, but they represent a means of communication for a sizable minority."

"I also think there are too many topics in the book to cover in one term," said Mann.

"The object is to select the ones of most interest. There is a host of topics and issues—an endless stream of arguments and positions in education which can be discussed and debated in class. Professors who are willing to take risks, and students who are honest with their opinions, can do a lot with this book."

At this point my graduate student asked: "Given the content and purpose of the book, what kind of guy do you think Gadfly is?"

"Anyone reading the manuscript gets the impression that Gadfly is a khaki kind of guy, not a French-cuff shirt and tuxedo guy—nor a guy who wears boots and earrings—nor dresses in black. He reminds me of some guy who used to drink tequila daisies in Tijuana."

"Is that Hemingway?" asked Dough.

"No, Hemingway used to drink margaritas in Barcelona."

"Who are you talking about?"

"Some guy named Peddiwell."

"Professor, did you ever find out where Gadfly teaches? Boy, would I like to sit in one of his classes. I bet he is a stitch, maybe even a hoot."

"I called all the colleges and universities around Mudd Puddle and Podunk. I even checked with Muddville, Pouhwheepsy, and Poughkeepsie, in the event there was a communication gap or misunderstanding with you and Gadfly. I also checked with several professors and professional associations. I cannot locate Gadfly. I think there is no evidence that Gadfly exists or ever existed.

"Now, Mr. Dough, tell me the truth: Did you write the book? Is the manuscript a product of someone's lectures, cut and pieced together? Did Dr. Mann put you up to this? Did someone really write this book on an airplane? Does someone still use legal-size pads to write a book?"

"Professor, let me answer your questions with a question: Where is your computer?"

"I don't have one."

"You're kidding. You mean it's being repaired."

"No! Within a few years half of all the people who word process on computers for more than two hours a day will complain of some form of carpal tunnel syndrome or repetitive stress injury, from numb fingers to inflamed wrists. I would rather not risk CTS or RSI. The recovery period, at my age, would take much longer than at your age."

"Professor, you sound a little irrational, if I may be so blunt."

"I'll tell you the truth. People sometimes refer to me as a dinosaur, others a saber-tooth tiger. Computers stifle my thinking process, particularly my creativity."

"Wow, how have you been able to write so many books?"

"You can't let the little things get you down."

"Like what?"

"Well, my ex still thinks I'm a jerk. I recently moved and now live next to an unsocialized kid who wears six earrings and can spell *constructivism* backwards and my new colleague in the adjacent office comes by each day to tell me about the theory of race, class, and gender and how it has supplanted education among younger professors. I hear the categories as one angry word, *raceclassgender,* and unsuccessfully try to refer to the old philosophy of reconstructionism and pre-postmodernism."

"I didn't realize that some professors become immersed with their ideas in the slavish pursuit of 'truth,'" asserted Dough. "With so many distractions, how are you able to write and publish so much?"

"I would rather not get too personal, but if you were fifty years old or more, you would know what I'm talking about. I'll just say: flax seed oil, soy, and vitamin E help, so does red wine, and plenty of exercise in horizontal and vertical positions."

"That is quite profound. What do you recommend I try first so I can start writing as soon as I finish my degree? Should I start with flax seed oil, possibly red wine? How about a compromising position—say a forty-five-degree angle?"

"Mr. Dough, the flax seed oil and wine are for *guppies*—people of my generation who used to be called *yuppies.* As for exercise, the best I have been able to do is a fifteen-degree angle—and that's on the treadmill.

"If you must have advice, and as you know I hate giving advice: The sky is the limit, when your heart is in it."

"What does that mean?"

"It means you have to want to do it, make a schedule and stick to it—no excuses unless you ache and can't get out of bed."

"That sounds a little too simple, professor. There must be more to writing a good book."

"Not really."

"I'm beginning to understand now how Gadfly could have used a legal-size pad to write the book," remarked Dough.

"Gadfly's book, or whoever wrote it, focuses on ideas and issues which in the long run will make the reader think more than any five-hundred- or six-hundred-page textbook, with glossy pages and colorful print, on a little of this and a little of that."

"Then I suppose Gadfly's manuscript should be a breath of fresh air," declared Dough.

"Maybe. Gadfly's manuscript forces both professors and students to come out of the closet and discuss many issues they are reluctant to examine in class. It requires people to take a position, at least to explore provocative ideas and positions without fudging. But some of the comments are off center and purposely desgined to upset some readers. It will be interesting to see how the book is received—considered as fluff and bluff or accepted in the marketplace of ideas, possibly a *succès d'estime.* And, we will only know, many years from now, if there will be other editions."

"Professor, one last question. It's really an afterthought. To what extent do you think Gadfly is different from other professors who write textbooks?"

"I don't know. Perhaps his irony and parodies are used to mask his own language mutilation and what Dr. Mann would refer to as his light research and simplistic dialogue. Some of us may view Gadfly as the Forrest Gump of education, others may view him as a cultural artifact akin to Cyclops or the Archie Bunker crowd, and still others may view him as a silly or even sinister deluder who should be run out of town like Ichabod Crane—on a horse with a pumpkin smashed on his head. Still others may liken Gadfly's book to one of Borges's *ficciónes*—to be amused by and to demonstrate the errors of our ways."

"Personally," I added, "I don't believe Gadfly can be characterized as belonging to the huntin', fishin', shootin' conservative crowd, or graduating from elite schools such as Andover or Harvard and believing that his private diaries are worth publishing, or as a card-carrying member of the liberal or intellectual group which reads *Atlantic Monthly, Harpers,* or *New Republic.* I would like to think he is like most professors, somewhere in the center and averse to extreme views and political dogma. The only discerning differences between Gadfly and other professors is he flies first class and still uses a legal-size pad to write his manuscripts."

"He seems to be quite independent and unconcerned about what others say about him," declared Dough.

"That's because he is probably tenured. As for not caring, most of us, including Gadfly, like to be stroked here and there, and sometimes here more than there."

"What are you trying to say? What does all this have to do with the author's judgments and practices, or his vignettes about education?" asked Mann.

"To keep it short and simple—the old KISS theory—I liked the book."

"You are acting like some professors I know, dodging direct questions and responding with pedantic language and intellectual banter."

"Let me apologize without admitting any guilt. Given the knotty plot of problems in education, and all the education commentators and critics hell bent on improving schools and society, Gadfly's satirical dialogue and didactic descriptions of teachers and schools are intellectually challenging and delightful."

"His so-called cool and cute prose fools no one with half a brain or anyone equipped with basic knowledge of the field," asserted Mann. "His book is a study of silliness and intellectual gobbledygook; it will lead to the intellectual impoverishment of course work, which in turn will lead to the unflattering assessment of teacher education."

"I've heard that argument before, some forty years ago, made by James Conant and James Koerner," I responded.

"That's true," declared Mann. "In fact, we still hear the same concerns today."

"Well, I think Gadfly clearly strikes a nerve at the heart of education. His jests are a welcome relief, given all the serious discussions in all the textbooks in education. We have enough serious textbook writers and angry critics in education. We have an oversupply of education hawks and parents and politicians who claim to know more about teaching than teachers themselves."

"Are you now criticizing all the critics of education?" asked Mann.

"Just the angry ones and extremists who put all the blame on teachers and teacher education, and wish to burn down schools or deschool society. These critics may represent five or ten percent of university people and education critics, but the remaining ninety or ninety-five percent who support our teachers and schools remain silent or are rarely heard because they tend to go along with the Establishment. Gadfly, at least, is willing to put all groups to a test with his challenging dialogue."

"We can go on forever. I think the readers would like to save time and get their medicine over with as quickly as possible. Can we end this discussion and let the readers decide on the merits of the book?"

"Sometimes, H. H., I wish you were a little more refined and uppercrust. You are constantly scoffing at the words and phrases of Gadfly. After all, if not for the likes of Gadfly, who else would confront us with the uncomfortable truths and hot-blooded 'isms' of education?"

"If you want to talk about truth, the truth is, I have resented the advantage you have had as the narrator of this introduction. You have set the tone and determined the course of the discussion about the book."

"But a good navigator is supposed to set the course of direction."

"I said narrator. And I was talking about Gadfly, and not *Moby Dick* or some ship of fools," responded Mann.

"Who knows Gadfly better? No one seems to have heard of him. At least, he was my student some time ago."

"It's been twenty years. You couldn't pick him out of a crowd of five people. He is an inconspicuous, unknown figure, teaching in the middle of nowhere."

"I resent your implications about small towns. You know good people do come from West Liberty and Wilmette, as well as from Podunk. Moreover, for all you know, Gadfly could be Dough or me."

"What happened to Rae?" interrupted Dough.

"You mean Ray. He retired two years ago. Remember, he was the professor who tried to defend his *Playboy* magazine collection as literary works. He had stacked more than 100 copies on his bookshelf, right in view of his graduate students."

"Professor, I was thinking of Rae and about the musical play, *The Sound of Music*."

"I can't take this dialogue anymore," declared Mann. "We are at a bottleneck. I, for one, feel you have lured me into the discussion as an expert and then turned me into a hostage so you could develop this introduction, and get into a mindless conversation with your graduate student."

"Well, every critic and every expert in the field unearth material that some dismiss and others welcome. I must confess I have had no intentions to toss you into a pit or seize you as a hostage. But I have enjoyed this little playful and paradoxical introduction."

"Is this my curse for being your colleague?"

"You are missing the point. This book needs to be read, analyzed, and debated. Actually, analyzed and debated may be too soft a phrase—it should be disputed and quarreled over. I hope every student will become part of the fracas."

"You realize, that after Chapter 2, this book becomes R rated, and some of the dialogue could be entered in the sport of education curmudgeons and pop-piffle speech."

"Professor, are you making a reference to education jargon?" asked Dough.

"I think Gadfly may, in between his purposeful-sounding expressions."

"What about you?"

"Well there are a lot of average Joe and Jane Doakes living out there between Mudd Puddle and Gotham City. These readers should have some thoughts. And, you know there are lots of wise professors who talk about the great mysteries of education. I'll let them decide for they like to keep on their intellectual toes and read the latest technical reports, and expand the knowledge base."

"As we search for knowledge and expand our horizons," said Mann, in a serious tone, "one must also understand that the new vision of today inevitably becomes the old vision of tomorrow. Similarly, this book, no matter how cutting edge, will eventually lose its magic status."

"You're right, H. H. It happened to Ozzie and Harriet; it happened to Johnny and Willie, even to George and Ringo. It could happen to anyone, and almost anything. When was the last time one of your education students read a book by John Dewey or Jean Piaget? Do you think our students remember more than fifty percent of the textbook titles or authors of the books they read last year?"

"Who are Johnny and Willie?" asked Dough.

"Ah, I can see you're not a country-western fan. Not knowing about Johnny and Willie, in most circles, is worse than not knowing about John and Jean."

Dr. Mann responded, "This whole dialogue reminds me of *Animal Farm*. Let's move on to the chapters and let the readers judge—whether they reject or accept the book and whether they view the author as a great pretender or as someone who has something worthwhile to say that needs to be said."

I
Philosophical/Social Foundations

Philosophizing About Philosophy

Philosophy is central to education because the philosophy advocated or reflected by a particular school district or school influences the goals or aims, content, and organization of the curriculum. Usually, schools lean toward a particular philosophy, but the teachers who implement the goals and curriculum reflect various philosophies. Studying philosophy not only allows us to better understand schools and their curricula, but also to deal with our own personal perceptions, beliefs, and values—the way we perceive the world and what we define as important.

Philosophy has always affected schools and society. Contemporary society, and the schools in it, are always changing, sometimes rapidly, certainly much more so than in the past. The special urgency that dictates continuous appraisal and reappraisal calls for a philosophy of education.

Philosophy enters into every important decision about curriculum, teaching, instruction, and testing. When an educational official or policy maker calls for stiffer standards, or emphasis of a particular course of study or content area, this represents a philosophy. The methods and materials a teacher chooses to use in a classroom reflect a professional judgment, which reflects philosophy. When a teacher decides to increase the homework load or assign a particular author, he or she is acting on the basis of philosophy. In short, choices reflect philosophy—and whether we recognize our own philosophy in education, it is out there and it influences our behavior and attitudes in classrooms and schools. Philosophy then operates overtly and covertly, whether we know that it is operating or not.

ISSUES

After reading the works of John Dewey, Robert Hutchins, E. D. Hirsch, and Paulo Freire among others for their philosophy of education course, the students—for their final paper—were asked the question "Why?"

It was the last day of class. Students were handing in their papers; the length varied from fifteen to twenty printed pages. No one had the imagination, wisdom, or guts to answer "Why not?"

For the remaining period, Professor Robert Hill asked his students to summarize their beliefs and attitudes about the importance of philosophy and their own philosophy of education.

Joel Chase, who was a science education major, was the first to volunteer. "Most schools have a philosophy that describes what they are about and what they are trying to achieve. Philosophy is reflected in the school's mission statement, if it has one, or in its goals of education. A school's philosophy is one of the first things state departments of education and accrediting agencies look at and assess when evaluating a school. Philosophy sets the direction of the school; it provides a frame of reference or a focus for students and teachers to follow."

Chase then pointed out that he was strongly influenced by the ideas of Mann, Dewey, and Kilpatrick. "I hope to teach in a progressive school where students share responsibility in curriculum planning, critically think and engage in inquiry-based learning, and participate in field-based trips and cooperative learning groups. Perhaps I am young and naive. If a school's philosophy differed widely from my own, then I would not want to teach in that school."

"Although most of us have some philosophy of education," commented Melena Rodriguez, "most of us in the class are still not aware of our own philosophy. We are all not like Joel, who seems sure about his philosophy. We are in our formative years as teachers, and we lack a definite set of beliefs about what knowledge and values are important, or how students best learn. Most of us in class have spent little time trying to clarify our philosophy; rather we read about the philosophy of others. Some of us even feel the course had little to do with helping us become better teachers, because there was little practical or how-to-do discussions."

Professor Hill responded, "You express two concerns; the first is common. A philosophy of education consists of what you believe is important about education, especially with regard to teaching and learning. You're not expected, after one or two courses in education, to have a clear set of values: to know what knowledge is most important, or to have a firm set of pedagogical principles. In fact, many teachers, if not most, are eclectics, that is, they do not have a precise philosophy of education and select ideas from various philosophies for their own classroom practices."

"Now for your second concern: Just how practical the course was," continued Professor Hill. "I think it is a matter of appreciating the big picture as opposed to learning tiny pieces of information which may or may not be helpful in limited situations. It is a matter of exploring and thinking about educational beliefs and ideas as opposed to learning do's and don'ts or tips on teaching. Some of the ideas we discussed have been around for centuries, and they influence schooling and society in America. To expect yourself to fully understand or appreciate every philosophy we have discussed is to expect what few of my colleagues are capable of doing."

"Can you elaborate a little more about the notion of eclecticism?" asked Nargis Punjwani, who was majoring in elementary education.

"I can, but I would rather you or someone else in the class discuss this idea," said Professor Hill. "What about you, Sam?"

"I'm not sure."

"Try your best," responded Hill.

"Is it like a teacher who contends that knowledge best exists in the classics, an essentialist belief, while believing that some answers come from within and through self-consciousness, an existentialist belief, and some are best derived from problem-solving and hands-on activities, a progressive idea?"

Professor Hill responded, "Not bad. Are you asking or telling the class?"

"Telling the class."

"Good. Can we improve your answer?" replied Hill.

"I'm not sure," said Sam.

"Nargis, what is your opinion about the first part of Sam's response?" asked the Professor.

She responded that the perennialists, not the essentialists, believed in the classics as the best source of knowledge, whereby Professor Hill briefly complimented her and went on to elaborate. "Most teachers, I believe, do not adopt one philosophy of education—that is, a strong set of beliefs systematized into a consistent framework. Rather, they are eclectics. Let's move on."

"Why is philosophy important?" asked Professor Hill.

Three students raised their hands, but Hill called on sophomore student Satoko Yamada, who did not volunteer. Yamada replied: "Philosophy gives meaning to our decisions and actions. In the absence of philosophy, the teacher is vulnerable to externally imposed prescriptions, fads and frills, to authoritarian schemes, and to what you refer to in class as 'isms' and extremism."

"Good," asserted Professor Hill. "But it sounds like a textbook answer. Now what does that mean in your own words?"

"Philosophy helps us search out answers to important questions about life. Without philosophy, we can easily be swayed by others, by extreme or silly viewpoints. Without educational philosophy, we lack direction in the classrooms and schools."

"How does Dewey enter into the picture about philosophy?" asked Hill.

There was no response, no volunteers from the students.

"Let me help you out," responded Hill. "Dewey was so convinced of the importance of philosophy that he viewed it as an all-encompassing aspect of the educational process—as necessary for 'forming fundamental dispositions, intellectual and emotional, toward nature and fellow man.' If one accepts this conclusion, it becomes evident that many aspects of teaching, if not most of the educational processes in school, are developed around philosophy. Even if we believe that Dewey's point is an overstatement, we should still recognize the pervasiveness of philosophy in determining our views of reality, what knowledge and values are worthwhile, decisions in education in general, and what is right and wrong with schools in particular, and even society if we wish to expand the discussion."

"Professor, since it is the last day in class, would you finally tell the class your preferred philosophy of education?" asked one of the students in the back of the room.

"I usually expect students to answer questions posed by their classmates. However, I like your question, so I will be brief and modify my routine," stated Hill. "My position is that no single philosophy, old or new, politically right or left, should serve as the exclusive guide for making decisions about schools. All philosophical groups examined in this course want the same thing, that is, they wish to improve the educational process, to enhance the achievement of learners, to produce better and more productive citizens, and to improve society. Because of their different views of reality, values and knowledge, however, proponents of particular philosophies find it difficult to agree on how to achieve these ends."

Hill paused and then added one comment. "Finally, it needs to be affirmed that philosophy without morality, or law without justice, is dangerous. It can lead to ideology, even extremism, whereby the rights of the individual are squashed by the mob, even worse by the state. And, we can invent all kinds of reasons and rationales for reducing the rights of the individual—for looking the other way, even for participating, as long as we have food on our table."

Ms. Rodriguez, who was majoring in bilingual education, spoke up: "That sounds a little like the history and politics of Western civilization since the decline of ancient Greece. It certainly characterizes medieval Europe, industrialized Europe, and twentieth-century Europe—with all its conquests and colonies, its wars and 'isms.' The birth of the thirteen colonies and the westward expansion of America is predominantly rooted in European traditions of war, racism, and the conquest of weaker races."

Hill responded, "Your point is provocative, and I'd rather not end the course on such a sour note. If I was a pessimist, if I wanted to turn memory into travesty, I could focus on famine, pestilence, war, ethnic hatred, 'final solutions,' and all the thousands of victims of war. I could fill all the bookshelves in our college library with the history of man's inhumanity to humanity. The entire world, including Third World and Eastern civilizations, has a history of slavery, barbarianism, peasantry, serfdom, indentured servants, and overwhelming poverty. The masses have always lived in the shadows of the monarchy and nobility, now called the politically powerful and capitalist class. I can talk about the philosophy of Karl Marx and modern day neo-Marxism in education; and I can talk about the dark side of the state and church, their conspiracies, and how each supported the other and squashed the individual.

"But this is not the time or place to talk about the horrors and dark side of society. I'd rather end on a positive note—and catch glimpses of hopes, aspirations, and goodness of humanity. I prefer to tell you about the wisdom of Socrates, Confucius, Averroës, and Gandhi; the hopes of Buddha, Christ, and Mohammed; the enlightenment of Locke, Rousseau, Descartes, and Jefferson; the music of Bach, Mozart, and Verdi; the writings of Shakespeare, Cervantes, and Dante; and the magic and myth of *Mary Poppins, The Lion King*, and *Crouching Tiger, Hidden Dragon*."

"What about the music of James Brown and Jimi Hendrix?" asked Claudia Washington, who rarely spoke in class. "Then there is Carlos Santana and Tito Puente."

"Are you serious?"

"Hell, yes! I wouldn't say it if I wasn't serious."

Hill was a little surprised and wrote off Washington's response as out of place. He could not tell if he was being baited or if she were serious. He merely responded, "Perhaps there is a generation gap."

"What about a cultural gap?"

There was no response. He felt he was being pushed into a discussion that was dysfunctional to his original point—and turned to Rodriguez.

"I am sorry to have digressed, but Rodriguez's point is powerful and reminds me of so many people who deserve to be remembered but remain unknown to us, and whose lives were taken away before they had a chance to blossom, and are forever anonymous to us."

"Now let me ask the class how they view the various philosophies," Hill added.

Gail Mendez, a history major, volunteered. "Major philosophical viewpoints that have emerged within the course may be viewed along a continuum—traditional and conservative versus contemporary and liberal—idealism, realism, pragmatism, and existentialism. These world philosophies form the basics of educational philosophies, sometimes called educational theories, along the same continuum: perennialism and essentialism as traditional and conservative, as well as progressivism, reconstructionism, and now postmodernism, as contemporary and liberal."

Chase, who sat in front of Mendez, remarked: "I assume controversy and debate arise within schools when teachers and administrators view educational problems or solutions in terms of different philosophical views. When there is a wide difference of opinion among school people or within the community, there is likely to be conflict."

"That is right," commented Professor Hill. "It might prove interesting to consider a number of current educational issues, such as creationism, school prayer, whole language, standard-based education, and testing, from different philosophical perspectives. If you know a person's educational philosophy, you often have a good idea about how he feels or where he stands on educational issues. Actually, you learn to anticipate your 'friends' and 'adversaries.' "

Yamada raised her hand and was recognized: "If we take your position, Professor Hill, that there is no preferred philosophy, then what is one to do when seeking direction about school problems and their solutions?"

"John Gardner said it best," replied Hill, "in his classic text *Excellence: Can We Be Equal and Excellent Too?*: 'No democracy can give itself over to extreme emphasis on individual performance and still remain a democracy—or to extreme egalitarianism and retain its vitality. A society such as ours has no choice but to seek the development of human potentialities at all levels.' "

Washington again spoke up and interrupted Professor Hill. "In a heterogeneous society like ours, this results in some hotly contested issues, including how much to invest in human capital, who should be taxed and how much, whether we should have more programs for gifted or disadvantaged students, to what extent we are to handicap our brightest and most talented minds to enable those who are slow to finish at the same time—so there are equal or near equal results."

"We cannot treat these issues lightly," responded Professor Hill, "because they affect most of us in one way or another and lead to questions over which wars have been fought in the past. To put it in a different way, all of these issues involve balancing acts and what effect these balancing acts have on individuals, groups, and society. These issues affect us on a personal level and on a professional level as future teachers."

Hill then asked the class, "What does this mean to you?"

Chase commented: "Many reconstructionists and postmodernists, not to mention perennialists and essentialists, have their own views about excellence and equality. Many of us in class are also unable to agree on what is equitable and just, and how much we can stretch the embodiment of reform and the fiber of society. How much should we spend on education? In terms of the greatest benefit for society should we spend two times as much on the handicapped student compared to the average student, as we do in most schools?"

"I think Joel is insincere and just playing with words to impress you," declared Mendez. "His insincerity and true colors are reflected in his use of the word *handicapped,* which is inappropriate."

"Handicapped students are handicapped no matter how you slice it or dice it," Chase responded. "It's also politically incorrect to use the word *disadvantaged* or *deprived* to describe what is now called an *at-risk student,* just as it is incorrect to use the words *watermelon, hysterical,* or *nuclear family* in some circles, even the words *mother* and *parent* in an interview because of the supposed belief that mothers and parents lack the time to meet the requirements for the job."

"I'm trying to be helpful," said Mendez. "I'm not part of the 'thought police' or 'gender goon squad.' "

"Dr. Hill, you should have assigned Orwell's *1984* for the class to read, given all these new words and double speak we need to learn to hide our thoughts and feelings."

"Joel, your point borders on sarcasm, but it is interesting enough for me to consider next term, that is, to prepare teachers for the new social and professional world they inhabit. Still, I think you may be creating a furor over a freckle."

"Well, I can't keep up with all the protected classes, including cross-dressers, transsexuals, and addicts, even people with asthma and allergies. Last week, my younger brother was told by his teacher he could not come to the classroom wearing Dippity-Do hair gel and Mennen deodorant spray because of the school's anti-scent policy and gender-free policy."

"We get the message. Does anyone have anything else to add?" asked Hill.

Punjwani, who had been quiet for most of the class session, spoke up. "It appears that too much egalitarianism can lead to mediocrity, indifference, and economic decline. On the other hand, excellence carried too far can create wide economic and social gaps, hostilities among groups, and a stratified society. I guess the idea is to search for the golden mean, although it means different things to different people."

"Very good," said Hill. "What else can we say about the philosophy of education?"

Beckie Langall, who was interested in elementary education, raised her hand and Hill called on her. "What we need to do, as future teachers, is to search for the middle road, a highly elusive and abstract concept, where there is no extreme emphasis on subject matter or student, cognitive development or social development, academic rigor or soft subject matter. What we need is a prudent school philosophy, one that is politically and economically feasible and serves the needs of students and society."

At this point, Chase declared that he had said essentially the same thing "and was criticized for being insincere."

"I think we understand that some books, including *Huckleberry Finn, Mary Poppins,* and all the books with the N-word in the title or content—from Dick Gregory to Randall Kennedy—have been plucked from the shelves in many schools. Likewise, some people in institutional and government settings have been chastised, even demoted or fired, for using an inappropriate word in public. Everyday we come up with new words we should not use. It's frustrating. We can even debate whether blacks should be able to use the word *nigger* in public discussion and whether females can use the word *bitch* and homosexuals can use the word *faggot.*"

Hill continued, "Believe me I have lived with those kinds of words and the resulting behaviors my whole life. I have experienced the outcomes, indirectly and directly, and both similar and different stereotypes are being portrayed today in so-called civilized countries, Third World countries, with ethnic and religious extremists, and with hate groups in this country. But let's move beyond troublesome words and allow Ms. Langall to finish her thoughts."

So Langall continued: "Implicit in this view of education is Dr. Hill's point: Too much emphasis on any one philosophy, sometimes at the expense of another, may do harm and cause conflict. How much we emphasize one philosophy, under the guise of reform or for whatever reason, is critical because no one society can give itself over to extreme 'isms' or political views and still remain a democracy."

"Ms. Langall, you said it very well," remarked Professor Hill. "Let me tell you a secret. Some teachers, like most of my colleagues, eventually adopt a philosophical view and that view guides their teaching and thinking of how students learn and what they should learn. While few of you will adopt a pure and well-defined philosophical position, many will lean in one particular direction. Ironically, some of you will not even be aware of your philosophical leanings, simply because they are not well defined. That is true, of course, of many experienced teachers."

Hill continued. "I don't know if it matters what educational philosophical view you adopt, if you adopt one at all, or whether you remain eclectic. What counts is that you understood that as a teacher you will be faced with choices and decisions and that philosophy is important in determining your choices and decisions. Few beginning teachers scrutinize a school's philosophy prior to being hired, rather they become increasingly aware of it after they are hired. It is worthwhile to understand your own philosophy, especially if you have a strong philosophy, and before you accept a position, make sure you work in a school and community that coincides with your view of teaching and learning. If your philosophical views are not strong, then you will probably feel comfortable with and fit in many more schools and communities than one of your classmates who has strong views. Joel's opening remark about seeking a school that coincided with his philosophy of education had meaning to him and might for others who have a well-defined philosophy.

"We are going to end early this time. I wish there were more time to deal with some of the viewpoints about different ideologies, cultural differences, and Western civilization. My dad lost his mother and father and his two brothers at Auschwitz, and my colleague across the hall lost his wife and only daughter in what used to be called Yugoslavia." Wiping away his tears, Hill looked around the room pensively and said, "I am the last generation that will be affected personally by the Holocaust, the last generation for whom it will be more than an intellectual discussion or moral exercise. But there will be other human atrocities, final solutions, and ethnic cleansings that your generation will have to face. As future teachers, you will have to interpret these events and put them into a global perspective—and deal with good and evil and the intentions of monsters and moral people. I wish all of you the best of luck in your next education course, as well as with your professional pursuits. I hope all of you develop the moral resources and philosophy to help your students develop into good people and a good society. All of you know my office number. Come in and say hello—and you don't have to have a problem to stop by."

Questions to Consider

1. How would you describe Professor Hill's teaching style? What do you like about it? What do you dislike about it?

2. How would you describe your philosophy of education?

3. Based on your philosophy, what knowledge is most worthwhile to teach in schools?

4. What are the advantages and disadvantages of having a well-defined philosophy or no preferred philosophy of education, as suggested by Professor Hill?

5. What problems arise when a society tries to promote both excellence and equality? If given a choice, should American society promote excellence or equality?

6. Was Professor Hill right in cutting off discussion about ideology, 'isms,' and political correctness and advancing the discussion to the brighter side of humanity? To what extent do our personal experiences shape our philosophy? Our view of the world?

7. Establish a file of articles that discuss school issues and appear in *Time, Newsweek, Wall Street Journal,* and *USA Today.* Analyze the philosophical positions of the articles' authors and their critiques or proposed reforms. Report your observations to the class.

Recommended Readings

James A. Banks, *Cultural Diversity and Education* (Needham Heights, MA: Allyn & Bacon, 2001).

John Gardner, *Excellence: Can We Be Equal and Excellent Too?*, 2nd ed. (New York: W. W. Norton, 1995).

John Goodlad and Timothy J. McMannon, *The Public Purpose of Education and Schooling* (San Francisco: Jossey-Bass, 1997).

Allan C. Ornstein and Daniel U. Levine, *Foundations of Education,* 8th ed. (Boston: Houghton Mifflin, 2003).

Howard Ozmon and Samuel Craver, *Philosophical Foundations of Education*, 6th ed. (Columbus, OH: Merrill/Prentice Hall, 2000).

2

The Influence of the
Educational Pioneers

Important ideas in education are usually associated with particular educators, thinkers, or writers. Education pioneers have shown the ability to formulate new and important theories, to distinguish important trends, and to examine crucial ideas and issues. Most pioneers or leaders in education tend to be one step ahead of the majority opinion—and rarely conform to that majority opinion.

Most educational pioneers espouse a particular philosophy or pedagogical principle and are usually in the forefront of an educational movement. Most important, pioneer thinkers give us direction and help in clarifying important ideas, concepts, and relationships in schools and society.

The discussion in this chapter spans 100 years, starting with John Dewey, perhaps the most influential educator of the twentieth century, and then turning to more radical pioneers in education—including reconstructionists who sought to change and improve schools and society and ending with modern radical pioneers, who might be labeled as *reconceptualists, critical pedagogists, neo-Marxists, feminists* or what some people simply categorize as *postmodernists*.

All of the pioneers mentioned in this chapter are concerned with political and social thought. The ideas of Dewey, and later Counts and Brameld, tend to be accepted today by most educators. The thoughts of more recent radical pioneers are considered more controversial. Most of the ideas of these new pioneers are viewed in terms of class, caste, and gender, and they have widened the scope of political and philosophical discussion in terms of liberation against capitalism, whiteness, and maleness. Those pioneers view schools and society in terms of subordinate groups kept down and controlled by a dominant group—a white, middle-class, male society. This type of revolutionary or radical thinking involves other social sciences as well and is gaining in popularity among liberal and younger academics.

More conservative educators view these ideas as politically radical, somewhat on the fringe, and an anathema to the meaning of American democracy. They also view many of these thinkers not as pioneers, but simply as people who are antiestablishment for the sake of being against the political and social system, because of immaturity, anger, or poor judgment. The result is that most conservatives prefer to distance themselves from these radical thinkers on a professional and personal level.

To what extent practitioners see the radical thinkers' work as worthy of attention is questionable, given the reality of the classroom, the bureaucracy, and the daily grind that characterizes much of the work of teachers, many of whom prefer to discuss new ideas relating to teaching and learning.

ISSUES

Professor New-Tone summed up his take on the great pioneers in education. "Time is of no account to great ideas. They are as relevant today as when they were first written 150 years ago or longer. The ideas of Comenius, Rousseau, Pestalozzi, and Froebel are as fresh and meaningful today, as they were ages ago. Their ideas are rooted in and express the child's natural goodness, faith in children and youth, the principles of human development and child psychology, and the methods of the child-centered movement and progressive education. Dewey, Montessori, Kilpatrick, and Piaget are twentieth-century giants. They were also progressive thinkers. Their ideas and methods have been widely adapted and used by educators and psychologists today in formulating childhood education, cognitive thinking and developmental theories, as well as philosophies and goals in education that have shaped American schools."

Across the hall, Professor Ultra-New-Tone was teaching another section of the same course. He also used the same text but his discussion was quite different. "The impact of the progressive educational pioneers in the schools was minimal. Their ideas made for good reading and forced people to ponder and think about methods of instruction, the role of teachers, and the significance of educational philosophy. But teachers did not change their methods; schools did not change." Ultra-New-Tone continued, "For hundreds of years, the seats remained bolted to the floor, teachers have talked too much, textbooks have dominated the lesson, and students were (and still are) expected to learn knowledge and memorize facts so information can be regurgitated in class discussions and on tests. New equipment usually found its way into some closet, locked up for most of the year. Not until the 1980s did the technological revolution enter the school doors, when the pioneers were long dead, and only because some computer companies and businesspeople—not educators—figured there was a market to exploit."

You could hear Ultra-New-Tone raise his voice. "If Rip Van Winkle had been a teacher and gone to sleep for twenty years, or even longer—say, one hundred years, and if he had awakened today, he could still return to the classroom and teach. Although the content would have changed, with the exception of the computer, the teaching tools and methods would be familiar to old Rip. He would know what to do with the desks and chairs, the chalkboard, the textbook, and so on. He could function in the classroom, perhaps even bluff his way so few people would know he was a relic from the past. Beyond the fact that the progressive pioneers of education make for interesting reading, they have had minimal influence in changing classrooms or schools. Just think when you were in the first grade, and ask yourself how much your teachers or schools have changed."

Back in Room 118, Professor New-Tone continued his lecture. "The ideas of the educational pioneers, especially Rousseau, Pestalozzi, Dewey, Kilpatrick, and Piaget have had a major impact on European and American schools. The foundation of

American schools and the continuous curriculum changes that have evolved—from teaching the three Rs to meeting the needs and interests of students—are rooted in the ideas of these great pioneers. Look at any philosophical, historical, or foundations text on education. Check the table of contents, the name index. More has been written about these pioneers than any other comparable group of educators. Any author who wants to write a foundations or introductory text in education needs to thoroughly discuss these pioneers and their impact on education. Every teacher should be familiar with and understand the works of these people. Most of the instructional and learning theories practiced by teachers today, especially at the elementary and middle school level, have a direct link to these great educators."

Across the hall in Room 117, Professor Ultra-New-Tone was also continuing his lesson. "The pioneers' treatment of children and description of teaching methods were romantic and idealistic. The problem is that most teachers, as they gain experience in the world of school reality, become practical and lose their sense of romance and idealism. The ideas of the pioneers made interesting reading, and still do, in college classrooms and among professors and their students. But their ideas were not implemented on any large scale, at least not in the public schools, regardless of the amount of literature and subsequent discussions of these pioneers in college classrooms. Their ideas never reached the inner-city schools of Harlem, New York, Southside Chicago, or the barrios of Los Angeles, nor did they ever reach the working-class schools of Astoria, New York, Blue Island, Illinois, or Pasadena, California. And that's where the school action is—in our inner cities and working-class neighborhoods, in the small towns and villages of America. Oh yes, there were and still are today a few suburban and private schools attended by rich kids, perhaps a handful, and a few more lab schools such as those in Cambridge, Massachusetts, Teachers College, Columbia University, University of Chicago, and Ohio State University, in which these new ideas, mostly child-centered and progressive, flourished. But these institutions were far and few between Harlem and Astoria, New York, or Southside Chicago and Blue Island, Illinois."

Ultra-New-Tone continued to criticize the progressive movement. He stated, "The real problem with progressivism became evident when the movement splintered into several wings, including the child-centered, activity-centered, experience-centered, creative, play school, and neo-Freudian groups. Dewey, in *Experience and Education*, criticized these groups for misinterpreting and misusing his ideas. Just as he condemned the old philosophies that pursued knowledge for its own sake, he attacked those who thought knowledge had little value. Not only did he warn against 'traditional ideas as erecting silence [and conformity] as a virtue,' he also criticized those who sought to liberate the child from adult authority and social controls. He declared 'progressive extremists' and 'laissez-faire' philosophies to be destructive to the ideas of progressivism, and he warned that 'any movement that thinks and acts in terms of an ism becomes so involved in reaction against other isms that it is unwittingly controlled by them.'

"Dewey was not alone in his criticism of progressive educators. As criticism mounted, Boyd Bode, another leading proponent of progressivism, warned his associates of the impending crisis in a book entitled *Progressive Education at the Crossroads*, published in 1938. He cautioned that 'progressive education stands at the parting of the ways.' The movement 'nurtured the pathetic hope that it could find out how to educate by relying on such notions as interests, needs, growth, and freedom.' In its social, psychological, and developmental approach to learning, in its 'one-sided devotion to the child, it betrayed the child' and deprived him or her of appropriate subject matter. 'If progressivism continued its present course without changing its focus, it would be circumvented and left behind.' Bode's words proved prophetic. More and more progressivists responded to the growing criticism and self-justifying theories that involved trivialities and errors. Progressivism encompassed too many different theories and practices, all labeled under progressive philosophy, which would contribute to its downfall."

Back in New-Tone's class, another statement could be heard: "All the great teachers today, all the 'Apple' teachers, and all the NEA and AFT master teacher award winners, exemplify the humanistic and cognitive principles of our educational pioneers. Every great teacher is learner centered and idealistic. Every great teacher expects students to think or reflect—in accordance with the theories and principles of our progressive educational pioneers. These pioneers changed our lives and the lives of hundreds of millions of students with their democratic ideas and principles of cognitive learning."

New-Tone continued to espouse the virtues of progressivism. "This movement experimented with alternative modes of curricular organization, utilizing varied instructional activities, life experiences, community-based education and field trips, problem-solving methods, and project methods (which got students involved in subject matter, social issues, and social problems). The philosophy focused on the student as the learner, rather than the subject. The student helped in planning curriculum, as opposed to leaving all the decisions to the teacher. Progressive education emphasized inquiry-based and independent learning methods as opposed to whole-group instruction (teaching to some mystical class average) and rote learning methods. It encouraged cooperative and small-group activities, rather than competitive and individualized learning, where students are divided into winners and losers."

Back in Ultra-New-Tone's class, you could hear him criticizing progressive pedagogy. "Progressive emphasizes *naturalism*, the theory that children learn naturally and that adults should not restrict the innate creativity of children or ignore their needs and interests. Schools of education have adopted this type of methodology at the expense of subject matter. Graduating from such education programs, the majority of teachers are opposed to drill, practice, and review. In fact, many so-called 'pedagogical experts' suggest that such procedures lead to busy work, memorization, and rote learning. Most elementary teachers succumb to the philosophy of progressivism, rooted in Rousseau's romantic view of children as unspoiled and natural."

By this point Ultra-New-Tone was raising his voice and turning red. "The claim that children learn naturally does not hold up, especially with regard to most inner-city and working-class students. The theory might work with rich kids who come to school from enriched cognitive backgrounds, where parents read to them on a daily basis and speak in whole sentences, but it doesn't make sense with children who need structure in their lives and who need practice and review to learn to read or do mathematics. We may be naturally wired for speech, but we aren't for phonics or long division. We have to be taught, and most kids need more practice with learning basic skills."

Ultra-New-Tone was now walking around the room; his voice booming. "The idea is for teachers to find interesting ways to practice and drill. This is the message set forth by early essentialist educators such as Arthur Bestor and Admiral Rickover during the *Sputnik* and Cold War era, and this is the philosophy of current essentialists such as E. D. Hirsch and William Bennett, and educational psychologists like Brophy, Good, and Rosenshine. Bennett and Hirsch advocate essential content, not process or so-called thinking skills. Brophy, Good, and Rosenshine seek more practice and review in the teaching process."

In the meantime, New-Tone was telling his class that "some of the worst aspects of teaching and learning today focus on facts and teaching toward high-stakes tests. What most standardized tests do is measure tiny pieces of information, low-level content. The testing and accountability movement presently engulfing us creates undue pressure on students, teachers, and schools to drill and teach toward the test. By putting test results first before the needs of students, education policy makers are making teachers and schools neurotic, and teachers and principals are making the kids neurotic. Worries about test results and rankings outweigh simple human values, critical thinking, creativity, and social development. We are sacrificing the support, care, and love of children for facts and test scores. Students deserve more than facts, facts, and more facts—nothing but facts and test scores. They deserve to be encouraged how to think, as discussed in Dewey's 1910 book entitled. *How We Think*."

Now New-Tone was getting all fired up and shouting. "In an effort to correct what many educators consider low-level content, fragmentation, and compartmentalization of subject matter," The professor remarked, "Progressivism encouraged an interdisciplinary approach, sometimes called a *broad field* curriculum design. Thus, the social sciences of geography, economics, political science, sociology, and history were fused into social studies. Linguistics, grammar, spelling, writing, reading comprehension, and literature were combined into language arts. Progressive educators also implemented a *correlation* curriculum design, creating links between two separate subjects such as English and history, history and art, science and math. For the subject-minded teacher, the basic content of the courses was retained, but it was organized with reference to common themes, subjects, and units. Finally, progressivism cultivated the democratic ideal, rooted in Dewey's *Democracy and Education* and the muckraker movement of the 1920s—a prelude to today's social reform movement in education.

"Although the major thrust of progressive education waned in the 1940s and 1950s, due to *Sputnik* and the advent of essentialism," New-Tone lamented, "the philosophy did leave its imprint on education. Contemporary progressivism is expressed in several movements, including those for a relevant curriculum, humanistic education, increased school reform and reconstructionism. In fact, one can argue that progressive proponents such as Dewey, Kilpatrick, Rugg, and Counts were early reconstructionists."

Back in Ultra-New-Tone's class, you could hear him still criticizing the progressive movement in education. "Progressivism was at the height of its popularity during the Depression, but a small yet significant group of progressive educators became disillusioned with progressivism and American education. They were considered radical for their day; they had FBI files, and they were later to be called reconstructionists.

"This group argued that progressivism put too much emphasis on child-centered education that mainly served the individual child and the upper class, with its play theories and private schools. What was needed was more emphasis on society-centered education that took into consideration the needs of society (not the individual) and all classes (not only the rich)."

"At the 1932 annual meeting of the Progressive Education Association, George Counts urged progressive educators to consider the social and economic problems of the era and to use the schools to help reform society. In his speech, 'Dare the School Build a New Social Order?' which was later to be published in a book, Counts suggested that the schools become the agent of social change and institution for social reform. In a rhetorical and highly charged statement, Counts stunned his progressive colleagues with the statement:

> If Progressive education is to be genuinely progressive, it must … face squarely … every social issue, establish an organic relation with the community, develop a realistic and comprehensive theory of welfare, fashion a compelling and challenging vision of human destiny, and become less frightened than it is today at the bogeys of imposition and indoctrination.

"The social issues of the 1930s, according to Counts, involved racial and class discrimination, poverty and unemployment—and progressive education had ignored these vital issues. The social issues today are similar, although the list is longer, according to the political left in education: reconceptualists, radical critics, critical pedagogists, and neo-Marxists. The big issues in education are still social and political—not whether there is excessive reliance on the textbook, stress on memorization, or grades. They deal with caste, class, and gender—and other issues dealing with population growth, disease, hunger, technology, pollution, and depletion of the earth's resources—all of which deal with equity and social justice.

"Theodore Brameld made the point in the 1950s," according to Ultra-New-Tone. "Teachers and students have a right to take sides, to stand up for the best reasoned and informed [position] they can reach as a result of free, meticulous examination and communication of all relevant evidence. In particular, teachers must measure up to their social responsibilities. Analysis and interpretation of social problems in class are only the first stage for schools in a democracy; commitment and action by students and teachers are needed. A curriculum based on social issues and social services is crucial.

"Neutrality in the classroom or schools," Ultra-New-Tone continued, "that which we often engage, under the guise of objectivity and scientific inquiry, is unacceptable for the democratic process. For Counts and Brameld, and now today's political left, progressivism has never gone far enough in reform because its proponents were and still are part of the Establishment."

Ultra-New-Tone argued that for political and moral guidance, we need to move philosophically left of progressivism for our approach to education. "Henry Giroux, for example, views the current practice of democracy as exclusive, rather than inclusive, in that many people are left out of the promises to which our system subscribes. The schools need to become more committed to 'educating people to be active and critical citizens capable of fighting for and reconstructing democratical public life.'

"Peter McLaren is more extreme. He states that capitalistic schooling is perverse and creates a culture of desire and consumption—not to nurture communal consensus and social harmony but to hide from students and the general public the inequities in our society, the contradictions in our stances, and our intolerance of differences. Yes, schools condition students to fulfill their human potential, but at great cost: obedience to social norms and standardized values.

"Ivan Illich demands a new just society that requires the present deschooling of society. He rejects the schools and calls for their elimination for liberation purposes. Learners would no longer have an obligatory curriculum imposed on them; they would be liberated from institutional and capitalistic indoctrination. There would no longer be discrimination and a class society based on possession of certificates. He relies on a grassroots curriculum that seeks to engage students and teachers in small learning networks at the community level—in stores, libraries, museums, art galleries, and so on.

"Michael Apple maintains that schools convey meaning and conditions that shape our lives and take control over us. The dominant social and economic system pervades in all critical aspects of the curriculum. Just as there is 'unequal distribution of economic capital in society, so, too, is there a similar system of distribution surrounding cultural capital.' In technological societies, schools become distributors of this cultural capital. They play a major role in distributing various forms of knowledge, which in turn leads to power and control over others.

"Paulo Freire talks about a 'pedagogy of the oppressed' for students and the poor and describes how people can move through different stages to ultimately be able to take action and overcome oppression. To effect major change, at what Freire calls the 'critical transforming stage,' people must become active participants in changing their own status through social action that aims at changing schools and society."

By the time Ultra-New-Tone had finished his lecture, he was banging his desk with his hands and his voice was booming as he informed his students that it was their responsibility to take the critics seriously and because of their youth they had the most at stake and the most zeal: "Before you are married and bogged down with children and a job, this is your time to be actively involved in improving society. This is the time in your life that you may charge the barricades."

Ultra-New-Tone tried to sum up his viewpoint. "The conservative philosophy is an extension of logic and math—a realm of pure inquiry, concerned with keeping clean the methods and tools with which we reason. In the face of their pretentious theories of reasoning and rational thought, conservatives leave behind the humanistic element, the notions of relativeness, context, and values which hold that all philosophies and theories are not determined only by static knowledge and empirical data. Progressivists are slightly more liberal than conservatives; they both live in the same world—and represent the Establishment. But mine is occupied by people and gods and haunted by subjectivity and art—not just Aristotelian logic and Newtonian science and math."

"Let me try to reformulate and reconceptualize my philosophy," continued Ultra-New-Tone. "We cannot all be progressive, just like we cannot all be radical or neo-Marxist. Some of us are doomed to conservative ideology, and others who claim to be more liberal or progressive are still part of the Establishment. Given the law of probability and the ever-shifting political and social views of professors, I hope as students you are not forced to listen too often to old-hat, stupid twaddle—ideas rooted in the past, in principles and virtues considered timeless. Change is inevitable, to use a cliché. Since the 1950s our significant knowledge—what I call scientific, technical, and social—has doubled every fifteen to twenty years. It can be affirmed that the amount of knowledge at the end of your life will be one hundred times what it was when you were born. Nonetheless, we have a significant number of education turtles (the ones claiming to be progressive) and ostriches (the ones admitting they are conservative) who refuse to change with the times and who portray radicals and neo-Marxists as screamers, howlers—or just plain nuts.

"Some of you may think I'm over doing it, but anyone who holds firm to tradition is probably stifling innovation and creativity without knowing it. Even worse, these teachers and professors tend to render students immune to new ideas, and they curtail conditions for educating the whole person. Anyone who holds to a traditional philosophy is shutting off conditions for student growth and curtailing the full development of human potential in directions that extend beyond cognition."

In the meantime, Professor New-Tone, across the hall, was summing up for his class. "Counts and Brameld were a little extreme and ahead of their times. But timing, you must understand, counts in the outcomes of life. The current crop of radical critics and neo-Marxists borrows and reworks the thoughts of old reconstructionists, but they express much more disdain for schools and society. They see teachers as prison guards of the system, schools as prisons, and students as prisoners locked up intellectually and politically. In particular, schools are considered highly discriminatory places that sort, track, and perpetuate capitalistic inequities—more precisely caste, class, and gender imbalances."

New-Tone continued: "The political left or radicals in education fail to understand that without consensus, without a middle ground or some balance that is acceptable to the majority, their views are nothing more than anger-based and fringe-based ones. Their ideas cannot be taken seriously by anyone other than a handful of doctoral students or college professors in some office corner or college classroom. Teachers and administrators who are in the business of teaching and reaching students, who have to operate in the real world of schools, have no time to get seriously involved in silly extremism. Teachers are dealing with bread-and-butter issues such as preparing lessons, managing students and organizing classrooms, developing instructional materials, grading homework, and preparing students for the next standardized test. Administrators are dealing with parents and community members, with legal and financial issues, and with personnel and student policies. They have little time to talk about tearing down schools or encouraging teachers and students to charge the barricades.

"Let me bring my lecture to a close. The reigning ideology in academia is something called constructivism and postmodernism. Both have a number of other names, from neo-Marxism to postcolonialism or, even worse, deconstructionism. Not many professors, teachers, or students fully understand what these philosophers philosophize partially because of their authors' anger, sentence structure, concept of knowledge, and sense of reality. In some cases, some of these critics may be missing something upstairs, given their obsessions about dominance and subordination, about reality and ideology. Their basic idea is that knowledge is a social construct, a belief system rooted in and influenced by time and place and social background such as race, class, and gender—all of which can be summed as *context*. In a nutshell, context influences knowledge and how we perceive and react to it. There is nothing inherently wrong with this premise, but the problem is that it can lead to the acceptance of nothing; everything is open to revision and reconceptualization—or worse, opposition and deconstruction (or elimination)."

New-Tone continued: "Taken to the extreme, we enter an upside-down world in social science, literature, art, and education. There is no way of establishing truth—not if everything can be viewed in context. Truth and reality are whatever the individual or group desires it to be. This university is not a university; it is a racist, class-based, sexist institution. Anything goes! All theories, principles, statements, or objects can be filtered, questioned, or reassessed by whatever social/cultural bias we want to see. Manson's world, Frankenstein's world, and the Taoist world on top of the Himalayas have as much reality as the world of Newton, Descartes, and Einstein."

"Although race, class, and gender are the main filtering agents for this theory, any variable can be added to the mix: culture, religion, geography, even weight, age, and marriage status. An argument can be made that thin people and fat people, young people and old people, or unmarried and married people are discriminated against or disadvantaged by society. It merely depends on how you perceive reality, what is truth, and what arguments or criticism you want to make. To be sure, all traditions, norms and beliefs, are open to argument and criticism. This being the case, everything I have said in class is open to debate, and there is no way to establish truth objectively, or a belief system. I might as well be teaching in Jack Nicholson's world of *One Flew Over the Cuckoo's Nest*."

Questions to Consider

1. If you had to make a choice, whose position would you accept as most accurate, that of Professor New-Tone or Professor Ultra-New-Tone? Why?

2. Consider your own elementary and possibly junior high school experience. How did the child-centered theories, or progressive theories, influence your teachers? Were your teachers more child centered or more subject centered in their teaching methods?

3. Now, consider your own educational experiences from grades 1 to 12. To what extent did the teacher or text (workbook) dominate the lesson?

4. There is a big difference between theory and practice; in fact, a good deal often gets lost when we try to bridge the gap. In what way does this statement reflect the differences between Professors New-Tone and Ultra-New-Tone?

5. How do you reconcile the views of Dewey and Bode, both of whom were progressive educators? How do you view the similarities and differences of Counts and Brameld, both of whom were reconstructionist educators?

6. In terms of reforming schools, to what extent do you subscribe to the philosophy of the radical critics and neo-Marxists?

7. Visit a nearby school and talk with teachers and administrators to find out the prevailing school philosophy. How would you classify their philosophy? To what extent does the school philosophy coincide with your education philosophy?

Recommended Readings

George Counts, *Dare the School Build a New Social Order?* (New York: Day, 1932).

Lawrence Cremin, *Transformation of the School* (New York: Random House, 1961).

John Dewey, *Democracy and Education* (New York: Macmillan, 1916).

Maxine Greene, *Landscapes of Learning* (New York: Teacher College Press, Columbia University, 1978).

Joel Spring, *Globalization and Educational Rights* (Mahwah, NJ: Erlbaum, 2001).

Teacher and Teenager Involved in Love Affair

Society is becoming less tolerant about bullying behavior, sexual harassment in school and work environments, and sexual affairs between teachers (or professors) and students. Although the lower courts seem to have rendered mixed decisions about a school's responsibility if administrators are unaware of the problem, legally and ethically the needs and expectations of students, parents, and the community are against relaxing vigilance toward sexual harassment, and especially sexual relations involving teachers and students grades K–12. Female students are also growing less tolerant toward male behavior that was once merely considered innocent flirtation or commentary made around the watercooler or locker room. Similarly, parents and communities are no longer accepting the old adage "boys will be boys" from school personnel. Stricter policies and procedures are being designed to minimize or eliminate this type of behavior.

Note that complaints of sexual misconduct on the part of teachers and administrators in school systems have increased in the last few years, according to *The New York Times*. The increase resulted from a concern that educational officials, parents, and community members have in the past neglected to report possible sexual offenses, because clear reporting procedures did not exist and plaintiffs were discouraged by school authorities; in some cases, school authorities did not report the incident to the police. It can also be inferred that despite an increase in complaints, cases of abuses are still going unreported. The flip side to the problem is that not all complaints can be substantiated, and some of the stories are exaggerated by "victims" who are looking to sue and collect money.

Nevertheless, several large-size corporations are hiring outsiders to check harassment claims with the rationale that many complaints are "too hot to handle," and also to make it easier for those who lodge complaints to avoid talking to an "insider" who may talk to other colleagues or who may have an impact on their careers. Although schools and colleges lack this procedure, had it been in place in the case study below, much of the conflict between school officials and parents would have been avoided. Still, the most important factors are for schools and colleges to improve the learning environment, reduce liability, clarify the murky environment by communicating clear procedures for sexual misconduct and harassment claims, and promptly and thoroughly investigate such claims.

ISSUES

The affair between the student and teacher made the local news. The twenty-eight-year-old tenured math teacher, Bob Martin, was being investigated for his alleged affair with one of his students, seventeen-year-old Lucy Khouvongsvanh. Despite repeated warnings from his supervisor at Edison High School that he was not conducting himself properly with students, Mr. Martin was permitted to teach. Not only did he continuously spend lunchtime with a group of female students in his room who were serving as his monitors, he also took Lucy out for pizza and movies on a few occasions. When it became seemingly apparent that he was carrying on an affair with at least one or more of his students, he was suspended with pay. But since no student or parent wished to file charges at that time and Martin immediately hired an attorney, he was reinstated until the end of the year and then not rehired.

Martin had no trouble getting another job at nearby South High School, since math teachers are in demand. Although officials at South High School followed standard procedures in checking his references, none of the letters in Martin's files, from his college where he received his degree or from Edison High School, mentioned anything that might cause suspicion or further investigation of Martin's behavior. The two Edison administrators who had written references focused on his teaching ability and kept silent about Martin's alleged romantic escapades because there was no clear evidence and no charges were made by the parents or students. Also, they felt that a teacher's personal behavior outside of school must be kept confidential unless someone requested specific information. Volunteering the information, even initiating a phone call, could be considered defamation. His sexual involvement had never been admitted or proven. In short, there was no careful check on Martin's references and no follow-up communication procedure between the two schools.

Five months later Lucy Khouvongsvanh was visibly pregnant, and her mother was now threatening to sue both schools; the first because it had sufficient information to suspect the teacher's involvement but kept it quiet, and the second school for not adequately checking references and putting other students at risk. Lucy's mother named Martin as the father. The local newspapers ran the story with pictures of Martin and Lucy, since she had now turned eighteen.

When the South High School principal was interviewed, he pointed out that principals often do not check the references of incoming teachers, and professors and administrators who write recommendation letters for young teachers couch their words very carefully and rarely, if ever, mention anything negative, since the Freedom of Information Act permits candidates to read their letters of reference. Unless negative comments can be fully substantiated, school administrators usually do not write these comments about a person.

The principal of Edison High School commented in the same news article: "Administrators try to resolve allegations of misconduct in an 'off the book' way, and often fail to tell other schools of a teacher's suspected misbehavior when he or she moves on. It is easier to say nothing, unless specifically asked, than to volunteer information unless a decision has been rendered by a court or mediation board, or there is supporting evidence from third parties."

And just when it looked like Martin might be indicted, he and Lucy announced their engagement, with the wedding to take place in June after her graduation. What first began as an illicit romance between a student and teacher was ending in a marriage. Henceforth, the charges against Martin were dropped by Lucy's mother.

Well, sometimes things just do not go away easily. A parent group at Edison became increasingly dissatisfied with the handling of the Martin affair. School officials were reluctant to take further action against a teacher who had an affair with an underage girl. The administration argued that the parents of Lucy originally refused to file charges, and that there was no clear evidence about his involvement until after Martin had left the school. Why publicize the school's "dirty linen" when Martin agreed to leave quietly without legal sabre-rattling? Despite the fact that Martin and Lucy were now engaged, and despite the school's "practical" position, the community mood was not forgiving. Martin had also been suspected of having affairs with other girls at the school. As one parent argued, "It is absolutely shocking that in this day and age the administration did not report the incident to the police." Out of frustration, as well as concern for the future, the parents as a group issued a one-page document, insisting the school complete the following actions:

1. Draft a statement that sexual misconduct constitutes a form of sexual discrimination that is illegal.
2. Provide a list of several examples of sexual misconduct.
3. Make a clear statement that sexual misconduct will not be tolerated by the school and school district and will result in prompt remediation, including suspension and expulsion.
4. Require all new teachers to take a psychological test and pass an extensive background check.
5. Require all student teachers to pay a $100 processing fee to the school district to help pay for the tests, since it was felt that the district was performing the job that colleges of education should be doing—as an entry requirement for certification.
6. Issue a teachers' handbook within six months, including the comment that any teacher involved in sexual relations with a student would be dismissed. Procedures for carrying out the investigation would be delineated, subject to speaking to an attorney.
7. Resolve all allegations and suspected cases of teacher–student romances. No "off the book" deals would be tolerated.
8. Require the school district to improve its communication with other school districts about former employees, and report to other schools suspected predilections when teachers move on.
9. Make the school district form an Office of Sexual Misconduct Prevention and hire an expert in sexual abuse and misconduct to coordinate the office.

When the demands were released in the local newspaper and on television, the roof fell in. The ACLU threatened the school with lawsuits, especially if demands 4, 5, and 6 were enacted as policy. The Edison students and parents had now lost confidence in the school officials in the handling of the Martin episode, and they threatened a student boycott if the district did not meet the parent demands. The nearby colleges reported that if a student teacher fee was instituted, they would withdraw their students—even if it meant extra time traveling each way for their students and professors. In the meantime, the administration defended their actions and indicated they would meet with the parents to try to work out the demands listed by the parent group.

At the meeting, one of the parents, Barbara Gitlin, argued that the Martin affair should have been investigated, and with proof of his affair with Lucy, Martin should have been suspended without pay and his license revoked. By taking the easy way out, the school now had legal exposure and public discontent. Even worse, it sent mixed messages about sexual abuse of students.

"Why, Martin left the school voluntarily at the end of the term without fanfare," responded one of the administrators. "Nothing is guaranteed at hearings or in court. What would have happened if we had learned that Lucy adored Martin because he supplied the affection that her own father denied? Or because the parents were divorced and she missed her father? What would happen if Lucy refused to testify? How long do you think the investigation or court hearing would take—one year, two years, three years? We responded quickly and negotiated a simple and practical settlement."

Gitlin was not satisfied, and argued the school district had made a farce of the idea of *loco parentis,* in place of the parent, and *loco communitas,* the teacher represents the community's morals. "Although there may be disagreement about what should be the proper relationship between student and teacher, it certainly does not include sex. And, although we might question the mores of some communities, the teacher is still expected to represent an ideal model of community-approved behavior and virtue. If we ignore the incident and all the other Martins of the profession, then it will put an end to public trust and respect for teachers within the community."

John Pincuski, an assistant principal, responded. "The type of enforcement or accountability you seek is less enforceable today than was once the case. We are not living in the *Ozzie and Harriet* generation; this is the post-MTV period. Britney Spears, *Cosmo Girl,* and Victoria's Secret set fashion trends; the skirts and shirts are inching up and the pants are slipping down."

Then, Theresa Cicchelli, one of the female administrators tried to tone down the heat. "I remember an old sage, Harry Broudy, in his book *The Real World of the Public Schools,* saying that determining just what is proper teacher–student behavior can lead to a Socratic debate or community uproar."

"You have to be kidding," asserted Gitlin. "We are talking about a teacher having sexual relations with a student who at that time was a minor. And, there is the overriding issue of men who use their position of power to exploit women."

Peggy Smith, a radical feminist, went farther in her analysis of the situation, referring to the male organ as "a worthless male appendage" and that the only useful function it had "in the future was as a sperm donor."

"I have heard enough about male power and exploitation of women, and I refuse to acknowledge Ms. Smith's remarks. Women involved with male students are treated less harshly than men," asserted Pincuski. "We are still living under the notion that men are always predators. Boys who have sex with older female teachers are not raped but supposed to be lucky. It's not a fluke that female teachers are sometimes involved in sexual misconduct. The only difference is that boys rarely press charges or blow the whistle on their female teachers. The female teacher has to become pregnant before the public takes notice."

Then Cicchelli stated, "Peg, I have sympathy for your concerns, but we have a few girls at South High who complain and cry so much I wish I had a makeup person around every time I have had to deal with them. Sometimes I wonder how much of their wounded-woman persona is real and how much is calculated. We have all female student types, ranging from the future Katie Couric—mature, self-confident, and urbane—to Monica Lewinsky, who flirts and then seeks our sympathy."

The principal, Stanley Smerdjian, commented: "Listen, there are no magic pills, no sure answers to this problem. Balance is crucial. Rather than stir up public discontent and get embroiled in discovery motions, depositions, and possible litigation, we chose the clean and simple solution. There was no clear evidence, no parent demands at that time. As for the letter of recommendation, we didn't want to risk a slander suit by Martin. He was an excellent teacher; he crossed the line, but we didn't want to destroy his career, since we had no proof at the time."

"If this was your daughter," asked Gitlin, "would you sing a different tune? Would you have a different attitude?" Gitlin reiterated that all principals and superintendents should spend more time protecting the potential victim or victims and less time covering up incidents. "Because of the age of the student, the police should have been notified."

The principal asserted that the law is unclear when a woman experiences sexual pressure from a man in a position of power. Roughly one million working women in the workforce are pressured each year to have sex with their supervisors. Thousands submit each year to unwanted sex as a client to a lawyer, physician, or psychotherapist. "Hundreds of thousands of female high school students are infatuated with their teachers, although just how many engage in sex and who solicits whom is hard to score. You can probably double the number of female college students who encounter some suggestive or flirtatious comments from a professor."

Pincuski interrupted: "I can do without this generalization. Men are sometimes victimized by sexually aggressive women who are often more manipulative or subtle than men. Female teachers, professors, and supervisors also have eyes, hands, and emotions. Female students and female workers also chase men in power for various psychological reasons. Some just want to be serviced, others have unhappy marriages and want to get even with their husbands, and still others enjoy sport sex."

"This conversation has become outrageous; you are bordering on a caveman mentality," asserted Gitlin.

"I got an A+ for political correctness during the last workshop. I also know the difference between female discrimination and feminist hypocrisy," responded Pincuski.

"Does this mean men like Martin face no sanctions or penalties?" asked Smith. "What happens if we had learned that Lucy had said 'no, no, no'?"

Eric Joreskog, the school superintendent, responded. "That's a great defense, according to feminists, and it works in some states and with some jurors. But enough social science data can be introduced to indicate that 'no' often means 'yes,' 'maybe,' or 'try harder.' Organizational penalties are often ineffective, and school districts (not individuals) can be sued by the plaintiff or defendant—depending on how the school district reacts. This is the real world, not the TV series *Law and Order*, where morality triumphs and the good guys win ninety percent of the time. We were lucky. Martin had tenure and left quietly. It could have been messy for everyone, including Lucy, and with students or parents taking sides, it could have lasted for years."

"So get to the bottom line: What is your position?" asked Gitlin.

"We agree with your first three statements," said Joreskog, "and we have similar statements about sexual harassment in place. If you wish, however, we will revise our statement to coincide with the language of your first three statements. In principle, I agree with two or three of your other statements as long as the language is modified. But we have no intention of being bullied. The best I can do is form a committee to deal with the matters and not make any promises about the recommendations or results.

"You're out of touch with the community, more so than some of the clergy I know. Any accusation of abuse or sexual misconduct by the clergy should be investigated by local law officials, rather than the church. The same is the case for teachers and schools. In fact, the public is demanding involvement in cases of abuse by priests and educators alike.

"You are on thin ice, linking parish life with school life, and what Catholic church leaders should do and public school administrators should do," asserted the superintendent.

"I realize the parents have good intentions, but I would advise that you tear up your remaining list of demands and avoid the coming showdown. Let the school district go on with the business of education. Martin is gone. *Loco parentis* and *loco communitas* are still alive at South High School," said the superintendent.

"In other words, you want to send no message. You want to continue to sweep things under the rug behind closed doors, and protect the old boys," commented Gitlin. "All you will do is form some committee and hope the immediate issue will be forgotten or diffused."

Smerdjian summed it up: "Think about what is at stake. Think about whether we need to air our political differences in public. Think about whether your cause is more important than peace. Personally, I would like to close the Martin case, especially since the two main players are engaged to be married."

Smith spoke again about most men being "lazy and incompetent," and "burned out by fifty years of age and relying on women who are paid half the amount, or even less, to do the detail work and run the daily affairs of an organization." She concluded that "men would do well to keep their genitals in their pants" so women, young and old, would not have to deal with them "and we would not have to debate the issue when no means no."

Smerdjian, who is fifty-five years old, shook his head, raised his eyebrows, and said nothing. Joreskog, who is also graying, stared at Smith and also said nothing.

The fact that both administrators said nothing prompted Smith to further push buttons. "You might as well as take your hands out of your pockets," pointing to Smerdjian. "It's not going to help you."

Again there was silence.

"You're a typical administrator, Stanley, avoiding controversy and selling out for some compromise or middle road that is morally questionable," asserted Gitlin. "I think there are too many Martins in schools and workplaces that go unpunished. They need to know they can lose their jobs, licenses, or be sued personally."

Gitlin spoke again: "Would you be willing to support a school policy that requires reporting all sexual incidents, real or suspected, to police officials for them to investigate, and failure to report such incidents would lead to a fine of up to possibly ten thousand dollars, possible loss of the job, and a six-month jail sentence?"

"No. The punishment is too harsh, but the idea is worth considering," said the superintendent. "I'm not going to yell '*FIRE*' because of some suspicion that there may be some smoke. I need to be sure the smoke exists."

"Are you at least willing to report all incidents to the police, and bar administrators from conducting their own investigations into these incidents?"

"No. My administrators would surrender their professional authority. Unless there is some evidence or witnesses that give similar accounts, I would rather not create a reign of terror or police state in our schools."

"I'll be candid," she said. "We've got to do something to get your attention. If it takes a lawsuit, so be it. There is no doubt the teacher had sexual relations with an underaged student. It is irrelevant that the student will not press charges; the school district should. If not, then the parents will take action."

The superintendent stepped into the conversation. "I fully realize that no teacher should have sex with a student, and no adult should have sex with a minor. While it may be easy to identify disturbing behavior in hindsight, proof is often questionable at the time of the charge. We acted in good faith and rid the district of the teacher—in a noncostly, quick, and efficient manner. Enough is enough! Go home and think about all the ramifications of student boycotts and costly litigation. Think about who loses and who wins. Think less about principle and more about practicality."

Questions to Consider

1. How prevalent do you feel the practice is of secondary school teachers (male or female) having romantic affairs with their students? Of the number of reported (nonreported) sexual affairs involving teachers and students, what percentage do you feel are male (female)?

2. Based on hindsight, how might you have handled the Martin escapade if you were on a special committee at Edison to review the matter and come up with recommendations for the principal?

3. Given the fact that Martin and Lucy were engaged, and no one wanted to press charges, was the administration correct in not pursuing the matter? Why or why not?

4. Of the several demands (recommendations) made by the community, which ones do you agree are legitimate?

5. The two parents, Gitlin and Smith, and the four administrators—Pincuski, Cicchelli, Smerdjian, and Joreskog—had very different views. Which views do you support? Why?

6. The principal and superintendent did not want to respond to Smith's remarks. Was this the right tactic? Had the principal or superintendent been female, would Smith have made the same remarks? If so, do you believe that the female school official would have verbally responded to Smith? How?

7. Based on library or Internet sources, develop a school district sexual harassment prevention policy. Report to the class.

Recommended Readings

Amanda Coffey and Sara Delamont, *Feminism and the Classroom Teacher* (New York: Routledge, 2001).

Philip W. Jackson, Robert E. Boostrom, and David T. Hansen, *The Moral Life of Schools* (San Francisco: Jossey-Bass, 1998).

David W. Johnson, *Reaching Out,* 7th ed. (Needham Heights, MA: Allyn & Bacon, 2000).

Nan Stein, *Classrooms and Courtrooms: Facing Sexual Harassment in K–12 Schools* (New York: Teachers College Press, Columbia University, 1999).

Roberta Wetzel and Nina W. Brown, *Student-Generated Sexual Harassment in Secondary Schools* (Westport, CT: Greenwood, 2000).

Cracking Down
on Student
Culprits

Dealing with classroom management and discipline is the number-one problem for beginning teachers in inner-city schools, because many students lack inner control and are unwilling to defer to teacher authority. Similarly, many teachers lack systematic methods for dealing with discipline problems, and because of cultural shock and lack of experience, they sometimes aggravate the problems that may exist.

Short and simple: In order to teach you must be able to manage your students. No matter how much potential you have as a teacher, if you are unable to control the students in your classroom, little learning will take place. Classroom management is an integral part of teaching, and techniques of managing students need to be learned—unless you happen to be six feet, four inches, and have a decidedly imposing frame.

Inadequate classroom management and discipline are widely considered by the public to be the major educational problem, even though the media have centered on school finance, student drug use, and student testing. In annual Gallup polls in education, taken among parents since 1969 and published by *Phi Delta Kappan*, student discipline, or the lack thereof, has been listed as one of the top three school problems each year for the last twenty-seven out of thirty-three years.

According to a recent National Education Association poll, the four major reasons the public gives for disciplinary problems are parents' failure to discipline youth in the home (84 percent), increased use of drugs and alcohol (83 percent), breakup of traditional families (72 percent), and schools' lack of authority to deal with the problem (67 percent). The attention paid by the media to the recent wave of school violence, since the Columbine killings, adds to the concern teachers and parents have for safe schools.

Although schools on the whole are considered safe places for children, the following discussion is about zero tolerance, which refers to policies that punish all students for certain offenses. The idea grew out of the federal drug enforcement policies of the 1960s and caught on in the public schools in the late 1980s and early 1990s, first in Orange County, California, then Louisville, Kentucky, and Yonkers, New York, and is seen as a way of dealing with students who are disruptive and who are involved with drugs or weapons. The recent string of school shootings has created uneasiness throughout the country and the trend among educators, parents, and communities is to adapt zero-tolerance procedures involving school violence, drugs, weapons, and also provacative or major fighting words intended to incite violent action, harassment, or hate-related behavior involving racial, ethnic, or religious prejudice or sexual aggression.

ISSUES

Kennedy-King Junior High School is located in a predominantly black part of Big-City, USA. This school is presently 80 percent minority and 20 percent white. In recent years there has been an increase in the use of drugs and alcohol and gang activity. The number of teacher assaults and student fights has increased slightly during the past few years. Last year, the school installed metal detectors to screen students for weapons.

The administration has called a special faculty meeting consisting of one dean, two guidance counselors, two administrators, and five veteran teachers to discuss the possibilities of implementing a *zero-tolerance policy* to punish students who cause repeated problems, especially those students "who are drug users, pushers, or gang-bangers," as described by the dean of discipline.

Everett Kohl, one of the guidance counselors, supports the idea of zero tolerance. In front of his colleagues, he voices his thoughts: "Media coverage creates the erroneous idea that inner-city schools are plagued with teenage criminals. The vast majority of our students do not cause discipline problems, use or deal drugs, bring weapons to school, or belong to gangs. There are a few 'rotten' kids, maybe five to ten percent, who cause ninety to ninety-five percent of the problems. We know who they are, since they are always in trouble. All we need to do is deal quickly and effectively with these few bad apples. Instead, we continue to give them one more chance."

Kohl pointed out that *zero tolerance* means just what the words imply, no second or third chances—automatic suspension for a prescribed number of days or expulsion for certain behavior or activities dealing with drugs, alcohol, weapons, gang recruiting, violent behavior, sexual harassment, theft, or defacement of school property.

Jarslaw Brezezinski, the assistant principal, then stated: "This means no exceptions; any infraction to any degree results in a hearing before a special committee of members who will represent school authorities, the board of education, and the local community. We are going to include parents, since their children have the most at stake, and so that there is no criticism that the committee is insensitive to the community. The idea is to regain control of the school."

Jennifer Jones, a young black teacher and critic of this idea, then stated: "This sounds like a simple idea, but it's not. There need to be some gray areas, where an option exists not to suspend students for minor offenses."

Responded Brezezinski: "I agree, no problem with this modification. Is there anything else you find objectionable?"

Ms. Jones continued, "Although none of you have mentioned students by race or ethnicity, I firmly believe this is unwittingly aimed at black and Hispanic students. My two brothers and I were honor students in high school. We occasionally smoked marijuana in our teen years, but were never gang members and never caused problems in school. We attended predominantly white schools, and you should have seen the way we were treated by the neighborhood police when we drove our mom's new car to school, or how some of the students reacted when we parked our car in the school parking lot. You have no idea how prejudicial some of our teachers were—they were dumbfounded that blacks could compete intellectually with white students in the honors classes. I just feel that attitudes in white society have not changed much in the last ten years, when I was in high school, and that a greater percentage of black and Hispanic students will become victims of zero tolerance."

Another teacher, Ms. Jane-Wo Yang, then said, "If we boil everything down into racial terms, and every time differences in outcomes are analyzed in terms of race or ethnicity, then we will always be stymied and our school policies will be ineffective. Jennifer, I am not going to quarrel with your personal experiences. I'm sure they are valid. But I feel that you have introduced a red herring into the discussion. If we are reluctant to address the issues that confront us or implement a sensible policy because of fear of being labeled racially insensitive or racist, then this school will disintegrate. This is what is happening in society when we talk about individual responsibility, morals, or family disintegration. We have a discipline problem in the school that is getting out of control. Personally, I'm afraid to walk to the parking lot alone, after school hours, and many of my friends and colleagues whom I usually have lunch with have been taunted and teased in the hallways with remarks and gestures by some of the male students. If this is not stopped, teacher turnover will continue and we will lose an increasing number of white students."

Walter Johnson, a black guidance counselor, then got up and said: "To some extent, I agree with Jane, and to some extent I agree with Jennifer. I don't think it's wise to talk about victimization of groups because it leads to political agendas and feeds a spoils system. However, I think if we clearly define our terms and policies, we can crack down on the culprits without victimizing students because of race. Someone who wears baggy pants, turns his hat to the right, or wears sunglasses does not have to be a gang member, but I would outlaw beepers and cellular phones; and I would enforce a clothing policy that outlaws hats or sunglasses in school because, in my view, adult authority is being tested—covertly and silently. We can always make medical exceptions, if there are any.

"I think we can apply zero tolerance to the right students and be color blind, too," added Johnson. "It amazes me how a teacher will stop a student in the hall without a pass, while ignoring a fight in the locker room or a group of boys taunting a female student in the lunchroom. It's almost as if teachers are afraid to stop the real culprits—or have learned over the years not to care, to be indifferent and uninvolved in order to get through the day."

"I'll be frank," said Tom Watson, a second-year English teacher. "The courts have undermined school discipline. The 1969 *Tinker* decision concluded that 'students and teachers [do not] shed their constitutional rights … at the schoolhouse gate.' And, the 1975 *Gers* decision entitles students to legal representation and, in lengthy suspensions (more than ten days), entitles them to a formal hearing, names of witnesses, and the right to cross-examine and confront their accusers, even if the latter seek anonymity because they fear retaliation. Then there are the numerous rights manuals which enumerate all the impermissible things educators are going to try to make students do. You don't have to answer a school official if he questions you. You can demand to see your school record. You don't have to submit to a locker search unless there is probable cause. If you get caught cheating, without documentation or witnesses, it is your side of the story versus the teacher's. If you don't like how the school makes you dress, you can sue."

"Tom is right," added Yang. "I look the other way when a kid cheats on a test because I'd rather not get involved in 'she said, I said' games with the student's lawyer. The cafeteria floor is full of trash, and so are many of the bathrooms, but if I single out a student he or she is possibly going to say, 'I didn't do it. Why are you accusing me? Are you prejudiced?'"

Brezezinski then asserted: "I think we are all overreacting and getting hung up on the threat of litigation. We have a discipline problem in school, and we either deal with it or allow the school to degenerate into chaos and obscene student behavior. Proponents and critics fail to realize that students have rights, and there are procedural processes to follow when students are sent to suspension or expulsion hearings. True, students can be represented by attorneys, who can also question teachers and administrators, as well as protect students. If we introduce and enforce zero tolerance, the school district will have to pay for the students' lawyers. As long as we agree that the school board, and ultimately the taxpayers, are going to pay these legal fees, then I say let's go forward. We should give students or their parents the right to choose any lawyer, if they wish, and then address the school policies or issues involved. The point is, we need to remove the 'bad apples' so the rest of the student body can benefit from a peaceful and productive school atmosphere. We need a safe and secure climate where teachers can teach and learners can learn."

"Instead of suspending or expelling problem students," asked Watson, "why not require parents to attend school with their child? Instead of targeting the student, we might make a parent accompany the child to all classes for five, ten, or even thirty days. We could do this for a number of offenses, including truancy and chronic offenders or other misdeeds. This would be a great way to improve parental cooperation."

Said Brezezinski, "I'm not sure how legal it is—punishing parents for the misdeeds of their children."

Added Jones: "Not only does this sound unfair for mothers of single-parent households who have to work, but also I'd like to see you tell a white person and professional he is to receive such a sentence."

Brezezinski asserted, "Some school people wouldn't mind seeing parents in school more often and even in class. The idea is creative, but I don't think the parents who work would like it, although it is indeed one way of getting them to take notice of what their children are doing and getting them to insist that their children shape up in school."

Watson sensed the committee members were wandering off the subject. He asked: "What do we do with the students who are expelled? Do they roam the streets? Do they get the opportunity to attend another school? Do they get a second chance to come back to school the next week or month? Provisions for expelled students must be worked out before we introduce the concept of zero tolerance."

The assistant principal answered, "Students under sixteen who are expelled will be transferred to one of five special service schools within the district for either emotionally disturbed children or behaviorally dysfunctional students. This is not a perfect match for all students, say, for someone who defaces school property or sexually harasses another student, but at least there will be provisions for the students who will be expelled."

"My big concern is the tendency to overreact to minor infractions, given the aftermath of Columbine," declared Jones. "I think zero tolerance makes no sense. Across the country emotions are high. We are jailing kids for minor offenses."

"What is a minor offense?" asked Johnson.

The discussion then became sidetracked. "At Twinkle Junior High, a girl's bag was searched for pot. She had a one-inch pen knife attached to her key chain along with tweezers. She was suspended for the remainder of the year—sixty-two days."

"That incident is one out of a thousand," responded Johnson.

"Really, what about Louie Huey, the eight-year-old boy at Dewey Elementary School, who drew a picture of a soldier in camouflage uniform with a knife in his hand. He was suspended for five days for drawing a weapon."

"I'm not sure the school was wrong in light of all the shootouts in school."

"Later it was found out that little Louie was drawing a picture of his older brother who is a decorated Navy Seal. However, the principal, Mr. Peppers, was quoted in the paper as saying, 'We can't tolerate anything that has to do with guns and knives.' Don't you think that statement is a stretch—and masks the issue that the suspension was for a drawing by an eight-year-old?"

"Maybe we need to look at the drawing, before we make any accusations," said Kohl.

"Oh. Are you worried about a copycat drawing?"

Yang then asked if anyone was going to River Town. "I read in the *Morning Star* paper that at La-Te-Da School in River Town a seven-year-old was hauled out in handcuffs because he pointed a chicken bone at a classmate and said 'pow.'"

"Well I read the same story in the evening edition. I thought the boy pointed a paper gun and said 'bang, bang, bang.'"[1]

"This is beginning to sound senseless," said Brezezinski. "As an administrator, I'd rather be criticized for being overcautious than not. It only takes one incident to turn a peaceful school in a charming neighborhood into a nightmare."

"But this is the big city," said Jones. "There is greater diversity—and people learn to be more tolerant. If not, the city would explode. If you consider history, the odds are twenty-four percent, according to the *Wall Street Journal,* that the president of the United States will be a target for assassination. The possibility of being killed in school is one in two million—or .00005 percent."

---

[1]The three aformentioned stories are based on real news stories; the content has been modified and adapted to reflect the text format.

"Common sense must prevail," continued Jones. "Our students have more to fear from adult mass hysteria and zero tolerance—which makes zero sense—than from their classmates who sometimes have more common sense than some of the parents and teachers."

Watson responded. "Talk about common sense and overreacting! What a lousy professional attitude! Do you always go around knocking your colleagues with off-handed remarks?"

"This is getting a little personal, and I don't think we need to dwell on Louie, Huey, and Dewey." Johnson refocused on school discipline problems which he felt were compounded by disruptive and potentially dangerous incidents on school buses and in locker rooms. He pointed out that nationwide some 13,000 students are annually injured in bus-related incidents. "Our school reported four major incidents last year, including a gang-related stabbing and a student pushed off while exiting the bus. When a student is injured, the first thing the lawyers want to know is if the school has a plan that ensures the safety of students."

"It's a real problem," asserted Kohl. "I insist we install video surveillance cameras on the buses to monitor student behavior and enforce a zero-tolerance policy. Given the disruptive behavior in school, we only need to give proper notice and follow precise guidelines. We should also install two-way communication links from the bus to the dean's office, in case of serious disruptions or emergencies."

"I don't think video cameras are a solution; in fact, they are double-edged swords," remarked Brezezinski. "They can be used as evidence against provocative or hostile students, but they can also be used as evidence that the school district did not provide adequate safety for a student who gets injured or beaten up by another student or group of students."

"What about foul language or trash talk directed at other students?" asked Jones. "What about students on buses poking someone on the shoulder? Where do we draw the line? When do we give students the benefit of the doubt? How about trying to help students who have problems, rather than suspending them? How about training bus drivers to deal with student behavior?"

"Given the nature of some of our disruptive students," said Yang, "the driver cannot be expected to handle all these problems. Moreover, I have no inclination to distinguish between smart-aleck behavior and serious misconduct. Students must learn to be civil, since disruptive behavior is contagious and snowballs. Students have to know we mean business." Brezezinski then asserted that school buses were potentially vulnerable to hostage takeovers, drug dealing, and gang-related activities. "I would encourage the local police to have their SWAT units train on buses for future emergencies. All it takes is one lunatic with a gun or knife to cause havoc."

"To be candid, hostage takeovers can take place anywhere in school, not only on buses," said Brezezinski. "Given the rash of school shootings, school personnel need special training on how to deal with violence on school grounds, including mock hostage incidents in libraries, lunchrooms, and classrooms."

"I find this discussion to be extreme and one sided," asserted Jones. "All the blame is directed at the student; no blame is directed at teachers or adults—some misread the situation or do not know how to respond in class or on school property and, therefore, aggravate the situation. Instead of preventing or controlling discipline, they unwittingly cause or add to the problem. You have already decided to overlook teachers' incompetence and convict the student."

"Jones has a real point," said Watson. "Teachers have *legitimate* power, by virtue of their position. But this type of power is not influential among older students who have learned that adults are not always right, all knowing, or fair minded. Teachers need to establish *referent* power as enjoyed by teachers who gain the respect and trust of their students."

"I understand your frustration," responded Johnson, "but the school has real discipline problems. I want to stay on target. Our locker rooms have become commonplace for student shakedowns, student gambling, student fighting, and student alcohol and drug traffic. We cannot use surveillance cameras in the locker rooms, because students change clothing. But I would give notice to all students that the lockers can be searched, given reasonable suspicion that student contraband exists. Also, metal detectors should be installed and students should be X-rayed before entering the locker room. Because of past disruptive behavior, I maintain the school has the right to implement these get-tough policies."

"Why can't we just hire competent security guards," asked Watson, "and establish appropriate roles for them?"

"How many—and at what cost? These types of guards are expensive," stated Brezezinski. "I would rather hire and train in-house security. But, we still need surveillance cameras and metal detectors."

"Walk-through detectors are costly and handheld wands are cheaper but less effective," remarked Kohl. "But it takes hours to line up and screen all students unless you have five or six rows or booths operating simultaneously, which only adds to the overall cost. The typical inner-city school, with a thousand or more students, only checks one student out of nine or ten. Even then, some kids still come fifteen or twenty minutes late to the first class. Video cameras and guards have other problems. Monitoring gets you so far until the time involved and cost get prohibitive."

Johnson then raised the issue of uniforms for all students, pointing out they are becoming the favored new dress code among many parents and school authorities since first implemented in the Cherry Hill school district on the south side of the city. "A few school systems in big cities have followed this lead at the elementary school level. I feel uniforms can be moved up the grade ladder to our junior high school."

"I agree," stated Kohl. "Uniforms are touted as the best thing since sliced bread was invented. School authorities claim they help reduce fights, weapons, and sex offenses. Because of the mass purchasing power of schools, they cost half the price of Gap jeans and Dr. Martens. It's not only the price that counts, but it is also a means of reducing social, psychological, and economical distinctions between boys and girls who buy at Kmart and Target and the ones who buy at Saks and J.Crew."

"As the parochial schools will tell you, when everyone is the same," continued Kohl, "then students have to distinguish themselves through achievement. Uniforms instill school pride, improve school attendance, save parents money, improve students' self-esteem, and give greater feelings of success and sense of belonging."

Brezezinski also espoused the virtues of uniforms. "Most important, students become calmer, more polite, and racial tensions and gang-related dress diminish. Uniforms are a win–win policy and can bolster a zero-tolerance policy."

"What about the ACLU? You know those lawyers are going to object," stated Yang, "claiming a violation of student rights and individuality. Uniforms will be viewed as an administrative tool to control students and prevent them from expressing themselves."

"Come on. Most preadolescent youth thrive on conformity," responded Watson. "Most would rather dress alike than unalike. Most would rather not worry about what to wear every morning. As for the ACLU, it will introduce the First Amendment protection of political speech and communication, but the courts here ruled that schools have a right to enforce dress codes to advance school policy."

"We may be oversimplifying the pros of uniforms," asserted Johnson. "Most of the stories about reducing school fighting, racial tensions, and gang activities are unconvincing, since the disruptive acts are not a result of the school environment, but closely related to family, peer, and community factors. Students involved in gangs will exhibit other ways to distinguish themselves—graffiti, hand signs, accessories, shoes, weapons. Uniforms are nothing more than a trendy idea. I think we need to enforce strict codes of behavior, not just dress codes."

"I think it's time we vote on some of these policies. Would someone like to start with a motion in favor of zero tolerance?" asked Brezezinski. "If it passes, then we will need to talk about procedures."

True to form, Jennifer Jones spoke up again against the task of the committee, the discussion that prevailed, and the motion to implement a zero-tolerance policy. "Although your concerns are valid, I still charge that the zero-tolerance policy, and the related discussion about violence, drugs, and gangs, as well as the need for surveillance, security guards, and metal detectors, all have racial tones that put down minority students."

Jones continued: "If this was a predominantly white school, many of the solutions would not be so harsh. Students, parents, and teachers would work together to solve the school problems. The policy to be implemented would provide for additional counseling: how students can get along in school, how they can work as a community of learners and as future leaders, and how they can assume responsibility and adult roles in school–community activities. The students would be treated as stakeholders, not as delinquents or gang members. The discussion would include positive reinforcement, not punishment; it would include success stories and shared enterprises, not coercive, police-like, and gestapo-like measures."

It was then Watson who remarked that the Columbine killings were a turning point—with chat rooms, web sites, and violent web games, weird clothing, and the media frenzy. "Zero tolerance is now acceptable in many schools across the country. School officials can no longer stand by idly ignoring the worst forms of adolescent acting out, sometimes with grim results. We have to react to someone who threatens to torch the school library, beat up the principal, harass or bully a student, or write graffiti on the school locker about Jews or blacks, or some gay person who wears lavender glasses. Intelligent, tough-minded policies are needed if kids cannot control themselves or if they can't be more tolerant and civil toward others."

"My only concern is that when people become frustrated, the whip has its appeal. My feeling is that we are looking for some knight on horseback to save us, and we may wind up with someone on horseback with a rattan cane," said Jones.

Brezezinski responded, "Are you implying that if we take stern measures in inner-city schools, if we try to enforce civil behavior and hold students accountable for their behavior, then we are racists?"

"I have a different set of benchmarks, a different view of reality. You think you have the answers and that you have *expert* power, but you are relying on *coercive* power, at least that is how most of the kids will view this new policy. I expect to be outvoted today, but I can tell you with a good deal of assurance the problems in this school, in this community, will not go away. In the long run," Jones concluded, "very little is accomplished by a show of force—much more is accomplished through love, mutual respect, and understanding. I question whether you truly understand, respect, or can appreciate these students."

Questions to Consider

1. What view do you have about the problem of discipline in the inner-city schools? Suburban schools?

2. Where discipline problems exist in schools, should a zero-tolerance policy be introduced?

3. Can school officials crack down on student "culprits"—and do so equitably?

4. Do you believe that parents should somehow be held responsible for their children's misdeeds in school? Why or why not?

5. Do you agree with the idea of "special service" schools or schools for emotionally disturbed or behaviorally disruptive students? Or should all students be included in regular schools?

6. Of all the characters mentioned, which two closely correspond with your views on discipline? (Brezezinski and Kohl represented one extreme, Johnson and Jones the other extreme, and Watson and Yang were more or less in the middle.) Why?

7. Write a description of the discipline policies that you can recall at the junior high or high school you attended. Compare your description with those of your classmates.

Recommended Readings

Lee Canter and Marlene Canter, *Assertive Discipline*, 3rd ed. (Santa Monica, CA: Canter & Associates, 1997).

Ronnie Casella, *Being Down: Challenging Violence in Urban Schools* (New York: Teachers College Press, Columbia University, 2001).

William, Glasser, *The Quality School: Managing Students Without Coercion* (New York: Harper, 1990).

Tom V. Savage, *Teaching Self-Control Through Management and Discipline* (Needham Heights, MA: Allyn & Bacon, 1999).

Theodore R. Sizer and Nancy F. Sizer, *The Students are Watching: Schools and the Moral Contract* (Boston: Beacon Press 1999).

Condoms
or
Abstinence?

For years parents and educators have been concerned that youngsters are having more sex with more partners and at younger ages. Although the causes are subject to debate, and reflect the mores, customs, and beliefs of our society, the consequences are evidenced in school by the growing number of teenage pregnancies and dropout rates resulting from such pregnancies. The strain is also felt by the social welfare system, with the growing number of single-parent households. The general opinion, at least by sex education advocates, is that students need to be educated about body parts, sexual choices, and safe sex, while others emphasize resistance skills and abstinence.

Although recent data from the Secretary of Health and Human Services indicate that teen sexual experiences and rates of pregnancy, birth, and abortion have declined since their highs in 1996, parents are still concerned about their children's sexual activities, and educators are split on whether the emphasis should be on how to properly use condoms and birth control pills or on morality and abstinence. Other factors that lead to controversy among parents and educators is whether the high schools should be in the business of dispensing condoms and just how graphic biology and health textbooks should be. Texas, Missouri, Maryland, and Colorado take the most conservative position and are likely to ban, eliminate, or otherwise seek changes and revisions in some texts that portray sexual organs, demonstrate the use of condoms, illustrate sexual positions, talk about oral sex, or discuss gay and lesbian marriages as an option.

There is also the problem of satisfying the majority of community members about sex education, which is not so easy when we add religious beliefs to the mix. Even more interesting is the claim by conservative groups that increased sexual activity among teens up to the mid-1990s can be attributed to sex education, sexual biology, and information on where to get and how to use contraceptives. In short, the more teachers talk about sex, the more involved students actually become with sex. Although sex education programs have been in place since the 1970s, the controversy about "the birds and bees" continues to ignite sparks. Does the recent decline in sexual activity and pregnancies among teens reflect the consequences of sex education, fears associated with contracting HIV and AIDS, increased feminism or independence among young girls, or a new morality shaping society? You figure it out.

You can bet that the Christian Coalition has one view, the American Family Association of Texas has another view, and so do the state education commissioners, state and local boards of education, the Association of American Publishers, teachers' unions, sex education advocates, the PTA, and the kids themselves. When the subject of teenage sex, pregnancy, and virginity arises, there are a host of hardliners for every position which are bound to keep the fans of *Hardball* or *Hannity and Colmes* riveted for a long time.

Of course, you don't need to be a cable or tabloid "junkie" to understand that since the Clinton–Lewinsky affair, coupled with the media fixation on the story, including the "old" media (newspapers) and "new" media (Internet), kids' awareness of the consequences of sexual misbehavior and immorality have been heightened. Ever since the White House scandal, the natural radar for sexual involvement and hypocrisy among adults has had a target-rich environment at dinner table conversations and in classroom discussions. Although the ex-president's behavior has little to do with the health and well-being of the nation's children, the politics and jokes about Clinton's adultery and lying have at best offered some "teachable moments" and at worst have had a corrosive effect on sex education classes.

It is not that news standards have necessarily slipped; rather, the nation's moral standards seem to have slipped. William Bennett might be right: The schools don't need to teach more about sex education; instead, they should be teaching about the virtues of temperance, fidelity, honesty, marriage, and parenting.

ISSUES

The parking lot was jammed at Apple Junior High School. It was twenty minutes before the meeting in this suburban village would start, and the school auditorium was already overflowing with parents who had come to hear the discussion on whether the junior high school curriculum should include sex education. Not since the discussions some three years ago on a balanced school budget and fiscal austerity had there been such a packed auditorium of parents to hear a school-related issue.

Thomas Hunt II represented the more liberal sentiments of the school board and eventually started the discussion by summarizing a *Phi Delta Kappan* report about the sexual activities of adolescents.

1. Seventy-two percent of high school students have had sexual intercourse by their senior year.
2. Thirty-three percent of junior high school students have had sexual intercourse by the ninth grade.
3. The nation has about forty-three million (increased to forty-seven million as of 2002) children attending public school, including fifteen million teenagers ages thirteen to seventeen; there are seven million teenage pregnancies (most of whom have dropped out of school); and another three million teenagers (most of whom are in school) have sexually transmitted diseases.
4. Most children and youth have received no parental guidance about sex. They are unwilling or uncomfortable to talk to their parents about sex and parents don't have the skills or comfort level to talk about sex with their children.

5. Most parents want the school to perform this educational function. Where parents seem divided about sex education is over curriculum content and the social messages the school sends to children.
6. Parents are either for or against abstinence among children. Those who accept participation want children to be knowledgeable about safe sex.

Hunt then added, "Ideally, children should learn about sex from parents, but it's not happening. Our students learn about sex from their peers, as well as from adult magazines and TV. The basic message is sex is good; it is pleasurable, and everyone hops in bed."

Barb Cienkus, one of the parents in the auditorium, then asserted: "I'm against sex education. By teaching our children about sex, we send the wrong message—that we are condoning it. Even worse, Dr. Hunt, you omitted one important aspect of the report you just summarized. It implies that since teenagers participate in sex, they need knowledge about condoms. I think it is a crime that some of the schools in New York and California actually dispense condoms to children who ask for them. You might say I'm old-fashioned, but I think we live in a sick society when school authorities encourage students to use condoms, and then ask if there is a color preference such as blue, pink, or green. Is this what is going to happen in our school?"

Another parent, Nasib Hassan, added: "Teaching about sex is a private matter between children and parents. There are also religious and moral factors that the schools are not equipped to deal with, that involve family and children, and which most educators merely ignore. I realize that my children and most other children would rather discuss sex with their friends, and possibly their teachers, and not with adults they live with. But I'm aware of what the Park Slope schools, in the next town, are teaching. The text pictures are highly descriptive and embarrass many children who have to read the text. The discussions are at best controversial and, if I may add, downright disgusting—where young girls who are twelve and thirteen have to see and be taught how a condom fits over a penis and where everyone in class has to demonstrate it on a wax model. It makes little difference that the classrooms are grouped by gender: that the girls are in one group and the boys are in another group."

Hassan wondered why two fingers, closely held together, could not be used instead of the model of a penis. (Most of the audience laughed; moreover, one person responded that some kids might actually assume this was the proper method for using condoms, which in turn led to more laughter.) She then proceeded to hold up a junior high school text that contained several explicit pictures of body parts and read selected paragraphs that dealt with sexual intercourse.

Another parent held up another text, used in a neighboring school district. As many as twenty-four out of twenty-five chapters dealt with normal or traditional topics about sex. But one chapter was entitled "Lesbian, Gay and Bisexual Partners" and included subtopics such as "Homosexuality and Safe Sex," "Power and Inequality in Sexual Relationships," and "Homophobic Feelings: Facing Unexamined Prejudices." One teacher wondered out loud about the merits of using such a text. Another teacher declared that the students needed a broad perspective on complex social issues and diverse sexual practices. "There is no such thing as the right viewpoint. I think we all have been victimized by this one, majority viewpoint. One chapter, about four percent of the text, will not bring down the Church or Western civilization, but it will help us deal with popular prejudices."

Mary Lou Coombs, an English teacher, claimed that the discussion was drifting into gay politics and that much of this drive for diverse sexual practices, as well as the graphic pictures and models, came from liberal-minded educators, rather than students, parents, or community members. It was time for the latter to speak up and take control of the textbook selection committees and curriculum committees.

Marius Milkovic, a parent and general contractor, was next to speak. "I don't think we can agree on what and how sex education should be taught, but it needs to be taught, since most parents don't do a good job about it with their kids. I guess the more descriptive the pictures and realistic the content, the more it is likely to offend. On the other hand, the more bland the text, the less likely it is to coincide with reality or diversity."

"I think the problem has more to do with school policy than textbooks," said Cienkus. "When I visit the school, all I see are exposed bellies, backs, and thighs. This would never pass unchallenged in my school days. We couldn't even wear caps or sunglasses."

"And what about see-through clothing and shorts above the midthigh. What we need," said another parent, "is a Ten Commandments for dress codes—to instill a sense of decency and morality."

"Let's face it," asserted Milkovic, "times have changed."

"Do you have girls?" asked Cienkus. "I'm no prude, but the other day I saw one girl come out of the school with a bulging cleavage that made my eyes pop. Another girl came out of the main entrance wearing a pink sweater two sizes too tight and not wearing a bra."

"It's possible that the girls were part of some play—*Grease* or *Westside Story*," insisted Milkovic.

"Get with it. Wake up. Sex is rampant," said Hassan. It starts with skinny clothes and exposed skin, moves into freak dancing and alcohol at parties, and climaxes on someone's couch or bed."

"Do you really think that these 'rub-a-dub' moves will lead to sex?"

"Honor students do it. Church-going kids do it. Just about everyone does it. A lot of kids only know two ways of dancing—slow dancing and freak dancing. What the schools need to do is to explain the difference between dating and mating" said Cienkus, "and about love and eroticism."

"Is that really a school responsibility?" asked Milkovic. "What about mom or dad?"

"I don't think students feel they can get straight talk from their parents about sex, birth control, condom use, and STDs."

Rajpal Tomarshwari, a counselor who was present at the request of the school board, tried to calm things down between Milkovic and the two mothers. "We need to discuss body parts and choices between safe sex and abstinence. We need to talk about the consequences of pregnancy. For girls there are the responsibilities of motherhood—diapers, a cramped social life, a change from being a teenager to a mom, interference with future education—and that there is a real personal loss in terms of education, career, and future household income. We need to discuss peer pressure, how to say no, and elaborate on the advantages of abstention, including the fact that it is time to come out of the closet and say it's okay to abstain until marriage. Many schools are not assertive in this area of sex education; rather, the teachers talk about choice and safe sex."

Mary Lou, again, criticized sex education and sex ideology. "All this talk about sex only increases sexual activity. When adults teach kids about sexual organs, discuss sex, and how to use contraceptives, the kids simply have more sex. Most sex education advocates will argue the opposite, but the research on this matter is hazy. By giving kids a choice about sexual decisions, all we have done is increase sexual activities and teen pregnancy. Whatever decline has taken place in teen sex in the last ten years or so has nothing to do with what parents or teachers are doing, but with the AIDS scare."

Cienkus had a different spin. "Kids will be kids. They are supposed to test their limits. If they don't, you worry about it. But the message now is that there are no limits. Anything goes. There are girls engaging in oral sex and claiming they are virgins. Then there is Jennifer Lopez with her hot rear end, wiggling her way to stardom. Of course, Monica Lewinsky is now a millionaire, an insult to every hardworking, professional woman. Even worse, part of the feminist crowd applauds her story and spunk—and new image."

"This may be in bad taste, but you sound a little jealous of Jennifer and Monica," said Milkovic.

"Are you stupid?" snapped Cienkus.

"I think kids can learn to enjoy sex without guilt or danger," said Catherine Holt, a guidance counselor. "Teaching teens about oral sex and mutual masturbation in order to help them delay intercourse benefits all parties, and reduces the rates of teenage pregnancies and abortions."

"I cannot believe what I am hearing," said Cienkus. "Is this your view, or the school's view?," she asked Holt.

But Mary Lou jumped into the discussion. "You don't have to be a Christian fundamentalist or a Tibetan monk to realize that we don't need comprehensive sex education, with pictures of sexual organs, models of penises, and demonstrations about using contraception. The idea is to teach resistance skills, saying no, and to teach children to have faith and pride in virginity. The hell with sexual choice, contraception methods which often don't work with kids, or letting kids come to their own conclusions and sense of self. This is progressivism at its worst."

"I think you all need to chill out, and have a little more respect and faith in our children," Holt responded. "Remember these kids are watching *Sex in the City* and *Will and Grace*. And if you really want to get bent out of shape, there is *Queer as Folk* on cable."

"What about teaching responsibility and better morals?" asked Cienkus. "What about adults exercising their authority? What about teaching girls to say no? What about teaching boys to keep their penises in their pants? Can we eliminate provocative pictures of sex organs from texts before adopting a textbook?"

"Many of your suggestions or questions are unrealistic, given the sexual mores and the media that bombards our kids with sexually explicit behavior," said Holt.

Hassan defended Cienkus and insisted on pledges of virginity. "I would warn all girls of the things our mothers said to us. 'If you give away the milk, no man will buy the cow.' Once boys have tasted the milk, they become bored and move on. The boy treats the affair as another notch in his belt, and the girl is possibly impregnated. The responsibility becomes hers alone. It was very different before Betty Friedan and Gloria Steinem, when women and their relatives demanded the man marry the impregnated woman."

"Besides sounding antifeminist, you sound like you are living in a time warp," remarked Tomarshwari.

"No I'm not. For all the ripping down of barriers that have taken place for women in the last thirty years, we may have inadvertently weakened something essential for our own mental health and happiness—romantic love and an enduring relationship with one man," responded Hassan. "Friedan and Steinem, along with all the *Vogue*-like magazines, told us our sexual yearnings were not wrong or bad, and that we should enjoy sex and not deny ourselves the opportunities to do so."

"Are you saying that feminism is the cause of teen sexuality and teen pregnancy?" asked Holt.

"I'd rather avoid that issue, because it will lead us down a side trail which will mask the current problem we have with the sex education classes," said Tomarshwari. "I'm just concerned with virtues such as moral responsibility and parental responsibility."

Mary Sophros, a housewife, part-time computer specialist, and parent of three girls, added to the theme of responsibility. "In the past boys have had minimal responsibility and have left pregnant girls and their families to fend for themselves. Few teenage boys have any commitment before sexual intercourse, and much less after pregnancy. We have to teach boys to be more responsible for their actions. Instead of bragging about their conquests and destroying the reputation of their classmates, they need to be held responsible for a fundamental and historical role in society—as protector and economic provider for their children."

Milkovic was quick to respond. "Let's stop bashing males; it is a little trying at 7:30 p.m. to hear grown women criticize teenage boys. There are many teenage girls, as well as older women in their twenties and thirties, who want to get pregnant. They are not all ignorant or innocent and they are not the ones being exploited. Some young girls engage in sexual activity because of a need for intimacy and see motherhood as a way of substituting love they never had at home. Some feminists see motherhood as an alternative lifestyle and a way of asserting their freedom from male control. Still other single women are worried about their biological clock and are not engaging in sex for pleasure but for procreation. These feminists and single women brush off fatherlessness as right-wing stuffiness or a sexist put-down of single mothers."

"TV treats fatherless families as fun—a single parenting woman as a new age model to copy," stated another parent and father of two children. "Dan Quayle was no match for Murphy Brown, and Baby Bush is no match today for all the women who advocate sexual freedom and the willingness to raise fatherless children. Sex education is needed—so long as we point the finger of responsibility in the right direction. There are usually two consenting parties with different needs and motives, but women have the ultimate choice of saying no. . . . Let's not forget that point."

"I think it is much worse for inner-city youth," mentioned Coombs. "Men who lose their role as providers become sensation seekers and wallow in drugs and gangs. Boys who lose their traditional masculine model as provider bond with other male peers in gangs and spend much of the time attracting women and seeking sexual conquests, since they are unable to fulfill their male identity through manly jobs and viable careers."

"That sounds like a theory for some college classroom. Are you excusing male responsibility?" asked Sophros.

Sophros's remarks gave Coombs the opportunity to continue with her thesis. "Much of the deviant and delinquent behavior within inner-city communities is related to the displacement of men and dissipation of their parental investment in marriage and children. Furthermore, our welfare system indirectly tells men not to worry because the government will take over their parenting and job responsibility by supplying a handout. We have created a new family unit—woman, child, and bureaucrat."

For the next fifteen minutes, the discussion drifted from the responsibilities of teenage pregnancy and family disintegration to the social problems related to father-less children and single-parent female households. Then the topic of sexual orientation was introduced into the discussion—followed by whether sex education should include different sexual practices and nontraditional families.

Tomarshwari argued that the discussion again had degenerated into the politics of the absurd, under the guise of social theory, liberalism, and gay rights, and that it was difficult enough to agree on topics and content related to traditional sexual orientations. The current discussion would only polarize the community. However, Jim Matthews, a divorced parent and attorney, pointed out that the topic was vital, that it was the new millennium and gays had constitutional rights. "To discuss sex or family life in terms of *Ozzie and Harriet* or *Father Knows Best* is irrelevant and possibly may be considered discriminatory by the courts; the school board may risk a lawsuit if only traditional lifestyles and spousal relationships are examined."

Then, the discussion turned to marriage education classes that had been implemented in the ninth-grade English curriculum. Milkovic objected because it was a six-week requirement for graduation, and that "there were too many touchy-feely topics in an already overcrowded curriculum." He added, "More time needs to be spent with solid content—reading, grammar, and writing.

Coombs, the English teacher, responded: "There is nothing wrong in learning how to talk and get along with the opposite sex. But, for the six weeks we discuss marriage, I assign readings from Shakespeare, D. H. Lawrence, and Freud. The need for the course is clear. Stop to think about the number of divorces in this country, and that many children no longer see or experience healthy relationships at home between mom and dad to serve as models.

"At the Park Slope schools, I believe they teach it a different way," continued Mary Lou who knew some teachers in the other district. "They focus on conflict resolution, listening skills, compromising—skills that, if mastered by adults while in their teens, should curb the divorce rate, or at least make teen sweethearts think twice about marrying too soon. In a consumer society like ours, there is nothing wrong with providing facts about marriage before trying it, just like people gather facts about computers or cars before buying them."

Asked Cienkus, "Aren't the schools trying to do too much, and interfering with personal, private, and religious matters? What about spending more time on real subjects such as English, history, math, and science? These marriage classes should take place after school, or possibly as an elective course, or as a topic in guidance counseling."

"What about diversity and gay rights? Are all marriages only between men and women?" asked Holt who was one of the more liberal staff members.

Tomarshwari, the other guidance counselor, responded: "The idea of giving secondary students a primer on matrimony is new, and *Time* magazine reports that some forty states have taken the plunge into marriage education as a recommendation or requirement for middle, junior, and high school students. Whether we incorporate this curriculum into sex education classes is an issue for the curriculum committee.

"Listen, sex, love and marriage are a part of all societies, and the prime method for perpetuating societies. I'm not a sex expert, only a guidance counselor, but we cannot ignore the divorce rate and how it affects society, so if kids in our schools take some make-believe vow with plastic rings and are instructed not to kiss, and then we teach the facts of marriage, that's fine with me."

"But that's part of the problem," Milkovic responded. "It is similar to the point made by Hassan that was ignored. So much above love, sex and marriage deals with cultural and religious traditions, as well as ethical and moral interpretations. This country prides itself on respecting diverse cultures and religions, and since sex and marriage views are so varied, I don't believe the schools can adequately represent all the different views. That leads to controversy and conflict."

It was eventually agreed that sex education would be introduced as early as the seventh grade, as a six-week health and hygiene mini-course. In the next grade, the course would last for an entire semester. Boys and girls would be divided into separate classes in these courses. Ninth-grade students would have sex education as a three-week unit in biology, and there would be no separation by sex. The content would focus on body parts, marriage, and families. The issue of reading materials and texts would be examined by a textbook committee comprised of teachers and parents. A dress code would be introduced: no spaghetti straps, no bare shoulders, no tank tops, no fish-net stockings nor T-shirts with lewd or suggestive messages, and no tight sweaters, or shorts and other clothing suited to a party or beach.

No agreement could be reached on whether the school should urge abstention as a matter of policy or whether contraception should be encouraged for those who wish to participate in sex. Under no circumstances would the school issue condoms. Marriage education would continue as a six-week unit in English. As for the discussion of nontraditional sexual practices and families, it was argued that preadolescents were not mature enough to examine these issues and that the notion of a lawsuit was frivolous, since the school had no policy for or against gay teachers or gay educational materials.

Questions to Consider

1. Do you agree that most parents are unable to have frank discussions about sex with their children? (Refer to your own experiences as a child or parent.) Do you agree that most parents want the schools to introduce sex education?

2. What limits, if any, should there be on reading materials and discussion of sexual parts and sexual activity with junior high school (high school) students?

3. Should junior high school (high school) officials make condoms available to those students who are sexually active? Why or why not?

4. Should junior high schools (high schools) provide contracts for students to abstain until marriage? Would such a policy extend beyond the responsibilities of the school?

5. Should schools offer courses for pregnant teenagers on motherhood during regular school hours? Should teenage boys be required (as opposed to be expected) to share in the responsibilities of fatherhood. If so, in what way?

6. Some strong views were expressed about sex education. Which two characters do you agree with? Oppose? Why?

7. Interview a school district official to determine his or her views on the subject of sex education and to what extent the person's views correspond with certain character(s) in the case study.

Recommended Readings

David J. Anspaugh and Gene Ezell, *Teaching Today's Health*, 6th ed. (Needham Heights, MA: Allyn & Bacon, 2001).

Virginia Casper and Steven B. Schultz, *Gay Parents, Straight Schools* (New York: Teachers College Press, Columbia University, 1999).

Danielle Crittenden, *What Our Mothers Didn't Tell Us* (New York: Simon & Schuster, 1999).

Frances A. Maher and Mary Kay Thompson Tetreault, *The Feminist Classroom*, rev. ed. (Boulder, CO: Rowman & Littlefield, 2001).

Lynda Measor, Coralie Tiffin, and Katrina Miller, *Young People's Views on Sex Education* (New York: Routledge, 2000).

II
Curriculum and Instruction

6

U.S. History CD-ROM
Stirs
Up Storm

Content is the "stuff" or heart of the curriculum. It is the "what" that is to be taught and learned. Content is the facts, concepts, principles, theories, and relationships of a subject—what Jerome Bruner referred to as "structure," Benjamin Bloom referred to as "knowledge and problem solving skills," and E. D. Hirsch referred to as "essential knowledge."

Groups charged with curriculum planning have choices and options in content selection. The selection process is influenced by their philosophical, social, and psychological views of learning (what some might call foundations of education). Theoretically, if you know some person's or group's outlook in these three foundation areas, you should be able to predict with good accuracy their views on content.

Actually, there is a problem of too much choice. There is too much content to include in a semester or school year, and somehow we must determine what is available and select what will enable students to learn. Progressive educators usually are influenced by the students' needs, interests, and experiences—and therefore are considered *student oriented*. Traditional educators usually are influenced by acquisition of prescribed knowledge, ideas, and values—and are considered *subject oriented*. The task of selecting content is made easier if educators involved in planning curriculum think of just how they are influenced by their own philosophical, social, and psychological outlooks, and to what extent they view their methods and approaches as progressive (or liberal) or traditional (or conservative).

In the case study below, the philosophical and political outlooks of the players involved are evident, and their particular views create issues that some readers may consider relevant and others outrageous. But what content is *selected* depends on philosophical and social views, and how it is organized depends on one's psychological views of learning. In the area of history, however, there is more room for disagreement over content, where discussions can become highly charged, than in other subjects such as math, science, and foreign language.

Ideally, the selection of content is determined by certain criteria: (1) *self-sufficiency*, based on helping learners attain maximum understanding through an efficient use of time and effort; (2) *significance*, to the degree content contributes to the basic knowledge and ideas of the subject; (3) *validity*, that which is accurate, not misleading or obsolete; (4) *interest*, content that is meaningful and related to the learner's life experiences; and (5) *utility*, that which enables students to use learned knowledge in their life experiences and activities. How a person defines validity and utility is influenced by his or her philosophical and social views. How a person defines self-sufficiency, significance, and interest reflects his or her view of learning.

How we organize or sequence content is based mainly on basic learning principles or sometimes a philosophy and should be divorced from politics. Four basic learning principles are (1) *simple to complex learning*, that is, content is best organized from simple to complex components depicting relationships among components; (2) *prerequisite learning*, which is another way of saying part to whole learning, and that learning must be understood before new information can be learned; (3) *whole to part learning*, that with understanding a general idea more information can be classified and learned; and (4) *chronological learning*, in which the content is sequenced as it occurs, based on the order of topics or events. These four learning principles deal with the *process* of learning, as opposed to actual subject matter or *content*.

Some educators argue that it is more important to stress process than content and others argue the opposite. The danger with this type of reasoning is that it de-emphasizes content or process, when in reality both should receive relatively equal weight in the classroom where teaching and learning come together and where the curriculum is implemented.

ISSUES

A storm of protest erupted at John Jay High School in suburban North Carolina when a CD-ROM consisting of recorded sounds, interviews, songs, and pictures and based on a survey of eleventh-grade American history, was initially approved by the history chair and a small group of history teachers (3:2 in favor) and introduced as a supplement to the history textbook. The $179 disk included discussions of homosexuality, birth control, and abortion that touched off an emotional debate among many parents of the community. Among the controversial clips was one claiming that the Vikings should be recognized as discoverers of America, not Columbus. The section on "Manifest Destiny" contained a picture of two partially nude men accompanied by the statement "Some men were drawn to the frontier because of their attraction to other men." The same section included photos of a group of women, looking the role of prostitutes, who played poker with gruff cowboys, along with the statement "These women swore in low, husky voices, carried guns in their garter belts, and looked at men as a commodity."

Another clip pointed out that "Immigrant women at the turn of the twentieth century searched for birth control devices to limit the size of their families because of economic hardships associated with large families." Miriam deFord, who has been credited with inventing in 1914 a diaphragm-like birth control device, was given more footage and discussion than Woodrow Wilson, Henry Ford, and the Wright brothers, all of whom played major roles in American history during the same era.

Still others were critical that there was no mention of Sam Adams and Thomas Paine, but Elizabeth Cady Stanton and Betsy Ross received major billing. Washington and Jefferson were considered little more than slave masters who had a tendency to chase women and whose historical contributions were cast aside into second place. With the exception of some material about the Magna Carta, signed by the Pilgrims on the *Mayflower* (which was wrong), nearly the entire body of early American political and legal thought was absent: the English revolutions, Locke's and Rousseau's notions of individual rights, the Age of Enlightenment, that is, our intellectual heritage—all of which were used for inspiration by our founding fathers to frame the *Federalist Papers*, Declaration of Independence, and Constitution. The U.S. Constitution was viewed as an ethnic European document, protecting the rights of Anglo men while disenfranchising and oppressing women, blacks, and Native Americans, and the majority of working-class populations. In fact, the CD-ROM narrative stated that "black and Native Americans were treated as less than a whole person (3/5ths) or simply as if they did not exist."

Sam Houston, Davy Crockett, and Jim Bowie were depicted as rife with American jingoism and prejudice, while Antonio Santa Anna and his 7,000 legions were merely trying to reclaim the land taken by Americans under the expansionist policy called Manifest Destiny. Buffalo Bill and General Custer were treated as white imperialists who were psychotic and had no regard for the environment, while Red Cloud and Crazy Horse were romanticized for defending their way of life. The Indians were seen as having a complex society with respect for nature and according to their women a greater degree of equality than in other societies at that time. John Calhoun and Robert E. Lee were each given less than one minute of coverage and were treated strictly as racists, while Harriet Tubman and Frederick Douglass each received three to five minutes of coverage. Jane Addams and Susan B. Anthony received more coverage than Henry Ford and John Rockefeller as did Cesar Chavez over Sam Gompers and John Hoffer.

Tubman, Douglass, Addams, Anthony, and Chavez received unqualified praise and were considered part of the group of twenty-five "People Who Made a Difference" in American history, thus receiving equal coverage along with Washington, Jefferson, and Lincoln. While Lincoln was initially viewed as the Great Emancipator, a discussion of his reasons for his failed marriage was followed by the statement "I don't think we are sure that Lincoln was strictly heterosexual." Even worse, Lincoln was subsequently viewed as a racist who initially supported segregation in the North, told "darky" jokes, and used the "N" word in public—and only supported emancipation at the end of the Civil War, and only after Congress enacted it.

The world of the 1930s was described as "unstable"; fascism and communism did not seem to exist. The rise of Nazism was examined in two sentences and linked "to the discontent and suffering of the German people caused by the harsh terms imposed by the Treaty of Versailles." The Holocaust was not mentioned, but Hiroshima was and the Americans were criticized for committing a terrorist act on civilian populations. More attention was devoted to the Depression, labor and ethnic strife, and women in the U.S. workforce than to Europe at war. The bombing of London, Dunkirk, the Battle of the Bulge, D-Day, and the North African and Pacific campaigns were not mentioned, but the German invasion of Russia received considerable attention. Stalin was perceived as a military and political genius who thwarted the German military machine and was misunderstood first by Roosevelt and Churchill at Yalta and later by Truman, which in turn led to the Cold War.

As presidents go, Eisenhower is depicted as representing the military machine and more concerned about building the U.S. interstate highway system to transport army vehicles and playing golf on weekends than leading the nation. Nixon and McCarthy are seen as overzealous politicos who hunted down communists everywhere in the movie industry, colleges, labor unions, and government—creating the "red scare" and having a devastating effect on the nation's political atmosphere. Reagan is considered a "popular" president because of his acting abilities who, like Nixon, was in league with big business, reduced the federal role in education, and slashed social/educational programs. Roosevelt, Kennedy, Carter, and Clinton receive accolades as humane presidents who represent the people: poor people, elderly people, the capably disabled, women, minorities, gays, and other diverse populations. The Bushes are described as "daddy Bush" and "baby Bush" and as destroying the last 100 years of progressive social and economic legislation through tax gimmicks designed to help the rich and special deals with the tobacco, oil, and defense industries.

In terms of the environment, the CD-ROM highlighted the work of Green Peace as uplifting and necessary while drilling for oil in Alaska and the oceans was considered one step below genocide and a violation of animal rights. We learn that the oceans wash our coast and feed our needs. They are given a gender too, "feminine." And the human creatures who overfish or pollute are labeled "men." The message is subtle but compelling—about rape. We learn about horseshoe crabs, eels, and wild salmon—all of which are vanishing because of fishermen and polluters; the accompanying pictures are all of men.

The World Trade Center and the 9/11 event is viewed in terms of a long and continuous misunderstanding between Islam and the West, starting with the Crusades and Inquisition. According to the CD-ROM, it would be foolish to view the event strictly as an extremist or terrorist view. One remark, made by the narrator was highly controversial: "We can think of the U.S. as an innocent victim only if we ignore the history of Western imperialism and colonialism and the global reach of U.S. capitalism and values—and their threat to traditional and religious societies."

The outcome of the adoption decision?: A battle over truth and coverage in history erupted, as an increasing number of parents heard the news about the new CD-ROM. The producers of the CD-ROM were contacted by the school superintendent, who indicated that he had received more than fifty complaints from parents about the revisionary treatment of U.S. presidents and references to sex and sexual preferences on the disk and the general anti-American interpretation of history. He was under pressure to reevaluate the school's decision to use the material. Mr. Beni Nagib, the executive vice president of the company, admitted that he had received complaints from various parts of the country, but he was not inclined to produce another version of the disk or to provide a refund for materials that were used. "It is still popular," he claimed, "in many other places, especially in big-city school districts and liberal communities."

Nagib added: "I think there is much more passionate interest around the present interpretation of the past than ever before, and the materials address issues and topics that in the past were excluded or glossed over. The project was written by several well-known history professors who were funded by the American Historical Association, the number one organization for developing historical materials for high schools. It closely corresponds to the interpretation of the National Standards of U.S. History, funded during the former Clinton administration. Unless you wish to squash academic freedom at the college level and freedom of the press at your school, I see no need to make any changes."

Back home at the school district, a small number of parents and teachers began to organize against the critics and objected to the idea of excluding the CD-ROM from the curriculum. Fred Ryan, a parent and restaurant owner, commented that "Many people believe that CD-ROM histories are providing students with a more vivid and interactive description of history, much more interesting and direct than books ever did. For perhaps the first time in years, history is coming alive for my child—a result of the CD-ROM."

One of the gay teachers, Mr. Peter Pink, commented: "I guess there is an outcry, today, about histories and books that focus on the views of minorities, women, homosexuals, and labor. But I like the idea that many different people built America, especially ordinary people. Political leaders, industrialists, generals, and white males get first billing in history texts; this six-hour disk is a supplement to the text; it stimulates discussion among students and says something very different than the standard text."

Alessandra Ruffolo, veteran history teacher, put it this way: "Although I disagree with some of the topics within the disk, such as birth control and abortion, as well as some of the nude pictures and the reference to prostitutes, this is one of the most exciting and interactive materials we have used in our history classes. The CD-ROM is a three-dimensional means of dealing with the past and allows students to work with primary sources in an interesting way." Ruffolo was of the opinion that the disk developed thinking skills necessary for real comprehension and appreciation of history. "History has come alive for my students in a way I could never make it appear with the standard text. My students really enjoy thinking about and discussing the CD-ROM."

"Some of us might disagree with the interpretation of people or events portrayed in the CD-ROM," said Pink. "Washington and Jefferson really lived up to admitted standards of greatness, Stalin was a tyrant, and Truman contained communism and was the original architect of civil rights legislation. But most stories of American heroes, whether we're referring to Washington or Kennedy, Custer or Ike, have little to do with expanding people's knowledge. The goals have been quite the opposite—to restrict knowledge as a way of controlling discourse on the subject, to inflate the character of our heroes and reduce their flaws. The new history presents an element of reality; it brings knowledge and ideas to the forefront that we have buried in order to create historical myths and folklore. Our students need this new assessment of history."

Bonnie Kushner, one of the liberal teachers and union representative for the school district, made her point in a distinctly political tone. "If we bow to conservative pressure, we will be no better than Nazi Germany, when the books were burned—or Communist China under Mao, when the Party insisted on Mao's interpretation of history as the official version that everyone had to cite. This disk has a distinct political view, and some people might call it revisionary and radical. But so what? All history texts represent political views. When a history book makes an approved state adoption list, don't you realize politics are involved? Do you think the United States has always been morally right in its treatment of minority populations and foreign countries?" Ms. Kushner had managed to get nearly three-fourths of the 11th-grade students who had taken American history to endorse the history disk over the standard text. The battle over the CD-ROM was building.

Ruffolo, who had minored in women's studies as an undergraduate, asserted that most history teachers are inadequately prepared. Many have minored in history and have academic backgrounds in related disciplines such as sociology, psychology, political science, and economics. "I remember Mr. Kenezevic, our football coach for ten years, who taught history as if it was a side job. It didn't matter how much he knew about history; the school was more concerned about his teams winning the district or state tournaments.

"People like him, even if they don't coach," claimed Ruffolo, "treat history in the same safe and sterile way—relegating women and minorities to second-class status, not knowing any better, not realizing the ways women and minorities have had to endure, how they were successful in their own ways, and how they impacted the American dream." She argued that the CD-ROM was a necessary instructional tool for many history teachers who ignore, negate, or unwittingly ridicule the role of women and minorities in American history.

Kushner then remembered another history teacher she had known, Mrs. Dolittle, who knew very little about geography. "She refused to acknowledge that as many as five states had cities called Springfield, that there were American cities called Frankfurter, Naples, and Toledo. I also recall that she was unable to name the six New England states. During class discussions, she was unable to locate Mt. Everest, the Baltic countries, and Victoria Falls on the map."

While Dolittle could distinguish between funky pop and sugary pop, she could not distiguish between "who" and "which" or "then" and "than." Although she wore the latest fashions, including gold-hoop earrings, red visors, and pink and blue-rimmed sunglasses, and carried Italian leather fringed bags, her street speech was utterly embarrassing and filtered into her teaching and conversations with colleagues: "gotta," "you know," "understand," "get it," "cool," "hip."

One of the men in the audience quietly remarked that it sometimes pays to make special allowances for "Hippie deluxe women who wear Prada white sneakers and Kenneth Cole pink blouses." One of the mothers was overheard whispering to a friend: "What about men with tight buttocks who wear Calvin Klein underwear and know the differences between wine from the vineyards of Côte d'Or and Saône-et-Loire?"

Someone else proceeded to direct the public conversation to academic standards. "How can the colleges maintain academic integrity when students challenge C and B grades, threaten litigation, and use affirmative action categories and federal student labels to support their appeal procedures and student rights? When prestigious colleges like Harvard boast about the success of their students and part of that success stems from its students' ability to put a high GPA next to their name, surely this filters down to other top institutions. How can we blame professors since they know that a high correlation exists between how students evaluate teaching performance and the grade they think they will receive? How do you blame teacher education institutions when state departments of education permit emergency certificates, allow teachers to teach out of license, and grant tenure to teachers who are computer illiterate or unable to speak formal English?"

Despite the support from some teachers and parents, the superintendent felt there was mounting pressure to censor the disk. Roberto DeSoto, a history teacher, was representative of the older, more conservative teachers. He argued that the National Standards of U.S. History, first appearing in the mid- and late 1990s, had sparked a firestorm of controversy both in Congress and among historians and educators. The standards were condemned by the U.S. Senate ninety-nine to one, and the senators insisted that any future recipient of U.S. tax dollars (grant money) "have a decent respect for U.S. history." He concluded, "The CD-ROM is an outgrowth of the new standards in history, as viewed by some revisionary or radical historians who have gained intellectual control over the field and think they are on the cutting edge."

According to DeSoto, some people argue that the CD-ROM, along with the history standards, does not ignore traditional historical events or people, but achieves a balance between them and revisionist thinking. Some might also argue that it paints a balanced portrait of the Native Americans, African Americans, women, other minorities, and homosexuals who built this nation. In the past, white heterosexual males have stolen the credit.

"But," as DeSoto remarked, "it is obvious to anyone who is not beating a loud or dangerous drum that the CD-ROM distorts American history; it mocks facts, places, and causes of history and judges the thoughts and deeds of our ancestors in a highly disparaging, leftist manner, advocated today by some radical, neo-Marxist, multicultural, and postmodern academics." DeSoto continued, "The video was made by a group of radicals and approved by three history teachers who believe that most of us need to be reeducated. I have heard these radical academics at conferences and I have read their treatises. Most of them are angry sickos who vent their craziness on the public under the guise of scholarship. They really seem to have a few screws missing upstairs."

Kushner argued that DeSoto's characterization of academics was unfair, designed to limit dialogue and discussion about the part of America that was unjust and undemocratic. "What these professors and intellectuals say is important, not only for the purpose of interpreting history and social events, but also for making us critically think about the kind of society we want. This is exactly what the CD-ROM is about." The fact that the discussion was taking place one week after Thanksgiving was embarassing. Kushner was the only history teacher who recognized that the Pilgrims did not sign the Magna Carta, that it was an English document and the foundation for their present laws.

Jack Schwartz, a parent and war veteran, then got up and when he finished the audience was in an uproar. "The problem with these professors and critics is that they never fought for their country; they were legal draft dodgers, like Slick Willie, with his special deferments and excuses. Most of these people, when they were kids, got beaten up in the school yard, and were laughed at because they were on the Latin team or tennis team. They don't like real men, like people who have defended this country or now hunt deer with bows and arrows. And if you think this is some grunt or caveman talking, then you are missing the point."

Schwartz now directed his thoughts to the CD-ROM. "I can tell you why there is no mention of the World War II campaigns and no mention of our military leaders. Because it was white men who bore the brunt of the hardships in these military operations and saved this country and the world from the horrors of fascism, Nazism, Japanese militarism, and later from communism. You don't have to be a card-carrying commie or Know-Nothing, just a simple vet like me, to conclude this history is subversive and mocks what I fought for and this nation stands for. You can tell me all you want about freedom of speech and that the history of this country is multicultural; so it is, but if any of my kids have to listen to this crap-o-la, what you call a CD, then I'm going after the superintendent and the school board. You haven't heard the last from the so-called silent majority, what some of you call flag-waving Americans or rednecks."

Schwartz was now turning beet red. "I want my kids to attend a normal school with normal standards devised by normal citizens of the community. Those pinko radicals might control the college campuses," continued Schwartz, "and they might influence intellectual thought in certain fields of study or college departments, but they are not going to control this community. We have a common history, a common language, and a common set of values which bind us together as one nation. Santa Anna, Crazy Horse, and deFord are not my heroes. To dismiss the achievements of Washington and Jefferson, to claim that Lincoln may have been a closet homosexual or racist, that Custer was some kind of nut, or that Roosevelt and Truman misunderstood Stalin, who was one of the biggest nuts in history, is downright stupid and absurd."

DeSoto, who had lost a sister (his three young nieces were now motherless) at the World Trade Center, took notice of the way the CD-ROM blamed the United States. "I think the 9/11 analysis is off the wall, and reminds me how some Americans once thought Hitler was justified in marching into Czechoslovakia and later invading Poland, or that Hiroshima was unjustified. The problem with this CD, besides being pure bull, is its view of the world; that is, evil emanates from two sources: the U.S. in general and white males in particular. It's perverse history, downplaying terrorism and ignoring religious fanaticism. Instead of building American spirit and sense of community, the CD-ROM is divisive and distorts history."

Robert Anderson, a local banker and representative of the Scandinavian Historical Society, then advised that "The Scandinavian community does not want to get into a pissing match with the Italian or Spanish community but Columbus was five hundred years late in making his discovery and actually learned about the new world by reading Viking writings. It's hard to say because it violates our sense of history, what teachers have taught us, but the story of Columbus is one of the great pranks and frauds in the history of the world—merely an excuse for Spain to conquer Latin America and rob the new world of tons of gold."

"But with that kind of statement you are going to upset the Italian and Spanish community," said Kushner, "which comprise about twenty percent of all the residents in this community."

"There is nothing wrong with facing the truth," said Anderson.

"Whose truth?" remarked Ryan.

Then Ruffolo asked Anderson if he had any relationship with the Arthur Andersen accounting firm that overstated the values of Enron, WorldCom, and Global Crossings, companies that had collapsed and defrauded tens of thousands of workers and small investors. "Are you just another one of those 'sharpies' and 'corporate thieves' we read so much about in business and money magazines? How dare you infer that Columbus was a fraud!"

You can guess the decibel level of noise that followed the remarks of DeSoto, Schwartz, Anderson, Ruffolo, and Kushner. The next day the superintendent conferred with the school board and found they were split about what to do. Most of the PTA members paralleled Schwartz's views and wanted the disks removed. A slight majority of the history teachers and students did not want the materials censored. Also, there was the issue of the school budget. If the disks were removed, then the district would be out more than $179,000, or 20 percent of the annual budget devoted to curriculum materials and texts.

Given the current pressure to reduce needless spending, the superintendent knew that removal would lead to a different form of criticism among budget-minded residents. But if the disks remained in the classrooms, he felt criticism would continue to mount and he would lose support within the community on other professional issues. The superintendent knew that other books in the library and departments assigned to students contained political and economic messages, obscenity, sex, profanity, slang, or could be considered ethnic, racial, or gender sensitive.

The damage was already done, but the superintendent knew he had to make a sensible decision; otherwise, the controversy would build a life of its own and get worse.

Questions to Consider

1. What could the school district have done before purchasing the disks to protect itself from the vagaries of the fledgling CD-ROM industry?

2. Who should be assigned to purchase curriculum materials: teachers, supervisors, parents, central administrators, others? Why?

3. What do you like the most about the new interpretation of history? What disturbs you the most?

4. If you had to support the idea of using or discarding the CD-ROM, whose ideas would you consider most important: those of Ryan, Pink, Ruffolo, Kushner, DeSoto, Schwartz, or Anderson? Why?

5. To what extent do you believe revisionary or radical professors dominate the subject area in which you are majoring?

6. A decision is needed. Consider your own political views. What should the superintendent do?

7. Interview two or three administrators from a local school district. Ask them who should plan curriculum and select related materials. Report to the class.

Recommended Readings

Dina L. Anselmi and Anne L. Law, *Questions of Gender* (Boston: McGraw-Hill, 1998).

James A. Beane, *Curriculum Integration: Designing the Core of Democratic Education* (New York: Teachers College Press, Columbia University, 1997).

Nathan Glazer, *We Are All Multiculturalists Now* (Cambridge, MA: Harvard University Press, 1997).

William F. Pinar, *Queer Theory in Education* (Mahwah, NJ: Erlbaum, 1998).

Walter Stephan, *Reducing Prejudice and Stereotyping in Schools* (New York: Teachers College Press, Columbia University, 1999).

Detracking and Doing Away with Honors Classes

The most common means of dealing with heterogeneity is to assign students to class and programs according to ability. In high schools, students may be tracked into college prepatory, vocational or technical, and general programs. In many middle and junior high schools, students are sometimes assigned to a class by ability and stay with that class as it moves from teacher to teacher. In a few cases, and more often in elementary schools, students are assigned to a class on the basis of a special characteristic, such as being gifted or bilingual or having a disability. Elementary schools may use several types of within-ability grouping. They may assign students to a heterogeneous class and then regroup them homogeneously by ability in selected areas, such as reading and mathematics.

Despite widespread criticism of between-class ability grouping (separate classes for students of different abilities), teachers overwhelmingly support the idea because of the ease in teaching a homogeneous group. Parents of high-achieving students perceive tracking to be in their children's best interests. Reality is also a consideration. By the time students are in middle school, the achievement and motivation gaps between the top third and lowest third of achievers have grown extremely wide, and teachers often cannot accommodate this range of student abilities. What happens is that the top third or the brightest students become bored in class and the lowest third or low-achieving students become frustrated because they are unable to keep up with their classmates.

The primary criticism of separating students by ability is that it results in low expectations for low-ability students, lowered self-esteem, less instruction time, less homework, and less learning—even worse, this type of separation has a compounding and stigmatizing effect on low achievers. The negative consequences of these practices disproportionately affect low-income students, minorities, and female students in math classrooms. Given our democratic ideals and the need to deal with diversity in schools and society, and given the notion that abilities are multifaceted and developmental, not genetic, the argument is made that differences in ability can become assets in the classroom rather than liabilities. Moreover, different students have different abilities that need to be nurtured.

Researchers have found that high-ability students benefit from separate ability groups because the curriculum and instruction are tailored to the students' abilities, and the classroom work and homework driving the group require extra effort. There are fewer competing values to curtail the academic ethos and less time is devoted to management problems, as well as review and practice. The pace is swift and the subject matter is more abstract.

But such arguments tend to run up against our own democratic thinking—that is, the ethos and drive to reduce inequalities and differences (including outcomes) that may exist between high- and low-achieving students. Ability-grouping critics contend that the gains made by high achievers do not compensate for the loss of self-esteem and achievement among low achievers who often find themselves slotted into groups where the instruction is less engaging. It is not clear, however, whether performance of low-achieving groups suffers because students themselves are less motivated or responsive, because of management problems, or because the instruction is really inferior as critics suggest.

Most of the advocates for ability grouping reflect on essentialist philosophy, and they were most influential during the post-*Sputnik* and Cold War era. Reformers such as Arthur Bestor, James Conant, and Jerome Bruner come to mind. Their idea was to upgrade the curriculum and offer more honors and advanced placement courses, and pay more attention to our brighter students. Today, a few essentialists, coupled with gifted education advocates, still prefer homogeneous grouping, including options for honor classes and advanced placement classes, based on academic performance. However, they are mainly on the defensive end of reform and have been criticized by Robert Slavin, Jeannie Oakes, and Alfie Kohn for elitist and sometimes racists views: that (1) ability grouping rarely adds to overall achievement in a school (although it may for a particular class), but it often contributes to inequality (highs do better, lows do worse); (2) homogeneous grouping or tracking is harmful to many low-achieving students in terms of self-esteem, expectations, and reduced work productivity; and (3) the wide range of abilities and aptitudes of poor, disadvantaged, immigrant, and bilingual children, and children with disabilities tend to be ignored in a homogeneous or tracking system.

As teachers, the definition of gifted and talented, and provisions for them, will vary according to school policy. You will need to know how to make recommendations, and what supporting information to supply, to earmark students for specific programs or classes such as honors or advancement placement, or for special reading and remedial classes. Recommending bright students may be limited to independent study in class and special clubs or field trips outside of class. Many schools adhere to specific guidelines, and some school districts and states provide wider latitude and discretionary planning about grouping. Indeed, the current situation covering homogeneous grouping and tracking leads to zealous debates among educators and reformers.

ISSUES

For the last two hours, a group of parents, teachers, and supervisors has been meeting about the possibility of eliminating all gifted and honors course work for the high schools of a big-city district (consisting of 59,000 students) in the Southeast. At present, only English honors courses are open to any student who wants to take them. The group is divided about mixing high and low achievers in the same classes. Parents of gifted children have been pitted against the majority of other parents, teachers are generally opposed to the idea, and the principals admit they are under pressure to "detrack" programs and increase mixed grouping of students.

Bob Kulieke, an honor-student parent, is now addressing the group. "My son is forced to take a 'dumbed-down' English course, dramatically below his capabilities, under the guise of promoting democracy in the school and cooperative learning. These new learning theories are silly: Kids are not smart or dumb, just different. There is a new definition of intelligence which boosts social skills, musical skills, and physical skills on an equal level with cognitive skills. We are in denial that kids are different and that they have different academic abilities and intelligence."

One of the principals, Maggie Van Tassel, who regularly reads the educational journals such as *Phi Delta Kappan* and *Educational Leadership,* was quick to respond: "Mixed-ability classes, what we often refer to as heterogeneous grouping, has been assessed as effective for the vast majority of students. Whatever gains may be made by high achievers in homogeneous classes do not compensate for the loss of self-esteem and achievement among low achievers who are often labeled as 'slow' and placed into groups where instruction is of less quality. Mixed-ability classes expose bright students to students with other kinds of intelligence, and there is nothing wrong in mixing students of different backgrounds and abilities under one school roof or in the same class."

A minority parent, Valerie Johnson, added with a note of alarm, "Sorting students into classes by test scores and ability contributes to inequality, and creates in the mind of many teachers a self-fulfilling prophecy that low-achieving students are not expected to do well, so why push them? The students wind up wasting their time with busy work or low cognitive materials which they would not get in a regular class. Heterogeneous grouping and program tracking are outmoded, elitist, and perpetuate racial dissonance."

"I've heard those arguments before, especially whenever educators talk about programs for the gifted, when we test and place students according to ability, or attempt to toughen standards. No matter how you slice it, the fact is that students have a wide range of abilities that is evidenced by the bell-shaped curve," said Kulieke. "There are major differences between rapid and slow learners, and my child and the other gifted kids in the school district do not have to become part of another social experiment or pet theory that denies obvious differences in academic abilities. Education is supposed to stretch the imagination and minds of students and make them think, not to bore or slow them down by making them do dumbed-down course work."

One of the supervisors, Asad Tiazi, added to Kulieke's position. "I read the same journals that our principal has read. Reports show that after one year of mixed classes, gifted students trail their peers who remain in homogeneous honors programs by at least one-half a year, and after two years by more than one and a half years."

"What do you expect?" said Denise Pennise, a fifteen-year veteran teacher. "It may sound easy in theory—to teach twenty-five or thirty students in the same class with wide ranges of abilities, but it doesn't work in practice, especially when you teach to the whole group."

"A lot of good teachers manage to do it," said Tommy Thompson, a parent and history teacher. "You break them up into two or three groups, and assign different work to different groups. Denise, I think you are making it sound more difficult than it is."

"Really, now," responded Pennise. "If a class is divided into two separate groups, each doing their own work at their own pace, students spend approximately half of the time doing work without direct teacher supervision. With three groups, they spend two-thirds of the time without direct supervision—often waiting for the teacher to finish up with another group. A lot of academic time is wasted until the teacher returns to the original group to monitor or provide feedback. How does this benefit the students?"

Tiazi, who heads the modern language department, pointed out that school officials around the country are responding to a group of "influential educators who are promoting the concepts of cooperative learning, detracking, inclusion, and diversity in classrooms and schools—all of which put pressure on school districts to reconsider honor programs and advanced placement programs." He concluded: "Most high school principals with whom I speak are considering stopping the practice of separate classes by ability in most academic subjects."

"Why?" asked one of the parents.

Tiazi replied that educators such as Jeannie Oakes and Alfie Kohn attack all forms of ability grouping as favoring white and middle- or upper-class students, as a form of elitism and racism. "According to these educators, whatever benefits high-ability students obtain do not outweigh the disadvantages for low-ability students—they only contribute to further inequality. The primary criticism of separating students by ability, according to these educators, is that it results in low expectations for low-ability students, less instruction time, less homework, and less learning. The negative consequences of these practices disproportionately affect minorities and lower-class students."

"There is little doubt in my mind," argued Kulieke, "that gifted, talented and high-ability students need similar peers and a challenging curriculum. The research also reports that these students perform better academically and socially in homogeneous groups because the curriculum and instruction are tailored to the students' abilities and the classroom work and homework challenge and stimulate their thinking and creativity. There are fewer competing values that might curtail the academic ethos, the discussions are high level and abstract, and less time is devoted to management problems or routine academic tasks."

Kulieke continued: "Other research data suggest that the reformers have presented a one-sided view that homogeneous groups harm low-ability students on an academic, social, and psychological level. Actually, there is more social interaction and less acting out with like-ability peers, more student participation in discussions, more suitable classroom tasks, matched by student ability and interest, more time devoted to practice, review, and homework—all of which tend to improve test outcomes. Also, teachers are more effective when they are not forced to divide their time and effort among students with wide academic ranges and abilities. But given our notion of democracy and the need to promote diversity in schools, and now the new notion that abilities are multifaceted, the argument is made that differences in abilities can become assets in classrooms rather than liabilities."

"The point is," said Van Tassel, "this is an age of budget trimming, and gifted programs are going to have to be cut. We cannot cater to students with special needs which involve costly programs unless they are favored by government categories or government-sponsored programs."

"The real problem is," said Hrunda Bhagat, a chemistry teacher, "that gifted students have almost zero advocates or pressure groups in their corner, and no federally mandated programs. With the exception of the *Sputnik* era, which lasted about ten or fifteen years, they have always been underdogs. When people advocate their position, charges of racism or elitism crop up, just like they have here."

Bhagat continued: "Even during the height of meritocracy, that is in the 1950s and early 1960s, when testing and tracking of students was acceptable and when most scholarships were based on ability, not need or athletics, only a small percentage of the gifted and talented population was serviced by programs—not more than five percent. A low funding priority and lack of trained personnel has resulted in a scarcity of programs. Not only do these kids and their parents lack political clout at the government level, there is also growing resentment among educational reformers to eliminate special programs for all bright students in the name of egalitarianism. And, although honor classes and advanced placement classes will probably not be eliminated at the local school level, there is real pressure to change and broaden the talent pool of students considered to be bright, even if it means redefining intelligence and academic ability."

Willie Nillie, a parent and local flower shop owner, maintained that students exhibit a wide range of talents and abilities, not only in academic areas but also in social, personal, artistic, and technical areas. "We need to broaden our definition of gifted and talented, beyond academics. This would work well with the advocates of inclusion, diversity, and multiple intelligences."

"I agree," said Van Tassel. "Sidney Marland advocated this idea back in the mid-1970s, when he was U.S. Commissioner of Education, a title that has been replaced by U.S. Secretary of Education. Although Marland came from the Winnetka schools, an academically elite school district, he advocated gifted programs in six areas: general giftedness, academic talent, creativity, leadership, art, and psychomotor abilities. Ten years later Howard Gardner expanded the concept of human abilities and developed the concept of multiple intelligences beyond the verbal and mathematical abilities that schools emphasize. Another ten years after that, Robert Sternberg urged that educators observe, test, and teach toward three different forms of 'abilities patterns': (1) analytical, good in analysis, evaluation, and judgment; (2) creativity, good in invention, discovery, and coping with novelty; and (3) practical, good in execution, implementation, and leadership. Without separating students into different ability groups, he argues that we should teach all students in ways that capitalize on their strengths, and also on how to compensate for and correct their weaknesses. Most important, the critics of tracking and homogeneous grouping would support this broad idea of abilities."

Thompson stepped out of his role as teacher and now commented as a parent: "I can't feel sorry for gifted children or even bright children. Most of them come from middle- and upper-class homes, and most wind up going to prestigious colleges and getting good jobs when they graduate. My child is average; he falls into the cracks at school; few teachers pay attention to him or even know him by name, and he has withdrawn from social activities in school to protect his dignity and self-esteem. He is forced, along with so many other average students, to get recognition and build his self-esteem outside of school. I have no sympathy for the top ten or fifteen percent of the academic students who usually control school functions such as student government, student newspaper, school orchestra, school yearbook, etc., and get most of the school's attention."

Ms. Johnson was just as critical. "It borders on selfishness, perhaps immorality, that we label about three to four percent of our student population as gifted and another ten to fifteen percent as talented, inferring that the rest of the students are ungifted and untalented—not worthy of special treatment. These percents are based on James Conant's book, *The American High School Today,* written at the height of the *Sputnik* and Cold War period. Many of us are still influenced by Conant's thinking, despite the fact it was written for a different era."

Commented Kulieke, "Your inference is an unfair one, given the extra annual twenty-five billion dollars we spend together on compensatory education, special education, and bilingual education, plus the additional college scholarships and grant money we allocate for student need. I think it is immoral to place gifted students into heterogeneous or inclusive classrooms and pay little attention to their special needs and abilities. It is like telling these kids to 'cool it. You have enough advantages.' No one points out that many gifted and talented students are bored with school, fail academic subjects, and drop out of high school."

One of the parents of a low-achieving student added, "My child has been assigned to the slow classes since junior high school. Repeatedly she has received the message that she is dumb. Teachers rarely call on her, and when they do they rarely give her time to respond. There is less stigma for her in mixed-ability classes. She is assigned more homework, and she is expected to do more work in class."

Tiazi, who was also a parent of a gifted child, responded. "Once more, as in so many social debates, someone with brains or more money is viewed in a mean-spirited way. I agree with Mrs. Bhagat and Mr. Kulieke. Smart kids are the underdogs; and if I may add, everyone who is not defined in a minority or disabled category is an underdog today in terms of how money or programs are doled out by the government. Well, if this year's experiment in English becomes standard practice, then parents like myself will either look at private schools or move to the suburbs. It's these social experiments that cause white flight, and not the attitudes of white or middle-class parents. My child deserves to go to the best college that he is capable of going to and should not have to be handicapped by classmates that cannot keep up with him or by charges of elitism or that he is mean spirited."

"I hate to be so blunt, but it is the parents of high-achieving children, your type, that create so much pressure and problems in school," said Johnson. "These parents view education as competitive. The object is not for their children to learn, but to obtain the right credentials—whatever it takes to get their children into the right college, to qualify for the right job. These parents insist that high schools maintain honors classes and advanced placement classes, letter grades, class rankings, and award assemblies—anything that labels and distinguishes their children from others."

Johnson continued: "I have no sympathy for parents who have bright children. I feel they are selfish and mean spirited, although they appear to be polite and preppy, and vocalize the right sound bytes. They support school integration as long as their children don't attend these schools. They support equal educational opportunity as long as their children are not placed in heterogeneous classes, where supposedly instruction is slowed down and content is watered down. Many principals, especially in the suburbs, are afraid to challenge these parents out of fear they will yank their children out of school, just like you threaten to pull your child. Even worse, these parents sometimes use their knowledge, political clout, and social connections to challenge teachers if their children's grades fall below a B, to pressure school board members or coaches to get them placed on school teams, and call friends and alumni to help them get into prestigious colleges—all designed to ensure their children win. These parents often don't want to see other children performing well, because it means their own children might slip a notch and not be on top of the hierarchy. If only three student admission slots are available at Stanford University, why do these parents want other children to succeed and spoil their children's chances?"

"Part of the problem," interrupted Pennise, "is that our best and brightest students, and their parents, are influenced by the best and brightest adults. Just think about the CEOs and CFOs of Enron, WorldCom, and Arthur Andersen—how they cooked the books and deceived their workers, shareholders, and the public in general. Some of us might excuse their crooked dealings as nothing more than what to expect from big business—that is, monkey business. But then there is Doris Kearns Goodwin and Stephen Ambrose, America's favorite historians, caught stealing whole phrases and passages. And some of America's favorite presidents—Kennedy, Johnson, and Clinton—couldn't control their biological urges and used the power of their office to seduce women."

"Are you saying these adult transgressions and lack of morality influence our bright youth?"

"Yes. But I'm also indicting the system and society; it is unfair to single out our gifted and talented students as selfish or mean spirited when you consider how some of our best and brightest adults behave and how their parents behave—the pressure they put on them to succeed."

Nillie spoke up. "I want to do away with honors and advanced placement classes, with teaching and learning reserved for bright students, and replace them with inclusive classes, so all students can experience the same classroom advantages the 'haves' experience."

But Kulieke, a parent of an honor student, had a different take about special classes and schools for bright students. "The policy statements of almost every school in the nation reflect a commitment to meet the needs of *all* students. Yet, the schools put major emphasis on educating low-achieving, poor, and minority students who don't qualify for entitlements and don't make comparable efforts for those already achieving above average or who don't belong to an entitlement class. Too many school administrators and educational reformers refuse to make modifications for high-achieving students or even care if these students do or do not achieve at potential. No one except their parents advocate for them; and teachers overtaxed by large numbers of students in mixed-ability classes usually cannot find time to modify content for these students. The outcome is boredom, tune-out, and wasted human potential."

Continued Kulieke, "We need to recognize and reward our brightest students, not criticize them or their parents for looking out after them since no one else will. We need more honors classes, advanced placement classes, and special high schools like the Bronx High School of Science and the Texas Academy of Math and Science, and more summer college programs for our best academic students. I'm for giving students on the academic bubble the benefit, as well as extra support after school and on Saturdays, to increase diversity. But I'm against recognizing basket-weaving and basketball, or inter-personal skills, what I call 'chit-chat,' as a criterion for entrance into an honors class."

"I'll sum it up in a different way," said Tiazi. "No gifted or talented student, no national merit scholar, no student admitted into Harvard or Stanford should ever be made to feel defensive or criticized as elitist or racist. When it happens, it is a nail in our national coffin, one reason why our most able students, the top three or four per-cent, perform at much lower levels than their counterparts in other countries—and it vividly shows up on international test comparisons."

Questions to Consider

1. Should high school academic classes be organized around ability or mixed ability? Why or why not?

2. Did you attend a high school that relied on homogeneous (heterogeneous) group-ing? Did you benefit (or not benefit) from the practice?

3. What are the advantages of homogeneous grouping? Heterogeneous grouping?

4. Assume you are free to adopt a homogeneous or heterogeneous grouping when you teach. What instructional methods would you use to facilitate your job?

5. As a future teacher, who do you tend to agree with: Tommy Thompson, the history teacher who favored heterogeneous grouping; or Denise Pennise, the veteran teacher who felt it was impractical; or Hrunda Bhagat who felt gifted and talented students were generally ignored?

6. Some of the parents had very strong opinions: Bob Kulieke felt that his son was forced to take "dumbed-down" English and that there was a need to recognize and reward our best and brightest for the good of society; Willie Nillie wanted to broaden the definition of the gifted and talented, which led to a discussion on mul-tiple intelligences; Tommy Thompson in his role as parent had little concern for the gifted and talented because they dominated school activities; Valerie Johnson felt that sorting by ability was elitist and racist. Whose opinions do you agree with? Whose opinions do you disagree with? Why?

7. Using the library or Internet, read an article on gifted and talented students. First analyze the article as if you were Azad Tiazi, the supervisor of the Modern Lan-guage Deparment, then analyze it as if you were Maggie Van Tassel, the principal.

Recommended Readings

Alexinia Young Baldwin and Wilma Vialle, *Many Faces of Giftedness* (Belmont, CA.: Wadsworth, 1999).
Elizabeth G. Cohen and Rachel A. Lotan, *Working for Equity in Heterogeneous Class-rooms* (New York: Teachers College Press, Columbia University, 1994).
Howard Gardner, *Frames of Mind* (New York: Basic Books, 1983).
Glenn Hudak and Paul Kihn, *Labeling* (New York: Routledge, 2001).
Samuel Roundfield Lucas, *Tracking Inequality* (New York: Teachers College Press, Columbia University, 1999).

Pushing
for
Tougher Standards

Three periods of education reform have emphasized tougher standards and featured words such as "beefing up the curriculum," "academic excellence," "mental rigor," "rigorous grading," and "standards." In all cases, these periods were characterized by a traditional educational philosophy (perennialism or essentialism). The first wave of reform was at the turn of the twentieth century when educators saw a need to bring unity to a chaotic and confused situation, because different subjects were being introduced at a rapid rate and subjects taught varied from school to school. There was no conformity as to subject requirements, time allotments, grade placement, topics, or content.

With these unsettled issues as background, the National Education Association (NEA) organized a series of influential committees between 1893 and 1895 to bring order to the curriculum, The Committee of Fifteen, spearheaded by two staunch perennialists (Harvard University President Charles Eliot and U.S. Commissioner of Education William Harris), urged that the traditional elementary school curriculum remain intact, with its emphasis on teacher authority, mental discipline (that is, mental rigor), the three Rs, as well as literature, geography, and history. Hygiene, culture, music, and drawing were given sixty minutes, or one lesson, per week.

In general, the committee resisted the idea of newer subjects and the principles of pedagogy or teaching that had characterized the reform movement of progressive pioneers (such as Pestalozzi and Froebel in Europe and Mann, Barnard, and Schultz in the United States) during the 1800s. The committee also rejected the idea of kindergarten and the idea that the children's needs or interests should be considered when planning the curriculum.

The Committee of Ten looked at reforming the high schools. Its recommendations best illustrate the tough-minded, mental discipline approach supported by Eliot, who was also the chair. The committee recommended four different programs or tracks: (1) classical, (2) Latin scientific, (3) modern languages, and (4) English. The first two required four years of Latin; the first program emphasized English (mostly classical) literature and math, and the second program, math and science. The modern language program required four years of French or German. (Spanish was considered too easy and not as important a culture or language as French or German.) The English program permitted four years of either Latin, German, or French. Both of these programs also included literature, composition, and history.

The Committee of Ten took a position and claimed that the latter two programs, which did not require Latin or emphasize literature, science, or mathematics, were "in practice distinctly inferior to the other two." In taking this position, the committee indirectly tracked college-bound students into the first two (or superior) programs and noncollege-bound students into the latter two (or inferior) programs. The committee ignored art, music, physical education, and vocational education, maintaining that these subjects contributed little to mental discipline.

The choice of certain subjects and the omission of others set the tone for the secondary curriculum for the next fifty or more years and indirectly set the tone at the elementary level, which fed the junior high and senior high schools. Even though very few students at that time went to college (less than 3.5 percent), this college preparatory program established a curriculum hierarchy, from elementary school to high school, that promoted academics and ignored the majority of students, who were noncollege bound. Today, even though we offer vocational, industrial, and technical programs, the academic program is still considered superior to and of more status than the other programs.

The second period for emphasizing academic standards was during the post-*Sputnik* and Cold War era, when American education and, in particular, progressive education became a target for criticism. With *Sputnik*, national pride was shattered, and there was the prospect that our oceans no longer protected us; there was the threat that our skies were penetrable. Then there was the Korean War in the 1950s, uneasiness with Mao's Red China, Khrushchev banging his shoe at the United Nations and yelling in front of the television cameras that Russia would bury us, Castro's Cuba and the Khrushchev–Kennedy missile crises.

Society pressed the schools to respond to our national concerns; in fact, some of us called it a crisis. The critics claimed there was too much emphasis on the "whole child" and "life adjustment courses" at the expense of critical thinking and academic rigor. In lieu of progressive pedagogy, playtime at the elementary school level, and a broad education at the secondary level which stressed the whole child, the need was to return to the basics (or three Rs) at the elementary level and essential subject matter at the secondary level: English, history, math, science, and foreign language, especially the latter three subjects. The need was to turn out sufficient scientists and mathematicians, and to push our bright students, in order to beat the Soviets.

This would become the reform period in American society where the idea of merit was fully accepted and promoted as a national goal, and when testing and tracking of students would be considered the norm without question. Powerful forces such as Arthur Bestor called for "a return to academic essentials and educational meritocracy." He declared that "concern with the personal problems of adolescents had grown so excessive as to push into the background what should be the school's central concern, the intellectual development of its students." The titles of his books, *Educational Wastelands* (1953) and *The Restoration of Learning* (1956), conveyed the message of the day. In *Education and Freedom*, Admiral Hyman Rickover questioned why Johnny could not read while Ivan could. For purposes of national interest, he demanded a "deemphasis of life-adjustment schools and progressive educationalists," and a return to the basics and "a beefing up of our science and mathematics courses." At the same time, he compared American and European schools and concluded, "The [American] student must be made to work hard," at his or her studies, and "nothing can really make it fun."

Our failure to heed Bestor's and Rickover's criticisms and warnings of the post-*Sputnik* era can be viewed by some as one reason why national attention has turned to a new wave of educational reform—the need for educational excellence and higher academic standards for all students. The educational concerns of the present period, and the policy reports between 1980 and 2000, all call for reforms to improve the quality of American education, and are highlighted by *A Nation at Risk*, published in 1983, *The National Education Goals*, published in 1990, and revised in 1994 and 1997, and the standards and testing movement of the new century.

In a nutshell, the previous concerns of the *Sputnik* era resurfaced in the 1980s, and have continued into the new millennium, under the themes of "excellence in education," "core academic curriculum," "standards-based education," and "education accountability." There is the same feeling of urgency. The only difference is that the outside threat, instead of being perceived in terms of guns and tanks and Cold War military defense, is now perceived in terms of economic competition and international test scores.

In the 1950s and 1960s, when there was concern that Johnny could not read or solve science or math problems and Ivan could, there were two great giants and two great ideologies squaring off at each other. At present, the United States bestrides the globe like a colossus. It dominates business, commerce, and communications. When it coughs or hiccups, the whole world hears the echo. However, we are still concerned about America's future workforce and ability to compete with the industrialized nations of Germany, Japan, Korea, and Third World countries like China, Taiwan, and Mexico.

Considering that we live in a highly technocratic, computerized, and scientific world, one in which knowledge has a great impact on our standard of living, and a world in which the push of a button can have an enormous impact on our lives, student enrollments in science and mathematics have serious implications for the future of our country. Although this statement could have been made twenty years ago (when *A Nation at Risk* was published) or fifty years ago (when *Sputnik* was launched), the words ring true today. Given that the world is now a "global village," one that is highly interconnected and can be radically changed in a flash by an electronic or communications malfunction or nuclear meltdown, the stress on science, math, and technology—and performance standards in general—is crucial.

ISSUES

When the dust settled at the latest national governors' summit, it was agreed to revive the campaign for tougher standards in the classroom: more rigorous goals, more homework, more academic subjects, tougher high school exit exams, higher college admissions standards, greater emphasis on computer technology, and increased teacher entry requirements and teacher accountability.

Dr. Jim Jenkins, the school superintendent in one of the suburban school districts of Seattle, read the governors' news release and decided to call a meeting with his teachers to discuss district standards. After distributing a two-page summary of the governors' proposals, he announced the launching of a district-wide committee to implement new standards and assessment procedures. The committee, to consist of five parents, five teachers, and three administrators, would have three months to submit its report to the school district.

Superintendent Jenkins ended the meeting with the following statement: "Several years ago, at the national summit, the governors created a set of national guidelines which were criticized by some groups as impairing local school district control, by other groups as offending minorities, and by still other groups as infringing on teachers' academic freedom. These excuses are red herrings. This state wants tougher academic standards, as well as monitoring procedures to assess the standards; the business community wants them too. We have a responsibility as educators to deliver these goods to our clientele."

The next day, in the teachers' lounge, several teachers and supervisors were discussing the superintendent's proposal. Said Olga Gajdosik, an art teacher: "The governors' recommendations for reform are too idealistic."

"Why do you say that?" asked another teacher.

Gajdosik responded: "They expect too much from students and teachers. They are too ambitious; nonetheless, their ideas are driving state reform agendas across the nation."

"I disagree," asserted Johnny Evers, who was starting his second year teaching. "The problem with the superintendent's thinking, the governors' thinking, and the whole notion of state reform and the resulting emphasis on academic standards is that there is an overriding view that schools lack direction and teachers lack accountability. The inference is that education can be improved through legislative policies, state regulation, and bureaucratic control. Their ideas are based on negativism—educators must shape up or ship out, maintain certain standards or be sanctioned. The new standards do not treat teachers as professionals, rather as semiprofessionals or semiautonomous workers in an organization that is administered from the top down."

"I'm concerned that this standards-based movement will turn into a witch hunt or one based around punishing teachers," said another teacher.

"I am afraid we will devote more time and effort to teach what is going to be tested," insisted Dereka Djakovija, an English teacher, "and it will detract from our ability to make pedagogical decisions. The ideal view of professional autonomy is that teachers do not align the curriculum with tests or teach toward tests, but develop their own curriculum to meet the needs of their students. I believe political and business considerations, and the pressure to prepare our students to pass new statewide exams, will outweigh professional autonomy."

"Nonsense. Education reforms come and go," said Abba Dabba-do, a history teacher. "One day it's rosy and sunny, and it's great to be alive. The next day it is rainy and someone points their finger at you. I would not get bent out of shape. Do you really believe that teacher jobs will disappear if test scores fall below a certain benchmark or if our students fail to improve? What business will change its plans to locate because there are a few students who fail to meet national or state standards set by some distant group of educators, even worse by some politicians?"

"I think the standards are too high, nearly impossible for most students to achieve," remarked Gajdosik. "If you look at these new standards, we have to start changing the curriculum in kindergarten and teach the students from the beginning with a curriculum that reflects the new standards."

"There is another problem," said Gajdosik, "the conflict between standardization and diversity. The standards movement promises to give all students the same knowledge and skills required for a sound education, but kids differ in abilities, needs, readiness levels, and learning styles. One standard for all students will not work, regardless of the number of tutors hired or adaptive materials employed. Student differences and learning rates vary to the extent that curriculum and instruction must be more different than alike for each student. Outcomes will vary, regardless of what content all students must master."

"No question the rules are changing," said Joe Tinker, a graying science teacher. "Students are being told that if they don't meet the new expectations, they will not graduate. Teachers and administrators are being told that where performance doesn't measure up, the school can be put under state review and possibly closed. Some school districts have set up extended school days and others six-day school weeks for kids who need extra help. The assumption is that the more instructional time a student has, the more likely that he will be successful. By the way, the pay is pretty good, if you want to volunteer to teach the extra hours."

"I think it is a matter of personal philosophy and perception about how difficult these exit tests are," said Frank Chance, a first-year math teacher. "More than twenty-five states now require students to pass exit tests for a high school diploma, but most reflect basic competencies, not rigorous standards sought by the governors or business community. We have trouble competing on a global level because our existing state standards are minimal. For every state that has imposed tough standards, twice as many have questionably low standards."

"I think this is all changing, as an increasing number of states raise academic expectations and the percent of students in each school that must meet the minimum standards," said Jian Jun Pong, the science chair. "If schools don't improve performance, they go under review with the ultimate possibility of being closed down."

"Many big-city school districts will never meet these state standards. I bet some big cities wind up with their own standards. The mayors of New York, Chicago, or Los Angeles are not going to allow the governors, under the guise of 'wascally wabbit' education, to interfere with their large, powerful school systems," said Evers.

"What kind of education?" asked Dabba-do.

"The polite terms are politics and education. I was just trying to lighten the education posturing."

"No doubt states and school districts need to set direction and goals, including similar academic standards and methods for assessing student learning," commented Dabba-do. "But establishing standards and monitoring policies are not simple tasks. They deal with sensitive issues concerning what standards, who develops them, how we test them, what we do with the results, and what kind and how much compensatory assistance we provide to students who fail the tests."

"You know everyone enjoys a good meaty reform program," declared Gajdosik. "But testing has been around for a long time and a very large testing industry has already been built around these tests. The new rage over testing is overkill in my view.

Young kids are being tested repeatedly and feel the pressure. Our schools are drifting toward becoming test-taking factories, and our teachers are no longer teaching but are instead preparing kids for tests."

"My concern is that this new testing program compares schools and school districts and leads to a 'don't test, don't tell' policy," said Pong.

"What does that mean?"

Pong explained. "When penalties, rewards, or school reputation is at stake, some of us look for angles to improve our ranking. We place low achievers in classes for students with special problems so we can exclude their scores, and we flunk other students to give them another year to mature and improve their skills. It's like the old sports game of holding players back to strengthen them so they can better compete. Still other schools rely on another policy, that of freely labeling students as learning disabled to provide unlimited testing time. The effect on raising test scores is significant. All of these subtle variations make comparisons among schools and school districts virtually impossible. The whole process has become a witch's brew. We zap many schools that play by the rules while ignoring other schools that inflate their scores by delaying testing of low achievers, providing extra test time for others by calling them learning disabled or labeling them ADA, or excluding them entirely from the testing process."

Chance then mentioned that a useful way to think about school reform and standards is to begin with practices that should take place in classrooms, and then build up to practices that should take place in schools, then school districts, then states, and finally the nation. "In other words, I advocate a down-up or grassroots model of reform to guide state or national reform efforts, instead of the current top-down model."

"During the last fifty years," Tinker remarked, "educators have learned that the best method for changing and improving schools is to involve teachers in collaborative efforts, in all phases of development and implementation of new programs, then to provide them with training and in-service education. But the new state rules, regulations, and sanctions will only lead to minimum commitments of teachers. The best way for enhancing student learning is to enhance teacher learning, teacher collegiality, and teacher input; the state standards and assessment policies result in teacher conformity and loss of teacher control and autonomy."

Pong stopped drinking his coffee and put his buttered roll down. "Standards exist in all of the major subjects. They were developed by professional associations which are open for us to join, and they were established with care and deliberation. There may have been some compromise so as not to offend any particular group, but I see little reason why the state or any other government agency must reinvent the wheel."

Djakovija, the English teacher, had a different slant on professional associations' standards. "The national standards currently in place have no impact on learning. They are vague and watered down. In my subject, they were formulated by the National Council of Teachers of English. They are written as bland statements designed to offend no one, such as 'students shall use spoken, written, and visual language to accomplish their own purposes'; 'students shall apply knowledge of language structure, language conventions, media techniques, figuration language, and genre to create, critique, and discuss print and nonprint texts.' The standards make no mention of required books to read, no mention of grammar, no writing or essay requirements, no grade-by-grade recommendation of tangible skills to learn."

Tinker, the science teacher, was more positive about the national efforts to reform and upgrade K–12 science, insisting that the standards effort has changed the curriculum from *reading* about science to *doing* it, by fostering more experimentation and hands-on activities, and by insisting that all students become *scientifically literate*. "Literacy means being familiar with the scientific world, understanding how science, math, and technology depend on each other, and using scientific knowledge and scientific thinking for personal and social purposes. The traditional science curriculum emphasized content and laboratory-based experiments. Science reform today links content with application in the real world; hence, it has moved from the laboratory to community-based projects."

Tinker continued: "The traditional science curriculum tried to train little scholars, based on the post-*Sputnik*/Cold War mentality, to beat the Soviets. It was fueled by Jerome Bruner's *The Process of Education*, that is, specific subjects had a structure: theories, principles, and concepts that should be taught. Each subject had defined boundaries, separate from other subjects. Today's curriculum encourages integration of science with other subjects and also encourages students to use science in their daily lives, to make appropriate decisions involving technology and social issues. Some science education experts refer to this new emphasis as *STS*—science, technology and society."

"The traditional high school course sequence, in place since the 1920s, offers biology, chemistry, and finally physics," he continued. "The new science curriculum questions this course sequence, since seventy-five of the agreed list of 152 basic concepts that scientifically literate people should know are in physics; yet, this course has the lowest enrollment and appeal among students. Its excursion into scientific literacy starts with physics, moves to chemistry, and then to biology or earth science."

"It is the same with math reform. Most changes in math have come from the National Council of Teachers of Mathematics (NCTM)," said Chance, the math teacher. "The NCTM has revised and upgraded standards in math by emphasizing mathematical reasoning and problem solving. It has helped align high-stakes standardized tests with agreed-on math content, and it has been instrumental in integrating math and technology, especially with computers and graphing calculators, for the purpose of storing common formulas and tables. The result has been a change in math pedagogy—less attention is paid to traditional knowledge-based topics. The NCTM has also encouraged math teachers to use real-world problems to teach all students, increase student expectations, toughen grading policies, and cover fewer topics in more depth within each course."

"Mr. Chance is correct," commented Pong. "Check the *Digest of Education Statistics*. It publishes the results of the National Assessment of Educational Progress. In the last twenty-five years, since 1973, the average math proficiency level increased twenty points for nine-year-olds, ten points for thirteen-year-olds, and five points for seventeen-year-olds. In science, it went up ten points for nine-year-olds, five points for thirteen-year-olds, and is at the same level for seventeen-year-olds. Furthermore, many more students are required to take these tests. You would have expected lower scores with an increase in student participation."

"Not necessarily, if teachers are now teaching toward the test or school principals are excusing some students who are considered learning disabled or limited non-English-speaking," insisted Evers.

"Now, now, let's not get smug or small-minded or accuse our colleagues of engaging in questionable practices."

"Well, people do what they have to do, and some people take extreme measures when their reputation or job is on the line," asserted Chance.

"I would rather not get into a long discussion of school districts and states where serious questions have been raised about the validity of gains in high-stakes test scores," Evers remarked. "I'd just say 'all that glitters is not gold,' including Texas, which tended to have higher NAEP scores than other states when Bush was governor."

"I recall those gains in Texas being called the 'Texas miracle'," declared Gajdosik. "Well, there have been enough documented cases of cheating across the nation. All you need to do is read the Rand reports, the *New York Times,* or *Education Week* to get the latest account."

"I prefer we stop this judgmental talk," said Chance. "Cleaning laundry should be a private matter. Personally, I think teachers have a tendency to criticize other teachers instead of protecting or supporting them."

Dabba-do, the history teacher, spoke: "I believe American history has been watered down to make room for courses in pluralism and ethnic and global studies. In some school districts, American History I is taught in the eighth or ninth grade and American History II in the eleventh or twelfth grade. So, the first 150 years of the nation's history is taught at the junior high level."

"Doesn't that have something to do with the spiral curriculum?" asked Gajdosik.

Tinker responded. "The idea is to increase depth and breadth of important ideas, or what Jerome Bruner called the 'spiral curriculum' and what Ralph Tyler prior to Bruner called 'curriculum continuity.' But when you teach content for the first time, there is no practice or opportunity to increase depth of understanding."

Dabba-do continued. "The fact is, only ten percent of high school seniors are considered proficient in American history while seventeen percent of eighth graders and eighteen percent of fourth graders reached that level on the National Assessment of Educational Progress, reported in 2002. In reverse, one-third of fourth graders lacked a rudimentary understanding of American history appropriate for their grade level. By the eighth grade, the figure rose to thirty-six percent and by twelfth grade it rose to fifty-seven percent. These are dismal scores, worse than any other subject, even worse than science and math."

"Given the events of 9/11," asserted Tinker, "I feel a little jittery about whether our high school seniors know enough about the nation's history and have the ability to understand the concepts of Western civilization, what this country is about, or what our international role should be."

"Let me give you more bad news," remarked Dabba-do. "When college seniors at the top-ranked 55 colleges were tested, according to a Roper assessment, seventy-eight percent had no idea that 'government of the people, by the people, for the people' was part of Lincoln's Gettysburg address. Just forty percent could associate the Battle of the Bulge with World War II, and only thirty-four percent knew that Washington was the commander at the Battle of Yorktown—the turning point of the Revolutionary War."

"The real issue is," continued Dabba-do, "that those of us who know better lack backbone and cave in to multiculturalist pressure groups at the expense of an education that should highlight Western culture and Western ideas. We need to teach our own history and be proud of our own heritage. Instead of only emphasizing tolerance, we need to emphasize intolerance toward failure—that's what is un-American."

"Among all the industrialized countries, the United States is probably the only one without a national curriculum and national test for academic tracking. The reason is simple: We have no national ministry of education. The Constitution gives the states wide latitude over education; in turn, the states permit local communities to share in its educational responsibilities. The idea of creating tough standards lies with the states, and not the federal government. This creates a problem, since state standards vary dramatically among the states."

"I don't think the issue is at the state level, rather it is at a local school level," said Michael Courtheoux, a veteran French teacher. "All the reform rhetoric and ambitious programs discussed by the governors, along with the new state standards, are of little value unless they consider what happens at the school level. The problem is that there are some 15,000 school districts, 85,000 schools, and 3.1 million teachers who have their own brand of education and idea of what works in the classroom."

"Mike is right! Reform must consider the daily practices of teachers in their classrooms and schools," insisted Evers. "Reform is also expensive. Additional costs have to be met by either cutting other programs or by raising local property taxes. Go sell that reform package to a paunchy middle-aged couple whose kids have graduated from high school and whose health benefit package was just cut at the workplace."

"Aside from the financial pressures, if students are held back because they fail to pass exams, the new standards may lead to more students needing to attend summer classes or even an extra year to graduate—causing more frustration and more students to drop out," commented Chance.

"I agree that school reform is a local issue, because we have so many school districts and school board members who make policy based not on research, but rather on habit, history, and local politics. Board members are rarely impressed by the recommendations of professional associations or educational researchers," asserted Pong, whose brother was an ex-board member and part of the old guard in another school district.

"Based on my brother's experience, board members are more impressed by someone who is polite, not honest. Board members are generally well-meaning people, but they are often naive or ignorant about what policies to adopt or what programs generate what outcomes. They are influenced more by Bill O'Reilly's thirty-second sound bites than the research of Ben Bloom or John Goodlad. Remember, school board members are a collection of local citizens comprised of businesspeople, sales and service people, and housewives—not educators. In addition, most parents and community residents have had their own experiences with teachers and schools which result in various personal views and hardened beliefs about what constitutes effective education."

"You can make the same statement about teachers. They know more about Bill O'Reilly's views than about Bloom or Goodlad, and that has serious implications about professionalism," said Courtheoux.

"Let's face reality. The problem is that the new standards and all the other reform packages rarely consider the host of educational deficits so many of our children have because of lack of family structure and parental responsibility," Gajdosik continued. "I'm not going to discuss one-parent versus two-parent households, since that raises too many eyebrows among minority groups, divorced women, and feminists. Parents today, including middle-class parents, seem to lack sufficient time or interest to nurture their own children's education. Instead of reading to their children and playing with their children, they rely on television, videos, and computer games to occupy their kids' time. Then the parents point the finger of responsibility at teachers and ignore their own responsibility. I think we are barking up the wrong tree. It matters little if we have national or state standards, or even local standards, if there is no fruit on the tree."

"That sounds so futile and begs the question about our professional responsibility as teachers," responded Tinker. "We are getting paid to do a job, and to ensure that students are educated to their maximum potential. I think we have been too easy with students, and our schools are too lax. What we need are standards which are tied to consequences. This means no promotion for social reasons, no watered-down content, no fuzzy standards, and no grade inflation. I'm an advocate of traditional teaching and learning: emphasis on the three Rs, more homework, teaching Shakespeare and not black English or Indian sign language, and penalties for failing tests."

Courtheoux made another point: "All this talk is mere venting and illustrates just how impotent we really are. State or national standards cannot work because the professional view of teachers is not considered. Groups of politicians, businesspeople, or academic professionals decide our goals and standards. They are written by people with social and political power, not by people who teach or understand what teaching is about. The curriculum is implemented by teachers in classrooms, not by groups of people outside schools. When goals and standards, and also curriculum content, include the teachers' voices, that is when school improvement efforts will work."

"I like your point about content," said Djakovija. "In fact, I see the content issue as a quality issue. States typically require a certain number of courses or credit hours at the secondary level in history, English, math, and science to graduate, and since the publication of *A Nation at Risk* in 1983 this number has increased, but states have left the question of quality up to local educators. I think there is a need to improve quality, not just quantity."

Djakovija continued: "Right now a measley one percent of twelfth graders writes well enough to be categorized in the advanced level of the National Assessment of Education Program, according to *U.S. News.* Only ten percent of eighth graders eligible for free lunch score at or above the proficient level. Our national tests show that our students don't have the right stuff."

"Did you know that in many industrialized countries such as Japan, Korea, and Germany, at least twenty-five percent of all high school students pass at least one advanced examination in math or science. In the United States, according to the *Digest of Education Statistics,* seven percent of high school students enroll in advanced placement science and five percent in advanced placement math, that gives them college credit," asserted Pong. "The average Japanese and Korean high school student takes one and a half courses per year in math and science. American students average less than three-quarters of a course per year in the same subjects—and it shows up later in our technological and manufacturing output. We fought the Gulf War with electronic equipment that was produced largely, about eighty-five percent, in Japan."

"What about the war in Afghanistan?" asked Courtheoux.

"Without sounding like a cliché, I think I've made my point," snapped Pong.

Gajdosik, the art teacher, responded. "This argument about toughening standards and upgrading the curriculum is old hat. We often fail to appreciate that education is more than cognitive or academic achievement. It involves social, moral, and aesthetic development. The secondary schools don't need to produce future scholars and scientists; that is the role of colleges and universities—when students specialize in their major field of study. We need to emphasize a broad education for students who will become literate in music, art, literature, as well as science and technology. Yes, music, art, even physical education, have a place in the curriculum. Picasso may not be as important as Plato, but he certainly influenced Western culture.

"We also need to recognize and bolster civic virtues, community values, and common decency, if we are to remain a democratic country with a common purpose."

"What does all this have to do with content, standards, and academic excellence?" asked Chance.

"I'll give you the short answer," remarked Gajdosik. "We need to recognize that there are many slow runners, or average and below-average students, who must become productive citizens if we are to prosper as a democratic society. We need to appreciate multiple intelligences and multiple skills, not only verbal and mathematical reasoning. There are too many C students who fall into the cracks and are discouraged by their schools, which emphasize the top fifteen or twenty percent of the student population."

"I agree," said Tinker. "Many A students wind up working for C students. Just think of Bush and Powell. You wouldn't find them in the library in high school or college. Then there is Bill Gates, who dropped out."

"The question is, can teachers adhere to high standards and still be responsive to the multiple needs of their students?" asked Dabba-do.

"How can we respond to student needs or interests when we are being forced to follow a script, with step-by-step lesson plans and predetermined guidelines?" asked Djakovija.

"Well, we need to help students reach higher standards, and aligning the curriculum to the standards is helpful," commented Dabba-do.

Evers, who was a little cynical for a young teacher, commented: "Under normal circumstances, the top students will meet the standards—and even exceed them. I'm worried about low-achieving students. Our standards should be bottom up, not top down. That is a different philosophy and approach to education, one that is more democratic and realistic. We can talk about tough standards until we are blue, but it matters little for students who cannot spell or pronounce the written language."

"Mr. Evers, I share in your concerns. I'm skeptical that the new plan will not produce much in the way of results," said Gajdosik. "It takes money to produce the results we are talking about. Higher standards mean very little if they cannot be supported with investments of capital—small classrooms, homework and tutoring classes after school hours, parental education, and retraining teachers to adapt to a new curriculum. Anyone can invent standards; the idea is to enforce them and to ensure that students can meet these standards. Did you know that seventy-five percent of American high school students complete less than one hour of homework a night? High school students in Japan, Korea, and Germany average about three to four hours of homework a night."

"Olga, your views are sound," responded Pong. "But I think the superintendent wants us to set new, tougher standards. He expects academic competency, and so do the state education agencies and local business community. I don't think music or art is part of Jenkins' agenda or Ford's agenda when it hires people to build cars. The idea of school reform is tied to core academic subjects, not breadth of subjects."

"I hope you don't feel offended, as an art teacher. But if we consider the sport of curmudgeons," said Courtheoux, "standards are about Cervantes, Hugo, and Shakespeare and why a playwriter or novelist ends at a certain point in his story, and not about Picasso and why the woman in his picture has one large and one small breast."

Questions to Consider

1. How do you feel about current academic standards? What is driving the push toward tougher standards?

2. At what level should standards be established: local, state, or federal? Why?

3. To what extent should the business community become involved in curriculum development? To what extent should parents become involved? To what extent should teachers become involved?

4. Which two teachers do you most disagree with? Why?

5. Which two teachers do you most agree with? Why?

6. Given the new emphasis on tougher academic standards, how do we balance the idea of educating the whole child? Given the stress on English, history, math, and science, how do we balance the idea of providing a broad education for all students that includes music, art, and physical education?

7. Using the library or Internet, read an educational article that discusses Bush's education reform package, the "No Child Left Behind Act," which includes annual testing in reading and math and requires schools to set—and attain—proficiency goals for students. What major points are made by the author(s) of the article? Politically, why is the act a compromise between school choice and increased education spending?

Recommended Readings

Jeanne S. Chall, *The Academic Achievement Challenge* (New York: Guilford Press, 2000).
Elliot W. Eisner, *The Kind of Schools We Need* (Portsmouth, NH: Heinemann, 1998).
Diane Ravitch, *The Schools We Deserve* (New York: Basic Books, 1985).
Marc S. Tucker and Judy B. Codding, *Standards for Our Schools* (San Francisco: Jossey-Bass, 1998).
Grant Wiggins, *Assessing Student Performance* (San Francisco: Jossey-Bass, 1999).

9

Accountability: The Finger Is Pointing at the Teachers

As the cup of hemlock touched Socrates' lips back in 339 B.C., history recorded for the first time the act of holding a teacher accountable for what he was teaching. Four hundred years later another great teacher was to be held accountable for his teachings. In 1925, John T. Scopes was held accountable by the local community for teaching about the theory of evolution, which resulted in a trial and his conviction. Each of us is able to recall cases even closer to home concerning the dismissal of a teacher on the grounds that his reading list, learning activities, or political, moral, or religious interpretations ran contrary to the values of the community. This concept of accountability (holding a teacher responsible for the views he expresses) is certainly not new.

A somewhat different view of accountability also has a history going back into time, that is, accountability for what should be taught and how it should be taught. In the medieval universities, professors and tutors were paid directly by the students. The law students of Bologna during the middle of the thirteenth century extracted this form of accountability, and revenged themselves on unpopular teachers by staging boycotts. In the United States, we can go as far back as the Old Deluder Satan Act of 1647. Enacted by the Massachusetts Bay Colony, it held each town accountable for teaching the children to read the Bible. A fine of five pounds was levied for noncompliance.

In the past, as illustrated by the above examples, the teacher or institution was held responsible for what should or should not be taught. However, the responsibility for learning what was taught resided with the learner. Regardless, a concept of accountability based on the ability of the educational delivery system to ensure successful student learning is a product of our times. It grows out of recognition of the magnitude of societal problems arising in part from the failure of our schools to come to grips with the learning problems of pupils who are not succeeding. It is evident to many that our educational institutions are failing to produce the egalitarian society heralded as perhaps the prime educational goal.

Anyone with common sense who is divorced from a political agenda understands that the complexity of testing and learning makes it nearly impossible to assign responsibility properly to various contributing agents to the educational process. That is, it is difficult to disentangle the efforts of several contributors to student learning, or even to try to separate the influence of a student's prior knowledge and what the school is trying to teach and its resources.

Surely most people agree that everyone, including teachers and school administrators, should be held accountable for their work. What many educators object to—even fear—is the oversimplified concept that defines accountability as the sole responsibility of the teacher or principal. Many different people have various impacts on student learning, and they should also be held accountable if we are going to employ a constructive model. The corollary to this is that behavior (learning) is never the exclusive product of one stimulus or set of stimuli provided by one person (teacher or administrator); it follows that no human being (school employee) should be held totally responsible for the behavior of another person (student). Those responsible for student performance include not only teachers and administrators, but also parents, community residents, school board members, taxpayers, government officials, and, most important, the students themselves—because the learners' health and physical conditions, cognitive abilities, motivation, self-concept, family background, and even age all affect learning.

Regardless of what accountability advocates urge, we need to think in terms of joint responsibility, and not just single out educators and make them scapegoats. For this reason, there is growing concern on the part of teachers and administrators, especially in city schools where the racial background of the educator is sometimes a factor in the hiring, promotion, and the dismissal processes, that accountability may be used as a political weapon against them—not for educational reasons.

Despite the reservations and pitfalls attendant on accountability, state legislatures and state officials of public instruction have moved forward with accountability plans of their own, apparently with little caution and little understanding of the implications of accountability. In response to the demand for accountability, state officials have enacted numerous statutes related to testing and accountability in the last several years. In addition, many state superintendent offices and state educational agencies are developing their own testing and evaluation programs that are in effect accountability plans. They are being driven by the "No Child Left Behind Act," enacted in 2001, which calls for testing every student in grades 3 to 8 in reading and math.

The majority of states have taken the position that accountability should be mandatory, leaving the specifics to the discretion of local districts. The laws range in content from definite and complex to vague and broad guidelines. It is difficult to categorize these laws. Not only do sections of the law sometimes have multiple requirements, but the interpretation of the legislation is not always clear.

What do school personnel have to say when surveyed on the subject of accountability? National Education Association (NEA) survey data suggest that teachers with negative views on accountability outnumber those with positive views by five to one. Both the NEA and American Federation of Teachers (AFT) have expressed reservations about accountability plans, often associating them with high-stakes testing, political grandstanding, and infringing on teachers' professionalism. The NEA maintains that the accountability movement is a "warped attempt to apply business-industrial models to learning," and that it threatens "more and more students and teachers [with] punitive, ill-conceived, and probably inoperable legislation and directives." Accountability misapplied, the organization continues, can lead "… educators and students to comply with inhumane, arbitrarily set requirements." And the AFT feels that "accountability offers ready teacher scapegoats to amateur and professional school-haters," and that accountability advocates are approaching the idea "with all the insight of an irate viewer 'fixing' a television set: Give it a kick and see what happens."

But teachers lack political clout; regardless of their views, the accountability band-wagon continues to grow louder. Ron Paige, the former Houston superintendent of schools and secretary of education under the Bush administration, warns teachers that educators should expect to improve their own performance; they need to meet high standards, and they need to embrace the attitude that all students can succeed. To put it in simple language, the politicians and voters want to hold educators accountable.

ISSUES

A somewhat cynical and oversimplified way of measuring teacher performance was stated with rare candor by well-known principal Charles Borgeson, who was retiring and speaking at his last news conference. He put it this way, or at least the big-city newspaper reported it this way: "Teachers about whom I heard bad things from students or parents, I rated poor. If they did not have tenure, then they were not retained. Teachers who were complimented by others, I rated average. I often felt they were either too opinionated or potential troublemakers. I never wanted to compliment them in writing or give them superior ratings, since the time might come that we would be at odds and they would use my own evaluation against me or the school district."

One reporter from the audience asked, "Who, then, received superior ratings?" Borgeson replied, "The teachers about whom I heard nothing. Of course, I had my own way of confirming these ratings. I would periodically walk the hallways, past the teachers' doors. If their classrooms were orderly and students were concentrating on their schoolwork, then there was no need to gather further information. Bureaucrats always want confirming and detailed information for their files. My instincts and experience served as my measuring tool for judging teacher effectiveness."

"What happened if the students failed, as they often do in big-city school districts like yours? Would these teachers be rated as superior?" asked another reporter.

"Like it or not, there are some students who continue to fail. It is difficult, today, to call them 'dumb' or 'lazy.' But they and their parents are responsible for their behavior."

Asked the reporter, "Are you saying that teachers should not be held accountable for teaching, especially in an age of consumerism and school choice?"

Borgeson responded, "I'll put it in simple terms. The teacher is accountable for teaching, and students are accountable for learning. I object to the egalitarian or liberal trend that shifts the finger of responsibility for learning from the student to the teacher."

"What do you say," said the reporter, "to parents of unsuccessful students who blame teachers when their children do not make normal progress in school achievement? These parents have faith in education as a means of making their children successful in life, and they feel schools are not meeting the needs and expectations of their children. They say school personnel should be held accountable."

Borgeson's boss, Superintendent Corky Wilson, commented, "No person alive can say with any assurance what programs in schools and communities work with students at risk. Since the War on Poverty started, in nearly every report or study, we have learned about the failure of one government program after another, including compensatory education, Chapter I funding, job training, urban renewal, and welfare—each of which cost the taxpayer billions of dollars. The studies by Coleman, Jencks, Moynihan, and the Title I and Head Start studies of the 1960s and 1970s staggered the nation by pointing out the powerful effects of home environment, peer group, and social class on achievement—and how they far outweigh the effects teachers and schools have. School critics have buried this data and still refuse today to admit that the school effect on students' performance is minimal, no more than fifteen to twenty percent of the total variance related to learning, and only a small part of this variation is attributable to teachers."

Borgeson put it in slightly different terms. "Advocates of accountability usually subscribe to the environmental theory of intellectual development. Good. But accountability advocates either have not done their homework or ignore that most environmentalists subscribe to Ben Bloom's summary of longitudinal studies as the most important piece of research in this area. Based on his research, Bloom points out that fifty percent of a child's general intelligence is developed by age four, another thirty percent by the age of eight, and the remaining twenty percent by age seventeen. His estimates are that thirty-three percent of general learning, as based on achievement indices, takes place between birth and age four, that another seventeen percent takes place between the ages of four and six, and still another seventeen percent takes place between the ages of six and nine. Thus, the most important growing period for intellectual development and academic learning is before the child enters school. He further points out that all subsequent learning is determined by what the child has already learned.

"What this suggests," the principal continued, "is that the most important years for changing learning outcomes are the early years. Most accountability advocates not only fail to recognize that educators are therefore working against overwhelming odds to effect changes with students who show deficits in learning, but also that the change problems become increasingly more difficult as we progress through the grades and attempt to hold teachers and administrators accountable for older students. Thus a ninth-grade class with a two-year average deficit in reading provides a more difficult change problem than a sixth-grade class with a two-year deficit. Similarly, two seventh-grade classes with the same reading average but with different ranges in test scores cannot be equated, although one might assume so since the averages are similar. The class with a lower range presents a more difficult change problem. With extreme cases, we need a more powerful environment to effect positive changes."

"How do you respond to 'more effective school research,'" asked the reporter. "It shows that poor and minority children can master the core subjects, including math and science, but some children need extra time and extra help such as tutoring. This research suggests that school success depends on the leadership of the principal and the school climate established by the principal, mainly where there is an orderly environment and good teaching is expected."

"Listen, the problems of poverty pile up, accumulate, and overwhelm most students, pure and simple. The 'culture of poverty' is all consuming—it affects the mind and spirit and the attitudes, motivations, and behaviors of the children and parents of the poor," responded the superintendent. "We impose an enormous burden on our teachers and schools when we expect them to make up for the inequality in American society."

Asked the same reporter, "What do you say to parents of children who achieve high grades and perform well on standardized tests, and who want their children to do even better so they can get into Harvard, Yale, or Stanford? They demand a lot from their children's teachers, and often put a great deal of pressure on the schools so that their children can compete more successfully for high marks on examinations."

Again the superintendent replied: "I have no sympathy for overbearing parents who overprogram their children and who put an incredible amount of pressure on their kids and on teachers and schools. These are the same parents who push their children to take three or four advanced placement courses during their senior year to get into Harvard or Yale, where the competition for admission is extremely selective and every candidate is looking for an edge or advantage. You have to discount much of the criticism of these parents, since they are rarely fully satisfied with their children's education. When these people complain, I expect my administrators to close ranks, say very little, be polite, and protect the person under attack unless the evidence is clear-cut."

Finally, the reporter asked if the superintendent was in favor of the new federal legislation that requires every state to annually administer reading and math exams to all students in grades 3 to 8.

"Listen, the testing results are going to be made public, which means that parents and community members will be grading teachers and administrators, too. In some school districts, heads will roll and jobs will be at stake."

"What about the fact that each state can select its own test and decide what is proficient?"

The superintendent answered, "I don't think the states will make it too difficult for themselves. A lot depends on the administrative leadership and clientele. I'm pretty sure the standards will differ. New York and Wisconsin may have one set that could be relatively similar, but quite different from that of Alabama or Mississippi. I bet Iowa, Nebraska, and the Dakotas have the best results because of demographics, and not necessarily leadership."

"Are you profiling certain students, based on race or class, as having some achievement gap, even before the test results are in?" asked the reporter.

"Listen, the facts are the facts, and I don't want to deal with a red herring or have some other ploy thrown into the mix. Academic achievement differences by ethnicity and race are clearly established. If I were a minority administrator, you would never have baited me about Iowa or Nebraska or used the word *profile* to get me into a box."

The interview with Borgeson and his superintendent created an avalanche of controversy over the issue of accountability. Within two days, the forces for and against accountability had lined up in the school district and the issue was reported in a follow-up article in the same newspaper.

One school board member, Nayeema Kaiseruddins, was quoted as saying, "It is important to relate dollars spent to student accomplishment, since sixty-five to seventy percent of the school budget is related to teacher/administrative salaries. The idea of holding teachers and administrators accountable is a wise policy, especially if we wish to focus on results."

But Tom T. Lasley, another board member, stated in the same news article, "Many variables impact student accomplishment. I welcome a joint accountability plan that considers the students, parents, teacher, administrators, board members, and community. The idea of only holding teachers and administrators accountable is highly political and unrealistic, especially without considering students; that is, the students' learning potential, what they bring to the classroom; students' family, the home experiences, stimulation and models provided by parents; the students' reading abilities, homework habits, and motivation for learning; the students' personality, self-concept, and interests; and the students' peer group, which sets standards of acceptable performance and behavior."

One of the parents, José Flores, maintained that "the heart of the educational system is in the classroom. It is here that teaching occurs and learning results. If anyone should be held accountable for academic achievement, it must be the teacher. Stringent teacher accountability would ensure that marginal teachers would not be retained. Why do we pay high salaries to teachers, in some cases $75,000 or more per year, who cannot get the job done? Why do we pay some of our principals $100,000 to $150,000, when student scores on standardized tests dip below the state or national averages? All professionals should be held accountable for performing their work well. If teaching is a profession, then once standards have been identified, it is the responsibility of teachers to meet them—and there is no reason why the teachers cannot set their own standards."

One of the guidance counselors of the school district, Albert Schlit, was also quoted in the news article: "The teacher works with many children, each of whom has different talents, different dispositions for learning, and a different home life. It would be unfair to expect teachers to meet high standards, or compare teachers, when the raw material is so variable and complex. If teachers are likely to be penalized when students do not perform well, then teachers will concentrate on teaching to the tests that measure student performance."

Schlit continued: "Our tests are not reliable enough, nor were they designed to observe changes in learning over short periods of time—say, eight or nine months. Our standardized tests were designed to measure where a student places at a given time in relation to other students taking the same test. In addition, when pre/post testing students, changes in standardized test scores for an individual may largely be the result of chance variation or guessing, because both scores are based on a small sample of test items. Three of four incorrect or correct items can change the score as much as one grade level on a typical standardized reading test."

Another guidance counselor, Michael Werner, quickly responded. "We have seen dramatic growth in the 'high-stakes' testing of students. Test results are now used to make important decisions about students, teachers, and schools. Did you know that more than forty states have mandated competency testing programs for students? In some cases, according to *Education Week*, students' promotion or diplomas are at stake; in other cases, the reputation of teachers and schools are at stake; and in still other cases (about fifteen states), cash bonuses are awarded to teachers and schools. But a drop in scores in some states means the school is in trouble; sanctions follow and outside agencies and consultants are brought in with authority over the principal, along with power to dismiss teachers."

"I don't think it's the extra money or bonuses that drive teachers and principals; rather, it's the fear of sanctions and job displacement," said Sergie Dostovsky, a reading teacher. "The result is that the test forces schools to focus instruction on the content of the exam; the test defines the scope of the curriculum, even the behavior of teachers or principals."

"That sounds like a polite way of saying that if you try to hold teachers accountable, they may review questions in advance, explain directions on questions during the exam, permit inappropriate breaks during the test, and conveniently extend the test time, and principals will encourage students to be labeled 'disabled' to permit them to take untimed tests or discourage other slow students from taking the exam—all for purposes of raising school scores," asserted Schlit.

"You said it, not me, and what you say is confirmed periodically in newspapers and news magazines. It's called 'cheating,'" said Dostovsky. "In fact, there are news items surfacing in many cities—reported in *Phi Delta Kappan, Education Week*, and the weekly news magazines—about teachers and principals directing students to change test items, and even changing the test items themselves."

"I guess who you hold accountable for test results—students, teachers, principals, etcetera—generates a good deal of controversy," said Schlit.

One of the community members, Harriet Hamburger, reflected the sentiments of the community. "Taxpayers feel the pinch of rising tax bills for the support of public education, and many of our older residents have high expectations of schools based on their own past school experiences; however, they also have other social and medical needs that compete for money with schools. They want to know what they are getting for the additional financial outlay to schools, and whether government spending increasingly can be shifted to meet their own personal needs. Like it or not, educators have to accept the fact that there is growing public resentment toward increased taxation to support schools, and the finger of responsibility is going to shift from the student onto the teacher and principal."

"This governor, Jesse Ventura of Minnesota, is a little punchy but he's a no-nonsense kind of guy," asserted Kaiseruddins, a school board member. "He called education bureaucracy a 'black hole' that consumes forty-four percent of his state's expenditures. He is against the teachers' unions, like many politicians, claiming we continue to put pressure for more spending on education without being held accountable. This kind of thinking would not fly in the private sector, Ventura argues. But he and so many other politicians who make similar statements about spending and accountability fail to grasp the simple fact that education is nonprofit; it is not a profit center, but an expense factor."

Lasley, another board member, spoke up. "It's a matter of the public becoming fed up. I'm tired of hearing why Johnny cannot read or that Johnny's international scores rank among the lowest in math, science, geography, and so on. I'm tired of hearing that about forty percent of our own students at all levels test below basic reading and math skills. It's demoralizing to read in newspapers about grade inflation and social promotion, and then when schools place students in slower tracks or remedial programs, there is the cry of discrimination. The terms *learning disabled* and *attention deficit disorder* are fancy ways of saying a child has trouble reading or has not been taught correctly. It's high time we hold someone accountable, instead of assigning these kids to dust-heap classes."

"I agree that it is important to test our students, to see how they perform and what kind of job teachers and principals are doing, since they are getting paid to do a job," insisted Flores. "We need accountability in education, but what we don't need is the federal government coming up with national tests—telling the states what to do or what should be taught through the test questions. We also don't need a witch hunt aimed at school people, given the fact that student, family, peer group, and community factors account for so much of the reason why students are failing."

The teacher union representative, Frank Frankfurter, also commented in the news article. "Accountability means different things to different people, and special interest groups have a vested interest in promoting accountability for one reason or another. What is good for one person or group, however, may not necessarily be good for education or the country as a whole. The concept, I'm afraid, is turning into a political football with disenfranchised groups and angry school critics already reaching the conclusion that teachers and administrators are the only ones responsible for student failure."

Frankfurter continued. "Accountability offers ready teacher scapegoats to amateur reformers and school critics, from the fellow who did not get along with his tenth-grade teacher to the corporate vice president who judges schools by the property tax rate. It is this accusatory climate, 'Let's get the teacher,' that puts teachers on the defense. Given the new millennium, where the public is in an anti-teacher-strike mood and school boards are successfully modifying teacher tenure, teachers become very jittery when they hear the words 'teacher accountability.' "

"As an active community member," Hamburger claimed, "teachers should decide on matters related to teaching and by what standards teachers should be prepared, evaluated, retained, dismissed, certified, and given tenure. Right now they have little say in these matters. To the extent they lack power, we can argue that teachers have been deskilled and deprofessionalized. The growing demand for accountability is just another nail in the coffin that infringes on the lack of teacher professionalism, whereby political and public agencies make decisions about their careers."

Flores was quick to point out that, on a practical level, "there has always been an implied form of accountability in terms of educational goals, compulsory attendance, student assessments, teacher codes of conduct, teacher ratings, supervision of teachers, evaluation programs, evaluation of school administrators, and budget costs. Accountability has always been with us, although until now it may have had a different name."

Dostovsky then reminded the group he was near retirement. "I've experienced different forms of accountability throughout my career. The only thing that's different now is the rate at which we are encountering it—how quickly school districts are responding to the standards-based movement and how quickly the states are devising tests, deciding what constitutes proficiency in order to measure academic progress and holding teachers and principals accountable for test results."

"I'm a little concerned, perhaps even a little paranoid," declared Lasley. "If a statewide or a national system of testing is inevitable, and I think it is, then how do we make it serve both accountability and instructional needs? Few educators right now know how to interpret or use the results of test data. The testing system we devise, if it is linked with accountability, must also be related to improving instruction, and this requires additional money for viable staff development programs."

As one of the skeptics and a veteran teacher, Dostovsky tried to sum up what teachers felt. "The principle of accountability is a given. But open to serious debate are the questions: Accountability for what? For whom? By what criteria? Most school tests, including those used for accountability purposes, reflect only a knowledge-oriented focus. Schools must also emphasize higher cognitive skills such as critical thinking, intuitive thinking, problem solving, creativity, learning how to learn, what-if arguments, and philosophical positions."

Dostovsky pointed out there were other important domains of learning that accountability plans did not address, because they were difficult to assess, such as interpersonal skills, socialization, cooperative behavior, communication, values, moral education and character development. "My biggest concern is that tiny, easy-to-measure objectives and short-term objectives will be emphasized at the expense of important, difficult-to-measure objectives and long-term objectives. What is measured becomes important to students and teachers, and I'm afraid memory, behavioral, and knowledge-based content will be emphasized at the expense of so much more important content."

Schlit was quick to speak up. "Accountability encourages instruction in narrowly defined behaviors that become immediate target outcomes and form the bases of assessment. This view toward teaching and learning is simplistic and overlooks the fact that there are human transactions in the classroom that cannot easily be assessed but may be equally as important as learning how to count or read."

"Like what?" asked Lasley.

Schlit responded. "When we deal with children in a learning environment, we are dealing with feelings, emotions, and attitudes, as well as spontaneous acts—all of which affect learning. The accountability movement ignores the reality of human interaction, that much of teaching and learning has little to do with intended goals and quantified outcomes. There is nothing more absurd than thinking that we can measure all or most results worth achieving; what we in fact end up measuring may be trivia, insipid, and low-level thinking while we ignore what is creative, innovative, and imaginative."

"Tests by their nature reflect only a small sample of what we are expected to teach students," declared Lasley who as a board member knew about more than just numbers and budgets. "Teaching to the test may be better than what goes on in a few, ineffective schools but in most cases, it represents a narrowing of the curriculum at the expense of understanding concepts, ideas, and the big picture. Teaching kids to perform better on tests by taking educated guesses, pacing, or reading instructions quickly may raise scores but has nothing to do with actual learning, what we really want kids to know."

"What I'm afraid is going to happen," said Frankfurter, "is that we are going to put pressure on teachers to teach toward the test and students to pass these tests at the expense of teaching and learning. The result is that teachers become frustrated and students dislike the idea of learning."

"You know, the type of test is also a concern," said Flores. "State and local tests vary too widely in terms of content. A single national exam is the way to go."

"I agree," commented Werner, the counselor. "Students score lower on the National Assessment of Educational Progress (NAEP) than most statewide tests. One nationally known expert pointed out that recently, in Wisconsin, eighty-eight percent of students met the state's reading standard, but only thirty-five percent reached NAEP's fourth-grade standard. Louisiana reported that eighty percent of the seventh graders passed the state test in math, but only ten percent did on the NAEP. In Oklahoma, there was a fifty percent gap between passing rates on the state and national tests; in South Carolina it was sixty-two percent."

"Are you saying that the state standardized tests are misleading—invalid or just designed to boost students' self-esteem rather than to measure real performance?"

"Not only are the test norms different, but it is also a matter of security and curriculum alignment, all of which impact test outcomes," said Werner.

"What do you mean?" asked Dostovsky.

"The test norms are quite different in Minnesota and New Jersey than in Texas and Kentucky, because of factors dealing with social class, minority status, and school spending. Teachers can sometimes obtain advance copies of state and local tests and review the material. Also, state as opposed to national tests are better aligned with the curriculum taught in local school districts, what some would refer to as 'instructional validity.' "

"Well," said Schlit, "I'm still opposed to the federal government meddling in education, which is a state responsibility. I'm against a group of bureaucrats from across the Potomac indirectly having the power to control the curriculum and put school personnel at risk of losing their jobs."

"No matter how you feel, high-stakes testing and national testing are growing trends," continued Flores. "We have more than forty million functionally illiterate adults. According to the *Digest of Education Statistics*, as many as twenty percent of our high school graduates are functionally illiterate, and as many as fifteen percent of our college graduates have only marginal literacy skills. Yet, our expenditures on education are the second highest per student among the industrialized nations. Someone needs to be held accountable, and the finger is pointing at teachers and schools—like it or not."

Questions to Consider

1. How would you sum up the principal's views on judging teacher performance? To what extent is he right or wrong?

2. How would you sum up the superintendent's views? To what extent do you agree or disagree with her?

3. How would you sum up the pros and cons of accountability?

4. Who do you think should be held accountable for student achievement? Why?

5. What are some of the measurement problems related to executing an accountability plan that involves teachers or principals?

6. Do you believe that teachers and principals should be sanctioned or rewarded on the basis of standardized tests? Why or why not?

7. The discussion included two teachers (Dostovsky and Frankfurter), two counselors (Schlit and Werner), three board members (Hamburger, Kaiseruddins, and Lasley) and one parent (Flores). Search the library or Internet for two articles on teacher accountability and summarize the view of the authors in relation to the characters (pro/con) of the case study.

Recommended Readings

Alfie Kohn, *The Case Against Standardized Testing* (Portsmouth, NH: Heinemann, 2000).

Linda M. McNeil, *Contradictions of School Reform: Educational Costs of Standardized Testing* (New York: Routledge, 2000).

Deborah Meier, *Will Standards Save Public Education?* (Boston: Beacon Press, 2000).

Gary Orfield and Mindy Kornhaber, *Raising Standards or Raising Barriers? Inequality and High Stakes Testing in Public Education* (Washington, DC: Brookings Institution, 2001).

W. James Popham, *Classroom Assessment: What Teachers Need to Know* (Needham Heights, MA: Allyn & Bacon, 1999).

10

Television as the First School System

Recent evidence makes it clear that television has become a "second school system" or cultural transmitter. Children under ten years old watch television for an average of 30 to 35 hours a week, or about one-fifth of their waking hours. By the time a child graduates from high school, he or she will have spent 15,000 to 20,000 hours in front of the screen. Before children reach eighteen, they will have seen 350,000 commercials urging them to want, want, want.

Rather than view television as a second school system, Neil Postman in *Teaching as a Conserving Activity* views it and other mass media (radio, comic books, movies) as the "first curriculum" because they appear to be affecting the way children develop learning skills and acquire knowledge and understanding. According to Postman and others, television's curriculum is designed largely to maintain interest; the school's curriculum is supposed to have other purposes, such as a mastery of thinking skills. In addition, watching television requires little effort and few skills; children do not have to think about or solve problems. Rather, they become accustomed to rapidly changing stimuli, quick answers, and "escapist" fantasies, not to mention overdoses of violent and sexual behaviors on the screen.

The average child now witnesses more than 8,000 murders and about 100,000 other violent acts by the time she or he completes elementary school. Estimates are that by age eighteen a youngster will have seen 40,000 murders and another 200,000 acts of violence on television. In a random look at ten channels on one normal eighteen-hour TV weekday, one study reported 1,846 individual acts of violence. Research cited in *Newsweek* suggests that repeated exposure to violence on television promotes a tendency to engage in aggressive behavior, such as getting into fights and disrupting the play of others. The Parent Teacher Association (PTA), consisting of more than 6.4 million members, has lobbied for years with limited success to curtail violent and sexual scenes on television, especially during prime time (7:00 to 10:00 p.m.).

Almost half of the adolescents surveyed in a recent study admit to the negative influences of television, noting that television's value system emphasizes antisocial behavior (e.g., drugs, violence, and sex are okay or even "cool"). The same percentage maintains that television viewing often detracts from participation in more constructive and worthwhile activities. These students equate television viewing with wasting time and being lazy. A small number complain that "plopping down" in front of the television and watching suggestive commercials increases their tendency to snack and eat junk food.

Given the dominant view of children as passive victims of television, it seems important to note that many children (as young as age 7) display considerable sophistication about the relationship between television and reality, and a high degree of criticism about the influence of advertising. They also seem quite adept at criticizing television for its artificiality—bad acting, inept story lines, and conspicuous consumption. Some of this reaction might be due to the fact that they are aware that adults, particularly teachers and parents, often disapprove of their watching television and believe that it has harmful effects on them. Just as adults frequently displace their concerns on children, older children and teenagers often assert that it is the younger viewers who are at risk, while they are more "adult" and less at risk.

Furthermore, not all research supports negative conclusions about the impact of television on student conduct and attitudes. If utilized properly, television can have a positive influence on socialization and learning, and can serve as a vehicle for information, education, news, and consumer literacy. Studies indicate that selected programs for preschool and primary grade children such as *Sesame Street* and *Electric Company* are associated with improved cooperative behavior and cognitive skills. Older elementary children benefit from *Square One TV* and local television tutoring programs. Adolescents and teenagers benefit from public broadcasting systems, which offers a list of several hundred documentaries on history, art, and science.

Most data suggest that for upper elementary and secondary school students, watching television more than 3.5 hours a day is associated with lowered achievement in reading and mathematics. But other than pointing out such a negative correlation, the research fails to consider how television detracts or competes with homework time and study time. Some research comparing U.S. students to students in ten other industrialized countries revealed that students from other countries "watch less television and spend more time on homework than their American counterparts." Other research suggests that in international comparisons American youngsters watch about the same amount of television as those in other countries.

The key appears to be associated with what American youngsters do with their free time. In other countries, youngsters are involved in substantial school-related and tutoring activities when they are "free." In America, youngsters might lag behind in international comparisons because they have so little "free" time to study; that is, they are involved in many social and extracurricular activities after school.

There is still another possible ramification of television and other electronic media as factors in shaping students' learning behaviors. The audio and visual stimuli might produce what Lev Vygotsky termed *spontaneous concepts*—concepts that are not systematic, structured, or generalized into a larger mental framework. Spontaneous concepts differ from scientific and abstract concepts, which are characterized by a degree of distance from immediate experience and which arise from reading text or being exposed to the teaching–learning process (where the learner integrates language or engages in a dialogue with the teacher or other students). Scientific and abstract concepts, if taught properly, involve *scaffolding*, that is, they help learners make connections and build on previous knowledge.

Learning takes place through the experiences the learner has. Piaget referred to *assimilation* of present experiences with prior experiences, and then the *accommodation* of the experiences with the conditions of the environment. However, television produces rapid stimuli that are too quick and superficial for integrating and organizing with prior experiences or for the viewer to actively participate and reflect. TV entertains us, and some of the pictures may shock us or stimulate our emotions or imagination, but the stimuli do not enhance connections essential for learning to take place.

Vygotsky's notion of spontaneous concepts suggests that television viewers process transient and low-level information and assume a passive role vis-à-vis any learning that takes place. On the other hand, reading and classroom discourse involve structured linguistic activities, active learning, and systematic thinking. We usually remember the main ideas of meaningful books we read, even several years later, because that experience was linguistically structured, required effort, and led to self-reflection. Television and videos rarely offer structured, active learning opportunities except and perhaps when reflection and discussion accompany viewing. That can be accomplished by showing selected segments or meaningful clips of media to allow students to process and discuss the content.

This discussion seems to oppose the notion of visual learning and learning style theory. Maybe. A picture is still worth a thousand words, but the need to explain the picture, to verbalize its meaning, and to reflect and think about it is still essential. All of these cognitive processes involve language and critical thinking, not just visual stimuli. Visual and auditory stimuli by themselves are important for a six-month-old child, as Piaget and other environmentalists purport, but a six-year-old and older learners need structural and meaningful experiences. They need to use language for the purpose of assimilating and accommodating learning experiences, as well as for abstracting and organizing relationships. The questions arise: Does television lead to real learning? Does television have a different influence on a first grader (child) versus a twelfth grader (young adult)?

You be the judge!

ISSUES

Last week's PTA meeting at Central Junior High School in North Carolina was the first of a two-part conference on "The Influence of TV on Your Child's Learning." The guest speaker, Dr. S. Evan Marcus, a communications professor from a nearby state university, commented that television had become the "first school system." By the time a child graduates from high school, "he or she will have spent more than 15,000 hours in front of the screen compared to 12,000 hours in school." Marcus went on to say that many kids are hooked on TV. "Millions of children watch TV late into the night and then yawn or snooze their way through class the next day. Television and other media sources such as video games and the music industry greatly influence the socialization of children and youth. For preadolescent and adolescent students, watching television more than 3.5 hours a day is associated with lowered achievement test scores."

Marcus ended his discussion by saying, "TV is alluring, distracting, and mesmerizing. It can make students lazy, unresourceful, and overdependent for entertainment. They become accustomed to simple plots, quick answers, and escapist fantasies—some of which can be harmful. They learn not to think or solve problems, to think in concrete terms, not the abstract, in the present, and not the future, to expect instant gratification, and not delay gratification."

The professor ended his speech and then distributed a list of twenty questions for parents to determine just how addicted their children were to TV. Parents were instructed to ask their children at home to complete the survey and to return it to the assistant principal who would then have the results tallied in time for the second meeting for the following week. You might want to complete the survey, too.

The Television Test: How Addicted Are You?

All of us need to think about the number of hours we spend watching television. Here is a test designed to make you aware of your viewing habits. Answer "Yes" or "No" to each question.

1. Do you watch more than three hours of television on a school day?
2. Do you watch more than five hours of television on a weekend or holiday when school is not in session?
3. Would you rather watch TV than speak to members of your family?
4. Would you rather watch TV than attend a school dance on Friday or Saturday night?
5. Would you rather watch TV than work by yourself on a hobby, puzzle, or game?
6. Would you rather watch TV or eat one of the following: pizza, ice cream, or a hamburger?
7. When you sit down with members of your family for lunch or dinner, do you watch TV?
8. The phone rings when you are watching TV, and you learn it's one of your friends. Do you continue to watch TV and ask your friend to call back or ask someone else in your family to take a message?
9. When you invite a friend to your home, do you usually watch TV (or videos)?
10. Do you automatically turn on the television when you come home from school or from a friend's house?
11. Would you rather watch TV than go to the movies with a friend?
12. Would you rather spend more time watching TV than talking to your mom or dad?
13. During the school year, do you spend more time watching TV than reading books and playing sports?
14. Do you spend more time watching TV than doing homework?
15. Do you watch TV while you do your homework?
16. If you were going to be tested on a school assignment that required you to read a book, and you could watch a TV version of it, would you watch TV instead of reading the book?
17. Do you have a television in your bedroom?

18. Do you watch television to help fall asleep?
19. Do you rush home or stop what you are doing at home to see a special program more than two times a week?
20. Can you imagine living without TV?*

Be honest. Score 10 for each "yes" answer. Now, what is your total score? If it is less than 70, then you don't let TV run your life. You are doing fine. If your score is between 80 and 120, then you are a borderline addict. You need to take a closer look at your TV viewing habits and see where you can eliminate some TV time. Most important, if you are ignoring mom or dad, or spending less time with your friends and watching TV, then you need to improve your social skills and you may be missing out on real fun. If you scored more than 130, then you are in deep trouble. It may be what the sponsors of TV ads want you to do, but you really need to evaluate the time you are wasting in front of the "boob tube" and how it is influencing your schoolwork and social life. If you scored 180 to 200, then you are in deep, deep trouble. You may even have some personal problems and are escaping from them by watching TV. Remember, it is never too late to change your habits—no matter how addicted you might be without realizing it.

Many of the parents were embarrassed; some were even shocked to learn the results of their children's responses. They proceeded to turn in the completed survey to the assistant principal who in turn tallied the totals. Of the 212 surveys that were returned, the average score was 118, and the median score was 131. As many as 31 percent of the students scored above 150. The danger signs were apparent.

The second meeting with Dr. Marcus was now scheduled to begin, and the parents crowded the auditorium. The parents seemed resigned to the fact that there was little they could do about the influence of television on their children, unless they were willing to eliminate television from the house.

Mr. Dan Marshall, a father of three children, seemed to represent the majority view as he commented, "This is an age of electronics. Our children's bedrooms are wired up, and they are used to seeing images on a screen, whether it's a computer, video, game, or television screen. There is little I can do, unless I want to turn back the clock to *Ozzie and Harriet* or *Father Knows Best* and start regulating their leisure activities."

Mrs. Dillie Lilly expressed another common view. "A lot of mothers in the auditorium are divorced and have to work, or work to supplement the family income. Still other women have become more career conscious. I come home at 6 p.m. and I have to first start making dinner. I cannot police my kids after school, and I have little time for them until dinner is ready. I'm glad they are home watching TV, rather than running around unsupervised on the street with their friends, possibly getting into trouble."

Another parent added a slightly different twist to the ramifications of television viewing among adolescents. "I don't think watching TV between twenty and twenty-five hours a week is so bad, nor do I think this interferes with schoolwork. Our kids are so wound up, programmed, and involved in sport programs and social activities

*About one-third of these twenty questions are adapted from Don Kaplan, *Children and Media* (New York: Instructors Books, 1986).

after school and on weekends. Still, others work part time. It is their endeavors outside of home, not television, that competes with schoolwork. If you add sleeping, eating, shopping, personal care, household chores, transportation, talking on the phone, surfing the Internet, and the like there is little time left over for homework."

"My concern is that there is something about watching television that is lonely—part of some form of escapism and introvertism. The only thing I can imagine that is more lonely for a youngster is to have lunch in school by himself," remarked Ray Calabrese, a divorced parent, Pee Wee hockey coach, and local Burger King restaurant owner.

"A little TV cannot hurt, especially if parents establish rules such as watching limited TV on school days, determining how much can be watched on weekends, the times when a child can watch, and that homework or performing chores comes first," said Marshall.

"My gosh, there is nothing lonelier than a boy or girl watching television on a Sunday morning, when the child should be playing with friends. TV becomes a drug; the more you watch, the more addicted you become. It leads to passivity, nonverbalization and nonsocialization," asserted Calabrese.

"Ray, you might be overdoing it. A little TV is okay as long as children are not captivated or hooked on soap operas or serials, and as long as they don't wind up watching TV when friends are over," said Lilly.

"Little children should be read to and talked to, rather than allowed to watch TV. Schoolchildren should be interacting with friends and doing homework, not eating pretzels or potato chips and not watching TV. More than one hour a day of TV should be prohibited. TV entertains and leads to the formation of wrong habits. By watching those thirty- or sixty-minute programs, kids expect immediate solutions to problems; they expect to be entertained; they expect not to have to talk to their brothers, sisters, and parents. Not only does this affect their ability to work out academic problems and create a need for instant gratification, but also it leads to a generation of lazy and nonverbal students," Calabrese concluded.

"All this from watching TV! You must be kidding! Is it the shape of the moon or the way Jupiter is lined up with Mars that is affecting your brain cells?" asked Marshall.

"Just listen to how half the boys and men you know speak: They either grunt, say nothing, or the wrong thing," responded Calabrese.

"That deals with socialization. Boys are boys; they are more physical and less verbal," said Lilly.

"Boy, had I made a remark like that about girls, you would be jumping on me," asserted Calabrese.

Mr. Wenfan Yan interrupted. He was one of the fathers in the audience, and was typical of those presenting the positive aspects of TV. "I manage to limit my children's TV watching to two hours a day, and they watch it only after they finish their homework. There are many excellent programs available for my children, including the Disney channel, public television, and various discovery, history, science, and news channels. TV is not going to go away; it has instant global impact, and with the arrival of wireless cable and broadcast satellites, the day is fast approaching when we will receive five hundred channels."

Lilly then spoke. "I allow my children to watch Al Bundy and Homer Simpson, which I admit is silly and antimale, but this is a part of the new common culture. Kids today know more about these two characters than they do about George Washington or Abe Lincoln. At least I make sure MTV and adult movies are not packaged in our cable subscription."

"You're lucky. We are spending more than seventy-five dollars a month for cable in my house," said Marshall. "Try to get your kids to watch The History Channel or Discovery Channel and it's like pulling teeth or asking them to drink cod liver oil. All my kids watch is MTV at least one or two hours a day, and they're hooked on Eminem, Limp Bizkit, and U2."

The conversation drifted to the Fashion Channel and *YM*, then Madonna and Britney Spears and whether their see-through clothing and freak dancing represented a new form of feminism or a continuation of female degradation, and then to what extent MTV and VH1 influenced teen fashions and the prevailing message that sex is recreation. One of the parents, Mrs. Yolanda Waxman, lamented about *Camelot,* the Beach Boys, and Tom Jones—describing all the wishing and hoping of the older generation and mentioning the banning of miniskirts at her school thirty years ago.

Another mother recalled the crush she had on James Dean and later Rock Hudson until she found out they weren't totally straight. Someone mentioned the controversy over gay Boy Scout leaders and whether they were aware of the new rule to fingerprint Little League coaches to see if they had a history of abusing children or to learn whether they were queer. One of the mothers resented the use of the word *queer,* and someone else asked if it was acceptable to fingerprint clergymen. One of the fathers, Jim Weber, spoke about the rivalry between CNN and Fox News, and that the anchor Paula Zahn had replaced Marie Osmond as his current fantasy. Another father lamented about his wet dreams and the crush he had on Shabana Shakil, his third-grade teacher, and reminded the audience that most young boys have had fantasies about one or two of their teachers. He asked whether Paula's two million dollar salary at CNN was justified, given the foxy appearance of Mrs. Montgomery, the English teacher at the school, who wore floral silk-looking blouses and scoop-necked dresses. Her $50,000 salary made it difficult for her to visit the *haute couture ateliers* at Christian Lacroix and Dior and it seemed a shame that, like so many of her colleagues, she had to settle for close-outs at Saks and *basic* cottons at JCPenney. The prevailing message was that teachers, even from Vassar and Smith, need only wear rumpy and dumpy threads, and the hell with self-respect and professional image.

After venting about their long-lost youth and their frustration over TV, the parents eventually raised two questions: (1) What can teachers and schools do to improve the TV viewing habits of their students? (2) How can teachers and schools encourage students to take advantage of the potential TV has for adding knowledge and understanding of their own culture (the arts, humanities, and science) and world around them?

Dr. Marcus threw the questions back to the audience and claimed it was the responsibility of parents to provide the proper guidance; it was not the responsibility of teachers or schools to police the behavior of children at home. He directed his thoughts to another problem. "Local TV stations do not always fulfill the stations' obligations, under the federal law, to serve the educational and informational needs of children. Local efforts of parents and educational groups are needed to hold stations accountable, because the Federal Communications Commission assumes each station is complying with the law unless it gets complaints from local groups."

Mrs. Waxman, who also happened to be the PTA president of the school, commented, "The national PTA and National Educational Association are leading the way to improve the quality of children's shows and reduce the violence and sex during prime time hours, but it is an uphill battle to get the word out to parent and citizen groups about the law."

But Marcus continued. "What I really object to are the children's shows that advocate toys, cereal, candy, and other products aimed at young viewers that feature the characters from the show. The amount of sex and violence during prime time is an outrage and reflects the new morality that now winks at the sexual escapades of our presidents, athletes, and actors."

"I'm more concerned about hard facts," said Yan. "According to the Centers for Disease Control and Prevention, ten million, or twenty percent, of American youngsters age twelve to seventeen have high blood pressure and high cholesterol levels that make them susceptible to future heart disease, cancer, and diabetes. The number of overweight teenagers has doubled in the last thirty years, with most of the increase occurring since 1990. We are witnessing an obesity epidemic, a growing number of teenage couch potatoes who are hooked on TV, video games, and personal computers."

Yan insisted that TV and computers are not the culprit, rather it is our fast-food diet and parental attitudes that send messages to children: "I'm tired, find something to do, go watch TV, go surf on the Internet."

"The point is," said Dr. Marcus, "kids don't burn off calories as they once did. TV, and possibly the Internet for some middle-class kids, competes for their attention, and they seem to be winning over playing basketball and soccer. Kids today rarely play ball after school hours, unless it is organized by the park district or school. TV has become an escape for many children who in my generation used to play in school yards and parks without adults watching over them."

"My big concern," said Lilly, "is that the TV advertisers realize there are some thirty to thirty-five million 'tweens,' kids from nine to fourteen, who have growing purchasing power. According to the *New York Times*, they spend more than $50 billion annually and influence more than $250 billion in family spending. With two-income working families and single-parent households, mom has less time to shop. The brands tweens prefer take on greater importance. Mom or dad may still drive them to the mall on Saturday, but they make decisions about buying Backstreet Boys or 'NSYNC, Tommy Hilfiger or the Gap, Trix or puffed wheat."

"Tween TV has become a revolution," she continued, "a jackpot to advertisers. Here is the rub. The favorite tween shows exhibit nonfunctioning families, silly and screwy men, young kids with green hair and nose rings, and a fair share of sexually active youngsters. My generation played Spin the Bottle and later was concerned about how to kiss and pet properly. My TV generation emphasized how siblings coped and solved conflicts with mom and dad. This new generation gets to see lots of crime, violence, sex, and drugs on TV. All you have to watch is MTV and VH1 and you get the picture—and why the three major networks lag behind."

Before anyone responded to Lilly, Weber asked, "What about queer television?"

"What about it?" responded Marshall.

"You know! Homo ... homo ... homosexuals."

"Well, the freckle on your neck is queer. Did you know your earlobes are not straight?"

"I'm talking about a queer TV channel—one queer program after another," responded Weber.

"Do you mean like a Spanish-speaking television channel?"

"Look, the Republicans have all the John Wayne and Charlton Heston movies. The Democrats have Jane Fonda, Robert Redford, and *West Wing*."

"Jane Fonda. Do you mean Hanoi Jane? Isn't she the person who caused us to lose the Vietnam War?" declared Weber.

"I thought it was McNamara, with his wrong numbers, who lost the war. Of course, he confessed forty years later, after 55,000 American soldiers died."

"Putting aside politics, aren't you concerned about family values?" remarked Weber.

"Get with it," said Calabrese. "When my girlfriend six months ago pulled me into the bathroom to show me the telltale pink line on a home pregnancy test, the last thing either one of us thought about was marriage. Both of us were still disentangling ourselves from our recent exes. The longest I have lived with anyone prior to my ex was five months."

"But what about the decline of the traditional family, the increase of homosexual behavior, teen sex, and HIV? Don't you think our children and youth are influenced by the loose values depicted on television?"

"Who would you blame: Little Richard and Elvis Presley or Pat Robertson and Jim and Tammy Baker? Maybe we should blame Ed Sullivan, for allowing Little Richard and Elvis the Pelvis on his show—for corrupting these kids from the heartland. Maybe we should blame John Dewey, since so many critics have blamed him for so many educational problems," asserted Marshall.

"The problem is," Lilly declared, "half of all youth under eighteen have been in a single-parent family for some part of their childhood. What some consider traditional or normal is out of sync with TV reality and modern times. The nuclear family, now about twenty-five percent of all American families, has been replaced by many different family forms—usually without a father at home."

"Television has certainly contributed to our moral decline. The behaviors and values exhibited on the screen belong in the sewer," asserted Weber. "*Murphy Brown* has been replaced by the *Geena Davis Show, Sex in the City,* and *Queer as Folk*. Fathers are unwed, sex is rampant, and normal men and women don't seem to exist anymore on the electronic screen."

"Come on, Jim. Given the politics of diversity, feminism, gay pride, the notions of normality and liberated behavior, sex transplants and Internet porn, the nuclear family seems on its way out. Even when couples remain married, what you might call a *traditional* family, there seems to be a plentitude of lust, a rash of extramarital affairs, sort of an epidemic that has infected the silent majority. These are the same people who yearn for *Ozzie and Harriet*. Although, today these people still attend church services, they no longer believe or care they may burn in hell. Now, you can't blame TV for all changes in family values.

"Let me just say, marriage today can be viewed as some sort of endurance test. It shouldn't be, but it is. I realize that the rules of politics have changed and are still evolving, but I resent the gender-visionary point of view where homosexuals are a protected class and women do not rely on men for economic support or even for having children, since sperm banks exist. We are pushing the frontiers of cloning and marching toward the day when women, some heterosexual and some homosexual, some married and others not even married, will be designing babies."

"I'm impressed," said Marshall. "Did you learn this from CNN and Fox News? Wow, maybe I need to listen to Paula Zahn instead of just watching her."

"It's ten minutes past the end of the conference session. Is anyone willing to sum it up?" asked the guest speaker.

Waxman volunteered. "TV, videos, and computers are here to stay. The electronic world is part of our culture. It is up to educators, not parents, to find ways to incorporate the electronic world into instructional methods that benefit our children and youth—in short, that has educational value for students."

Marcus concluded: "Food for thought for the next conference. But I hate to put the responsibility on the shoulders of schools, like we do with so many other ills of society that we find hard to resolve. Right now, however, I'm going home to watch the end of the Yankee baseball game."

Questions to Consider

1. What guidelines or recommendations for viewing TV would you suggest as a parent?

2. What guidelines or recommendations for viewing TV would you suggest as a teacher?

3. How can teachers utilize television for educational purposes? How do you intend to use TV in your own teaching?

4. Based on the questions in the survey, are you a TV addict?

5. Do you have an interest in curtailing the number of hours you spend watching TV? How many hours do you average per week watching TV? Reading a book for enjoyment?

6. To what extent do you feel that TV is contributing to a fat and flabby generation of children and youth?

7. Based on library or Internet sources, develop a school plan to help students who watch too much TV reduce their viewing hours.

Recommended Readings

Stephen M. Alessi and Stanley R. Trollip, *Multimedia for Learning*, 3rd ed. (Needham Heights, MA: Allyn & Bacon, 2001).

James M. Cooper, *Technology and the New Professional Teacher* (Washington, DC: National Council for the Accreditation of Teacher Education, 1997).

John F. LeBaron and Catherine Collier, *Technology in Its Place* (San Francisco: Jossey-Bass, 2001).

Eli M. Noam and Jens Walterman, *Public Television in America* (Washington, DC: Brookings Institution, 1999).

Linda E. Reksten, *Using Technology to Increase Student Learning* (Bloomington, IN: Phi Delta Kappan, 2000).

11

Distance Education Is Closer Than We Think

Among the major changes teachers must deal with in the twenty-first century is the new view that the ability to acquire information will be replaced by the ability to retrieve and use information. New technologies transfer teaching and learning (1) from whole-group instruction to individualized instruction, (2) from one-size/one-paced instruction to customized/self-paced instruction, (3) from passive learning to active learning, (4) from absorbing facts from teachers and textbooks to navigating the Information Superhighway and World Wide Web, and (5) from the teacher as a transmitter to the teacher as a facilitator.

Tomorrow's teachers will use computers, web sites, videos, cameras, and teleconferences for teaching and learning as well as videodisc portfolios for evaluation. Students and teachers will share information and communicate with other students and teachers from around the world. Both teachers and supervisors must become effective technology users, and principals must encourage and ensure in-service training in technology use. For the most part, technology staff development for teachers has been fragmented—not content specific, not ongoing, and not adequately challenging or up-to-date. *Time* magazine puts it another way: In 1998, schools spent $88 per student on computer equipment but only $6 per student on computer training of teachers; currently, 80 percent of schools have Internet access, but only 20 percent of teachers feel prepared to use technology in their classes.

The typical approach has been to provide in-service training for teachers and let them train their students. Unfortunately, this method is slow and unreliable and assumes (from an educator's point of view) that the source of knowledge lies with the teacher or adult, not the student or learner, and that teachers should dole out information to students in a lockstep method. Educators think of using technology in the classroom as analogous to teaching children how to read or write. We fail to understand that some children grasp the use of technology more quickly than adults, including their teachers, just as they learn a foreign language more quickly than their parents or other adults.

By the time teachers have learned the new technology, what they know is often obsolete; learning to use the new technology must be an ongoing process. Also, some teachers lack the motivation to transfer the new knowledge to their students. Many are stuck in a time warp of whole-group instruction, as opposed to allowing students to learn at their own pace via computerized and digital instruction. The same teachers often rely on the explanation/demonstration mode, which assumes the teacher is the source of knowledge as opposed to giving students the power in having expanded access to information and a wider selection of data. When educators completely move into the twenty-first century and allow students to do the same, then many students will use information on the Internet and World Wide Web that exceeds the teachers' knowledge. Computer guru Seymour Papert, in *The Connected Family*, puts it this way: "The contribution of digital media to education is a flexibility that could allow every individual to find personal paths to learning. In the future ... every learner will be 'special.' "

The full shift in using technology enables students to personalize their learning based on their specific backgrounds, abilities, learning styles, and interests, as opposed to "one size, one speed" for all learners. It suggests, also, that learning is a lifelong process, not confined to classrooms or schools. It shifts control from the teacher to the student so that the latter is able to access information far beyond the teacher's knowledge. In the near future, it is hypothesized that the teacher's role will not be as crucial, dominating, or valuable in the teaching–learning equation—a notion hard to digest but true with computer-proficient students.

Elsewhere, in still another publication, Papert contends that the present viewpoint, which questions whether computers or digital information improves teaching or learning, is dated and actually downright stupid. He argues that relegating the most powerful technology ever invented to serve modest academic goals is dated and calls for educational leaders to make the most of the new electronic world, to invent new visions, new goals, and new pedagogy. Children and their parents who have grown up with computers at home, Papert warns, will be less inclined to let teachers and administrators off the hook about "backward" learning. As the technology revolution continues and new knowledge rapidly increases (we are living in an age where it is doubling every fifteen years or so), the baby boomer teachers and post–baby boomer teachers are either going to have to expand their technological horizons or possibly lose their licenses to teach.

Don Tapscott, in his bestselling book, *Growing Up Digital*, refers to the "Net Generation": teens who use e-mail, communicate via chat clubs, electronically check sports scores and weather forecasts, listen to music and movies, gather school information on the web, and feel being online is as "in" as dating, partying, or chatting on the phone. These youth are the most potent force for computer use in schools. They have grown up with digital equipment—video games, CD-ROMs, DVDs, cameras, and music—and they are going to force educators to shift from teacher-centered to learner-centered education, and, if we may add, from textbook instruction to electronic instruction, from classroom education to distance education and from physically confined classrooms to virtual classrooms.

The technology available to the Net Generation is everything the baby and post–baby boomers' television never was: interactive, participating, individualized, self-paced, and a tool that children can control. We might question whether Internet use actually fosters critical thinking and problem solving, or whether it leads to aimless surfing, but Tapscott argues that the interactive medium is a natural self-esteem builder, whereas TV viewing is not. He contends that as youth spend more time online, they spend correspondingly less time watching television, which we know correlates with lack of achievement on standardized tests. In the final analysis, we can no longer teach a generation of students weaned on the new technology by using pedagogy based on teacher talk, in which the teacher dominates the lesson and is the dispenser of knowledge. Put in different terms: As goes technology, so goes teaching. Like it or not, educators either join the Net Generation and adopt the digital media, or be branded as obsolete and discarded.

ISSUES

"Technology keeps staring us in the face," said the principal of Lincoln Elementary School. "We have to face reality. The pencil no longer makes the point. Textbook teaching is boring and dated. Teachers talk too much. Technology can improve and update teaching and learning. It's just a matter of putting all the pieces together—computers, televisions, phone lines, and web links—in proper fashion."

Taking the notion of technology further, the principal told the teachers at the monthly faculty meeting that he envisioned the school would soon be linked to the nearby university not only by video and television, but also by a computer network to share instructional materials and other information, as well as to train teachers. "The driving force behind the idea," the principal said, "is to economize and save resources and to cooperate with the university in grant writing for new equipment and software, as well as to make use of their technical consultants. It is too expensive to install cable networks or distance learning equipment on our own. Budget restraints have reduced us to working with nearby school districts and colleges—almost like a regional learning consortium—to share web sites, chat rooms, and human resources.

No one raised any questions at the faculty meeting since the school district was a top-down administration and had an older faculty that had learned that it was easier and more practical to go along with the administration than to challenge them. But in the teacher's lounge the next day, the conversation was heated.

Peg MacDonald, a fourth-grade teacher, expressed her view. "What our kids need are caring and supporting teachers, not some teacher from a distant place who doesn't even know them by name. Technocratic teaching may work at the high school or college level, where students are older and more mature, but at this level, children need to be nurtured, not placed in front of some electronic device."

Tetsuko Hokura, a sixth-grade teacher, agreed with Peg for different reasons. "What the principal said yesterday sounds good in theory, but it will not work in practice. Although we live in a world dominated by technological complexity, most of the older teachers are not computer literate, and they are reluctant to admit it or do something about it. They are too comfortable in their teaching career to change, and they have their own teaching style and habits. I just don't foresee them taking advantage of distance education."

MacDonald interrupted. "Our students, and not our computers, are the best learning machines. We should never lose sight that digital learning is superficial, that it's great for retrieving information, but that the integration of learning experiences requires active, constructive processes where new information is assimilated and modified with prior knowledge. Learning with computers and other technological media such as videos or television draws on images that are transient and depict rapid motion; therefore, they are out of sync with the learner's capabilities to integrate prior knowledge. Information in a text is more structural and static, and time is available to review, slow down, and integrate information. The fast pace of technology and the host of visual symbols engulf the viewer with too much information, too quickly."

Hokura responded. "Forgive me, Peg. Considering that many children and youth have 'wired bedrooms,' furnished with a television, VCR, computer, and printer, the idea of the printed medium in the form of books is becoming a relic of the past. Peg, you are either going to have to learn, as a teacher, how to integrate teaching and learning into this new electronic culture or run the risk of becoming irrelevant to these children and their parents."

Bruce Tuckman, a third-grade teacher, supported the principal. "Telecommunications, global television, and satellite networks are the pathway for knowledge—whatever a computer or TV screen can receive—from info-services to entertainment. Home and business subscribers point and click their way onto the Internet, while many teachers still rely on filmstrips and the chalkboard as their tools of technology. We have to change and understand the new media and communication systems and use them for educational purposes."

"I agree. Teachers talk too much. Textbooks and chalkboards dominate the lesson. Most of us rely on teaching methods once used in little red school houses, where the medium was the teacher's spoken word," stated Hokura. "Technology engages many more youngsters, and changes the students' role from a passive one to an active one. Many kids I know learn visually as well as verbally, and they like to use their hands as well as their heads. Kids with visual and artistic learning styles and creative talents go untapped or unrewarded in a teacher-talk, textbook-based classroom."

Petro Kanellopoulous, a veteran teacher who was playing cards with three other colleagues, joined the conversation. "Tetsuko, you're a little harsh on us older teachers who still rely on the Bic pen, but I understand the point you are making. We all need to update our skills on a regular basis, otherwise we become old hat and irrelevant. I believe that teachers need to create partnerships with teachers in other school districts and with area colleges. Distance education is happening now, and it will continue to grow."

"A two-way interactive system could connect our school through a maze of computers, video cameras, TV monitors, and telephone lines," said Tuckman, who now was filling in a crossword puzzle. "Linking up with schools outside the district means we could share instructional expertise. It would certainly be great for small high schools that sometimes struggle to offer elective courses such as Japanese or Latin and advanced placement courses such as chemistry or calculus."

"I agree," said Hokura. "There is a rich body of information that students could use if they could only gain access to it. They could even communicate with other students across the country or even across oceans. What a great idea to adopt a group of foreign students in another classroom or school so as to enhance global understanding."

"Well, I'm not sold on the whole idea," commented MacDonald. "I think telecommunications and electronics change so rapidly that whatever equipment and software we buy will already be dated on delivery. The whole enterprise is too expensive and will strain our budget for equipment and materials. And I don't trust partnerships with big business, because so often they are driven by profit motives. It's like putting your trust in Rupert Murdoch or Enron and WorldCom."

Tuckman was quick to respond. "I'm going to say two things that will not make me popular but are at least honest. Teachers love to complain when they talk shop, especially when they talk in the teacher's lounge; therefore, I discount a lot of the criticism. Second, TV, computers, videos, and VCRs are educational tools that teachers should be using in their classrooms. Pencil and chalk technology represents a bygone era. This is the twenty-first century and we need to get with it and become a part of the Information Superhighway. If we ignore the electronic world that we live in, then the lives of PlayStation, Nintendo, and Sega will win the battle for our students' minds."

"You know," mentioned Hokura, "many legal battles are being fought across the country over equal funding between rich and poor school districts. Many court decisions involve multimillion dollar awards to build new facilities and equip schools with the latest electronic and computer technology. Many inner-city schools, in the near future, will be spending a great deal to update their computer facilities."

"Well, it's nice that attention is being paid and funding provided to improve the education facilities for all children," declared Tuckman. "Right now minority students and poor students don't have the same access to computers as middle-class students. We need to equalize opportunity; equal access to knowledge is also crucial for leveling the social and economic playing field."

Hokura reacted. "There is a great deal of school construction taking place to replace older buildings in the Northeast and Midwest and to compensate for expanding student enrollments in the South and Far West. We have the opportunity to rethink school buildings, to create new architectural designs, and to install electronic connections that can transform teaching and learning. Our classrooms can be connected to the best museums, libraries, and colleges."

"What all of you are saying makes sense," asserted MacDonald, "but the issue is not just understanding the pedagogical importance of technology. First, who will train teachers in how to use this new technology? The answer has political and professional implications. Second, technology and the new electronic and information systems are tied into big business—billions of consumers and billions of dollars. Video and TV technology has turned our children into consumers and not thinkers, into watching a medium dominated by graphic violence and sex, into playing interactive warrior combat games. I have kids at home who spend more time playing *Quake* and *Doom* than reading or doing homework. The new Information Superhighway serves commercial interests, not educational interests. It is driven by profit and entertainment, not by teaching and learning. I don't know if we should be quick to join the new electronic bandwagon without asking some hard questions that have educational and ethical overtones."

"I don't think we can resist the inevitable. Distance education is a factor that we need to adjust to and utilize in our professional practice," commented Jack Isower, the librarian. "But there are so many hidden legal traps involving distance education:

whether the school or university that is transmitting the program has obtained all the rights to use the intellectual property and has protected the material from misuse. There are several copyrights to obtain before transmitting, including the right to reproduce the work, to transmit it, to perform the work in public, to display it, and to create another work derived from the original work."

"Jack, you sound like a freshman lawyer, gung-ho, but you're missing the forest while focusing on trees," responded Tuckman.

"Listen, details are important," added Isower. "Most teachers and school officials don't fully recognize the legal problems involved with the Information Superhighway, including, if I may add, the need to protect the materials from being misused or misappropriated by other institutions, teachers, or users. If the material being displayed is not owned by the transmitting institution, it may be held liable for copyright infringement."

"Point made," interrupted Peg MacDonald. "I'm more concerned that the advantages we think exist for distance education and computerized instruction among adults—particularly convenience, variety, individualized or self-paced education, and lifelong education—do not apply to children and youth. Learners never achieve mastery by the click of a mouse, a visual file, a chat room, or a walk through cyberspace. They must become deeply involved, experiencing failure and success, practice and review, discussions and integration of new information with prior information. Our electronic culture prohibits personal contact, verbal dialogue, and deep understanding. It is the teachers' passion for teaching and connection with students that result in real learning. This is achieved in classrooms and small groups through discussion and dialogue, not in cyberspace; through eye contact, not e-mail or by looking at a video screen or logging onto the Internet."

Hokura nodded in agreement and raised the issue of "virtual" worlds. "It's one thing to have *virtual libraries*, or libraries without books, where computers give college or high school students access to a collection of online materials and gateways to the Internet, but I'm against *virtual classrooms* for younger students. I realize that it is cheaper and more efficient to get books and journals and other materials, especially rare collections which eventually yellow and turn brittle, in electronic form than it is to warehouse, store, and distribute them to one user at a time. But it is another thing to have virtual classrooms for children just because the market is driving it for adults."

"I think we now have the ability to participate virtually through anything," said Isower. "This means students can now dissect a frog or a pig in biology without worrying about animal rights activists, or smell the dead animal that causes some students to get 'grossed out.' We can deal with sensitive issues such as interviewing AIDS victims through e-mail and chat rooms."

"I don't know what is sensitive about an AIDS victim or animal rights activists, but the notion of e-learning is increasing rapidly, creating new education paths and training opportunities. I'm not just talking adult learning, but also learning for children and youth," asserted Tuckman.

"My feeling is that the child's needs and interests come first, especially at the elementary level," responded Hokura. "We need nurturing teachers, not high-tech teachers. If given a choice, I'd hire a smiling, nontech teacher over a nonsmiling technocratic teacher any day of the week."

"I don't want to sound like a dinosaur or Lilliputian," asserted MacDonald, "but we need to think through the pedagogical benefits of this electronic culture in relationship to the developmental needs of our younger students, especially at the primary grades. Call it virtual classrooms, distance education, computerized instruction, or web links—I don't care—they all foster two-dimensional learning and linear brain functioning. Humans need to be actively engaged for meaningful learning to take place."

"I agree with much of what you say," remarked Tuckman. "Some of this information technology results in fragmented and superficial learning. Like it or not, however, welcome to the world of online learning! Those of us who grew up with computers will go along with the information flow; the skeptics, critics, and naysayers will be written off as alienated or antiquated. Join the twenty-first century and accept the electronic culture or move aside."

At its best the Internet can educate more people faster than any tool I know," remarked Isower. "But I'm concerned about the worst case scenario, that the Internet can be used as a cesspool, to spread rumors, and increase ethnic and religious hate—as a vehicle for unfiltered and filthy information. Even worse, the aura of technology surrounding computers and the Internet encourages the ignorant and least educated to be impressed by information gleaned from these sources."

"Well, as Dewey said it," asserted Hokura, "education is neutral. If he were alive today, he might say the Internet is neutral. I guess what we need are software programs to filter out those vile ideas."

"I don't want to touch First Amendment rights, and the notion of free speech," said MacDonald, "but I don't think you can prevent or stop all of the hatred that infects people's minds by downloading some software program. I think we have reached a period, worse than Orwell's *1984*, in which our kids are suspectible to some scary information on the Internet. In short, the Internet is not the be-all, end-all panacea."

"Before we wrap up this discussion," Kanellopoulous said, "I want to return to the issue of technology and equal opportunity."

"Why?" asked MacDonald.

"I'm thinking of John Dewey and his ideas that education should be planned and developed in context with the life experiences and needs of the learner."

"Get with it! This is the twenty-first century—Dewey is no longer relevant," snapped MacDonald. "If you mentioned E. D. Hirsch or John Goodlad, people might listen to you. If you mentioned Seymour Papert or Don Tapscott who describe computer and Internet trends, people might listen even more."

Kanellopoulous pointed out that black Americans and, to a lesser extent, Hispanics are still involved in an ongoing struggle against racism and discrimination, and that they have overlooked the electronic world as a means for upward mobility. "You know, Apple, Hewlett-Packard, and Oracle were all started with almost no capital by young adults fooling around in their garages and homes. Where are the black and Hispanic youth? Playing basketball on asphalt streets or baseball on dirt streets. I'm reminded of the film *Revenge of the Nerds* and the creation of the cyber-elite. Being a nerd is simply not 'hip' in the ghetto, and is often out of place with kids who wish to avoid the wrath of gangs and underachieving, thuggish kids at school. Being a computer-proficient nerd also goes against the hip-hop diaspora of cash, flash, and trash-talk. As a result, many black and Hispanic kids have little idea about cyberspace, much less experience connecting to a library and finishing their assignment with a multimedia report involving text and graphics."

"That sounds pretty racist," said MacDonald.

"Only because you see me as a white person. If I were black, you would probably say that my ideas are fresh, insightful, and worthy of consideration. Look, the history of African Americans and technology has been devastating. Mainstream technology has been used in the past to enslave black people. The compass brought them to America, and guns were used to keep them subjugated. Technology is also a class thing. Poor people and people of the inner cities have little access to technology, and those that do are consumers—not designers, implementers, or innovators. As a group, poor people suffer from technological illiteracy. As minorities fight over race-related issues related to welfare, affirmative action, integration, and testing, they lose sight of the fact that they have become second-class citizens of the technological age, which in turn will detrimentally affect their status and relationships as Americans and global citizens."

"Your view on computers and minorities is overkill; some people might call it dialectical politics," stated MacDonald.

"I'm not sure what you mean, so I'll leave it to the theorists to explain it."

"But once you are sensitized about race issues, you cannot ignore it. It's always there," responded MacDonald, "in your face."

"Does that mean every education issue has a black or Hispanic relationship?"

"Where did all these ideas come from?" asked Isower. "It really sounds like you've been hanging out in some cotton gin town or redneck saloon."

"You can slash and smash, but facts are facts," stated Kanellopoulous. "There are few, if any, blacks or Hispanics cashing in on the tech revolution. I can't count one. Can you? Instead of buzzing through cyberspace, black and Hispanic kids run around on basketball courts and ball fields, hoping like hell to become the next Kobe Bryant or El Duque and make millions of dollars in professional sports. It's the easy way out, but it works for one out of a hundred thousand or more minority kids. Those are terrible odds! Today's students should be shooting fewer hoops, playing less baseball and football and instead learning to surf the Internet and use computers for personal and school purposes. Ethnic pride, racial thinking, and competitive sports help people cope and survive in ghetto conditions, but it does little to prepare people to think about innovations in society."

Kanellopoulous continued. "The great equalizer has become the computer, and it can allow many minorities to vault over decades of injustices. But when you think in terms of ghetto culture, you fall into a black hole—no pun intended. Life passes by; opportunities go unnoticed. This kind of self-limitation may be used to excuse one's technological ineptness, but it does not win points in a capitalistic and competitive society. Information is now king, and computer use is the avenue to the information highway. What counts today is computers, not racial or bilingual rhetoric. I want minority kids to tap into knowledge-based institutions, and use cable connections in schools and at home in order to log onto the larger world of unlimited knowledge and assume greater responsibility for their own learning."

"Look, almost half the kids who live in ghettos can't even read or write. I think you have become intoxicated by some high-tech expert," said MacDonald.

"My feeling is that school reform must use television, videos, and the web to modify images, voices, and sounds to fit different learning styles and inspire different learning."

"Baby, you're off the mark," responded MacDonald. "You're so far ahead of the pack, so consumed with high-tech lingo, you missed the boat. You have to get poor minority children to read and write first, before you worry about the new technology and the Information Superhighway."

"I think Bruce summed it up earlier," declared Kanellopoulous. "Join the new century—adopt and adapt—or be left in the dust as a relic. And, if you want to break from your Rip Van Winkle mold, use computers to teach kids how to read and write."

Questions to Consider

1. At the faculty meeting there was no discussion about the merits of distance education and the Information Superhighway, but in the teacher's lounge the discussion was heated. How typical do you believe Lincoln Elementary School is? What does this say about Lincoln teachers? About the school climate?

2. How valid do you believe the generalization is about older teachers being computer illiterate or, even worse, not willing to change? What percentage of teachers do you believe fits into the computer illiterate category?

3. Do you believe the majority of teachers will incorporate the Internet into their instruction by the time you begin teaching?

4. Can schools and business become partners in distance learning to the extent that students and teachers benefit?

5. At the end, the discussion centered around the different views of Peg MacDonald (go slow attitude) and Bruce Tuckman (a positive attitude), Tetsuko Hokura and Jack Isower (technical and legal), and Petro Kanellopoulous (minority considerations). Whose views are you mostly in agreement with? Why?

6. How do you personally expect to use computers and the Internet with your teaching practice? Explain.

7. Use library and Internet sources to come up with a plan that schools might develop to respond effectively to students who lack computers at home. How do computer experiences of children and youth differ in urban and rural areas? By class, caste, and gender? Explain why these differences exist.

Recommended Readings

Dennis Anderson, *The Internet and Web Design for Teachers* (Needham Heights, MA: Allyn & Bacon, 2001).

Jane Healey, *Failure to Connect: How Computers Affect Our Children's Minds* (New York: Simon and Schuster, 1997).

Seymour Papert, *The Connected Family: Bridging the Digital Generation Gap* (Marietta, GA: Longstreet Press, 1996).

Anthony G. Picciano, *Distance Learning: Making Connections Across Virtual Space and Time* (Upper Saddle River, NJ: Merrill Prentice Hall, 2001).

Don Tapscott, *Growing Up Digital: The Rise of the Net Generation* (New York: McGraw-Hill, 1997).

III
Teacher Professionalism

12

Why Teach?

When you ask teachers why they chose teaching as a career, more often than not various stock answers are provided, ranging from desire to teach, the love of children, the importance or rewards of teaching, to the opportunity to influence society or future generations. The question is somewhat rhetorical and self-serving—like asking someone why they are strolling in a park or why they like good wine or good sex. A lot of reasons can be given, consciously and unconsciously. Conscious reasons usually express what is considered conventional or appropriate, rarely what is controversial or eye opening. Unconscious reasons are rarely discussed in the professional literature, perhaps because educators would rather deal with practical issues or prefer to avoid issues that deal with the psychology of life and its hidden motives, tensions, and conflicts.

Answering the question of why we teach involves examining our life's goals and expectations, our real feelings and emotions, and our attempts to deal with the significance of our own personal choices and professional identity. Unquestionably, risk is involved in trying to unravel the truth about our choices and careers; indeed, the idea of self-discovery elicits an awareness about life that some of us may feel uncomfortable with or may not want to deal with in a significant way. To probe the *why* and *what* of teaching, to examine the reasons for teaching, or to truly evaluate how we teach and whether we are truly satisfied with teaching is to better understand ourselves, a process that many people would rather avoid while others yearn to discover these answers.

The search for meaning is a search for self-understanding and self-hood and, can be painful, according to Arthur Jersild, a well-known psychologist and author of *When Teachers Face Themselves.* "And although it is healing, the person who undertakes it is likely to feel worse before he feels better." His position is that we all need to face ourselves, not avoid it, even if it hurts. We all need to press into the deeper reasons of why we teach and what we expect to accomplish. Our own self-understanding will enable us to gain insight into our student–teacher relations and, if I may add, our collegial relations.

Before we teach then, we need to analyze our motives and discover ourselves as people and as teachers. The teacher you choose to be or actually become requires you to look regularly in the looking glass. Too many teachers choose to float through their careers without ever questioning their motives, or they might first seriously consider their motives as a teacher ten or twenty years into their careers.

Part of the reason why we teach is related to social mobility, but teaching is by no means the only career that has attracted ambitious young people seeking upward mobility. There is also a tendency toward self-selection into various professions on the basis of membership in the profession of other family members, particularly parents. Doctors' and lawyers' children frequently enter into one of their parents' professions because of the influence parents have on the formative years of a child's growth and development, because they are often encouraged for financial reasons to do so by their parents, and because children are influenced by modeling significant others such as parents. A similar tendency exists in teaching, although it is probably no longer as strong as it may have been, especially with the numerous options women now have to enter other professions that they did not have before the era of Betty Friedan and Gloria Steinem.

The pattern of following in the footsteps of parents who happen to be teachers is less likely these days among college-educated parents because teaching provides only so much upward social mobility for youngsters; those to whom teaching offers that opportunity most often have parents in working-class occupations or come from first-generation immigrant families. Actually, the research suggests that the influence of former teachers tends to be much higher than parents' influence in making the decision to teach. Data also indicate a positive influence from professors of education who make teaching appear to be an attractive and rewarding profession.

National Education Association surveys conducted in 1971, 1976, and 1995 attempted to get at reasons for teaching. Respondents revealed the three most common and constantly ranked reasons: (1) a desire to work with young people, (2) the value of teaching to society, and (3) interest in the subject matter (which is obviously mentioned more by secondary teachers rather than elementary teachers). In addition, research reported by this author elsewhere, in the *Foundations of Education,* also indicate other reasons for teaching: that potential teachers see teaching as fulfilling, important, and challenging. Although many student teachers do not envision teaching as a job with high levels of status and income, they report that these factors are not particularly important to them. One might interpret these attitudes as a display of idealism and further hope that these young adults will maintain their positive attitudes as they mature as teachers and as they begin to raise families.

Finally, one of the hottest trends in teaching is the large number of early and mid-career changes among people in businesses, allied health, and government who are opting out of their present roles and becoming teachers. In some cases, they were disillusioned in their initial occupational choices and others have decided there is more to life than making money. Some have given up higher salaries but see real rewards in managing and teaching twenty-five or more kids in a class.

A related group entering teaching is older professionals and retirees from all fields, especially the military and police departments and health and nursing, who have opted for another career. These people entering teaching later in life already have a bachelor's degree and are mature and experienced and seem highly dedicated. They are looking to keep active, feel they can make a contribution to society, and enjoy teaching children. The field of teaching is fortunate to have these people and more than half of students currently enrolled in master's teaching programs started their careers in another field. More than 275 university programs across the country offer this type of certification program, which emphasizes teaching methods and pedagogy, but not subject matter. These types of programs, it should be noted, are different than alternative certification programs which recruit recent college graduates and quickly put them into the classroom, without the requisite number of education courses, in order to ease the shortage of teachers.

ISSUES

A number of teachers were sitting around the lunch table in the school cafeteria in a Milwaukee inner-city school and talking about why they and their colleagues decided to teach. Muhammad Shazi, a music teacher, was finishing his coffee and made this comment, which got the discussion going: "In recent nationwide surveys, the great majority of teachers find their work 'very satisfying.' When asked if they would become teachers again, more than half, and in some surveys as many as two-thirds, said they would."

"What are the attractions or reasons for finding teaching so rewarding, according to these surveys?" asked Walter Williams, a black history teacher.

"The top reasons, in the surveys, are love of teaching, love of students, love of the subject, and a desire to serve society or to help others. Most secondary school teachers have an affinity toward the subject they teach, and most elementary teachers love the kids they teach."

"Your list of reasons for teaching doesn't even scratch the surface of why I went into teaching," said Jim Crowley. "I chose teaching as a matter of security, pure and simple. I'm an artist first, but very few artists can make a living. I support myself through teaching and paint after school and exhibit on weekends. I may not seem as dedicated as some of my colleagues profess to be, but I do a damn good job teaching art—better than most art teachers—since I'm actively involved as an artist and I can combine theory with practice."

"I'll tell you why I chose teaching," asserted Tillie Lee Werner, a speech teacher. "I was twenty-eight years old, selling insurance, and everyone around me was chasing 'the almighty buck.' I got tired of the nine-to-five grind and two-hour lunches with balding male clients who were hitting on me and chasing their secretaries. I felt like I was accomplishing very little. I was disillusioned about private industry and found myself daydreaming in the evenings about teaching. But it wasn't easy to make the switch. I was scared. I had to reflect and ask myself what I wanted to do with my life."

Werner continued, "I guess I was lucky. I love teaching. I'm not talking about the subject matter or students, although they are important. I'm talking about the act of teaching—the joy of having kids think, inquire, and imagine the process of analyzing an abstract idea at the level of the children so they can understand it."

"Rachel, why did you enter teaching?" asked Werner.

"Well, to tell you the truth, it was not for any of the noble reasons we often read about: love of teaching, love of children, or to help improve society," Rachel Stehl, the PE teacher, replied. "It was my junior year in college, I recall, and I didn't know what I wanted to do. I had to select a major. My best friend, Karen, was studying education as a safety net, in the event she could not get admitted into law school. I decided to follow suit and enroll in education courses with her. I guess everything turned out for the best. Karen now practices law, and here I am with you."

"Erica, what made you go into teaching?" asked Werner. Erica Drucker sighed: "I'm one of those dedicated teachers you read about. I really wanted to teach my subject. I love books, and I wanted to instill a love of literature in my students. To tell you the truth," she continued, "I never thought I would be teaching in such a tough school, with so many children who can't read at grade level, or even near grade level, and with so many disciplinary problems. To be honest, I'm frustrated. I really wish I could discipline less and teach more."

"I agree with Erica's feelings and Muhammad's survey information," said Williams. "Most teachers teach for altruistic reasons and are committed to helping others. For every teacher who is simply marking time, say, because it's a way of working and raising children or because they are trapped by a pension, there are four or five who are committed to the profession."

"Although I'm not sure about your percentages, I think your description is more accurate with younger teachers," remarked Crowley. "Time has a way of neutralizing altruism. I believe the same routine, year after year, the daily grind, the nature of bureaucracy—its rules and routine, paperwork, and the assembly-line effect, as well as the fact that not all colleagues are collegial—influence your thoughts about teaching as the years pass. As we get older, some of us become trapped by our pension, like Walt believes, and our original enthusiasm wanes."

"You paint a factory model of school that many critics talk about in the professional literature. But the vast majority of these critics never taught and are merely expounding sociological and psychological theory," said Shazi.

"I think it is only natural for people in many professions to get burned out, to lose some of their adrenalin and original zeal after fifteen or twenty years of doing the same thing," remarked Nicco Toi. "Teachers shouldn't become so defensive about this change in attitude. Instead of denying it, I think they should accept it as natural."

"If you're concerned about the hormonal changes your body is going through, you should know you're in good company. As we get older, many of us have second thoughts, doubts, and concern about our professional careers and identity," said Werner.

"I agree," remarked Erica. "Teachers have their own personal concerns, somewhat different from other professions, which we sometimes conceal. I think there is a sense of loneliness and anxiety as time passes, and we lack direct professional channels for expressing our concerns and reflecting. Some of us, I believe, have a lot of unconscious, hidden hostilities toward youth, as we age and become aware that our lives are passing by."

Werner responded, "Why this gloomy outlook?"

"It's just that some of us wind up teaching children that are bound to fail, because the circumstances are such that they cannot help but fail. Unable to reach and teach these children, we give up on them. It's not only frustrating, but it also leads to questions about our own personal limitations and professional self-worth. Some of us begin to make excuses, others become detached as a defensive mechanism from the children we teach and the colleagues we encounter on a regular basis. All of these factors take their toll and result in loneliness, despair, and burnout."

"I agree," said Williams. "A loss of zeal over years is common for most people; it is a part of aging. Moreover, when someone is approaching fifty years old, it is not uncommon to think about a pension. The danger arises when young teachers become trapped; for example, they might grow to dislike teaching but remain in the profession because they are afraid they cannot do anything else or they feel they only have ten more years to collect their pension."

"I would like to change the discussion from when we are approaching retirement to when we are in our youth. I've heard it said somewhere," said Anna Layden, a science teacher, "that early teaching models are triggered in later years. The chance of teaching as a career is rooted in childhood tendencies to talk, prompt, and correct others. Once in front of the classroom, teachers incessantly talk, call on students, and correct students. Thus, for some of us, the decision to teach predates college or high school and goes back to childhood. Parents are much more influential than former teachers in influencing their children to teach, especially their daughters. I think a lot of this had to do in the past with the limited number of career choices available to women. Today, a lot of bright women who normally would have chosen teaching as a career are entering other fields of study."

"Your implication, Anna, is that the teaching profession is losing a lot of bright women, and since teaching is largely a female profession, about sixty-seven percent, the entry standards and people entering teaching will be lower. But I don't see that happening," said Werner. "Standards for teacher preparation are growing more rigorous, because of the national and state reform movements in education and the increased role of accrediting agencies. In fact, the scores that education students make on standardized tests have been increasing recently. A lot of this has to do with the improved salaries of teachers and the status being awarded teachers."

"I think Anna is right about the early influence of parents," said Wanda Pulaski, who was now studying for her doctorate in education, although in an earlier period in her life she was undecided about teaching. "There is research dating back to the 1960s and 1970s, with Benjamin Wright and Dan Lortie, up to the present, that indicates about twenty-five percent make their decision to teach before finishing elementary school, and sixty to seventy percent before finishing high school. My decision was influenced by my parents, their family traditions, and their respect for education. It was also bolstered by my fourth- and fifth-grade teachers who today would be called *school marms*; indeed, they were dedicated and nurturing teachers who made me realize how important teaching is."

"I'll be honest with you," said Shazi. "It was my junior year in college, and I was undecided about what I was going to do after graduation. I minored in education because I was unsure about which profession to enter. I enrolled in the first two education courses to explore what teaching was all about. It wasn't until my third course, the second half of my junior year, that I became committed to the idea of teaching."

"I guess I'm more like Wanda," remarked Williams. "I knew I wanted to become a teacher in high school. I was influenced, in my formative years, by my history and English teachers. They were great teachers with a sense of humor. I learned a lot from them."

"The point Walt and I are making," stated Pulaski, "is that many teachers make an early career decision to teach. I'm not criticizing Muhammad, but I will take a poke at these instant teachers who come from various alternative-certification programs. Many of these programs attract enthusiastic teachers from top colleges. Typically, they enroll in a quickie education program, but almost everyone in some 'reform' mode or who oversees public education at the state level has a high opinion of them. But they have had little prior interest in teaching—minimal time, effort, and preparation. There is no real commitment on their part—no real professional preparation. Give them a rough assignment, and it is easy for them to get up and leave, despite their initial enthusiasm."

"It sounds like you don't care for the Teach for America Program, or alternative certification, which exists to meet the needs of disadvantaged and underserved populations in urban and rural America," said Shazi.

"Under the new rules, it is easy for a math or science major to get a teaching job, that is, in areas where we are concerned about shortages. But expertise in math or science, or any subject, is not the same as pedagogical knowledge or experience. Trial and error rarely produce good teaching. These new recruits don't have a clue about how to teach students who have serious personal needs or reading deficiencies."

"You sound quite cynical," declared Stehl. "Aren't you being a little unfair, given their positive motives and enthusiasm for teaching?"

"No," said Pulaski, "I'm just being realistic and honest with my feelings. I'm not going to just agree with so-called 'university experts' or state bureaucrats, many of whom never taught a day in their lives."

Pulaski continued. "Teach for America gets the most media attention, and it's usually very positive because it recruits young 'missionary' types into inner-city classrooms for two-year stints—about seven thousand teachers so far. Let me just say, according to the *New York Times,* their retention rate is below the national average—some nineteen percent of these recruits don't even complete their initial two-year assignment. Its easy come, easy go."

"That's unfair," said Crowley. "It goes back to the perennial issues: Not everyone is cut out for teaching; experts cannot agree on teaching and training methods; and no one can agree whether teachers are born or bred. Young teachers can learn how to write lesson plans, but some of us are just lost when a student says to our face and in front of other students, 'Fuck you,' 'Make me,' or 'I don't care.'"

"Look, the problem is simple," remarked Williams. "These recruits get a five- or six-week crash course at the university and are expected to seek out experienced teachers and to lean on corp alumni for support. Well, that doesn't usually work in tough schools."

"In my book, attitude counts a lot," asserted Crowley, "and these recruits, for the greater part, have the right attitude. They also have excellent academic backgrounds and can easily pass required state competency exams."

"Tell me, Walt, why did you go into teaching?" asked Pulaski.

"Well, the pay is pretty good, there is good job security, and I enjoy my summer vacations. I've been to Europe and Latin America six or seven times. Some of my colleagues tell me that I have the wrong attitude. But I still think I'm a good teacher."

"You know, I have to give Walt an A for his honesty and practical reasons for teaching. It's not ideal; it's not going to win him any favors or awards, but I think," said Shazi, "that there are a host of economic reasons why people choose teaching as a career, just like there are economic reasons for choosing other occupations. In our case, job security, pension, a short working day, and long vacations have always been considerations. Although job security is not as certain as it was in prior years, once tenure is awarded our security is enhanced; most important, salaries and working conditions have improved largely due to the influence of teachers' unions. Sometimes, however, we are made to feel guilty or defensive if we discuss the advantages of the union or if salaries are discussed in public."

Walt then turned to Erica. "I can tell you are nervous about having to teach your next class. Is it really worth it?" he asked. "You might want to think hard about transferring schools."

"You're right," responded Erica. "I really can't control my students, but I really want to teach. I've tried everything. I've been to the principal's office four times this year. I've read two books on classroom management in the last two months. My method courses didn't really prepare me for this type of school. I feel lost. Maybe I don't have what it takes to teach."

Pulaski interrupted. "Listen, Erica, you're a great teacher. You're just in the wrong school. Don't give up on the profession, but think about transferring to another school where the kids will appreciate your teaching and where they read at grade level. I understand that you care, and Walt doesn't seem to care as much as you. But you have trouble teaching, and he doesn't. It's merely a job for him. I guess some of us can be less committed and less concerned and still do a relatively good job at teaching."

"You better believe it," insisted Walt. "I don't take my school work home. My workday ends at 3:00 p.m. I have another life outside of school, and I don't mix my personal life with my teaching responsibilities. Why should I? I don't get paid after three."

"Gee," Erica said, "I always take work home. There are essays to grade, homework to mark, then there are quizzes, lesson plans, and clerical assignments. How do you do it, Walt? How are you able to finish all your work in school?"

"It's simple. I have three monitors who come in forty-five minutes early to help me grade papers and tests. I only give short-answer quizzes so my monitors can use a key to grade the papers. They also grade my homework. I have them spot check only one or two questions where the answer is closed ended. As for lesson plans, I use my old ones. The causes and results of the Civil War haven't changed for the last hundred years."

Pulaski commented, "I love your attitude, Walt. You are sure to win the Teacher of the Year award!"

Walt pointed to Wanda and asked: "Do you still write new lesson plans?"

She responded: "I update them periodically—maybe not as often as I should."

"The key is," said Walt, "I know my subject. I don't have to prepare like some of you. My depth of knowledge makes me a better teacher than most of my colleagues who spend hours reading and reviewing before teaching. What I do, however, is that when some activity clicks with the kids, I note and elaborate on it for the next year. If it bombs, then I insert notes or make changes for the following class or term. When a joke goes over well in class, I note it on the margins so I can tell it next term."

"Your attitude is detrimental to students," said Stehl.

"Oh, really! I have fun with my kids. All work and no play makes for a dull teacher and a dull classroom. I may not prepare like some of you. I may not stay late with my students, but my students and I connect. I don't have to use black rap or jive to connect. It's an honest relationship, and we understand each other."

"How do you deal with all these new standards and prescriptions on what to teach and for how long to teach particular content?" asked Stehl.

Walt responded in simple Walter-like language. "I haven't yet changed my personality or my methods, and no one is going to direct my schedule down to the minute. When that happens, it's time to pack up and cut out."

Pulaski turned to Erica. "Walt is Walt. I doubt if he will ever change. I guess he is living proof that dedication and good teaching do not necessarily go hand in hand. There are probably thousands of teachers like him, perhaps even thousands of police officers, nurses, social workers, even physicians and judges, who work with children and have similar attitudes about their jobs. They don't really care like some of us, but I guess they do a decent job."

"Maybe even a good job," said Walt.

"There is some truth in what Walt says," remarked Shazi. "I knew some young idealistic teachers who were overwhelmed by the demands of their new job and never left school before 6 p.m. Well, they dropped out of the profession and dropped their master's degree programs."

"You know I haven't said much in this discussion," commented Layden, "because I have more concerns about safe sex and finding a husband than dealing with professional problems. First, I have to say that almost everyone knows about the national shortage of teachers, some 200,000 to 250,000 new teachers are needed each year until 2010, and school districts are trying to entice bright recruits. But a good many young new professionals, brimming with idealism and determination, enter the classroom and are immediately told they have to follow specific guidelines set by the school district or state. Creativity and independence are discouraged. Rigid guidelines are imposed. Maybe it's okay to have one or two Walts in every school to keep us from following a minute-by-minute script."

"What does your personal life have to do with our discussion?" asked Werner.

"I'm just trying to be honest with my feelings, and I thought it was legitimate to be honest as well as human, rather than hold back and create anxiety. You know, my parents have been married forty-seven years, but I don't know if I want to wait until I'm married to have a baby. My dad is a minister, and I don't know how to tell him my feelings, but I thought I could express them here."

"Well, I'm one of the last of the Mohicans and still believe in being 'nuclear,' at least when it comes to families," responded Erica.

In the meantime, Werner tried to sum up the feelings being expressed. "There are many motives for choosing a career in teaching. Those who are thinking about entering the profession—and even those who are currently teaching—should ask why they made, or are about to make, this choice. Being honest with yourself and understanding your reasons for teaching will help you become a more effective teacher. It will make you more sensitive and aware of people, including your colleagues and students, and you should be able to better assess your own attitudes and behavior as a teacher."

Shazi then remarked, "Precise analysis of our reasons for teaching is difficult, but it is beneficial to discuss them, to be honest about them, and not to feel guilty about some of the practical reasons for teaching."

"Doesn't anyone want to deal with personal issues such as sex and marriage?" asked Layden.

"Not really," said Werner, "this is not the place."

"The point is," said Crowley, "people can choose a career in teaching for practical reasons or because they appreciate long summer vacations at the lake or because they reject the pressures or uncertainty of private industry and still do an excellent job teaching. Someone else who claims to be highly dedicated and loves to teach can be placed in a difficult teaching situation and not reach or teach the students. Of course, dedication and love of students and subject go a long way in influencing teacher behavior, teacher–student interaction, and teacher professionalism."

Questions to Consider

1. At what point in your life did you feel sure you wanted to teach?

2. Why did you choose teaching as a career?

3. Given the fact that we live in a materialistic society, where professional status is also influenced by the amount of money people earn, to what extent should economic factors play in a person's decision to teach?

4. Erica Drucker is obviously having trouble with her students. Is it time for her to look for another school? Can she succeed in a "better" school? Does she have the right personality for teaching?

5. Is Walt's attitude as negative as it appears on the surface? How much of what he says is merely bravado, defensiveness, or possibly the fact that he might prefer teaching in a "better" school?

6. Some of the teachers (Crowley and Williams) chose teaching as a career for practical reasons, others (Werner and Stehl) because they were unsure or undecided on a career change, while others (Drucker, Layden, and Pulaski) expressed positive motives and knew very early in life they wanted to teach. What conclusions can you reach about career aspirations or reasons for teaching and teacher effectiveness?

7. Interview several teachers at a local school to determine their reasons for teaching. Compare your findings with those of students in your class.

Recommended Readings

Michael W. Apple, *Teachers and Texts* (New York: Routledge, 1986).

William Ayers, *To Teach: The Journey of a Teacher,* 2nd ed. (New York: Teachers College Press, Columbia University, 2001).

Arthur Jersild, *When Teachers Face Themselves* (New York: Teachers College Press, Columbia University, 1955).

Parker J. Palmer, *Teaching from the Heart* (San Francisco: Jossey-Bass, 1999).

Stanley J. Zehm and Jeffrey A. Kottler, *On Being a Teacher* (Newbury Park, CA: Corwin Press, 1993).

13

Teacher Preparation:
What Courses?
How Many?

Despite all the talk about the reform of teacher education teacher training has not changed much during the last fifty years. Although variation may be seen in emphasis, sequence, or titles of courses, and deans of schools of education may often boast that their programs are the most innovative or best prepare their undergraduate clients, a basic framework exists among the 1,250 colleges and universities involved in teacher preparation. The names of the courses have changed and fewer education courses are required than fifty years ago, but the program usually falls into three broad areas: liberal arts and science, academic major (or teaching specialization), and professional education courses, consisting of foundations, methods, and student teacher experiences. Some institutions today may also offer a required course in reading, special education, or bilingual education, largely determined by state requirements.

For the last century, educators have argued over the requirements and emphasis in each of the three areas. There has also been concern about fragmentation, the lack of liberal education courses, the academic quality of education courses, and whether education theory can be translated into practice. Another concern is the historical rivalry, jealousy, and turf wars that erupt among professors of arts and science and professors of education. The controversy between both camps reached its height during the *Sputnik* era, corresponding with the publication of James Conant's *The Education of American Teachers* and James Koerner's *The Miseducation of American Teachers* (both published in 1963 and both critical of teacher programs, teacher education courses, professors of education, and state education officials involved in certifying teachers). The rivalry continues today, although it is less heated.

Since the publication of *A Nation at Risk* in 1983, teacher education proposals have been characterized by four constant themes: (1) increase courses in the teaching specialization, (2) reduce teacher education courses, (3) upgrade teacher education courses, and (4) raise admission or selection standards for teacher education candidates. Related themes include testing teachers in basic skill areas, holding teachers accountable, and raising teacher salaries to attract better qualified recruits.

During the 1980s and 1990s, the Carnegie Forum and Holmes Group published several reports which, in general, advocated (1) a five-year program for all teacher candidates, (2) extensive clinical training and supervision, (3) a teacher internship accompanied by mentoring or coaching of beginning teachers, (4) expanded researcher-practitioner partnerships, and (5) professional development centers in the "field," offering staff development experiences for all teachers.

The Carnegie Forum, in conjunction with the National Education Association and American Federation of Teachers, has been also instrumental in developing the National Board for Professional Teaching Standards (NBPTS), which has developed a voluntary certification system that establishes high standards of what teachers should *know* and be able to *do*, assesses and recognizes effective teachers, and establishes a governing board (comprised mainly of teachers) to endorse these standards.

In the new millennium, two educators stand out as key players in reforming teacher education. John Goodlad, who recently retired from the University of Washington, has written several books on improving teaching and schooling. In *Teachers for Our Nation's Schools*, (1994) he criticizes American educators with "moral delinquency" for the deplorable state of affairs in teacher education, pointing out that teacher educators lack a clear mission and are divided among themselves about how to improve teacher preparation programs. Goodlad also asserts that professors of liberal arts merely criticize without offering viable options, and state officials and policy makers impose contradictory, politically laden, and bureaucratic regulations that only add to the confusion. He offers nineteen postulates or recommendations for improving teacher education.

In several of Linda Darling-Hammond's publications, including the most prominent ones, *A License to Teach* (1999) and *A Right to Learn* (2001), she points out that (1) teachers who are fully prepared and certified are more effective with students than teachers without full preparation; (2) teacher effectiveness accounts for the largest variation in student achievement, more so than what the schools do (e.g., schools might introduce smaller classes or more reading programs); (3) the least qualified teachers (in terms of preparation) and least experienced teachers typically are assigned to inner-city schools where students have the most learning problems; and (4) teacher preparation represents one of the most important resource differentials between middle-class and lower-class schools and in part explains the academic differences between both students.

ISSUES

What is the proper mix of (1) general or liberal education, (2) specialized courses or courses in a specific area, and (3) teacher education or professional courses? This was the first question asked at the university-wide academic committee meeting at Northern State University.

History professor Janice Applewood-Hayes was first to comment. "Mastery of subject matter to be taught is all that is required for good teaching. I don't understand why we need all of these education courses; they don't prepare teachers to teach subject matter. All they do is create obstacles for students who want to teach and preserve jobs for professors of education as well as state officials who guard the gates by evaluating education programs and courses and grant certification."

Associate professor Heiu Chow replied, "My colleagues in the School of Education view good teaching as primarily a matter of pedagogical expertise, that is, understanding and implementing methods and basic principles of teaching. A good teacher considers *what* is to be taught, what we call subject matter or content; and *how* it is best taught, what we call pedagogy. It is possible to be an expert in subject matter, a literary giant or top-rated scientist, but be unable to convey the knowledge to learners. A good teacher needs to understand the principles of teaching and learning, to get students to critically think and problem solve in any subject."

"I believe the difference in opinion expressed by Professors Applewood-Hayes and Chow goes back to the 1950s and 1960s," said sociology professor María Lopez. "James Conant, in *The Education of American Teachers,* described a long-standing quarrel between professors of education who defended education courses and often wanted to increase the number beyond state requirements, and arts and science professors who saw little value in these courses and wanted to limit them."

E. F. Pajak, professor of language, then interrupted. "But Conant, as president of Harvard University, also argued that most education courses were 'Mickey Mouse'—those were his words—and that the foundation courses such as philosophy, history, and psychology of education should be taught by professors of arts and science."

"That is true," said Lopez, "but Conant was a professor of chemistry for more than twenty years before becoming president. In my opinion, he was merely reflecting his biases as a science professor. It is only recently that the conflict between education and arts and science faculty has subsided. In some institutions, the education faculty has similar status because of the recent hiring of many education professors who are more research oriented than their predecessors."

Pajak answered, "Conant also pointed out that student teaching was the most important education course. Even today there are many education reports published by the Carnegie Foundation and the National Education Association that conclude student teaching is essential and should be improved for purposes of reforming teacher education."

"I have no argument with this position. Student teaching provides the opportunity for education students to observe and to teach under the supervision of experienced teachers—in short, to translate education theory into practice," asserted Chow. "Student teaching is usually limited to one term. I advocate that we extend it to a school year and that student teachers be assigned two different schools. At least half of the experience should take place in an urban school, preferably an inner-city school, since the U.S. student population is increasingly becoming minority, immigrant, bilingual, and in need of teachers who understand their culture."

"Quantity of instruction is one issue, but so is quality," said education professor Terry Snower. "The relationship among the student teacher, cooperating teacher, and supervising professor is crucial to the student teaching experience. Although student teaching is a time for trial and error, for making mistakes and learning from them, how well future teachers develop during this period will have a lot to do with the help they receive from the cooperating teacher and supervising professor."

Snower continued, "The problem is that some cooperating teachers are unqualified or disinterested in working with student teachers and feel it is more of a burden than reward to work with these students. We need to encourage and compensate qualified teachers to mentor our student teachers. They play an essential role in the teacher education program, and it often goes unrecognized or is minimized by professors of education. In fact, such terms as *trumped, subordinated,* and *deprofessionalized* have been used to describe the past relationship between teachers and professors."

Snower pointed out that senior professors should be encouraged to work with student teachers and cooperating teachers. In the past, many senior professors were reluctant to work in the schools, and junior faculty, adjunct professors, and part-timers were employed to do this work. "Senior professors should be rotated to work with student teachers and teachers in the field. Why not? The new research on teaching and teacher education includes teachers' voices, teachers' stories, teachers' reflections, what we used to call action research or field research. All of these new trends welcome practitioner-researcher collaboration, education professors learning from teacher perspectives, and insights to acquire greater research credibility."

"We also need to get our education students into classrooms much earlier than when they student teach. They need field experiences early in their careers, and on a regular basis," commented Chow. "Field experience provides an early understanding of the reality of classrooms and schools and can help education students decide if teaching is really for them, rather than postpone reality until the student teaching period, often the last year of college, when it is too late to switch fields."

"What education students need is more liberal arts and subject specialization, not field courses that lack academic substance," responded Lopez.

"Not so, according to most professors of education," asserted James Biddle, an education psychology professor. "Field experiences provide opportunities for prospective teachers to familiarize themselves with the workings of the classroom from a teacher's perspective and to integrate theories of education and teaching principles learned in textbooks by observing and talking to teachers. Without these experiences, preservice teachers have greater difficulty linking theoretical knowledge and pedagogical skills, gained by textbook readings and discussions in education courses, with real events and situations in the classroom. In fact, until preservice teachers can integrate what they read with the reality of teaching, almost everything they read as principles or methods of teaching remains theoretical. Even worse, they will have trouble fully understanding and appreciating the content of their education courses."

"Are you saying preservice teachers cannot make the connection between theory and practice, between college classroom content and real classroom experiences?" asked Professor Snower.

"That's one way of saying it. Maybe on Friday night, after two or three drinks, we will gain a better understanding," said Biddle.

"Let me say it another way," said Professor Applewood-Hayes. "Preservice teachers lack certain benchmarks and practical experiences to fully integrate for future use what they learn in education courses; even worse, they don't even know what they don't know because they know so little about life in classrooms as a teacher."

"Are you inferring that the academic content of teacher education courses does not prepare beginning teachers for the realities of the jobs and that we need to emphasize field experiences and student teaching?" asked Snower.

Lopez responded, "There are philosophical ideas and learning principles that can be taught to education students in advance of practical experiences in the classroom. But theory and practice go hand in hand; in fact, good theory is based on practice. The problem, however, is that most professors of education rely on theory, or the academic content of their courses, whereas teachers come to rely on everyday common sense and practical methods to guide their teaching."

"Let me change the subject," commented Ziggy Yates, a professor of English. "The problem with teacher education is related to the entire course sequence. James Koerner, in *The Miseducation of American Teachers,* tabulated 1,600 transcripts of student teachers in thirty-two colleges of education in the late 1950s. He found that twenty-two percent of the total program of secondary teachers and forty-one percent of the program of elementary teachers were devoted to education courses. The percentages were even higher among those attending teachers' colleges. In these schools, more than twenty-five percent of the secondary education program and forty-five percent of the elementary program were allocated to education courses."

"In the last forty or more years, especially since the *Sputnik* era, there has been a substantial reduction in the number of education courses required in the place of generalized and specialized courses in the arts and sciences," said Chow. As of 2000, most colleges and universities required eighteen educational semester credits, or about twelve percent of the total program for secondary teachers and about twenty-four credits, or about twenty percent for elementary teachers."

"The point is," said Yates, "there are still too many education courses. Although the trend is to reduce the number of education courses, many institutions, including our own university, still encourage courses beyond state certification requirements."

"You're speaking like a true professor of arts and science," replied Chow. "I suppose you want to further reduce the number of required education courses."

"Your own professional colleagues view good teacher education in two sharply contradictory views, including a substantial number who maintain that mastery of the subject matter to be taught is essential and, at the other extreme, those who view good teacher preparation as primarily a matter of pedagogical expertise," commented Yates. "The Holmes Group, a number of reform educators based at prestigious research institutions, represents the first position and prefers that teachers invest their preparation time in earning a baccalaureate degree in academic disciplines and later a master's in education. This position is acceptable to arts and sciences professors."

"The second position," continued Yates, "that pedagogical knowledge and skills are more important than subject matter, is best illustrated by the recent research on teacher effectiveness and master (or star) teachers that suggests there are generic methods of teaching that cut across subject matter and grade level. It is also represented by the field of *cognitive psychology,* with its focus on general thinking skills and learning strategies. This viewpoint, I assume, is the one that most of your colleagues in the School of Education advocate. However, most of my colleagues in the arts and sciences reject this emphasis on process and pedagogy at the expense of content and academic rigor."

"There is a middle position," interrupted Pajak. "That is, generic teaching strategies—once considered applicable to teaching any subject—must be modified to fit the particular subject. And, if I may add, they must also fit the grade level or developmental stage of the students. This position, argued best by Lee Shulman and Lauren Resnick, suggests that students cannot critically think in their subject without a knowledge base; content provides the tool for understanding the world around us as well as for developing and applying our mental processes. This idea seems to operate more at the secondary level and would be acceptable to most arts and science professors and old-time essentialist educators such as James Conant and Jerome Bruner and current essentialists such as E. D. Hirsch and Diane Ravitch, who are also subject oriented and believe that academic disciplines have their own structure, their own theory, principles, and concepts."

"Listen," said Lopez. "I think there is no clear evidence that greater emphasis on subject matter for prospective teachers results in improved teaching, or that greater emphasis on pedagogy makes a difference. Most people make certain assumptions based on their professional background and biases and merely advocate that particular platform. I also see no reason why courses defined as *professional* or as *education* courses cannot be as intellectual or rigorous as courses described as *liberal arts.*"

"Anyone who takes a middle position would probably agree with you, María. However, I still have a problem with course content," argued Yates. "Not only is there wide variation among states in terms of certification requirements, but also within states among colleges and universities preparing teachers. The content of these education courses also varies considerably from institution to institution, and even courses with similar titles in the same institution usually vary in content, since the professors who teach them cannot agree on a common body of knowledge that they all feel should be held by teacher candidates. Furthermore, standards in these courses vary, depending on the institution and the professor, so that it is difficult to determine what has been taught and learned in these courses."

"I think you can make this criticism about many fields of study, not only education," commented Applewood-Hayes.

"You have a point," replied Yates, "but the admission requirements for teacher preparation need to be upgraded. Too many C students are permitted entry into teacher education programs. Education is sometimes considered a last resort for students who have no idea what they wish to study or who switch majors in their junior or senior year."

"That criticism is representative of a different era," commented Chow, "especially when there was an undersupply of teachers. Although, today, there is great diversity in admission requirements into teacher education programs, most departments of education have raised the grade point average (GPA) in the last ten years from two to two and a half or higher on a four-point scale. Nationwide, according to *Education Week,* approximately twenty percent of all students applying for admission into teacher education are rejected. This represents a significant increase in the rejection rate, largely reflecting the national reform movement to upgrade the profession, especially admission requirements, and the recent increase in teacher education enrollments, which is expected to continue in the near future. Increasingly, our best and brightest students are majoring in education, because of the improvement of teacher salaries and fringe benefits."

"I think you are a little nuts," declared Yates, "if you feel that our brightest students are entering teaching. Salaries are capped and designed to demotivate bright and creative students from thinking about teaching. A beginning sanitation worker in New York City currently makes more money than a freshmen teacher."

"Money is not the only thing in life or the only criteria for deciding on a career," responded Lopez.

"We need to enforce academic standards, otherwise, the blind will wind up leading the blind and the semi-illiterate will be teaching the illiterate," insisted Yates. "Schools of education are noted for relaxed requirements, and for passing almost everyone, including students who cannot write a compound sentence. Too many education graduates cannot pass simple basic skills tests in reading and math, and too many big-city schools wind up hiring these teachers because of the need for a warm body in the classroom. Everyone and every institution looks the other way, including schools of education, accrediting agencies, school districts, and state lawmakers, partially because of teacher shortages in selected geographical areas and because there is a minority gap in test scores that few people wish to frankly discuss."

"Most of the problems about quality would be resolved," said Applewood-Hayes, "if prospective teachers were required to demonstrate a specified level of competence by the end of the preservice stage in order to be allowed entry into the profession. I am referring to a pen-and-pencil test in an academic area, as well as a classroom performance test, and possibly an essay test, too."

"Let me emphasize your point," said Yates. "There are schoolteachers in many big cities that can barely speak or write formal English, and others who have failed basic skill tests several times before passing, and still others who would not pass if they were tested."

"We have to make better decisions on who teaches," asserted Lopez.

"I've heard that story before," responded Yates. "The fact is that minority candidates fail teacher tests in basic skills at much higher rates than white candidates. I can cite one state after another where this has happened. The states which have narrowed the gaps have done so by establishing lower cutoff scores, not by improving the education of minority candidates.

"Are you aware that some big-city school systems, such as Los Angeles and New York City, are hiring beginning teachers before they complete student teaching, just to fill classrooms with bodies? How do we respond to lower minority test scores in an era of teacher shortages and affirmative action which protects groups defined as minorities? How do we deal with bilingual teachers who cannot speak or write formal English? How do we improve standards for all teachers?"

"I don't think lowering cutoff scores on tests, refusing to test teacher candidates, or using racial ploys or cries of discrimination are sound answers," said Applewood-Hayes.

"Many of our school districts have not found a way to get rid of incompetent or academically unqualified teachers," declared Pajak. "In other professions there is no tenure and it is much easier to say good-bye to poor workers. We have to find an objective way to make decisions about who gets into the profession and about competency and productivity. But the unions enter into the picture, and then there is the problem of judgment or whether a school principal is politically motivated or biased."

"Teachers have rights, but students should come first," said Snower. "It may take two or three years for a determined principal to fire the worst teachers in a school because of all the legal hoops involved. As for less than average teachers, it doesn't pay; it is just too complicated and time consuming."

"I don't think the unions trust principals or superintendents," mentioned Applewood-Hayes. "Performance will always be an issue. The idea is to reduce the problem by upgrading certification requirements and testing teacher candidates. The need is to better screen candidates before they enter teacher programs."

"Are you correlating academics with teacher effectiveness?"

"My ideal teacher candidate is someone who is intellectually, emotionally, and socially fit. Intelligence is only one criterion for consideration, but I would demand a minimum level of literacy and test for it," declared Yates.

"Do we need to discuss the reliability and validity problems associated with testing?" asked Pajak.

"Listen, we test our students on a regular basis, so why can't we test teachers," asked Applewood-Hayes, "to ensure they are qualified in the three areas mentioned by Ziggy. I want a whole person to teach, someone well rounded, not just an intellectual."

"Are you trying to refine teacher education?" asked Biddle.

"No," said Applewood-Hayes, "but we need to shift the dialogue from politically expedient methods to more rigorous methods of preparing teachers. We have to clean up our colleges of education, like Abraham Flexner's recommendations for medical education some one hundred years ago. We have too may education mills, turning out many unprepared and unqualified teachers. We have too many alternative certification programs that place minimal emphasis on teaching skills. Knowing one's subject is crucial, but the methods of teaching are vital, too."

Snower then pointed out that many states, about forty, were moving in the direction of alternative certification to meet the demand for new teachers, especially in math and science. "You realize, under the standard certification rules, Bill Gates could not teach computer science and Albert Einstein would not be able to teach physics. Let's face it. Good teachers can come from several educational and professional backgrounds."

"The problem I have with your reasoning, and all the reform-minded critics," said Yates, "is the interference from the lay public, the press, and state education policy makers who want to establish backdoor methods of entering teaching. This kind of interference would never be tolerated by schools of medicine, law, business, or engineering. Everyone seems to have this strange notion that we can make 'instant' teachers or take uncertified teachers and expect them to perform as good as certified teachers."

"Listen, if retirees or businesspeople wish to switch careers, they should have to prove themselves the same way other teachers have had to," asserted Chow. "No shortcuts!"

"You sound like a teacher union representative," said Lopez.

Snower responded. "No, I'm trying, so is Professor Chow, to upgrade standards. Ziggy is right. Doctors and lawyers have clear entry points, uniform education programs, and licensing tests."

Professor Pajak interrupted, arguing that it was not the *process* but the *input* that counted. "The debate needs to be shifted from how we prepare teachers (process) to who we admit (input) into teacher education programs. We cannot have better schools until we have better teachers, and we cannot have better teachers until we have qualified candidates, and we cannot have better qualified candidates unless we test and screen them."

"Regardless of the test we use," commented Snower, "if it is a test where jobs or promotions are at stake, it is sure to invoke controversy about group outcomes—whether the test is valid, fair, or reliable. Other than a test of professional knowledge in education, and possibly an essay, it is premature to test beginning teachers at the end of their teacher preparation. I would delay judgment until the end of a two- or three-year *internship* under the tutelage of experienced teachers. This would permit teachers to learn on the job, the only place they can really learn, and would require some demonstration of classroom competency at the early stage of their careers and at the end of the internships."

Biddle spoke up. "I think the opinions at this meeting are so diverse that we might learn from John Goodlad's recommendations, at least there would be a vehicle for communication and compromise among professors of education and arts and science. In his book *Teachers for Our Nation's Schools,* he delineated nineteen postulates for improving teacher education, including a Center of Pedagogy, to implement the postulates, and to be staffed by a team of liberal arts professors, education professors, and practitioners (teachers and administrators) from the schools. This group would decide on how prospective teachers would be prepared, what courses would be required, and how cooperating teachers and schools would be utilized for teacher education. It would also screen candidates on the basis of moral decency, enhance research and reflective practices, and expand departments of education to include liberal arts professors and school practitioners, and take responsibility for the first year of teaching."

"All this sounds wonderful," commented Chow. "But I see this as a method for diluting the influence of departments or schools of education. I realize that education professors and liberal arts professors need to communicate and cooperate, but not at the expense of departments or schools of education. I remind you that professors of law have control over law schools and professors of business have control over business schools. The point is, education is a professional field, like law and business, and control needs to be firmly established by professionals within the field and not by arts and science professors."

Chow continued, "Professors of arts and science can have input in the academic component of the study of teaching. However, when it comes to foundations of education, pedagogy of subject matter, teaching methods and principles, field experiences and student teaching, and overall professional responsibilities and ethics, teacher educators—that is, education professors and professional accrediting agencies and state departments of education—need to control their own policies and practices."

Lopez asserted, "We don't want to leave it to chance or accident whether beginning teachers acquire professional knowledge suitable for good teaching. Teaching is part science and part art, and the scientific component can be taught to education students in terms of pedagogical principles."

Again Biddle interrupted: "If the scientific aspect of teaching cannot be taught, then schools of education should close shop."

"Professors of education and experienced teachers are best equipped to do the job," said Chow. "What I would like to see is more dialogue between professors who deal with theory and the practitioners who are involved in the practice of teaching. It would also be helpful if we could improve the dialogue between professors of arts and science and professors of education."

Both Pajak and Lopez chuckled, reminding the others that the issue dated back to Conant's observations when he was president of Harvard and wrote *The Education of American Teachers*. "Some things at colleges and universities are just slow to change—or just don't change."

Questions to Consider

1. What is the best mix of liberal arts, specialized courses, and education courses?

2. What education courses have been most helpful for you as a preservice (in-service) teacher?

3. Which professor's point of view do you agree with most? Why?

4. How can we limit the long-standing quarrel between arts and science professors and education professors?

5. Among the professors of education (Drs. Biddle, Chow, or Snower), whose view do you prefer? Why?

6. How can we improve the communication and cooperation between professors of education and experienced teachers?

7. The Carnegie Foundation, Educational Testing Service, and National Council for Accreditation of Teacher Education have developed their own models for teacher education. Check the library or Internet and summarize one of these organizational models for improving teacher education. Discuss your findings with the class.

Recommended Readings

James B. Conant, *The Education of American Teachers* (New York: McGraw-Hill, 1963).
Linda Darling-Hammond, *The Right to Learn* (San Francisco: Jossey-Bass, 2001).
John I. Goodlad, *Teachers for Our Nation's Schools* (San Francisco: Jossey-Bass, 1994).
Holmes Group, *Tomorrow's Schools of Education* (East Lansing, MI: Holmes Group, 1995).
John Sikula, ed., *Handbook of Research on Teacher Education* (New York: Macmillan, 1996).

14

Finding a Teaching Position: Cakewalk or Hurdle?

Given the conventional wisdom that some 200,000 to 250,000 teachers are needed annually for the next ten years, because of increasing student enrollments and teacher retirements from the baby boomer generation, the perception is that new teachers can easily find positions. Revisionary and separate analyses by the two most prominent experts on teaching trends, Linda Darling-Hammond and Arthur Wise, indicate that whatever shortage may exist is only in some geographical areas such as in parts of the South and West, as well as in big cities and inner-city neighborhoods and in specializations such as science, math, and bilingual and special education. For the most part, surpluses exist in most of the Northeast, Middle Atlantic, Midwest, and Rocky Mountain areas, as well as in wealthy suburban school districts and in many secondary subject areas such as English, social studies, art, music, and physical education.

The number of new teachers prepared each year is estimated at 175,000 to 190,000. About 15,000 to 25,000 are hired as experienced teachers from (1) another state or another school district, (2) a pool of experienced teachers returning to the profession, or (3) a pool of substitute teachers who are looking for a full-time appointment. About 10 percent of newly hired teachers are initially hired without a professional license, with minimal preparation or with an alternative certification. The majority of these new teachers fill positions in inner cities and poor rural areas; schools that need the most qualified teachers usually wind up with the least qualified.

For the most part, teacher shortages exist in places that few people want to teach in because of stress, poor teaching conditions, lack of support, cumbersome bureaucracy, and/or low salaries. The turnover, obviously, is dramatic in those schools, causing the need for more teachers and creating a cycle whereby there is a lack of experienced teachers in the central cities and rural areas, adding to problems of inequality.

Only about 75 percent of newly prepared teachers find a job after graduating from a teacher preparation program. The need is for either schools of education or state departments of education to restrict the pool of candidates who can enter teacher preparation programs as they do in the medical profession. In areas of specialization, where a shortage is expected to exist for several years, scholarships or some kind of bonus or differential pay is needed to increase supply. The need also exists to ensure that midcareer recruits meet the same standards as traditional candidates and that abbreviated programs, including Teach for America, although they may be implemented with altruistic reasons, be upgraded or closed down. We need a contemporary

147

Abraham Flexner, who some one hundred years ago, on behalf of the medical profession, exposed medical schools and their practice of training ill-prepared physicians. Many schools were labeled as "mills" and were shut down by the medical association.

Now, on a more practical level, one that deals with the issue of getting your first job, it is important to recognize that procedures and criteria for hiring new teachers are not standardized. Beginning teachers do not always have a clear picture of how to present themselves and what qualities to stress.

Most school administrators say the credential file and interview are most important. The credential file often determines whether a candidate will make it to the interview, and the interview often determines whether the candidate will get the job. In some big-city school districts, the interview process does not exist. Bodies are needed, to be blunt, and if the candidate has the right courses and fills out the appropriate forms (although the latter may be cumbersome), he or she will get the job.

For the greater part, however, expect a close examination of your credentials in order to get to the next stage, an interview. In a survey conducted by Joseph Braun of 271 elementary and secondary principals, Braun found that the five most important variables in reviewing a candidate's application were (1) correct spelling and punctuation in the candidate's application letter, (2) candidate's work with children, (3) letters of recommendation(s) from administrators, (4) neatness of materials, and (5) evaluation of student teaching from the cooperating teacher. (Ironically, academic background and computer skills did not make the top five list.) The variables considered most important about the candidate's interview were, in rank order, (1) honesty of responses, (2) interpersonal skills, (3) use of oral English, (4) personal appearance, (5) anticipated ability to adjust to the community, and (6) sophistication of responses.

Regardless of what you think about interviews, they remain the most direct and important screening tool available to the vast majority of school districts (with the exception of very large ones that still rely on bureaucratic forms and pen-and-paper tests). You need to know what to expect from interviewers. According to one school administrator, writing for the *American School Board Journal*, veteran interviewers:

1. Focus not on questions of competency (that should be investigated before they meet with candidates), but rather on those of philosophy and the roles of how you might fit into the system.
2. Are impressed not by verbal glibness, but rather by physical attractiveness and personal charm.
3. Are not rigid about time, but rather are willing to allow you to ask questions and clarify points.
4. Sometimes have you meet individually with key members of the staff or screening committee, say, before or after the formal interview.
5. Make notes after the interview to recall impressions and characteristics to distinguish between you and other candidates.
6. Send candidates material about the school system, which is important to read (to show you care) and ask related questions about sometime during the interview. The material should help prepare you with basic school demographics, goals, problems, and challenges that you will face in the school (or school district).

The teacher's job includes many nonteaching activities outside the classroom. This fact often comes as a surprise to beginning teachers who were not introduced to the varied responsibilities of teachers, since their methods courses and student teaching experiences focused on classroom activities and pedagogical skills. The courts generally place three legal duties on the shoulders of teachers: instruction, supervision, and provision of a safe environment for students. In addition, the courts have defined and upheld the school district's assignment of extra teaching duties, and the professional teaching organizations have recognized them as within the scope of the teacher's job, so long as they are reasonable adjuncts to the normal school day, not discriminatory, demeaning, or unusually time consuming.

In using the criteria cited by the courts, one school principal, writing for the *NASSP Bulletin*, elaborated on ten extra assignments or duties teachers can expect to perform: (1) take over study hall, (2) supervise student organizations or clubs, (3) supervise field trips, (4) attend parent–teacher meetings, (5) provide bus supervision, (6) supervise the school's breakfast or lunch program, (7) supervise the school's detention program, (8) supervise teacher aides, (9) supervise at athletic games, music performances, school parties, pep rallies, and other school-related programs, and (10) serve on schoolwide or district-wide committees.

Other duties, not specifically listed here or not always specified in the school manual or rules, are also within the scope of the teacher's job. Although they are not always spelled out in the contract or specifically listed in conjunction with the position, teachers can be expected to perform duties outside the classroom, especially if they are associated with student health or safety, academic, or social growth. The best a new teacher can hope for is for the school district to spell out these extra duties at the interview stage, or certainly at the acceptance stage.

Good luck in finding the job that you want.

ISSUES

It was May, and a group of students enrolled in different sections of their last education course required for certification were in the student cafeteria comparing "war" stories about their job search. Barbara Bowman, a twenty-one-year-old English major, already had four interviews and two job offers, subject to getting her certification. She described her success. "I was fortunate to work for Professor Hunkins for two years as a work-study student. He teaches in the graduate school and knows many teachers and principals who are enrolled in the master's and doctorate programs. I asked him for a favor one day when I was in his office. He made six calls to principals and superintendents to find out if there was a job opening in language arts or English. As you know, he has a great reputation. In a matter of one hour, he had scheduled four interviews for me. The trick, he told me, was to get to the interview—to be pushed to the head of the crowd. Then, of course, I was on my own."

"With your personality and positive outlook on life, I guess it was easy for you," commented Carl Furillo, also an English major. "I never nurtured the kind of personal contacts you did. I have to follow Professor Nirmala's advice in class."

"What advice is that?" asked Ofek Christensen, a history major.

Furillo, who was getting certified as an elementary reading teacher, replied, "The credential file and interview are key for getting a job."

"What is the credential file?" asked Hieu Lim, a music major.

"The important items are transcripts, letters of reference, and your resume. Transcripts speak for themselves. General letters, I'm told, rarely convey fitness for a specific position; they send a vague message and employers perceive that a candidate is applying to many school districts. Targeting is important; letters should be written to a specific person, not to 'Dear Sir' or 'To Whom It May Concern' and communicate qualifications in ways that relate directly to the needs of a particular school. The resume should detail education, employment, or teacher-related experiences, and skills related to the position. It should also include special categories such as camp experience, sports experience, military service, honors, and even hobbies that might relate to the job."

John Penick, a future math teacher, who was having no trouble getting interviewed, asserted that his education professor, Dr. Alam La Faz, made the point that "school interviewers are always looking for something extra, such as if you have coaching experience, acting or drama experience, writing or editing experience, or whether you are computer proficient, in order to utilize their teachers as a coach or director of an extracurricular or after-school activity. It is the special skills and experiences that distinguish the individual candidate from the rest of the pool of candidates."

"The interview is most important, according to Professor Frank Fields," said Furillo. "He divides questions in an interview into four types: (1) *Questions designed to help relax candidates.* These are usually general questions. For example, did you like your student teaching experience? (2) *Questions designed to assist candidates to express themselves openly.* These are general questions. For example, how would you describe your philosophy of education? (3) *Questions designed to evaluate the candidate's competence.* These are specific questions. For example, how would you teach a gifted learner or slow learner? (4) *Questions designed to evaluate the candidate's enthusiasm about teaching.* These can be general or specific questions. For example, what activities would you use to make the classroom an exciting place for learning?"

"When I went to my interview," commented John Bakula, a former accountant and midcareer teacher candidate, "I brought a portfolio of my teacher-related materials, including education research papers, lesson plans, and unit plans I developed in my methods class; pupil evaluations and supervisor evaluations of where I student taught; and videocassettes of two lessons I taught. It was a big success. Without being overbearing, I marketed myself—and it worked."

"What is a teacher portfolio?" asked Furillo.

"There is no rule or format," replied Bakula. "It usually includes a collection of items that help explain professionally who you are and the products of your work. It supplements the resume, and often says more about you than a resume. It can be sent along with the application for personnel people to review at their leisure. However, I used it at my interview to elaborate on what was in it."

"The portfolio also worked for me. You can't overdo it or brag about all your strong points in a letter of inquiry or on your resume," said Brad Meisel, a special education major. "I used the portfolio, however, to stress specific strengths and include student-teaching products related to the job opening. Though you cannot oversell yourself in a letter to personnel, you can do it in the portfolio, at least to a much greater extent."

Bakula added, "Talking about strengths, if you are computer proficient, then I think you need to stress it in the resume, the portfolio, and interview. The schools are plugged into technology and need teachers who can work with computers and teach kids about them."

"I have already been to two interviews," stated Furillo. "Although some interviewers ask superficial questions and are influenced by the physical characteristics and personality of the applicant, most interviewers ask specific questions and later discuss and evaluate the responses of the candidate. Actually one of the schools asked me two or three questions about my computer literacy and whether I knew enough to tutor some of the older teachers who were reluctant to learn to use computers."

"I spent thirty minutes in the placement office, as well as some time with my clinical professor, and I was able to anticipate several questions I was asked in my interview," asserted Bakula, who wanted to teach at the middle school level. "I had expectations that I would have to field questions related to my (1) teaching philosophy, (2) needs of the students, (3) subject matter, (4) lesson planning, (5) which activities I could direct, and (6) plans for professional growth. Four of these type of questions came up in my interview."

"I'm not sure whether I agree with both of you," said Penick. "I think physical characteristics and personality count more than knowledge or ability. If you can impress someone on a personal level, so they feel comfortable with you or even like you, then the rest falls in place; in fact, everything else is secondary."

"I think we all agree that the interview is crucial," commented Christensen. "The key question is, How do you get the interview? Barbara's method is probably the best, but most of us were not as smart or able to work part time for Dr. Hunkins."

Lim responded, "My professor, Dr. Athena Papadopolous, pointed out in class that there is a need to plan our job search and to use as many sources as possible: (1) college placement services, (2) state department of education recruitment offices, (3) school district employment offices, (4) newspapers from nearby large cities, as well as the *New York Times* (Sunday section) or *Education Week*, and (5) personal contacts such as teachers you know or professors at the college."

Responded Bakula, "The Internet is a lifesaver. Not only did I learn about specific vacancies from the Internet, but I was able to send my papers by e-mail. I applied to eighteen different school districts in less than an hour. It sure beats talking to a computerized voice or some tired secretary who connects you to the wrong person, or stuffing envelopes, parking, and standing in line."

"That's a great idea," said Lim. "Most school districts are hooked up to the Internet. I guess it's just a matter of finding the right search engine and web connection. Even if jobs are not posted, you can certainly find out plenty of information about a particular school district and its needs, prior to looking for a job or prior to an interview."

"You know a lot of jobs are still obtained by word of mouth or who you know," said Meisel. "A recommendation from a well-known person is worth its weight in gold."

"If you want to talk on that level, then a phone call by someone connected or friendly with a key administrator works wonders," declared Penick. "Some of the senior professors who work in doctoral programs have personal contacts with administrators from nearby school districts. Barbara is right. It's worth getting to know these professors so you feel comfortable asking them if they are willing to make one or two calls on your behalf."

Lim volunteered her thoughts. "I think the key is to do your student teaching at a school in which you might want to teach and where you think there will be an opening in your field the following year. Look for a large school with a large faculty so that the chances for retirement or replacement among teachers is good. Or, try to get placed in a growing school district that will need new teachers. Once you are placed in the school, the idea is to develop a good relationship with your clinical teacher and department supervisor who may play a part in the hiring process."

Penick was quick to object. "The idea sounds good in theory, but it is not always practical—at least not at this college. The director of student teaching, Dr. James Sears, assigns us where he can place a large number of students to facilitate the job of the clinical professor. He is not interested in individual requests."

"The right excuse or exception often works; it only takes a little imagination," said Christensen. "However, I would like to go back to the application. For most of us, if the application is not outstanding, we will not get a chance to be interviewed."

Lim responded. "My professor ranks in order the factors of the application that are important: letters of recommendation from those who are familiar with your work with children or adolescents, then your professors' recommendations, next evaluations of student teaching from your cooperating teacher, and finally previous employment experience."

"What about grades, honors and awards, and the reputation of the college or university you graduate from?" asked Bowman.

"Those factors rank lower, but for a good reason," asserted Lim. "Remember, teaching is a people industry, and getting along with students, parents, colleagues, and supervisors is important, more so than grades or your knowledge and what is revealed by your transcript."

"I still think knowledge of subject matter is important, especially at the high school level. Grade point average must count. Teaching ability must be essential," responded Bowman.

"Listen, everything you mention counts, at least to some extent," said Lim. "But people, I believe, are more impressed by social and personal skills than academic scores. It is the impression you make and how you get along with people at the interview and workplace that count for getting hired and promoted."

"I met my brother's high school principal at a party," said Meisel. "She gave me some good advice about interviews. First, she said it is the most direct and important screening tool for the vast majority of school districts, with the exception of the big-city ones that still rely on some qualifying exam or bureaucratic procedure for placements and assignments."

Meisel continued. "Principals consider most important (1) maturity and poise, (2) personal appearance, (3) academic background, and (4) ability to get along with students and colleagues."

"What about old-fashioned common sense and preparation?" asked Long Luu, a math and computer major. "Being clear on your own philosophy of teaching and learning, and how your philosophy fits in to the school system, is important; reading in advance about the school's or district's demographics, problems, and achievements and show that you are familiar with this information; understanding how you fit into the district or community; dressing as a professional; being friendly and polite; asking questions and answering questions; getting to know the interviewers by their name and addressing them by name—these are basic ingredients for a successful interview."

Penick spoke up. "I think the easiest thing is to go to the teacher education placement office, which usually has a list of openings by geographical location, grade level, and field of teaching. The office is very helpful and will assist you in writing letters of application and in making professional inquiries. As for myself, I am actively looking for a position. I am not waiting for chance. I am taking an active role, applying for many jobs at once, and not waiting for results before trying another district. In fact, I expect to have two or three job offers before I make up my mind. Grabbing the first offer is not always the best strategy, especially if you are uneasy about the school or if it is early in the job hunting stage."

"I can't be as cavalier as you, John. I hope to teach social studies and there is an oversupply of teachers in my field. I may have to take the first job offered," remarked Christensen. "Just how fussy or tough you can be depends largely on whether there is a shortage of teachers in your field. Of course, supply and demand curves vary by subject, grade level, and geographical location."

"I really don't think there is a problem finding a job," said Luu. "The teaching force has been graying for the last fifteen or twenty years and the average teacher is over forty-five years of age. Large numbers of teachers are approaching retirement, and the nation's school-age population is booming. In California, for example, reduced class-size legislation requires student–teacher ratios of twenty to one and, accompanied by teacher attrition, has fueled desperate, last-minute hiring. In 2000, more than 29,000 teachers in the state were working with emergency credentials, that is, hired with no student teaching experience. And, as goes California, so goes the nation. Texas, Arizona, Florida—big growth states with skyrocketing school-aged cohorts—may soon adopt California's approach to luring emergency and alternative-certified teachers with minimal training or experience."

"Where did you get this information?" asked Bowman.

"It's in all the papers and news magazines. You don't have to be an education major to know what's happening," responded Luu. "The big-city schools always have shortages, because of turnover problems. In Utah, all a substitute teacher needs is a pulse and a high school diploma. In parts of Virginia, all that's needed is two years of college to substitute. In more than twenty percent of the school systems, science and math teachers are being hired without having majored in science or math. New York City is hiring European math and science teachers, even Australians via a teleconference to teach math and science. Retired teachers and off-duty police and firefighters are being recruited around the country, especially in high crime schools that are hard to staff. The states are increasing the loan forgiveness program for math and science teachers and for anyone willing to teach two years in the inner-city or rural schools. Experts say that the teacher shortage will continue until 2010."

"Do you always talk like that?" asked Furillo. "You talk like you're some professor reading from some notes."

"Just citing the facts, only the facts."

Bakula, who was the oldest member of this group, was a little pessimistic about the need for teachers. "Every few years we seem to go through a teacher shortage, partially to get more money, more programs, more publicity. Even former President Clinton got into the act a few years ago and approved billions of dollars in federal aid to recruit more new teachers."

"Are you saying there is no teacher shortage?" snapped Furillo.

"Well, if there were a real teacher shortage, many of us would not be worried about landing a job," remarked Meisel. "It really depends on how you analyze the statistical data and what you mean by the word 'new teachers.' "

"I think Brad and John may have a point and it seems to correspond with Professor Fields' recent lecture. Federal projections, by the National Center for Education Statistics, report that the annual need for teachers will *decline* as the current enrollment surge advances through high school during the next decade. So, at best, the teacher shortage is for a short interval," stated Luu.

"You know, the word *new* stuck with me," said Furillo. "It made me pause. I also had Professor Fields and he made us aware of government publications, including the annual *Digest of Education Statistics*. Let me summarize one of the tables from my notes. In the 1990s, depending on the precise year, thirty-four to fifty-two percent of new teachers were former teachers reentering the profession. Another twenty to twenty-six percent were doing something else than going to college the year before teaching. Many were older people—retirees from the military or police force, people with experience from other fields, people who had been downsized or were looking to switch careers, and people who had raised their children and wanted to teach. Only twenty-eight to forty percent had just finished a teacher education program."

Furillo continued: "Every year for the last twenty years, more than 100,000 people received teaching credentials, but more than one-third never went into teaching. Between two and three million people are qualified to teach, but have not taught. The claim about a teacher shortage is oversimplified; it really comes down to certain subject areas, such as science and math, and certain specializations such as bilingual education and special education."

Bowman responded: "All your factoids are interesting, but they don't turn me on. Getting a job as a teacher boils down to persistence, personality, and connecting with the right people. I guess if you're a science teacher, it doesn't matter. If you're a bilingual person, it doesn't matter. If you played soccer in college, it doesn't matter, as long as the school needs a soccer coach. English teachers, history teachers, and elementary teachers without a specialization will find it harder to get placed, so they need to make more phone calls and get their resumes sent out earlier. If you are focused and determined, you will land a job."

Questions to Consider

1. What can you do to improve your personal credential file?

2. How might you better prepare for a teaching interview?

3. Can you anticipate five questions that might be asked in an interview for a teaching job?

4. How might the topics or issues of the interview differ in an inner-city school compared to a suburban school?

5. To what extent do you believe a teacher shortage exists?

6. Some of the characters in the case study tended to stress personality, effort, common sense, and so on as more important than grades in finding a teacher's job. What is your opinion?

7. Check the Internet or contact the state department of education and rank order the top ten teaching fields or specializations that seem to have the most job openings in your state. Compare your findings with others in your class.

Recommended Readings

Joseph Blase and Peggy C. Kirby, *Bringing out the Best in Teachers* (Thousand Oaks, CA: Corwin Press, 2000).

Barbara L. Brock and Marilyn L. Grady, *From First-Year to First-Rate*, 2nd ed. (Thousand Oaks, CA: Corwin Press, 2001).

Ann Lieberman and Lynne Miller, *Teachers—Transforming Their World and Their Work* (New York: Teachers College Press, Columbia University, 1999).

Courtney W. Moffatt and Thomas L. Moffatt, *How to Get a Teaching Job* (Needham Heights, MA: Allyn & Bacon, 2000).

Educator Supply and Demand in the United States (Evanston, IL: American Association for Employment in Education, 2000).

15

Adjusting to Your New Job: A Matter of Philosophy and Principle

Imagine that you have just graduated from an accredited college and teacher education program and you are ready for your first teaching job. Regardless of the adequacy of the training, and regardless of whether you had an A average, B average, or less, you are all in the same boat. You and your former classmates are about to make the transition from theory to practice, from the college classroom where you spoke in philosophical and hypothetical terms to the actual school classroom where you will deal with real problems and real people.

Once you are given the keys to your classroom and an attendance roster of your students, you are on your own. Someone says "Good luck," and you either sink or swim. In theory, you are prepared to swim. Your training should make a difference, but all of us know that there are some teachers who are familiar with the latest theories and know all the "dos and don'ts" in teaching but are unsuccessful with students. There are other teachers who break many rules and are not familiar with the latest theories, yet are very successful in the classroom.

As you enter the classroom, reality sets in very quickly. Are all the lights working? Are the shades in place? Do you have adequate blackboard space? Do you have chalk? Erasers? Does your desk have drawers? Can you move the tables and chairs in your classroom? Have your instructional supplies arrived? Do you have textbooks? The first day counts, so does the first week, and so does the first year.

The key to your success has less to do with your knowledge of Dewey or Piaget and more about your understanding of what is expected, your workload, and the kind of students whom you will teach. Your success and development as a teacher will largely hinge on the extent and type of support you receive from colleagues and supervisors. Your training may have prepared you for the big picture, and it may have given you some ideas about pedagogy, but your improvement as a teacher will depend on the help you receive as a beginning teacher. You will need time away from the classroom to reflect on practice, to discuss and resolve problems, and to obtain feedback and assistance from a cluster of colleagues.

As an education student, it is easy to think that you are better equipped than others to be a teacher. And, as a young student, it is reasonable to criticize many former teachers you once had and say, "I can do a better job." Well, when reality sets in, you will not only have to worry about reaching and teaching students, but also how to get along with colleagues and supervisors, follow school policies, deal with administrative constraints and bureaucratic regulations, respond to memos, forms, and reports, deal with your workload as well as extra duties, adopt the curriculum to the needs of your students, and deal with students from different cultures and backgrounds. Beginning teachers often simplify their world and feel teaching is all about students and subject matter, not realizing that there are many teaching and teacher-related items that count and mount in number.

Numerous reports from professional groups, including the Carnegie Foundation, the National Council for Accreditation of Teacher Education (NCATE), and the American Association of Colleges for Teacher Education (AACTE), document the shock of the new teacher that accompanies the realities of the school and classroom. Organized staff development programs, professional development centers, and mentor programs for beginning teachers have increased in recent years, and many big-city school districts have recognized and introduced an induction period, the first two or three years, during which new teachers receive assistance from colleagues, retired teachers, and college professors working together. Nevertheless, all of these new programs for continued learning and professional development are still exceptions, not the rule, and in many cases don't always help as evidenced by the large turnover of teachers, especially in the inner-city schools.

Common causes of failure among new teachers have been identified by a number of researchers, among them Good and Brophy's *Looking in Classrooms* and Ornstein and Lasley's *Strategies for Effective Teaching*. Among the general causes of failure are (1) assignment to difficult classes; "good" courses and "good" students are assigned to teachers on the basis of seniority; beginning teachers are given the "leftovers," "slow" students, or "difficult" classrooms; (2) isolation from colleagues and supervisors; new teachers are often left on their own, unless trouble becomes evident, and their classrooms are often away from the main office; (3) poor physical facilities; classrooms, room fixtures, and equipment are often assigned on the basis of seniority; (4) extra assignments; burdensome extra duties lead to low morale, and new teachers are often assigned the tough assignments or the ones senior teachers prefer not to have, such as yard or hall patrol, or a homeroom; (5) lack of understanding of the school's policies or expectations; school officials often fail to clarify the school's goals, priorities, and expectations, not to mention a host of legal policies that the teacher needs to quickly understand and cope with; (6) inadequate supervision; new teachers often complain there is little supervisory assistance and that classroom observations are usually limited to one or two per year, even during the first year.

In general, having to learn by trial and error without support and supervision has been the most common problem faced by new teachers. Expecting teachers to function without support is based on the false assumptions that (1) teachers are well prepared for their initial classroom and school experiences, (2) teachers can develop professional expertise on their own, and (3) teaching can be mastered in a relatively short period of time. Researchers find that little effort is made to lighten the class load and limit extra class assignments to make the beginning teacher's job easier. In the few schools that do limit these activities, teachers have reported that they have had the opportunity to "learn to teach."

Studies of elementary and secondary schools have shown that teachers expect to learn from one another when the school provides opportunities for teachers (1) to talk routinely to one another about teaching, (2) to be observed regularly in the classroom, and (3) to participate in planning and preparation. Teachers who are given the opportunity to (1) develop and implement curriculum ideas, (2) join study groups about implementing classroom practices, or (3) experiment in new skills and training feel more confident in their individual and collective ability to perform their work.

The case study below deals with two new and idealistic teachers, each with unique problems of getting adjusted. The first case takes place in a pleasant, suburban school district where morale is high and teachers are collegial. Nevertheless, Stuart Baden has trouble adjusting to his new job because his teaching philosophy conflicts with that of his supervisor. In the second case, James Smith, a black teacher, gets his first job in a New York City school and runs smack into reality—colleagues whose competency is questioned and a host of issues related to poor working conditions. In both cases, the problems characterize the experiences of beginning teachers and circumstances that sometimes make the first teaching assignment difficult to adjust to and results in disillusionment and indifference.

ISSUES

Stuart Baden, steeped in the latest educational learning theories of Benjamin Bloom, Howard Gardner, and Daniel Goleman, is a new and motivated teacher hired by the Pleasantville School District, about fifteen miles south of "Motor City." From among eighty-five candidates, he was hired to teach junior high social studies. The selection committee was impressed by his social and personal skills, his zeal for teaching, and his positive attitudes toward students and life in general.

Pleasantville is a high-paying school district with the potential for population growth and an increasing tax base to support schools and teacher salaries. Students are academically oriented and test at the top eightieth percentile nationwide on the Iowa Reading Test and eighty-fifth percentile on the National Assessment of Educational Progress (NAEP). Most of the teachers are in their late forties and early fifties and enjoy working at Pleasantville. Teacher morale is high, and many of the teachers socialize together on weekends. More than fifty percent of the teachers know their colleagues' children by name and have regularly shared family pictures of them.

After four months on the job, Baden has come to the realization that his educational philosophy and learning theories conflict with the views of the majority of the staff as well as those of his immediate supervisor, Mrs. Susan B. Laird, who has been chair of the department for ten years. He has had two formal teaching observations and conferences with his supervisor, and feels that a negative bias was reflected in the outcomes of the evaluation due to their different views about "good" teaching. Laird tends to be a behaviorist and believes in strict discipline, plenty of homework, practice, and review. She asserts: "Preadolescent students need to be shaped by the teacher; otherwise, they will take advantage of you and make excuses about why they are late for class or unprepared. Students need to be held accountable for their daily assignments and homework needs to be checked regularly by grading, oral reviews, or pop quizzes. Your objectives need to be clearly stated and learning should be outcome based."

Baden believes that learning should be fun and children should read for enjoyment and not have to learn phonics. Instead of practice and drill, he views the big picture and main ideas as essential for learning. He does not believe in daily review assignments in class or homework on a daily basis. "If the students enjoy the class, and understand their work, then they will become self-motivated and learn on their own without coercive measures. Although education should have purpose or intent, it should not be broken down into tiny pieces of information or necessarily be measurable."

Because of their divergent views on teaching and learning, Baden has asked to meet with the principal to seek his advice. Ivan Mavroudis is part of the "old network" at Pleasantville and supports his chairs, but he is somewhat flexible and indirect in his approach with people. After twenty minutes of discussion in his office, the principal recommends that Baden work things out with his supervisor and get to know his colleagues better. "Most of us are aware of the latest learning theories, but they are only theories. We have a good group of teachers at Pleasantville. They enjoy their work, like the students, and get along with the parents."

Baden responded: "I wish my colleagues and supervisor were a little more flexible and open to more innovative ideas about teaching. The job is becoming frustrating. I feel the relationship with my supervisor, namely, our philosophical differences, is influencing my evaluations."

"Nonsense," declared Mavroudis. "We hired you because you are motivated and positive in your outlook on teaching. I think you have lots of potential, but you are a new teacher and you need to reflect. If you wish, I'll be glad to observe you, and then answer questions and make recommendations. You think about it."

The next day Baden chatted at lunch time with an experienced teacher, P. J. O'Rourke, whom he felt he could trust. After telling O'Rourke his problems, the veteran teacher commented: "This is an older, entrenched teaching staff with little turnover because the pay is good and students are motivated to learn. The teachers here are used to doing things their way, and you're a rookie with little status. Also, Mrs. Laird is not going to change, and the way you describe her is pretty accurate. You really have different ideas about teaching and learning—she is quite traditional and detailed and you are progressive and remarkably creative. She is a behaviorist, and believes in structured and organized learning activities, and you are more cognitive and abstract in your views about teaching. As for Old Man Mavroudis, he will protect the chair, and at the same time be friendly and vague with you. That's how administrators talk, and that's how bureaucracy works, at least at Pleasantville."

Baden answered, "If I listen to you, there is little hope."

"Well, I guess you have a dilemma," commented O'Rourke. "You are young and idealistic. Either you modify your idealism and fit in, or you remain firm in your convictions and possibly look for another job. I guess it is a matter of character and age. Most people, as they get older, accommodate and make some compromises in order to maintain their jobs, especially if it's a good job. And teaching at Pleasantville is about as good as it's going to get."

Baden decided to visit his two former favorite professors of education, Dr. Helen Bezijian, of the Foundations Department, and Dr. Beni Shuto, of the Curriculum Department. After listening to his story, Dr. Bezijian pointed out that Baden was young and had a long teaching career ahead of him. "Being happy and having a good relationship with your colleagues and supervisor are very important. If you feel that you must adjust your beliefs to fit in, then I say you should look for a new job. If you remain at the school, then you will only become demoralized as time passes. There are other schools and supervisors in neighboring districts that will appreciate your educational theories of learning."

Dr. Shuto had a different view. "It may be a seller's market if you teach math, science, or special or technical education. The problem, however, is that I fear the demand for social studies teachers is minimal, at best moderate. Even if you find another job, there is no guarantee that the grass will be greener, and it may be some time until you find another job. Remember, the pay is excellent, the students are motivated, and the parents are cooperative. I think you need to allow two or three years to go by before you make any decision about leaving the school or looking for another teaching job."

———————■———————

Another rookie teacher, Mr. James Smith, with a bachelor's degree from Fisk and a master's from Rutgers State University, had no trouble finding a job. The color of the teacher matters in inner-city schools, and since it takes a politically acceptable form, Smith was in great demand. He had six job offers to teach music in Yonkers and Philadelphia schools and in nearby suburbs. He chose the New York City school system to be close to his parents, and chose a predominantly black school to serve as a role model, which he felt was important.

During lunch period, after only one month on the job, Smith and four of his black colleagues had become regular customers at Gotham's Grill. The conversation centered on "shop talk," and Smith was informing his friends that he was disillusioned about his job.

"Why?" asked Felix Jackson, another freshman teacher.

"This thing about black models is oversold," remarked Smith. "I can't say this in a public forum, but the white teachers and administrators have just about disappeared from the school system, and the scores of the students are among the lowest in the state. The same reading pattern exists in almost every major city. Just recently, it was reported in the *New York Times* that thirty-five percent of New York City third graders were reading one year or more below grade level, compared to six percent for the rest of the state. By the sixth grade, the discrepancy was more dramatic. In short, the race of the teacher has little to do with the educational performance of black or Hispanic students. What we need are teachers with superior verbal skills who are also knowledgeable of their subject area. Jerome Coleman's 1966 classic study of equal educational opportunity made this abundantly clear, as did William Wilson and Thomas Sowell, two black educators, who made the same point several years later."

Smith continued: "The passing rates of white teachers on state and national teacher exams of basic skills is two-hundred to three-hundred percent higher than those of black teachers. In Arizona, a few years ago, the passing rates were seventy-three and twenty-four percent, respectively, in California seventy-six and twenty-six percent, and in Louisiana it was seventy-six and fifteen percent. Teachers expected to educate kids need themselves to be educated. Well-intentioned policies, such as affirmative action, will not solve our educational crisis."

"Nobody wants an incompetent teacher, but I don't know if there is a relationship between a test score and incompetency. Putting teachers in the classroom and evaluating their ability is a more realistic way of assessing competency," said Valerie Tak, a third-grade teacher.

"What happens if you hire a teacher, and then find out he or she can't spell or speak formal English?" responded Smith. "Do you think it is easy to ask the teacher to leave or find another profession? We need some kind of screening device, with real teeth or benchmarks."

"I thought the idea was to attract teachers, especially minority teachers, not shut them out," asserted Jackson.

"I also resent your generalizations," asserted Tak. "I can hold my own on any pencil-and-paper test which, in my view, has nothing to do with teacher performance. The fact is, many white teachers assigned to inner-city schools experience cultural shock and are unable to cope. Most of these teachers, for the greater part, have an attitude problem. The kids pick up on the attitudes of these white teachers."

"The truth is, sometimes I feel the blind are leading the blind in this school," asserted Smith. "No one wants to deal with the problem. We merely claim the tests are discriminatory and ignore the message about teacher literacy. No one wants to talk about the academic performance of our own colleagues, and when test results are mentioned we come up with all kinds of excuses and explanations such as the test is biased. In the long run, the kids lose."

"Given the teacher shortage, especially in big cities like ours, why do you want to come down hard with a big fist?" asked Jackson. "We need to attract more minority teachers, not exclude them. The teaching profession needs to become more diverse. Diversity promotes health, vitality, and creativity within the system."

"Sometimes I think diversity is used to mask affirmative action policies, or even quotas, because it is a term that is considered politically acceptable," declared Smith. "Most of the white teachers I know feel diversity is used to justify lower standards and overlook second-rate performance. The biggest problem I have is that instead of dealing with students as individuals we see them and lump them into groups—black, Hispanic, white."

"Personally, I think you have an identity crisis," said Diana Washington, who taught reading.

"I would rather not get into a black psychology session with you," commented Smith. "Instead, I'll tell you what else bothers me. I had no idea after my methods courses how complex teaching is and how difficult it is to teach children who lack inner control and basic academic skills. Student teaching was helpful and it provided a dose of reality. But not until the room keys and roster of students are given to you, and you are on your own, do you realize the difference between the practice and theory of teaching."

Tak, who was finishing her sandwich, rhetorically asked Smith if he knew about the recent teacher shortage, and the subsequent large number of inner-city teachers who had obtained positions with alternative-certified and emergency licenses. "These teachers never completed student teaching, and some never even had more than one or two education courses. These teachers are rushed and pushed into the classroom, and they are seriously unprepared."

"Don't they get support from the schools?" asked Smith.

"That varies with the way the wind is blowing," remarked Jackson. "In some schools these teachers are resented because they were licensed without formal training or with minimal training. In other schools, they are welcomed. Some schools provide them with support, even a mentor. In other schools, they have virtually no assistance from colleagues, no contact with the supervisor or principal. They are on their own."

"The license policy you outline only increases my frustration about the job," responded Smith. "These 'instant' teachers, what I call 'snap-pop' teachers, diminish the image of our profession, as well as our salaries, because if there were fewer teachers, the schools would be forced to raise the ante to attract more qualified teachers."

"The point is," said Tak, "we need to create supportive professional experiences for beginning teachers regardless of how they enter the field. Beginning teachers need realistic and ongoing mentoring experiences."

"Most of these raw recruits wind up in big-city schools," asserted Smith, "where the shortages are acute because of teacher turnover. The system infers, in its covert-racist way, that inner-city kids don't need experienced or well-trained teachers. Instead of paying what it takes to get experienced teachers, it pays less money and hires beginning teachers, many with emergency licenses."

"We are faced with a *fait accompli*—an increasing number of big-city school districts welcoming emergency- and alternatively certified teachers with minimal or no education courses," said Tak. "It's not our problem, but an issue among teacher educators. Should they cling to traditional teacher preparation programs, or should they modify programs to meet emergency conditions, actually lowering professional educational standards? As it stands now, the school districts hire who they want—with or without the stamp of approval of teacher education institutions—teachers trained by traditional or nontraditional methods."

Smith asserted that professors would "figure out how to protect their jobs." He felt completion of education course work and supervisory clinical experiences were essential for proper preparation. "Permitting teachers various alternative certification routes not only hinders professionalism and salaries, but also teacher education institutions. This alternative certificate hurts the status of the teaching profession.

Washington interrupted: "It all boils down to control. Should school districts be permitted to hire who they want, even when teachers are not certified by traditional standards? Should a teacher shortage allow teachers to enter the profession through the back door, that is, without full certification? Not until we gain control over licensing standards, not until teachers guard their own gates like physicians, attorneys, and accountants do, will we be a true profession."

"What does this have to do with teaching our students?" added Washington, who signaled the waiter to order dessert. "I mean, let's get real, let's talk about the heart and soul of teaching. Teaching in this school has little to do with what is taught in teacher education programs."

"I think it's the day-to-day problems that add up and take their toll on teachers," commented Jackson. "All of us are isolated when we teach, and when I'm not teaching there is no formal mechanism to work with experienced teachers, no daily communication among my peers. The facilities of the classroom are second rate. The better classrooms and equipment are assigned on the basis of seniority. This is also how they assign students. As a freshman teacher, I have some of the toughest students—and so does James. The school is sixty-five years old and blanketed with graffiti. The school's expectations and goals are not clear; there is minimal communication between me and my supervisor; he has little time to work with and nurture me or anyone else, since he is burdened with mounds of paperwork. The evaluation system is intimidating; the principal arrives unannounced and teachers are judged without provision for commenting. No matter how you toss the dice, teacher professionalism can be improved."

"What really bothers me is the extra class assignments and duties such as hall patrol, yard patrol, cafeteria patrol, and study hall," asserted Smith. "Teacher aides help, but there are not enough of them. The bottom line is that assignments given to beginning teachers should not be so burdensome that they affect our teaching. I'm stuck with cafeteria patrol. It is one of the toughest assignments. No college course prepared me for this assignment. I think the school assigned me to the job because they view me as a big enforcer type who can control the kids."

Said Washington, "The teacher's job includes many nonteaching duties outside the classroom. This fact often comes as a surprise to beginning teachers who are not introduced to the varied responsibilities of teachers, since their methods courses and student teaching experiences focus on classroom activities and pedagogical skills. You're no exception. You ought to be glad you are not in the suburbs, where the expectation is that teachers regularly work on school-related committees and tasks after school without extra pay. Most big-city teachers get paid for staying after 3:00 p.m. It is spelled out in the contract."

"I realize we are responsible for many nonteaching supervisory activities, ranging from study hall patrol and homeroom assignments to working at athletic games and in detention halls," asserted Smith, "but none of these duties were specified in the school manual or rules or during my job interview with the principal."

Washington responded, "Our school is no different than others. Extra assignments and duties are rarely spelled out in the contract, and rarely listed with the position opening. I do think the school authorities could and should have spelled out these extra duties at the interview stage with you, or certainly at the acceptance stage."

"James, you are overly sensitive about too many things," commented Jackson. "You are not going to change the system, and you are not going to improve the quality of teacher selection, teacher preparation, or teacher professionalism. Try to be more relaxed, broaden your professional experiences, maintain a balance between work and social activities, and keep on communicating with your friends just to help clarify your problems. You need to start talking to your colleagues, even though you feel they are not as literate or effective as you would like them to be. It's unhealthy to isolate yourself at work, to have only a few folks like us you can eat lunch with. Relax a little more, smile, and smell the roses."

"What roses? I would be glad to work after school hours for free on some committee if I was paid $15,000 or more per year as they do in the suburbs," snapped Smith.

"The problem seems to be," Jackson went on, "as a freshman teacher you came to the job with high expectations, high hopes, and high motivation. You have been introduced to reality, and some of your initial idealism seems to be waning. That's kind of natural. Just don't allow the bureaucracy to beat you down."

"Right now, I'm more concerned about professionalism than paycheck," said Smith. "I now understand why so many teachers leave the profession or peak early in their career. I am going to do my thing. I will join the union, rely on the power of numbers, and try to improve the profession."

"You know what, we have less than five minutes to get back to our classes. It's time to exit the restaurant before the late bell rings," declared Tak.

"Wasn't that Pinot luscious? I could taste the gobs of black cherries with the lively finish," said Smith as they exited.

"Ah, now you're beginning to relax," responded Jackson. "Tomorrow, let's try the Rochioli vineyard and solve the nation's education problems."

Questions to Consider

1. How can Baden try to work things out with the older, more entrenched teachers?

2. Although Baden claims he was seeking advice, did he make an "end run" around his supervisor? Is it worthwhile for Baden to modify his teaching style if Laird is as inflexible as O'Rourke claims?

3. Advice is given by O'Rourke, Bezijian, and Shuto. Whose views should Baden follow? Why?

4. Smith expressed strong views about verbally literate and academically competent teachers. What are your feelings concerning these twin issues?

5. Washington had strong opinions about alternative-certified and emergency teachers. What is your opinion?

6. Is Smith pessimistic, idealistic, or realistic? Will Tak's notion of mentoring new teachers help? Is Jackson correct in telling Smith he is fighting a losing battle, that it's easier just to go with the flow?

7. Use the library or Internet to find and read three or four articles about the problems of beginning teachers. Make a list and be prepared to discuss the five most frequently mentioned problems.

Recommended Readings

Jerome S. Allender, *Teacher Self* (Boulder, CO: Rowman & Littlefield, 2001).

F. Michael Connelly and D. Jean Clandinin, *Shaping a Professional Identity* (New York: Teachers College Press, Columbia University, 1999).

Gerald Grant and Christine E. Murray, *Teaching in America* (Cambridge, MA: Harvard University Press, 1999).

Allan C. Ornstein and Thomas J. Lasley, *Strategies for Effective Teaching*, 3rd ed. (Boston: McGraw-Hill, 2000).

Seymour B. Sarason, *You Are Thinking of Teaching?* (San Francisco: Jossey-Bass, 1993).

16

The Reality
of
Teaching

If, in your education course, you are assigned to review some of the problems of beginning teachers, you will most likely read about the feelings of isolation, poor understanding of the school's expectations, assignment to difficult classes, burdensome workloads and extra assignments, the inordinate amount of paperwork, lack of supplies, materials, and equipment, poor physical facilities, and lack of help from experienced teachers or supervisors. All of these problems contribute to new teachers' feelings of frustration and failure. If the assignment was at an inner-city school, the likelihood is that some of the beginning teachers also voiced concerns about classroom management and discipline and the inability of students to read, to understand the material, and to maintain their attention or focus in class. The result is that many potentially talented and creative teachers find teaching unrewarding and difficult, especially in the inner city and, depending on what research you read, nearly forty to fifty percent of newly hired teachers leave the profession within five years.

As future teachers, it is understandable to have anxieties about the difficulty of teaching, since most people do have concerns about the unknown when they are about to embark on a new job, especially if it is their first job. Of course, the standard criticism is that education courses do not prepare teachers for the realities of the job. However, you can make the same criticism with other professions and other jobs. Course work, by and large, provides theory and abstract knowledge. You still need to apply what you have learned in college classes to the real world; indeed, the transition from theory to practice is not always easy or meaningful.

Another factor that often surfaces in education courses is that many young students feel optimistic. College students at the pre–student teaching level tend to have confidence in their own abilities and believe they are better equipped than others (older people) to be teachers. What young student cannot, after all, reasonably criticize many former teachers and say "I could have done a better job"?

Despite the optimism of education students, numerous reports over the last several years document the shock new teachers experience that accompanies the realities of school and classrooms. Organized in-service programs and internal support systems for beginning teachers are scarce. Mentor relations between experienced and beginning teachers and support for colleagues for continued professional development are expanding, but are still the exceptions.

Without question, there is recognition for an *induction period*, the first two or three years of teaching that is critical in developing teachers' capabilities, and that beginning teachers should not be left alone to sink or swim. Several state education agencies have recently developed internship programs for new teachers, while other school districts have increased staff development activities. However, most important for the professional development of new teachers are the internal support systems and strategies that the schools adapt, that is, the daily support activities, continual learning opportunities, and regular in-service programs.

One support activity among many is for beginning teachers to share classroom experiences, to tell their stories, and to reflect on ways of addressing problems within an in-service or staff development program and within the structure of their school district. In effect, beginning teachers need to come together to share, organize, and apply what they know about teaching in a sort of self-help program. In the case study below, the teachers are grappling with, reflecting on, and venting about their problems, experiences, and feelings without the presence of a supervisor. The personal stories, and their feedback and interpretation from peers, seem to have a nurturing and supportive effect.

ISSUES

"I thought I knew what teaching was really about and had a good understanding of what it is like to teach. I thought I was well prepared by my teacher education program and could easily make the transition from theory to practice, from the role of education student to teacher. Well, once I was presented with the keys to my classroom and the roster of my students, reality set in very quickly," said Anna Lupe, a first-year teacher at Jefferson Elementary School.

"I know the feeling," asserted another elementary school teacher. "I had a basic idea about what takes place in the classroom, since my student teaching experience was quite extensive, but I had little knowledge of the multiple roles of teachers. I was unaware, also, of the extent of preparation that goes into lesson planning, especially in the early stages of one's career, and the need to pace yourself and manage time during and after school so you don't become drained or burned out."

Rudolph Adamczyk, a freshman middle school teacher, agreed. "Sometimes I feel so tired when I come home that I have to lie down and take a nap. Teaching is much more draining than I ever realized. I think I talk too much in the classroom. I have to learn to allow students to talk more and think for themselves, as opposed to my doing most of the work in class."

These were some of the comments made by a group of beginning teachers at the school district's workshop. The year was half over and all the new teachers were required to meet for two days between the semester break. It was a time for teachers to meet as a group and to reflect and evaluate their teaching experiences.

Pat Dooley, a high school math teacher, was next to speak up. "My biggest problem is the amount of paperwork I have to complete. No education course ever prepared me for it, much less mentioned it; however, I spend four to five hours a week on school forms, records, and reports. It never stops. I'm always running to my next door neighbor, an old pro, for help. The paperwork is mind boggling—dealing with pupil attendance, pupil records, textbooks and supplies, time schedules, guidance and health data, personnel information, transportation forms, roll books, and on and on. In the past four months, since I started, I have filled out more than seventy-five different forms in duplicate or triplicate." She added, "Thank goodness for my neighbor. Everyone needs a buddy teacher or understanding supervisor to survive the paperwork avalanche."

"What about all the administrative memos and directories that you have to read and follow?" said Gordon Van Geerling, a middle school teacher. "Almost every day, there is a memo in my mailbox about some school activity, event, or assignment. The best memos are those that instruct teachers about a shortened day and that each period will be reduced by six minutes, except periods five and six, which are lunch periods, and that period three will meet at the time of period eight, and to omit the eighth period entirely."

"I know what you're saying," commented Sally Zapata, a second-year reading teacher. "There are some memos I have to read two or three times to fully understand what is required. You should have seen the last one on grievance procedures. It was a five-page memo, consisting of headings, subheadings, and sub-subheadings."

"No, I think the best memos are those which refer you to last week's memo for further information or to paragraph 14d of the teacher's handbook. When I get those types of memos, I often run to my chair for help," said Van Geerling.

"Well, I have a real teaching problem," commented Singha Fijay. "As a new teacher, I feel that I was assigned to difficult classes and one of the worst classrooms—next to the bathroom. Periodically, you can hear the flushes. I believe the good students are assigned to teachers on the basis of seniority and they also have better classrooms and equipment. Providing leftovers to new teachers damages morale."

"I'm glad you mentioned this point," said Frank Costelli from Dewey Elementary School. "I feel isolated from colleagues. Teaching can be a lonely occupation, whereby you sink or swim on your own. I wish there were more contact with experienced teachers and more opportunity to socialize with the faculty, other than just during professional preparation periods and lunch." He added, "I'd also like a formal mentoring or coaching system, whereby experienced teachers, preferably those who teach the same subjects or grade level as I do, could provide professional companionship and discuss issues and problems; observation and feedback, especially related to my lesson planning and teaching; and general assistance, for helping me adapt to school situations."

Van Geerling spoke up. "You know, New York City instituted a mentoring program involving retired teachers who work two days a week with new, inexperienced teachers."

"Part of the problem is that supervisors are overworked and don't seem to have time, or make time, to visit our classes. My supervisor has observed me once, and she told me that two visits a year is what to expect unless I have trouble with the students or complaints from the parents," said Zapata.

"Well, I think most people in most professions complain when they get together," asserted Costelli. "I believe this is just a gripe session, which parallels other occupations when people talk shop."

"My biggest complaint is the quality of food in the teachers' cafeteria," asserted Adamczyk. "It reminds me of army food—full of grease, fat, and starch, and geared for the "mature" person who is soft and pudgy. The food and atmosphere doesn't have to be like a picnic at the *Jardins des Tuileries* in Paris or Kensington Gardens in London, but the food and lounge should have a little more taste and style, possibly even evoke a little passion."

Zapata spoke up. "This time I agree with Rudy. You don't need to be a big food buff to realize that good food stimulates socialization and increases morale. The cafeteria should be a place to come, not to eat and run, where teachers can talk shop, reflect, and discuss problems."

"As new teachers, we all make mistakes and we all need assistance. I wish we had a mechanism for analyzing what we are doing in the classroom, so that we can learn from our mistakes," said another teacher. "I think all of us develop some bad habits that we are not fully aware of and need ongoing observation and feedback from experienced teachers and supervisors to modify those bad habits. We all need to be more reflective and honest about our own teaching. It would be nice if we could look in the mirror, and see how others see us, and improve our skills."

As the session continued, there was agreement among the new teachers that they needed to improve their professional skills, and enhance socialization and interaction among colleagues. A list follows of recommendations the group agreed the schools could implement for achieving these goals:

1. Schedule beginning teacher orientation in addition to regular teacher orientation. Beginning teachers need to attend both sessions.
2. Appoint someone to help beginning teachers set up their rooms.
3. Provide beginning teachers with a proper mix of courses, students, and facilities (not all leftovers). If possible, lighten their load the first year.
4. Assign extra class duties of moderate difficulty and requiring moderate amounts of time, duties that will not become too demanding for the beginning teacher.
5. Pair beginning teachers with master teachers they can meet with regularly to identify general problems before they become serious.
6. Provide for coaching groups, tutor groups, or collaborative problem-solving groups for all beginning teachers to attend. Encourage beginning teachers to teach and observe each other.
7. Provide for joint planning, team teaching, committee assignments, and other cooperative arrangements between new and experienced teachers.
8. Issue newsletters that report on accomplishments of all teachers, especially beginning teachers.
9. Schedule professional events, involving beginning and experienced teachers, such as tutor–tutee luncheons, parties, and awards.
10. Provide regular (say, twice monthly) meetings between the beginning teachers and their supervisor to identify problems as soon as possible and to make recommendations for improvement.
11. Plan special and continuous in-service activities with topics directly related to the needs and interests of beginning teachers. Eventually, integrate beginning staff development activities with regular staff development activities.
12. Carry on regular evaluation of beginning teachers; evaluate strengths and weaknesses, present new information, demonstrate new skills, and provide opportunities for practice and feedback.

"I like the list we generated," said Lupe, "but these kinds of lists often don't lead anywhere, because a lot of people don't really want to change, especially if they feel comfortable doing what they already do, and schools, in general, are conservative and slow-moving institutions. People often say they welcome change, because it is politically correct, but they would like to say go change the other person and leave me alone."

"What you say is partially true," answered Adamczyk. "I think, however, young teachers are more motivated and willing to change than older teachers."

Lupe commented: "Isn't that a generalization? Isn't that an age discrimination remark?"

"The point I'm making is not discriminatory. It is hard to change old habits and customs. Now, let me give you another dose of reality," said Adamczyk.

"Another negative statement?"

Adamczyk referred to an old book he bought for $1 at the book fair, called *The Schools* by Martin Mayer and written nearly fifty years ago. As a former school board member and school critic, Mayer argued that students are lucky to have two great teachers in their K–12 school experience. Another teacher from the group then commented on the definition of greatness and referred to Vito Perrone's notion of teachers who have heart and about the need for teachers to know their students and to be their advocates.

Zapata was a little more precise in her view of teacher competency. "I think teacher competency covers the entire spectrum of the bell-shaped curve, and this notion of competency applies to other professions as well." She continued: "Most teachers are average; that is, they fall somewhere in the middle of the curve. Some are less than average, some better than average. A small percentage are simply incompetent, and another small percentage are great."

"Statistically, you are right," said Dooley, "especially since we are dealing with large numbers. But few professionals like to consider themselves average in performance, even worse, less than average. Your idea, Sally, is hard for us to accept and it may even lead to denial for some of us in the room. In fact, the younger we are, the more gung-ho we are, and the less likely we are to accept this analysis."

"Perhaps this is one reason why the educational textbooks I read as an undergraduate student were almost always positive about teachers and teaching," remarked Fijay.

Adamczyk spoke up. "I do believe that Ted Sizer's book about *Horace's Compromise* is more enlightening regarding the reality of teaching; it really affected me as a student."

"Why?" asked Lupe.

"Horace teaches five English classes and 120 students, in an upper-middle-class suburb, and he knows he is lucky compared to many big-city teachers who have union "negotiated" loads of 175 students. However, he has compromised his professional principles and the way he would like to teach because of time and circumstances. He figures he is committed to thirty-two hours of teaching, administrative assignments, class preparation, and extracurricular activities. Averaging five minutes per week for correcting each student's homework, essay papers, and reports, he adds another ten hours. Supervisory duties, professional meetings, student meetings, periodical parental meetings, and student letters of recommendation result in another ten hours: fifty-two hours, total, not including lunchtime, coffee breaks, and travel time."

Adamczyk pointed out that Horace would love to read more in his field and take more professional courses; he would love to visit and observe his colleagues' classes and spend more time planning and revising curriculum. He would like to meet all his students' parents, and most important counsel all his students, since even the smart and socially adjusted ones need some direction and help with questions about school. He would like to assign more homework and grade it in more detail rather than taking shortcuts with a check or minus. He would prefer assigning weekly themes or essays and making more detailed comments, since the students need regular feedback on how to write. He would like to spend thirty minutes preparing for each lesson, rather than ten. He would like to spend more time writing each year the fifty or so student recommendations for college; in fact, he would like to interview each one before writing the letters.

"Horace would like to do a lot of things he doesn't do," stated Adamczyk, "but there are only twenty-four hours in a day. No one seems to get upset about his compromises. His students go on to college, a few come back to say hello. Horace is a mild-mannered person; his colleagues like him, his principal likes him, and he doesn't make waves."

"If I was a principal of a school, I would consider this book to be subversive," said Zapata.

"Let me say that the teaching profession is characterized by many dedicated teachers who make similar compromises," stated Lupe. "We are frequently criticized in the press and professional literature. American students score low on international tests. Johnny cannot read. Mary cannot write. Grades are inflated. Teachers score low on GRE tests and basic skill tests. We must respect the diverse needs and learning styles of our students. We must better relate to parents. We must be more scholarly, more strict, more progressive, more socially sensitive. We must improve our professional preparation. We must be held accountable. The reformers and critics—they really don't know the facts. They have ideologies and agendas. Many of them never taught, and the ones that did haven't been in a classroom for decades. Most of us go with the flow. What else can we do? What can we say—and to whom? If I got excited over everything that is wrong with the system, I would have a heart attack."

Costelli spoke up. "No doubt there is truth in what you say, but I would prefer talking about our successes; the students we influence, the cumulative impact we have on society. I love teaching kids. I would not change my profession for a minute. I have hard-working students and wonderful colleagues, most of whom are dedicated. I think teachers are heroes and we should be portrayed as such."

"Both of you raise interesting points," responded Van Geerling. "I recall Seymour Sarason's book, *Teaching as a Performing Art*, which I read in one of my education courses. He describes teachers as *performers* who are artists and actors. What he means is that as performing artists or performing actors, we seek to both *instruct* and *move* our audience. In our performance, we try to alter the students' relationship between sense of self and the significance of subject matter, and thus increase their learning. But it takes more than knowledge of the subject to accomplish this task, what Sarason calls *book knowledge*. We need to understand how children think, feel, and learn, and we need to be caring and compassionate. The colleges can teach us book knowledge and about child development, but caring and compassion reflect our life experiences and personalities, not what can be learned in teacher preparatory programs."

"Let me guess. Are you inferring that we need psychological testing or psychological screening of teachers?" asked Dooley.

"I might not go for that, because there is some questionable reliability and validity to these tests. But not everyone has the temperament to teach and not everyone who wants to teach should be encouraged to teach."

"Are you saying, then, that unless we are caring and compassionate we are not qualified or fit to teach?" again asked Dooley.

Van Geerling responded, "I would not lock the profession into two or three personality types and conclude that all other types are second rate or unqualified to teach, but unless one enjoys teaching and working with children, there is little reason to enter the profession. If there is no passion or zeal to teach, then the problems we are talking about mount and detrimentally affect our performance."

"Listen, you don't have to be a rocket scientist or full professor to come to the conclusion that we need screening procedures to filter out future teachers who have inappropriate attitudes or characteristics," responded Fijay.

That remark ignited Zapata. "You're barking up a slippery slope, characterized by subjectivity, ethnic politics, and dubious validity. Do you really think a particular test or screening device can accurately tell us who should teach and who should not? A cognitive test is one thing, where answers are either right or wrong and easy to score. But the procedure you talk about, which leads someone to say you are fit or unfit to teach, is bound to cause conflict and litigation."

"Well, everyone talks about John Dewey, including Sarason," declared Lupe.

"So what else is new?" remarked Dooley. "Actually more people speak about Madonna and Tiger Woods."

"Are they doing it?" asked Costelli.

"No, no, no. I'm just making a point about the priorities of society, our values, the influence of the media—where education fits on the totem pole," said Dooley.

"Just for the record. Not everyone swears by Dewey," asserted Fijay. "The old essentialists during the *Sputnik* era blamed him for 'soft education' and the reasons why Johnny could not read, but Ivan could. I read Diane Ravitch's recent book about school reform. She villainized both Dewey and progressive education, blaming them for the decline in academic standards."

Lupe responded. "Look, Dewey is the *numero uno* educator of the twentieth century. His theory was that education had to be related to the child's experiences. He affirmed there was an 'organic connection between education and personal experience' and that 'all genuine education comes about through experience.' "

"Relating subject matter to the learners' experiences or personal life doesn't always work. The connection has to be made between the teacher and students before real learning can take place in the classroom," Dooley asserted.

"What kind of connection are we talking about?" asked Costelli.

"I'm referring to a rapport and trust between teachers and students, a strong bond, actually a passion for teaching and reaching students, understanding the students' world, what makes them tick and click and light up. To some extent it corresponds with Rudy's view, only he was a little negative in the way he described some of us; and how we teach."

"Where does this idea of connection come from?" questioned Van Geerling.

"The idea is based on my own life experiences as a teacher mixed with some formal knowledge about teaching. We all need to read books about teaching that make us reflect and face ourselves."

"Frankly, Gordon, I don't think it matters what you read. The commitment and joy of teaching, the intellectual, imaginative, and creative elements of teaching, the love of children and subject matter—these feelings and emotions cannot be learned by reading about them. It's an attitude; it comes from the heart, not the mind. Teaching is a matter of caring about and connecting with students; it has to do with the whole person—who he or she is—and little with our training methods."

"What you say, still, reminds me of a classic book an old professor of mine once recommended," said Van Geerling. "It was by Arthur Jersild, *When Teachers Face Themselves*. Jersild's basic premise was that self-understanding was essential and quite different from the methods, lesson plans, and skills emphasized in education courses. All of these methods and techniques we learn have their place and are useful at certain points, but what is really needed for teachers is a 'personal kind of searching' that enables each one of us to identify our own concerns and our students' concerns. I really believe each of us, as teachers, is involved in a timeless search to find the meaning: Why teach? What does it matter? What difference will it make? As Jersild says, 'The search for meaning is not a search for an abstract body of knowledge,' not for a new teaching technique. It is a personal search, a journey we should all take to know ourselves better, to clarify our roles as teachers."

Anna Lupe tried to sum it up. "Having discussed all our problems as new teachers and having listened to the discussion about the psychology and meaning of teaching, I'm not sure if the problems we talk about suggest that the selection and preparation of teachers is inadequate or misguided or instead suggest that we are reflecting about some touchy-feely, idealistic view of what teaching should be about."

"I'm not naive," Lupe continued. "I realize many people have vested interests in education courses, but I also wonder if we are not trying to envision a concept of a master or self-actualized teacher that is based on fantasy, novelty, or theory."

"You have a point," remarked Adamczyk. "We need to focus our attention on realistic changes, what the school district can do now, regarding some of our concerns. If not, many of us will simply burn out. Too many older teachers I know merely look forward to early retirement. I hope this doesn't become my future."

Questions to Consider

1. What are some ways for coping with problems or concerns related to the job of teaching?

2. How realistic do you consider the problems or concerns raised by the new teachers in the in-service session? Of all the problems or concerns raised by the new teachers, which three concern you most? Why?

3. Of the twelve recommendations designed by the group of new teachers, which five do you feel are most important? Why? Which five are least important? Why?

4. How do your views of teacher competency square with Mayer's view of great teachers, Perrone's teacher with heart, Zapata's view of the bell curve, and Dooley's view of being average?

5. In what ways does Sizer characterize most of your past teachers? In what ways do you expect to be different and not compromise your teaching? How does Sarason characterize teaching? In what ways do you agree or disagree with his metaphor?

6. In general, do you feel the teachers in this school district are realistic, pessimistic, or idealistic? Why?

7. Interview several teachers in a nearby school. What policies do the teachers say need to be implemented to improve teacher morale and teacher performance? Discuss these policies with the class.

Recommended Readings

Philip W. Jackson, *Life in Classrooms*, 2nd ed. (New York: Teachers College Press, Columbia University, 1990).

Susan Moore Johnson, *Teachers at Work* (New York: Basic Books, 1990).

Vito Perrone, *Teacher with a Heart* (New York: Teachers College Press, Columbia University, 1998).

Seymour B. Sarason, *Teaching as a Performing Art* (New York: Teachers College Press, Columbia University, 1999).

Theodore R. Sizer, *Horace's Compromise* (Boston: Houghton Mifflin, 1984).

17

Teaching Conditions and Contracts

A number of education commentators have attempted to view the education profession in terms of ideal or distinguishing characteristics, and to either rate or describe teachers based on these characteristics, to accord it recognition as a semiprofession or profession. The work of James Conant, *The Education of American Teachers* (1963), Ronald Corwin, *Sociology of Education* (1965), and Myron Lieberman, *The Future of Public Education* (1960), characterize this early period. Teaching was not considered a profession in the fullest sense; it did not possess many of the characteristics professions are supposed to possess. At best, it was viewed as a semiprofession.

Forty years later, as we enter the twenty-first century, new books have been published about teacher stories, teacher voices, teacher reflections, and teachers at work. They give an inside glimpse of the professional lives and identity of teachers. But not much has changed within the profession, as reported by prolific and well-known educators such as F. Michael Connelly and D. Jean Clandinin, *Shaping a Professional Identity* (1999), Christopher Clark, *Talking Shop* (2001), John Goodlad, *Educational Renewal* (1998), and Ann Lieberman and Lynne Miller, *Teachers—Transforming Their Worth and Their Work* (1999).

The theme of professionalism and teachers' professional world and work, their identity and self-worth, comes down to power (also called *empowerment*), prestige, and money on a practical and material level and working conditions (sometimes called *climate*), professional autonomy, and collegiality on a human and situational level. If we escape from the educational jargon, professionalism simply deals with money and working conditions, as was the story some forty years ago.

Although the student is technically the client, and teachers should be sensitive to the needs of their students, the real client is society. Since society is always changing and can be viewed in local and national terms, the profession lacks clear norms of what is expected and teachers are bound by the historical, social, and local conditions of society.

Most professionals in other fields render a service to their clients without the clients' exercising control or judgment over them. Professionals recognize the need to service their clients, but not at the expense of their own self-interest; there is a point in the professional–client relationship where the professional's self-interest suffers, when service to the client is governed by the whims of the client or public. Professional status requires that the professional person maintain independence of judgment and not permit the clients' interests or the politics of a lobby group or community group to influence her decisions. The professional is supposed to have the knowledge and expertise to make judgments, and the client is not qualified to evaluate the services the client needs. The professional who permits his clients (or the clients' parents) to tell him what decisions to make does not provide optimum service to them and does not maintain high status or independent judgment.

Teachers assume, or are led to believe, that the public at large and the local citizenry have the right to share in decision making in terms of what books to use and what content to teach. This assumption prevails because of the notion that the public is the prime beneficiary and it provides the children to teach and the money to pay their salaries. The professional situation worsens when teachers are challenged by parents or the community—told how to teach, how to evaluate their children, or how many minutes or innings their children should play on some school basketball or baseball team.

The physician, lawyer, accountant, and engineer also provide a service to their clients and are paid for it, yet no one in his right mind expects the client or public to prescribe the drug, write the clauses for a contract, or determine how much taxes are owed or how the roof should slant. This protects the client (and the client's parents) from being victimized by their own lack of knowledge, as well as from the power struggles of organized pressure groups, while it safeguards professionals from the unreasonable judgments and demands of the public.

In contrast to other professions, a great proportion of teachers' service is legislated and enforced by lay groups who constitute membership in local and state regulatory agencies. Decisions within these agencies are made without or with minor teacher representation and are usually politically laden, not professionally motivated to serve teachers.

The expectation that teachers are supposed to act as models to emulate *in loco parentis* and *loco communitas* also increases the power of lay groups over teachers, especially parent and community groups. These doctrines, during the first half of the twentieth century, have resulted in teachers being expected to respect the mores, customs, and social sentiments of local communities, to discharge their role by staying out of bars, cocktail lounges, etc., and dressing and acting a certain way, in conformity with local custom. The teachers' special efficacy in honesty, hard work, and sexual chasteness was promoted in the ideal and popular image of the American teacher: overworked and underpaid, dedicated and dowdy, a spinster and schoolmarm, illustrated by Miss Dove, Miss Brodie, and *Our Miss Brooks*—all of whom were eager, a little neurotic, wore bland and colorless clothing, and had their hair in little old-maid's knots.

Television programs and the movie industry presented more positive images of male teachers, à la *Mr. Chips*, which may reflect something about Hollywood and that the complaints later raised by woman activists were on target. James Francisco played *Mr. Novak* and Sidney Poitier played in *To Sir with Love* in the mid-1960s; and then there was Lloyd Haynes in *Room 222* and Bill Cosby as quick-witted teachers who exemplified positive black role models, reflecting the civil rights movement of the 1960s and 1970s.

Perhaps the best way to appreciate the changing image of teachers in American society is to note three profiles of the "average" teacher. The first one goes back to the pre-1950s, when the teacher was thought of as a meek public servant, controlled by autocratic administrators and school board officials, who was dedicated, poorly paid, and usually a female. The second image, from about the late 1950s to the 1980s, was of a self-determined individual, militant (teacher strikes in the 1970s and early 1980s reached a high point of more than 100 per year, passing the 200 mark in 1975 and 1980), and bent on improving salaries and working conditions. The third and most recent image is (1) that there are wide standards, expectations, and degrees of expertise and competency among teachers; (2) that teacher education programs, licensing procedures, and certification regulations need to be aligned and strengthened on a national level; (3) that some form of assessment and accountability needs to be implemented that will result in high-quality teachers, and (4) that teachers and administrators need to work together to service the needs of their clients and to improve school–community relations.

ISSUES

Parkside School District is located in the heart of the farm belt, comprising five elementary schools, two junior high schools, and one high school. It covers a thirty-five-mile radius, employs 250 teachers and twenty administrators (including eight principals), and enrolls some 3,500 students. Since 1990 the average age of the community has increased by about half a year per year, and student enrollments have decreased about 1.5 percent per year. The people in the county take great pride in the fact that the high school football team has won the regional title three out of the last seven years. Only once a year, when the ACT and SAT scores are published, does the local paper, the *Guardian,* take strong note of the academics: high school scores are in the top 25 percent nationwide. Elementary students are tested on the California Achievement Test in the third and sixth grades. Their scores are even more impressive: Students' average scores are in the top sixteenth percentile on a nationwide basis.

The newly elected school board is two years old; it is comprised of three local businessmen and bankers, one fourth-generation farmer, one retired attorney, and two housewives. Only three of the seven board members have children in school. The board members were elected on a platform for trimming the school budget and introducing cost-effective education.

The teachers are frustrated over working conditions and salaries. Their complaints can be summed up in three ways. During the last five years they have been required to participate in ten additional committee meeting days after school without pay. Their annual sick leave with pay has been reduced from ten to five days. Their professional free time during school hours, a time usually devoted to lesson planning and grading papers and homework, has been reduced from twelve hours to five hours a week. Although the consumer price index has increased an average of 4.5 percent during this five-year period, the annual salary increases have been 2 percent, amounting to a net loss of 12.5 percent in real income.

Most of the experienced teachers, especially those without working spouses, are becoming increasingly militant. However, the younger teachers, who have been in the district for only a few years, are less militant; the ones without tenure are reluctant to express dissatisfaction and are in no mood to support a strike.

Ramaz Rejiman, a history teacher for some eighteen years at Parkside High School, is one of the representatives of the militant faction. At a district meeting organized to discuss the teachers' platform for negotiations with the board, he pointed out the following: "Since 1981, when the air traffic controllers went out on strike and subsequently lost their jobs, there has been a growing antiunion, antistrike sentiment in this country. There was a time when the public appreciated labor and respected the right to strike. The unions have been crippled by big government, big business, and the press—and the ripple effect on teacher organizations is clear. The number of teacher strikes in the last ten years is half that of the previous ten years. Education is vital to this country, and the citizens must be willing to support it. I say it's time we get a decent salary increase or we strike."

Stephanie Knight, one of the younger teachers without tenure, then stood up and commented, "The law in this state prohibits public employees from striking. The school board has become increasingly conservative and will merely get an injunction and force us back to work while we negotiate. We will only look silly, being forced to return to the classrooms. And, for those who defy the court order, many of us may lose our jobs or be fined a penalty. Why can't we act in a professional manner and bargain in good faith with the school board?"

By now the split among the older and younger teachers was becoming evident. "That seems reasonable, at least in theory," said Bill Bass, a veteran physical education teacher with twenty years of experience. "The board, over the past several years, has kept a lid on teacher salaries and has eaten away at our previously hard-won improvement of working conditions. This new board is no different; in fact, it is probably worse. The problem is that the community has a blue-collar mentality. We earn considerably more money than the average resident. Although everyone talks a good game about the need for good schools, many of these people feel our workday is too short, our vacations are too long, and we don't deserve more money. The board knows this attitude exists, and even encourages this sentiment."

"You're right," remarked Rejiman. "The attitude among many residents is that the teachers' salaries, if properly weighted by a 180-day work year and supported by iron-clad tenure, is a job worth much more than the dollars cited in news articles and at board meetings."

"When you compare teachers' salaries with those of other professionals, and you throw into the discussion how important teaching is for society, we are definitely underpaid and underappreciated," said another teacher.

Yegor Dubinin, a young English teacher, responded, "If the school board will not work with us, and if they want to cut educational spending, then why can't we organize and elect a friendly school board? Most of us live in the county. Why can't some of us or some of our family members run for election?"

Dubinin continued, "Both the NEA and AFT, at the national level, usually brag about how many congresspeople and governors they help elect. They tally the results and keep records as if it were some world series where the object is to determine which organization helped elect more politicians. I'm sure the union would send representatives to help us organize and elect our own pro-teacher board."

"Who cares?" asserted Rejiman. "The politicians we send to Washington often prey on young women and the local politicians we elect often lie, cheat, and steal—or are just plain airheads. Machiavelli was right. Power corrupts. People can be bought and sold and become the tool of somebody else."

"I never read Machiavelli in my education courses," said Knight. "Is he some left-wing or revisionist educator I should know about? You know, some of these neo-Marxists really challenge the system, although I admit that I have trouble understanding their prose."

"What does all this have to do with our situation?" asked Bass.

"I guess it reflects my frustration with the unions, the administration, and the system in general," responded Rejiman. "Most top dogs don't care about the rank and file, but instead care about preserving their own power and position. I question if the union leaders in Washington have time for us or care what happens in the Corn Belt. I also question whether our own superintendent cares about or even knows us by name. He is far removed from the classroom and seems more concerned about community relations and whether someone calls him to complain that too much salt was used to clean the snow and that it's an environmental hazard, or whether insufficient salt was used and it's an insurance risk.

Dubinin responded, "Somehow the system overshadows what we do in the classroom, how we teach, and how we feel and interact with our students and colleagues. Sometimes, I sit home and just think about the loss of professionalism—our loss of pride, dignity, and self-worth as teachers. I'm not sure now if money is the issue or if it just comes down to the old Rodney Dangerfield punchline, 'I can't get no respect.' Maybe I'm just tired of battling the system for a few dollars. All I know is, it used to be much easier to wake up in the morning and come to school. Something inside of me has died as a teacher. It's like that old Carole King tune, 'I really tried to make it,' but after a while the system beat me down, and squashed much of the joy out of teaching—at least it has for me."

"Is Carole King some educator I should know about?" asked Knight.

"That human dimension is important. I know what Rejiman is talking about," declared Bass. "Too many schools fail to build a community that fosters teacher collegiality—just feeling good about coming to school and working with students and other teachers. The *official* rules focus on control and excessive regulations at the expense of the *ideal* view of schools that stresses a social process which occurs naturally and continually through collaborative activities."

Bass continued, "I guess it's a matter of moving from theory to practice—or creating new schools and new systems. But that's not easy when you are overwhelmed by poor working conditions and low salaries, especially if you teach in schools where students lack basic skills and control in the classrooms and school hallways."

"What about Yegor's original point? Do we focus on electing board members who understand our concerns, who will treat us as professionals; that is, give us the respect we think we deserve?" said Knight.

"Earth to Mars. Do you really think this will ever happen?" responded Rejiman. "Do you really feel the public will ever understand how much it really needs its teachers and treat us accordingly? I think their football team comes first."

"That election is two years down the road, and there is no guarantee that we can win or successfully support board members who are pro-teacher or pro-education.

What do we do now?" questioned Bass. "I cannot risk striking. I'm divorced and the only breadwinner in my family. I have two children to support, and my oldest son will be attending college next year."

"I agree," said Annette LeFluer, who has been elected Teacher of the Year on two occasions in the last six years. "I love teaching. I am as dedicated as any other teacher in the district. But we cannot exist on love or dedication. Robert Morgan and Albert Safer, the two bankers on the board, both drive big, new cars. My car is five years old. Aren't teachers entitled to buy new cars every three or four years? Do we always have to be asked by others to make sacrifices for the love of teaching? I'm tired of hearing teaching has its own rewards. The era of the schoolmarm and Mr. Chips ended a long time ago. I wish the public would wake up: It's the new millennium."

"You know, every once in a while you read an article that teacher salaries in some small suburban school district in the Northeast or Midwest are approaching $100,000. That's yellow journalism," Bass insisted, "an exceptional case, based on the wealth of a local economy. All my life I've had to work two or three extra jobs to make ends meet for my family. I've been fighting for increased wages for the last twenty years, and I am proud of the gains we made and in the old days salary increases have outpaced the consumer price index. However, my big concern is the $100,000 headlines, will stimulate community resentment toward what teachers earn."

"You cannot really blame the community," asserted Greta Klaus, a science teacher. "Historically, teachers have not been considered important figures worthy of emulation or high renumeration. To some extent this corresponds with the nation's anti-intellectual attitude that persisted until the Kennedy era, when finally the 'best and brightest' minds were recruited to serve the administration.

"From the beginning," Klaus continued, "the schoolmaster of colonial times ranked low in status, qualifications were minimal, and bonded servants coming to America who were tailors or locksmiths commanded higher salaries than schoolmasters. By the mid-nineteenth century, women were sought after to staff elementary schools because they were considered 'more virtuous than men, their manners more mild and gentle,' and they were willing to accept one-third to one-half the salary of men.

"At the turn of the twentieth century, illiterate ditch diggers and factory workers earned more money than teachers did. Although teachers today have relatively high status compared with other occupations, they do not receive salaries in keeping with their status. Many skilled blue-collar workers, such as plumbers, electricians, and construction workers, even nonskilled workers such as bus drivers and sanitation workers, rank lower in status but receive higher salaries in most cities and states."

"Why this history lesson?" asked LeFluer, a math teacher?

"Because it is the history of a low salary base that must be overcome. It is hard to catch up when salary increases are tied to the consumer price index and the previous low salary base."

"But that does not fully explain our salaries today," remarked Bass.

Sara Patel, a foreign language teacher and counselor, offered another explanation. "Low teacher salaries prevail because the profession has been dominated by women for the last hundred years because no other career options were open to them. Traditionally, women have been paid less than men for similar jobs, and female-dominated jobs, often called semiprofessions, have been low paying in general. Since the 1980s, female career options have expanded dramatically, but the downside is that the profession is losing a lot of young, bright women to other occupations."

"Are you saying, Sara, that today's female teachers are not as smart as the last generation of teachers?" asked LeFluer.

At first Patel did not want to answer the question, so she directed a question back to Greta that had nothing to do with the original question. "You're friendly with Agnes. Do you think that she really lost all that weight over the Christmas holiday or did she get a tummy tuck?"

"No question she is a different person," responded LeFluer. "She also seems to have lost all her signs of aging. Her skin appears much smoother and firmer. Maybe it's that special diet. She only eats Harmony for breakfast. It's a vanilla almond oat cereal rich in calcium and antioxidants."

"Talking about calcium, have you checked for bone loss?" asked Patel. "My doctor is just wonderful. She recommends hormone replacement therapy. I've been on it for the last five years, and I feel it's great. It prevents bone loss and reduces my hot flashes."

"I'm sensitive about my wrinkles and bone loss, but I think the original question needs to be addressed: Whether female teachers are equally smart today as they were when we attended college," responded LeFluer.

"Do you really care?" asked Patel. "To be honest, my mood swings affect my relationship with my husband. I wonder if it has any effect on my students."

"I think this conversation is inappropriate and has little to do with our professional lives. We should get back to the original point," asserted LeFluer.

"There is nothing wrong or silly about our discussion. It deals with the natural course of aging, with emotions and anxieties, and with personal identity and attitudes of self-acceptance. All of these feelings affect our behavior in the classroom and at school."

"This entire discussion about wrinkles, weight, and bone loss is out of place," insisted LeFluer.

"Will the public ever see the light? Will teachers ever be treated with the respect and status they seek? Will teachers ever be treated as full professionals?" asked Bass, who now felt it was safe to enter the discussion.

"I think it comes down to money. Money leads to prestige, and both money and prestige have a lot to do with respect and acceptance and how the public views us and subsequently how we view ourselves," responded Dubinin.

"The fact remains that we have to negotiate every two or three years with other pressure groups for a portion of the public pie," responded LeFluer. "So many of us are forced to supplement our income, especially among those who are family bread-winners. After a while, it affects your morale and your energy, and commitment to teaching. It's not a factor when you are in your twenties or whenever you first begin teaching, but it creeps up on you when you are in your thirties."

Bass then expressed his feelings. "The fact that everyone seems to be an expert who thinks they can tell teachers what to do plays on my mind. I read the constant criticism of teachers in papers and magazines—why Johnny can't read, how we must relate to students and to the community; we must be better prepared, more scholarly, more compassionate, more accountable. All of these things build up. They lead to frustration or indifference, at least for me they do. I've learned to hide my feelings, because very little can be gained by venting, and no one really wants to hear or face the facts."

"It's like saying 'how are you' as you pass a colleague," said Dubinin. "No one really wants to know how you really feel, or that October was not a good month, that your daughter needs braces, Thanksgiving was a letdown, your back aches or you need a root canal. You just learn to say 'I'm fine,' even when it's been a hard day in your history or math class."

"You have a valid point," responded Patel, "but social roles and historical employment practices play the major role in determining working conditions."

"I have another point to make," said Dubinin. "Many of you in this room seem disillusioned and demoralized. You fail to consider the impact we have as teachers on children and society in general. Teaching has real meaning to me. We touch and shape so many lives. Through the students we teach we influence the course of history. Every doctor, lawyer, CEO, and U.S. senator or governor has been influenced by their teachers, some teachers more than others, but there is no escaping our influence."

"I have another good story. If you listen to the voices of teachers or read the surveys of teachers who are willing to enter teaching again, you would better understand the passion and enthusiasm of those who teach. These stories and surveys give you a lift and remind you why you entered teaching in the first place," asserted LeFluer.

"I know some of you are going to label me as uncaring and uncommitted," said Rejiman, "but I think the problem is that attitudes and feelings change. Even under the best circumstances things become 'old hat' for most teachers. As the years come and go, classroom and school patterns remain about the same—flat, dull, or neutral. The content of the courses changes slightly from year to year, so there is a little tweaking of lesson plans. Although each year there is a new crop of students, there is repetition in teaching that leads to a certain amount of boredom, burnout, and staleness. After a couple of years, there are few surprises—little novelty, little imagination, little creativity involved in teaching the same thing over and over. There is the normal flow of events, the same stress on rules and routine, the same virtues of punctuality, politeness, and honesty which characterize most classrooms. I really believe there is something in teaching, like a lonely Sunday morning, that creeps up on you and affects your mind and body, your compassion and zeal, as a teacher. I think you have to be highly unusual to maintain the original commitment and dedication that so many of us once had toward teaching."

Klaus then remarked about the number of public school teachers, totaling about 3.1 million, and that possibly too many people have entered the profession. "The larger the profession, and teaching is the largest one in the nation, the lower the entry requirements and the more its members approximate the ability levels of the general population. Historically, low entry requirements adversely affected supply–demand factors and public perception, which in turn has had a depressing influence on teacher salaries. The public needs to be informed that our education requirements now match those of accountants, architects, and engineers. Earnings of the latter group start out the first year about twenty to thirty percent higher than that of teachers and average about fifty to sixty percent higher after ten years."

"What is your solution?" asked LeFluer.

"I realize that private industry can afford to pay its professionals more money than the nonprofit sector," said Klaus. But we need to take the cap off teacher salaries; it should be possible for some of us to earn $125,000 to $150,000 based on merit. Even if only one teacher out of one hundred was earning this figure, it would elevate our status and morale.

"Don't put too much stock on some silly pronouncement by some ribald, aging professor. Stick to what is feasible and rational," declared Klaus.

Dubinin, one of the officers of the teachers' association, then took the floor. "We are merely venting our frustrations and drifting from the task at hand. We called this meeting to establish a unified platform about our working conditions and salaries for next year's contract. We are dealing with a school board that is bent on reducing education spending; that means we will probably be one of their targets, since sixty-five to seventy percent of the school budget goes to salaries and fringe benefits."

Rejiman, another union officer, then suggested: "For starters, let's compare the district salaries with adjacent districts, as well as districts within the state. Let's compare property taxes among the districts. Let's compare residents' income who have four and five years of higher education with our education and income, thus bypassing most of the labor force of the community that we are compared with. Our student achievement scores are tops. Let's compare our school district achievement scores with districts of comparable student scores and then compare teacher salaries. Or maybe, we can compare our salaries with school districts in New Jersey, New York, or Illinois, where some teachers earn $90,000 to $100,000 a year."

"This means we would focus on a few wealthy school districts," insisted Bass. "The school board would reject this comparison. Also, the consumer price index is much lower in our region. Why not compare our school district salaries to others with similar average household incomes and cost of living indices? I also like the idea that we elevate teaching to the income level of the administration. I would modify Greta's idea and recommend that one teacher at every grade level, or maybe five to ten percent within the district, earn as much as the principal's average salary within the district, which is $122,500."

"In this school district, football scores seem to count more than achievement scores—at least with the majority of the community," commented Patel.

"The point is, we need to agree on a plan of action," said Dubinin. "That means, if we are to strike, all of us must strike. If we are to negotiate, then we need to get our ducks in a row, and only designated representatives should speak to the press. Now, what shall be our course of action?"

Questions to Consider

1. How typical, in your view, are the teachers' complaints about working conditions and salaries? How typical is the school district?

2. To what extent is Rejiman correct in feeling that the public is against teacher strikes? To what extent is Knight correct in arguing that teachers are at risk when they strike? Why are they more at risk in small districts?

3. One teacher (Klaus) advanced the possibility of teacher salaries reaching $125,000 to $150,000, while another teacher (Dubinin) was concerned that teacher salaries were being targeted because it represented a large portion of the school budget; still another teacher (Bass) talked about teachers having to work a second or third job to make ends meet. What is your view about teacher salaries?

4. One teacher (Patel) maintained that the intellectual caliber or bar of the teaching profession has suffered in recent years. What is your view on this supposed trend?

5. How realistic is the idea about electing pro-teacher school board members to improve teaching conditions and salaries?

6. In determining salaries of teachers today, how relevant is the fact that in the past (as well as today) women dominated the teaching profession?

7. If you were selected to help write a rationale for increasing teacher salaries, what information would you present to bolster your argument? Would you use Rejiman's data? Why or why not? How about Bass's idea?

Recommended Readings

Joseph Blase and Jo Blase, *Empowering Teachers,* 2nd ed. (Thousand Oaks, CA: Corwin Press, 2001).

Christopher M. Clark, *Talking Shop: Authentic Conversation and Teacher Learning* (New York: Teachers College Press, Columbia University, 2001).

Linda Darling-Hammond, *Solving the Dilemmas of Teacher Supply, Demand, and Standards* (New York: National Commission on Teaching and America's Future, 2000).

Myron Lieberman, *The Future of Public Education* (Chicago: University of Chicago Press, 1960).

Carol J. Reed, *Teaching with Power* (New York: Teachers College Press, Columbia University, 2000).

IV

School Policy and Reform

18

Financing Teacher Salaries

Dan Lortie, in his classic book titled *Schoolteacher* (1975), claimed that teaching is an "unstaged" career, meaning that advancement is limited and responsibilities rarely change from the first year to the last year of teaching. Similarly, teacher salaries are based on well-defined and limited stages of advancement, primarily education and experience. Fifteen years later, Susan Moore Johnson, in her book *Teachers at Work* (1990), made a similar observation: Teachers often become disillusioned by uniform roles, responsibilities, and rewards; teachers refer to "low salaries as one of the most frustrating features of their workplace."

By 2002, not much had changed. Teachers are underpaid, and the public gets what it deserves—not the best and not the brightest candidates who wish to teach. Nationwide, the salaries of teachers averaged $43,000, not much different than the average salaries of many semiskilled and blue-collar occupations that require much less education and have little pressure or responsibility.

Of course, a good deal of variation is seen among states and within states between school districts. The average salary in Alaska, Connecticut, New York, and New Jersey is 90 to 100 percent higher than the average salary in Mississippi, New Mexico, North Dakota, and Utah. Salaries in suburbs adjacent to major cities in New York, Chicago, and Los Angeles run 25 to 30 percent higher, especially in wealthy school districts such as Rye and Manhasset, New York, or Niles and Winnetka, Illinois. In these suburban school districts it is not uncommon for veteran teachers, with twenty years of experience and a master's degree, to earn $100,000 (which is about 30 to 40 percent higher than the salaries of neighboring city teachers). Given the difficulty in teaching and reaching inner-city students, the high turnover rate among teachers in inner-city schools, and the increase of at-risk students in inner-city schools whose futures depend on the kinds of teachers they encounter, an argument can be made that the highest paid teachers should be in the cities, not in the suburbs. Of course, politics and education go hand in hand, and policy is not always made to benefit the poor or underclass. Put in a different perspective, beginning salaries for teachers in New York, Chicago, and Los Angeles are between $3,000 and $10,000 less than the starting salary of a police officer, and $2,000 to $5,000 less than a transit worker in these cities, and the gap increases over time.

The fact is, teachers have never been paid salaries comparable to other professionals with similar education. Even in colonial times, the schoolmasters' salaries compared unfavorably to those of other professions. Willard Elsbree, in his 1939 book titled *The American Teacher*, pointed out that teachers rarely received even half the salary paid to ministers in the New England and the Middle Atlantic colonies. In the middle of the nineteenth century, Elsbree concluded that only male teachers in city schools received enough to subsist on: $14 per week, and females, a little less than $5. Teachers in small towns earned about $4.50 a week—less than blacksmiths, barbers, and painters.

In 1920, the average teacher earned $75 a month and in many small school districts, the teacher had to agree, if she was a female, (1) not to get married, (2) not to keep company with men, (3) to be home in the evening by 8:00 or 9:00 p.m., unless attending a school function, (4) not to loiter in ice-cream parlors, (5) not to smoke cigarettes or drink alcoholic beverages, and (6) not to dress in bright colors, nor dye her hair, nor wear dresses shorter than two inches above the ankles. Of course, we need to understand small-town U.S.A. in the context of the days of the Model-T Ford and Sinclair Lewis's *Main Street* and *Babbitt* and the puritanical value system that prevailed.

Obviously, the above conditions no longer exist, largely because of the growth of teachers' unions, which have played a major role in improving working conditions and salaries. Between 1900 and 1940, the wages of teachers tripled and between 1960 and 1980 they tripled again, from an average of $4,995 to $15,970, reflecting in part the growing militancy of teachers' unions, as well as the corresponding growth of professional training required to enter the profession. For example, according to the NEA, in 1961, 15 percent of teachers did not hold bachelor's degrees, compared to just 1 percent in 1976.

From the mid-1960s to the mid-1980s, Frank Endicott and later with his colleague Victor Lindquist published an annual report on starting salaries (with a bachelor's degree) for five occupations, including teachers. The other occupations were accounting, business, engineering, and sales/marketing. For each year, except in the mid-1970s, the spread between teaching and the other four occupations widened. In the beginning (1965), the gap between teaching and the highest starting occupation (engineering) was $139 a month. By 1982, the spread was $774 a month. Today, the average starting salary for teachers is $35,000 but for accountants it is more than $40,000 and for engineers it is more than $50,000. The gap widens when such variables as graduate education and experience are taken into account.

Twenty-five years ago, when the author wore cutoff jeans and sandals and teachers averaged $15,032, he published *Education and Social Inquiry* (1978) and advocated a $50,000 a year "master" teacher contract (3.3 times the average teacher salary) and $75,000 (5 times the average teacher salary) for one teacher per 100 teachers for each school district. The idea was to lift the cap for teacher salaries so as to recognize superior teaching, enhance teacher prestige, and motivate entrepreneurial and older teachers who had become frustrated by low pay to remain in the profession. These were the same teachers who in their earlier years were idealistic, when they were not married or did not face their own children's college tuition bills.

Extrapolated to today's climate (with the average teacher salary at $43,000), the master teacher could earn 3.3 times more or $142,000 and salaries could run as high as $215,000 for 1 out of 100 teachers—a big shot in the arm for prestige and for attracting high-quality candidates.

On the surface, these figures sound a little preposterous, given the notion that teachers are supposed to enter the profession for altruistic reasons such as love of

teaching or love of children, desire to impart knowledge or shape the youth of tomorrow, to influence or improve society, etc. But low pay and uniform pay that fails to distinguish between effective and ineffective teachers, dedicated and undedicated teachers, leads to disenchantment and indifference as the years pass. It affects not only the
pocketbook, but also the mind. As a point of comparison, today more than 1 out of
100 plumbers, electricians, or bricklayers (with less education) who work for themselves earn more than $215,000 per year. More than 1 out of 100 accountants, busi-
ness majors, engineers, and sales/marketing personnel earn more than $215,000. If
we want the "best" for our own children, and if we prize education, then we should
pay teachers a salary that will attract talent and also enhance the supply of teachers so
we can make decisions about quality. The old cliché rings true: We get what we pay for.

In the past, we have paid teachers as if they were second-class citizens, largely
because the profession was (and still is) dominated by women who have been traditionally underpaid for their work in the job market. Even though teacher salaries have
always been low, Kenneth Galbraith has pointed out that as late as the early 1970s the
salaries have ranked at the top 5 percent paid to working women, in part because
women have not had the same opportunities to advance in other fields. Thus, the
gains in salaries for teachers over the years have in the past been more accepting for
women than for men teachers. Similarly, there has always been more prestige for
women (because of limited professional opportunities) than for men in teaching,
which in turn helps explain why the profession today is more than 70 percent female.

Some fifty years ago, Richard Hofstadter pointed out that the admission of women
to the teaching profession in the nineteenth century was urged by school boards,
because women were considered to have pure morals, be gentler and kinder toward
children, and would be inclined to work for less money than men; in fact, female
teachers were paid about half the amount as male teachers. Michael Apple, in
Teachers and Texts (1986), made a similar point about women in society being
unpaid in the home and underpaid in the working world. Teacher salaries must be
considered in terms of gender politics and relations of domination and exploitation. In
short, salaries for teachers merge with the traditional relationship between husband
(the "real" breadwinner) and wife (who worked to supplement the household
income), the higher paid male school administrator and lower paid female teacher, as
well as current feminist issues related to the workplace.

The female factor in teacher salaries may not operate today, but the historical and
cumulative effects of underpaying females do influence current salaries and what we
think teachers are worth paying. The fact that schools will need about two million
teachers during the next decade means that school districts are scrambling to find
ways to attract new teachers, such as wooing them with higher starting salaries, housing and mortgage assistance, special scholarship programs for high-need fields and
locations, and signing bonuses to work in inner-city schools.

But school districts are also taking shortcuts by encouraging quick alternative certification programs, awarding emergency certificates, and hiring European teachers
who speak English and retired teachers on a part-time basis. This is especially true in
big cities like New York and Los Angeles, which are experiencing major shortages of
teachers. Some school districts have also addressed "merit" increments, but the merit
raises are marginal and the political difficulties of making judgments about teacher
effectiveness plague the profession. Thus, the majority of school districts retain the

"objective criteria" for paying teachers—teaching experience and credits earned—even if they are only marginally relevant to teacher competence.

When the dust settles, it is hoped that the nationwide demand for teachers will lead to significant increases in salaries. Indeed, there is also need to explore the relationship between working conditions, teacher turnover, teacher pay, and the need to raise starting salaries to attract and retain good teachers.

ISSUES

Poor George. The Smallville District he teaches in is in deep financial trouble. Although population growth has been constant in the last ten years, the extra student enrollments have burdened the school budget. Consisting of 2,375 students, 125 teachers, and fifteen administrators, three elementary schools and one high school, it must now find a way to trim the school budget of $2 million, or approximately $1,000 per student.

As a point of comparison, the average teacher salary is $1,100 more than the state average and $1,750 to $1,900 more than the three surrounding school districts. Classroom ratios coincide with the state average, that is, 19:1, and the five schools are between fifty and seventy years old. There are six proposals to reduce spending, all of which were presented for review to Superintendent Nova Demerdjian and the school board.

Proposal 1: This proposal focuses on teacher salaries and related perks. Salaries would be frozen for one year. The amount of money teachers would pay for insurance coverage would increase from 25 to 50 percent (saving $350,000). One-term, or half-year, paid sabbaticals and reimbursement for professional travel, graduate school tuition, and professional books and subscriptions would be frozen for two years (savings $500,000). A new girls' gym to replace the old one would be put on hold for an indefinite period (saving $700,000 but here there is risk of losing Title IX grant money. In addition, five teachers and one administrator slated to retire would not be replaced (saving $475,000/year); the outcome is that classroom ratios would increase from 19:1 to 20:1.

A master teacher category pattern would be also established for each of the five schools to recognize highly talented and effective teachers. One teacher per twenty-five teachers would be eligible in each school for this special recognition identified through (1) parent ratings at the elementary level and student ratings at the high school level, (2) peer evaluations, and (3) the principal's evaluation. The three rating groups would be weighted equally, with the evaluation instruments and standards to be developed by the teachers themselves for the purposes of content validity and professional empowerment.

Each teacher identified as a master teacher would receive a 25 percent increase in salary and would be expected, in addition to his or her regular duties, to spend one professional period per day mentoring inexperienced teachers and teachers who received low ratings. Besides increasing the ceiling for teacher salaries, the master teacher salary would help reduce the uniform reward structure and cap on teacher salaries. No longer would all teachers hold the same rank, and those with expertise would become part of the school reform or improvement process. Competition in education is healthy and inevitable, and this type of competition would reward outstanding teachers. The concern is, however, that we lack a reliable and valid means by which to evaluate teacher effectiveness accurately and fairly so that the master teacher designation will be based more on politics.

Proposal 2: This proposal focuses on academic conditions. In addition to not replacing the positions mentioned above, it would eliminate another six teaching positions. The outcome is that classroom ratios would now increase to 21:1. The school calendar would be increased from 175 days (3 days below the state recommendation) to 182 days, thus increasing state aid for the district. Teachers would have a longer school year, seven extra school days. But with the extra savings and monies earmarked by the state, teacher salaries could be increased 5 percent.

The intent of this proposal is aimed at increasing the school calendar, assuming that with extra instructional time students should learn more and the cumulative effects would show dividends in the current measurement-driven climate of educational achievement. The proposal infers that people are drawn to teaching by the love of learning or desire to work with children and there is no need to encourage an entrepreneurial spirit that rewards exceptional talent.

This proposal is somewhat directed against Proposal 1. There is little desire to promote parent or student ratings of teachers because those client groups are deemed unqualified to measure teacher effectiveness. Even worse, it is maintained that peer review for salary purposes would lead to various forms of favoritism and politics and ultimately be divisive. It's one thing for teachers to work collaboratively, but they should not be expected to rate each other for purposes of employment or rewards. Besides, the legalities of the evaluation procedures could become an issue if one of the low-performing teachers challenged the outcomes.

Proposal 3: This proposal's goal is to streamline the curriculum. It proposes to freeze new textbook orders for two years throughout the entire district. All math enrichment and music enrichment programs for the talented and gifted, as well as staff development programs, would also be eliminated for three years. The elementary school after-school program, from 3:00 to 5:00 p.m., and the high school intramural sports programs would be eliminated for two years. In addition, students, unless they qualify for free lunch, would be expected to pay user fees for science lab equipment (estimated at $125 per year), and students who play on a school team would pay $75 to $200 per year to participate, depending on the activity. A "safety net" would be provided for special circumstances so as not to put financial pressure on a family that might not be able to afford the extra fees. The user fees would be implemented for an indefinite period, in part depending on parental reaction. All teaching slots would be retained; however, up to 2 percent increases could be allocated for next year's teacher salaries.

Proposal 3 is perceived by the school board as nonthreatening to the majority of students, parents, and teachers. It slightly affects talented and gifted students, but that group represents only 3 percent of the student enrollments. The user fees are directed at the families who can afford the extra payment. No teacher will be hurt by layoffs and classes will remain small since all teaching slots are to be saved.

The intent behind this proposal in opposition to Proposal 2, is that teachers work long hours after school preparing lessons, grading tests and papers, filling out records and forms, and keeping up with the field by reading or attending evening classes at nearby universities. In addition, in many suburban and rural school districts, including this one, teachers are expected to stay late to work on professional matters. The reality is a sixty- to sixty-five-hour workweek, an exhausting schedule that schools of education fail to mention to new recruits and the public refuses to recognize. Teachers don't need to work additional hours or days for an increase in wages—the same salaries enjoyed by their contemporaries in low-pressure, low-responsibility semiskilled and blue-collar jobs.

Proposal 4: This proposal is simple: It would close down the second oldest elementary school, the one with the fewest student enrollments (380 students) and eliminate all twelve nontenured slots within this school. The older, tenured teachers would be transferred to schools within the district. With the closing of the neighborhood school, about 70 percent of the 280 students would be required to take a ten to fifteen-minute bus ride to one of two adjacent schools; the schools then would be at their maximum enrollment levels. With the money saved, teacher salaries could be increased 4 percent for the coming year.

The advocates of Proposal 4 object to Proposal 3 and feel that a 2 percent increase across the board is "peanuts" for teachers who are already underpaid and that it will affect morale throughout the faculty. In fact, it is actually considered by the teachers to be a "slap in the face." But Proposal 4 borders on surgery, according to critics. It will not only lead to school overcrowding, but it will disrupt existing friendships and peer relations created by classroom and school experiences among the 380 students in the old school. It is bound to demoralize nontenured teachers for the remaining year; most important, it will send a message for years to come with future young candidates that careers in teaching are not secure at the Smallville School District.

Advocates claim that educators attempt to pretend that public schools are exempt from the laws of supply and demand; at the local level jobs can be reduced to cut costs. Given the nationwide shortage of teachers, however, the proposal seems out of sync with reality. Surely, it will create a lopsided number of veteran teachers and when they retire, mostly within a compressed time period, there will be not enough seasoned teachers to maintain stability within the district. This situation is augmented by the fact that nationwide 30 to 50 percent of new teachers leave the job during the first five years because of dissatisfaction with salaries or conditions. (The differences in percentages reflect different surveys.) At Smallville the percentage is 36 percent. The fact is, growing school enrollments caused by population growth and birth rates are expected to increase the need for additional teachers in three or four years at Smallville.

Proposal 5: Proposal 5 has some similarities with Proposal 1. It links salary increases to annual teacher evaluations, based on five sources of information:

1. Student ratings of teachers related to lesson preparation, instructional methods and materials, classroom management, testing practices, homework, and ability to make lessons interesting;
2. Peer teachers who observed and evaluated teachers;
3. Student achievement data, which would carry the most weight, at least one-third;
4. Self-evaluations based on personal goal setting for the school year, as well as professional growth; and
5. Supervisory evaluations based on two observations per year.

Instead of automatically giving teachers the same raise, based on education or experience, teachers would be classified into one of four categories:

1. Below average, failure to meet district standards, no raise (limited to 20 percent of the faculty);
2. Adequate performance, 2 percent increase (limited to 50 percent);

3. Superior performance, 4 percent increase (limited to 20 percent); and
4. Master teacher performance, 6 percent increase (limited to 10 percent of the faculty).

Regarding this proposal, the concern among teachers is that the students are too immature to judge good teaching and that, as one teacher said, "the ratings would boil down to teacher popularity and personality, not competence." Peer evaluations would lead to favoritism among selected teachers and ill feelings and jealousy among colleagues within the school. Most important, there is fear that ethnic and gender politics will bias the evaluation outcomes. There is also concern that many teachers will be demoralized by no raises or small raises, causing dissention and divisiveness. Of course, almost all of the parents and board members support the idea and link it to the concept of professional growth, accountability, and competition. Although the idea might not be popular among teachers, they would be permitted input on all phases of the evaluation program. In similar fashion, teachers would evaluate principals.

Proposal 6:   Proposal 6 avoids pitting teachers against each other within the school building by evaluating the school outcomes in terms of state standards. Student achievement on standardized tests would be tied to teacher performance as a group, and subsequently to salaries for all teachers within each school. Thus, teachers would be committed to helping each other and working as a team to improve the quality of education within the school. Salaries for teachers would fluctuate as student scores decreased or increased, from a floor of minus 2 percent to a ceiling of plus 8 percent. Instead of students competing for grades, the coin would be reversed: Teachers would be competing with other teachers in other schools within the school district. The minus 2 percent salary would be a method for motivating or improving poor performing schools and putting some of the responsibility on teachers.

Here the concern among teachers was that most changes in test scores do not reflect the efforts of teachers but more potent factors such as parents, home life, peers, television viewing habits, and other nonschool factors, as well as a host of test-related factors such as guessing, coaching, regression effects, and test administration, all of which are magnified when differences in performance are compared over short periods of time or when converting raw scores to grade equivalents (i.e., 6.2 reading level) or composite scores (i.e., 28 ACT score).

Controversy surrounded Proposals 5 and 6. There was some concern that teachers would focus on knowledge, not problem solving, creativity, moral education, aesthetic appreciation, student feelings, attitudes or values, social and personal development, and so on. Teachers would teach toward the test, constantly review and drill tiny facts, and encourage memorization of information—all to show gains on post-test scores. High-performing schools could not easily raise student performance, since they were already near the top, whereas low-performing schools statistically would have more opportunity for students to improve. As student scores increase, there is greater likelihood they will plateau or drop the following year because statistically there is less chance for improvement—a Catch-22 for effective teachers and schools. The evaluation program, it was argued, "put money in the pockets of consultants at the expense of teachers whose income and careers could be threatened."

The majority of parents and school board members liked Proposals 5 and 6, because they went hand in hand with most states which are working on or have already adopted statewide standards and related accountability procedures. Since the compensatory education movement during the last forty years, we've addressed our failing schools the same way: Spend more money, without focusing on results. As one parent said, "Now taxpayers want to know why test scores go down in some schools while expenditures continue to go up, and school board members want to know how students are doing before they ratify teacher contracts or renew the superintendent's contract."

Granted, standardized tests are not the most valid way to measure student achievement or teaching effectiveness, but there is no perfect way to evaluate students or teachers. "At least the school's curriculum would be aligned to state standards," asserted one board member. "Teachers would be expected to pay attention to the standards and teach essential content. If students failed the state "report card," or if scores dropped, the teachers would be held accountable. If the scores improved, then the teachers would be rewarded."

Note, however, that the school board was unwilling to vote for any proposal, and left the final decision in the hands of the teachers, since their salaries would be directly affected and the board did not want to jeopardize morale or give the impression that teachers had no input.

Questions to Consider

1. Which proposal do you prefer? Why?
2. Which proposal do you dislike the most? Why?
3. Which proposal would probably create the most tension between teachers and parent groups? Why?
4. Recall the consumer (or client). Which proposal would be least beneficial for students? Most beneficial?
5. Which proposal would be considered most controversial for the community in which you live? Why?
6. According to the author, the last two proposals are the most controversial for teachers. Do you agree? Why or why not?
7. Search the Internet or contact your state department of education to determine teacher salaries among school districts in your state. What similarities/differences exist in teacher salaries within and among school districts? What are the reasons, in your view, for the differences in salaries? Are higher teacher salaries essential for maintaining high-quality teaching? Why or why not?

Recommended Readings

Kern Alexander and David H. Monk, eds., *Attracting and Compensating America's Teachers* (Cambridge, MA: Ballinger, 1997).

Michael W. Apple, *Teachers and Texts* (New York: Routledge & Kegan Paul, 1986)

Marci Kanstoroom and Chester E. Finn, *Better Teachers, Better Schools* (Washington, DC: Fordham Foundation, 2001).

Dan Lortie, *Schoolteacher* (Chicago: University of Chicago Press, 1975).

Allan Odden and Carolyn Kelley, *Paying Teachers for What They Know and Do* (Thousand Oaks, CA: Corwin Press, 1997).

19

Year-Round Schooling Debate: Two Distinct Sides

People want to change or reform education; yet they are also afraid of change, especially if it comes too quickly or if they feel they have little control or influence over it. People become accustomed to the status quo and prefer to make modifications in new policies, programs, or behavior in small and gradual steps. Most people, when they talk about change or reform and say they welcome it, often would prefer that other people within the organization change.

The world of the teacher does not allow for much receptivity to change, and one of the characters in the case study that follows keenly illustrates this position. Both Michael Fullan and John Goodlad have described the teachers' daily routine as presenting little opportunity for interaction with colleagues. This isolation results partly from the schools' organization and self-contained classrooms and partly from their teaching schedules.

Seymour Sarason has also commented on the isolation of teachers in the school organization and how the isolation negatively impacts change. He contends that the reality of the school has made teachers feel that, professionally, they are on their own. It is their responsibility—and theirs alone—to solve their problems.

These facets of life in classrooms and schools cause teachers to view change or reform as an individual activity. Viewing their struggles as solitary, teachers often develop a loneliness that turns into hostility toward some administrators who preach change or reform. Similarly, teachers develop a resistance toward change agents and reformers from outside the school system who seem insensitive to the teachers' plight.

Part of the problem with change and reform is that it rarely addresses changing the education system; instead, it deals with increasing the budget or doing what we have been doing "only doing it better." The case study below does not seek to overhaul or change the system, but to instead do more of the same, which will also cost more money. Furthermore, there is no indication of just how teachers will be involved in the planning stage; in fact, their role seems identical to that of the past. The teachers are seen as spectators, not key players involved in change.

The particular type of change deals with modification of the school schedule, that is, adding additional days or hours to the school calendar. Several U.S. government reports, including *A Nation at Risk* (1983) and *Time for Results* (both the 1991 and 1994 reports) have recommended extending the school year or school day to provide more time for teaching and learning. Some researchers have also recommended extending the school schedule for at-risk students who need extra instructional time to master the fundamentals. And, given the movement toward high-stakes testing and standards-based education, which holds teachers and administrators accountable, an increasing number of school officials are providing options for, or in some cases are requiring, extended school in afternoons, on Saturdays, and in the summer.

However, extending the school schedule, especially to a year-round school schedule, is controversial not only because it adds instructional costs but because it also disrupts child–parent activities. Action for extending time for learning is gaining momentum as testing students and publicizing the results motivate school personnel—through shame, political pressure, or possible loss of jobs—to improve.

ISSUES

Concern over the test results of third- and sixth-grade students who took the National Assessment of Educational Progress (NAEP) test in reading, math, and science had residents in most school districts, as well as policy makers, wondering whether the public school year should be increased for students in an effort to better prepare them for secondary education and the future workforce. These concerns resulted in a growing public dialogue to introduce year-round schooling in Merryville.

Advocates of the idea pointed out the following:

1. The United States is one of the few industrialized nations where summer breaks last as long as ten to twelve weeks. Prolonged summer vacations are representative of a historical period when the United States was an agricultural nation and children had to help their parents harvest summer crops. Today, the vast majority of parents (both mothers and fathers) work year-round and make special arrangements for summer activities for their children.

2. The average number of school days per year in the United States is 180. The longer school terms of Japan (240 days) and Western Europe (200 to 220 days) lead us to conclude that one reason for the poor performance of U.S. students on international tests is the shorter time in schools. As we move up the grade level, the achievement gap worsens between American students and their international counterparts. One reason is that the cumulative effect of additional schooling in Europe and Asia adds up.

3. Students who have more time to study specific knowledge, skills, or tasks should learn more than students who have less time to do so. Common sense suggests that if instructional quality is kept constant, then extra instructional time should have positive effects on students' output.

4. At-risk students need extra time attending school to counteract the effects of their environment and subsequent lack of academic skills. A year-round school would increase the time in school for these students and opportunities to learn more.

5. A year-round school would be cost effective, since the facility is usually empty during the summer. When schools are left empty in the summer, the taxpayer winds up spending more money per day for education.

6. A year-round school should provide more flexibility in the schedule, thus students could take more varied courses and more academic time could be allocated to reading and math.

7. Not every student would have to attend year-round schools. There could be a choice between the traditional school calendar and year-round school. Modifying school time is part of the restructuring movement, which can take many shapes and forms, including an extended day (to 4:00 or 5:00 p.m.), an extended week (five and a half or six days of school), an extended year (i.e., based around fourteen- or fifteen-week trimesters), or all-year schooling.

8. It would be easy to operate an all-year school under a *charter* contract. The typical charter school is exempt from many burdensome state and local rules in exchange for being held accountable and demonstrating that its students have met specified goals. If they don't, the charter can be revoked and the school closed. Those parents who want all-year schooling could have the option to send their children to a charter school that promoted this concept.

The critics of the idea argued point for point:

1. Most students look forward to their summer holiday, and many families plan summer vacations and camping and recreational activities during this extended period. There is more to learning than just academics; summer is a time to develop social, recreational, and leisure skills for future living.

2. The same results can be achieved by increasing the school day (which averages, among public schools, five hours and thirty minutes) by an additional forty minutes. This would add 120 hours per school year (40 minutes × 180 days), or 22 extra days per year (dividing 120 by 5.5), totaling 264 school days over 12 years, and nearly 1.5 extra years of schooling. This has immense future consequences in terms of international test scores, human capital, and national productivity. Just think what it would mean to have nearly 13.5 years of schooling in 12 years! Increasing the school day by 40 minutes has the same effect as increasing the school year 22 days. The schools are not set up for the extra days, but can surely modify their school day by an extra 40 minutes.

3. Extra instructional time does not guarantee increased student achievement; in fact, additional time with poor instruction can lead to unintended and dysfunctional learning effects. It's more important and cheaper to increase the quality of instruction through staff development than the amount of time spent on instruction by hiring more teachers.

4. Many programs exist for educating at-risk students. Considering year-round schooling as another compensatory program or only for students who are failing results in duplication of efforts and clouds the objectives of extended schooling. The idea is to reach all students, not just those who are at risk or failing. Extra school time for at-risk or failing students is only part of the equation. What they really need is

more academic time; actually, more required instructional time or minutes in the day devoted to reading, language, and writing skills.

5. School plant costs per extra hour is minimal, compared to adding extra days. Personnel costs are the largest part of any school budget, and theoretically would be similar for 120 hours or 22 school days per year. However, maintenance, insurance, and utility costs would increase much more by adding days (as opposed to additional hours, even though the sum total would be the same). The extra expenses could require additional property tax revenues and, in turn, increased public resentment for raising property taxes.

6. A year-round school would make it difficult to perform extended renovations and capital improvements. Teaching and instruction might be periodically interrupted for maintenance and repairs.

7. Educational alternatives and choices are becoming a reality in the United States; in fact, several states already have voucher programs and many more have tax credits that can be applied to private schools. Many alternative schools and choices are available for parents and students; extending school time or the school calendar is only one option. The easiest and least costly choice is to vary the length of instructional periods or require that more academic time per day (not add extra days) be devoted to core academic subjects, say, six per day, and less time for watered-down electives, minor subjects, recreational activities, study hall, etc.

8. Charter schools siphon money away from existing public schools. Under the guise of introducing competition for public schools, they are usually run by the private sector, which is profit driven. The public has always had the choice of year-round schooling; it would have merely approved a bond issue, which in turn could lead to higher property taxes. Sell that to the public, if you can. Actually, high school students already have the option to attend summer school classes—and very few (about 10 percent) do.

Three teachers sitting in the teacher's lounge were talking about the pros and cons of year-round schooling.

The first teacher, Dennis Consalvo, was indifferent to the idea and said, "There are many ways to reform or restructure schools — and year-round schooling is only one method. The key to improving schools and fostering achievement is for educators and parents to create and govern schools they want—to take a real interest in educating children. Successful change depends on a collaborative effort among teachers and the community: a relationship where concerned adults care about schools, share common goals and values, and plan and solve problems together."

Arkadiusz Myszkowski, the teacher's colleague, said, "Your ideas seem to reflect a good deal of wisdom. Why don't you become more involved?"

"To tell you the truth," replied Consalvo, "I have lesson plans to prepare and exams to grade. I really don't have time."

"You need to make time," said Myszkowski.

"You sound like some of the professors I used to have when I was an undergraduate long ago. I now have family responsibilities. I would rather not get involved in politics or heated debates about education. The reason why Johnny cannot read or why so many students are failing in schools has little to do with school time or the school calendar. The *process* is not the issue, the problem is the *input*. Schools have not changed their instructional delivery system since the conception of public education. With the exception of movable desks, modern lighting and plumbing, and pastel-colored boards, what else has changed? What *has* radically changed in the last several decades is student enrollments and family living patterns; the input is different compared to when we went to school."

"Are you saying that all this talk about reforming and restructuring schools is for naught, merely an intellectual exercise?" asked Peter Klujian.

"The school officials will do what is politically expedient, short and simple, despite all the fuss," declared Consalvo.

"What about teacher input?"

"I have been teaching for nearly twenty years. I have seen many new ideas and reform movements come and go. Some critics blame status quo elements on teachers or teacher unions, others put the blame on superintendents, school boards, and state education agencies—as being selfish, conservative, or antireform. I don't think it matters who you blame for our educational ills; it boils down to media rhetoric and political squabbling."

Consalvo continued: "Actually, there are some of us, including myself, who believe the schools do a relatively good job—given the diverse population they serve, the multiple needs and abilities of the students, and the multiple responsibilities and roles the schools have incurred. Not everyone succeeds in school. Granted, some achievement test scores have declined, but consider the increase in poverty, crime, drugs, teenage pregnancy, and single-parent households—and then ask who is to blame. Schools in middle-class communities do a pretty good job for most of their consumers. The successful outcomes of schooling are evidenced by the fact that this nation outproduces all other nations, big and small, and many nations are more homogeneous than ours. To tell you the truth, I'm content to go home and not get involved in some pent-up educational demand or trendy idea."

"You sound pretty cynical."

"No, I just feel so much of education reform is based on flim-flam and willy-nilly ideas. Educators who espouse these reform slogans will never admit to their own ignorance. All they argue is for increased spending."

"You sound like you're an *O'Reilly Factor* fan," declared Myszkowski. "I don't know who is more pompous, Jesse Ventura, the governor from Minnesota, or Bill O'Reilly."

"Listen both of those fellows are trying to hold the education bureaucracy accountable," remarked Consalvo. "For me education can become a bottomless pit, where the kids are used as pawns to get more money out of taxpayers."

"Actually, you sound more like some redneck with a pick up truck and a six pack," insisted Klujian.

"I'd rather not get into hyper-liberal talk. The fact is, after spending $125 billion in compensatory spending during the last twenty-five years, we have virtually nothing to show for it. The 2000 NAEP scores for the nation's fourth-grade readers, released in 2001, show that sixty-three percent of black fourth graders, fifty-eight percent of Hispanics, and sixty percent who receive free lunch scored below the basic competency level, which means they can't read."

"Does that mean we give up and stop trying?"

Consalvo responded again: "Look, more than $80 billion in compensatory spending was spent in the past decade. We tripled compensatory spending, mostly, for reading and literacy programs, and have had no change in output. The NAEP average reading score was 217 points out of 500 for fourth graders in 2000, the same as it was in 1992."

He continued. "So, now, why spend more money on more school days without calling for some accountability? Your reform idea calls for more spending and more of the same, which produces no results."

"What about the idea of extending the school year?" asked Klujian.

"Why?"

"If you want to learn how to swim or play golf, you need to put in extra time to practice," asserted Myszkowski, "If you want to learn how to read, kids need to put in time and some kids need extra time."

"I'm going home to eat and have my six pack," Consalvo responded. "Then I'm going to put my feet up on the coffee table and watch the *O'Reilly Factor*."

"Let's get serious. Increasing the school year to 200 or 210 days is costly, but the educational benefits should be weighed in terms of the money society spends on unemployment, welfare, public housing, and the penal system. I'd rather spend extra bucks on extra education. In the long run, society saves money," responded Klujian.

"We need to define learning in terms of what we want to achieve," said Myszkowski. "Every higher unit or increment of learning should be weighed in terms of cost. In other words, what does it cost to raise reading or math scores in the school district from one point to another point, say, from the present grade level to an ideal level? Right now, we don't have good information on what it costs to make incremental improvement."

"Maybe we have reached a flat level," she continued, "for some students where more money does not result in more gains. If we weigh down a swimmer, there is only so much improvement he or she can make. If we tie one hand behind a tennis player's back, there is only so much improvement he or she can make. Well, the culture of poverty may be the overriding factor preventing educational improvement."

"Common sense dictates that extra instructional time would improve academic outcomes," asserted Klujian. "If instructional quality is kept constant, then extra instructional quantity should have positive effects."

"What about school leadership, clear school goals, staff morale, a skilled teaching force, positive teacher expectations, emphasis on basic skills, extra homework, and no-nonsense discipline?" asked Myszkowski. "All of these reforms cost very little and would not upset the school schedule. Maybe it boils down to the quality of instructional time, not the quantity of time. Maybe teachers need to learn to make effective use of their time and ensure that students attend to academic tasks or content."

"And, maybe it boils down to student input," responded Consalvo.

"And," said Klujian, "maybe it boils down to schools requiring teachers to spend more time in specific curricular areas. Right now, if you visit the typical elementary school, one fourth-grade teacher may spend ninety minutes per day on reading and language arts, and another teacher seventy-five minutes on the same subjects. You can also observe two teachers spending similar instructional time in the same curriculum area and focusing on different resources, activities, and content."

Klujian continued: "The same problem is seen at the junior high or middle school level. I know one research study involving a sixth-grade class where instructional time in reading over a school year ranged from 68 to 137 minutes. That's a difference of 69 minutes per day. There were similar ranges in mathematics among teachers in the same school district: 20 to 73 minutes or a difference of 53 minutes. One teacher, in short, may spend two or three times more academic learning time per day on reading and math than another teacher."

"I agree," interrupted Myszkowski. "Before we go madly off extending the school day or school year, maybe we need to ensure similar academic instructional time and similar content for students. Standard-based education should help bring uniformity into the curriculum."

"I'm going home. I think all this talk about reform is too complex and chaotic. I don't think that teachers have time nor should be expected to cope with the seemingly messy problems of education reform," concluded Consalvo. "Furthermore, we don't get paid enough money to worry about these weighty matters."

Questions to Consider _____

1. Are you an advocate for increasing the number of school days? Why or why not? (If yes, by how many school days?)

2. Are you an advocate for increasing the academic time in the school day? Why or why not? (If yes, by how many minutes?)

3. Would year-round schooling be more efficient on a per diem basis than the regular school calendar?

4. Which type of student would benefit most from year-round schooling?

5. What are your feelings toward Consalvo, the teacher who had no time to get involved in school reform, who actually felt schools do a good job for most students and who wanted to freeze education spending?

6. What is your view about Klujian who wanted to spend more money on school reform or Myszkowski who felt we may have reached a flat area in academic outcomes, that is, more spending has minimal or no effect on improvement of academic test scores?

7. Using the Internet or library resources, find a recent article on year-round schooling. What are the issues discussed? Advantages? Disadvantages? Would you want to teach in such a school, assuming payment for extra teacher services?

Recommended Readings

A Nation at Risk (Washington, DC: National Commission on Excellence in Education, 1983).

Gerald W. Bracey, *Bail Me Out!* (Thousand Oaks, CA: Corwin Press, 2001).

Ronald S. Brandt, *Education in a New Era* (Alexandria, VA: Association for Supervision and Curriculum Development, 2000).

Michael Fullan, *Change Forces* (New York: Falmer Press, 1993).

John I. Goodlad, *Educational Renewal* (San Francisco: Jossey-Bass, 1998).

Baseball in Yankee Heights—and the Cost of Schools

The author of this text grew up in the 1940s and 1950s, a world where David Riesman's *The Lonely Crowd* was a best-selling sociology book read by artists and intellectuals in the West Villages, Harvard Squares, and Hyde Parks of the country. When I started teaching, it helped explain a new generation of middle-aged men and women, like "Willie Loman" and "Mrs. Robinson," all of whom are represented in the case study below.

Riesman formulated three major classifications of society in terms of how people think and behave: traditional, inner, and other directed. His "inner-directed" society, which I still remember as a youngster, was highlighted by Puritan morality, work ethic, individualism, achievement and merit, savings and future orientation, with mom and dad and other adults (teachers, police officers, clergymen, etc.) knowing best and influencing the attitudes and behaviors of children and youth. It was the Eisenhower years: Minorities were "invisible," out of sight, segregated, and on the other side of the urban tracks or buried in rural towns, away from the highways. Gays and lesbians were in closets, also locked out of sight, and a woman's place was in the kitchen, characterized by the Betty Crocker syndrome. On television, American society was being played out on *Father Knows Best* and *Ozzie and Harriet*. The only form of youth rebellion that I can remember was portrayed in the James Dean films and *West Side Story*. Elvis Presley and the Beatles had not yet appeared on the *Ed Sullivan Show*, and neither had Calvin Klein or Armani ads appeared in the *New York Times* or *Chicago Tribune*.

Norman Rockwell's paintings of the 1940s and 1950s have become better known than Riesman's writings, since the artist was understood by the masses whose family life and values he depicted in his pictures. He illustrated a Newtonian world where values were regularly transmitted by the family, peer group, church, and national institutions. Boys were boys and girls were girls—and they could squabble in the school yard without threat of litigation.

Rockwell's pictures of Stockbridge (and other small towns) were safe, orderly, and antiseptic: Trees were trimmed, houses were cute and picture perfect—reminding us of colonial America. There was no display of poverty or social unrest. Children played together, went to church with mom and dad, and ate dinner at the table as a family. They had regular haircuts and checkups with the local dentist and doctor; later they went off to college (dressed in a suit) and fought our wars (without burning draft cards or defacing the American flag). Children were "normal"; families were "normal" and social protest was not part of Rockwell's landscapes.

Rockwell's world—sentimental, romantic, white, small town, and Christian, in short, a nuclear family highlighted by regularity and predictability—belongs to a bygone era. It has been replaced by the harsh realities of a postmodern world—diverse, pluralistic, urban, and nonsecular, with different family forms—where normalcy is considered atypical or out of step but irregularity, even deviancy, is considered normal or cutting edge, as evidenced by new art, music, the fashion world, and the entertainment industries. Andy Warhol, Dennis Rodman, Eminem, Madonna, and Cher are models to emulate in this new world, which some traditional folks might say is perverse or stretching the boundaries of decency. These "models" go to great lengths to be cool; their worst fear is to be uncool, or even worse, boring, for they would lose their audience and millions of dollars. Their behavior—unusual, exaggerated, peculiar—is all about money and remaining in the limelight.

The characters depicted in our case study represent the opposite society. They are conservative, bland, and boring. The women are polite and preppy and the men are corporate blue and gray, Monday through Friday. They live in the "cult of prosperity," best depicted by Scott Fitzgerald's *The Great Gatsby* and by the lesser known authors (who were still giants) such as John Dos Passos in *Manhattan Transfer* and Theodore Dreiser in *An American Tragedy* who depicted the disintegration of human character to a competitive and materialistic environment. It is also a world of liberal Protestant churches, where residents are concerned about social and civic improvement, where women still get something out of working crossword puzzles and reading *Architectural Digest*, and where men read *Barron's* and smoke Montecristo cigars or possibly Cuban cigars on the patio, sun parlor, or golf course.

The people in the case study are not like you, and you are not like them, although there are many scenes that you can relate to because the setting takes place on a suburban baseball field. But the people sitting in this particular ball field live in a "Yankee town," a lost world or one that is disappearing from the American social setting. The people here exhibit different language and behavior than in most suburbs. Even though a baseball game is unfolding, the conversation displays little emotion (that is part of being cool), and the chatter is civil and the topics are safe and surface-like: about the weather, schools, camp, the scouts, furniture, barbecues, golf games, and popular books (nonpolitical, nonintellectual).

For our purposes, part of the conversation deals with school finance, which helps us understand some of the school budget and building problems confronting the nation. But, remember, these people are not like most of us, unless you have lived or now live in Lodgemont or Tuxedo, New York; Ridgefield or Greenwich, Connecticut; Hamilton or Western Dover, Massachusetts; Kenilworth or Winnetka, Illinois; or Hancock Park or Hillsborough, California. If you are like most Americans who have grown up on Main Street, Mott Street, or Division Street, it is doubtful if you fully understand these people.

ISSUES

Yankee Heights, located twenty-five miles from downtown Chicago, has grown from 5,350 people to 11,550 within the last ten years. Property values have soared; the median cost of a house is $710,000. The enrollment of the four elementary schools reflects the town's growth; each exceeds 500 students, although they were originally designed to house no more than 350 students.

A new school seems imminent, since the number of parents with young children now outnumbers the other residents of the community. However, questions dealing with site selection and cost have become hotly debated among residents and are keenly reflected in the parents' conversation at the local park district fourth-grade pee-wee baseball game, where the Bisons are trailing the Lions by four runs in the last inning. It's one out, and runners are on first and second.

Heather Smith, the mother of Jason who is at bat, is sitting along the third base stands and speaks loudly: "Come on, Jason. Hit one for Mommy. You can do it!"

Sandra Walker-Beefer, who is in the middle of a divorce and sitting adjacent to Heather, comments, "I love your son's mushroom haircut. What stylist do you use?"

"Andreas," replies Heather. "Besides giving wonderful haircuts, he is very cute and has great buns. He must be about forty years old and he's single."

Sitting on the other side of Heather Smith is Gary Yaeger, the Bank One V.P. at the nearby Payville township branch. He is the father of Michael, who is scheduled to bat next. "What's happening with the plan to build the new school? Have they decided where to build it?" Yaeger asks.

"Strike one," yells the umpire, who is none other than fourteen-year-old John Shankovic from Rockefeller Junior High School.

"There was a meeting two days ago at the town hall and some professor from Northern State spoke about the expenses of new school construction," said Smith.

"What did the professor say?" asked Yeager.

"Ball one," came the umpire's call.

"Good eye, Jason. Wait for a good pitch," yelled Mrs. Walker-Beefer. Then, in a calm and subdued voice, she answered: "Building a new school is no simple task. The rules are complex, the stakes are high, and the considerations are political."

"So what else is new?" commented James McFrey, a downtown attorney, school board member, and father of William, who was on the field at short stop. "You can make the same statement about building a new Wal-Mart."

"Try answering these questions," replied Smith, as the umpire yelled "Strike two," and she loudly echoed, "Protect the plate, Jason."

"What questions?" said McFrey.

"How many students will the school accommodate? Where will the building site be located? How will attendance boundaries be drawn? How will property values be affected? How will the costs be funded? How will property taxes be affected? How will voters react? Which companies will get the contracts? How many minority contractors must be hired? The list of questions, with potential for vague and politically toned answers, is endless."

In the meantime, Hu-Fay Yen's mother, who was sitting next to McFrey, asked: "Why is my son playing so deep in right field, and by the foul line?"

"Actually, he is out of place," remarked Yaeger. "He needs to move over toward second base and come in closer about fifty feet. It's the coach. He doesn't have experience. I don't think he ever played baseball; even worse, he rotates all the children in the field so no one gets a chance to learn to play one position. No wonder why we lose so many games."

"I think the coach is just trying to be democratic and not hurt anyone's feelings," said McFrey. "The kids are only nine years old."

"I think they should play to win; it is good conditioning for what lies ahead in life," remarked Kathy Elliot, the wife of a real estate developer, whose son was playing left field.

"Do we have to rush the kids through childhood? I wish the kids learned more about cooperation and less about competition," commented McFrey. "So many of these kids, who are innocent now, will be cheating on tests in high school—all because of competition to get into prestigious colleges. Who do you think they model?"

On the next pitch, Jason hit a grounder to short, which was gobbled up by William McFrey. It was a perfect throw to first, but it was dropped by Tracy Martin. The bases were now loaded. No one dared to comment about Tracy's blooper. However, Yaeger asked: "Why didn't Bill throw the ball to second base and get the easy force out?"

"That's simple. The second baseman didn't realize he had to cover second—that the runners were forced," whispered Smith.

"The real problem is, little Gary doesn't like to play second base. He wants to play short stop, and with this rotation system, he rarely gets to play his favorite position," commented Barbara Wilson, Gary's mom. "Do you know he collects old baseball cards, and he has an Ernie Banks and a Pee Wee Reese in mint condition?"

"Who is Pee Wee Reese?" asked Walker-Beefer.

"I believe he played short stop for the New York Yankees—or was it the St. Louis Cardinals?" said Yaeger.

"No, Reese played for the Giants," said another parent.

"I think you are both wrong," commented McFrey.

"Gee, I thought at first he was a character in *Shopgirl* or *Journey*."

"Wasn't *Journey* a great novel?" remarked Heather. "I love Danielle Steele. She really tells it like it is. To tell you the truth, I could relate to … uh, who was that anchorwoman who begins to question her marriage with her husband? Wow, did he make money."

"You know, *Shopgirl* was just as interesting. That woman, I forgot her name, she really captured the attention of that older millionaire from Seattle. That's my kind of man," said Sandra.

As the next batter, 130-pound Robert Buck, got up to the plate, the conversation shifted: "Do you know how complicated it is to figure out the expense of a new school?" said Wilson.

"What's so complicated?" remarked Trudy Grobmann, whose son was playing third base.

"It is possible for one school serving the same number of students to be three or four times more expensive than the other."

"That's difficult to imagine," said Tracy's mom—Jan Martin—as the pitcher released the ball and Robert Buck hit a high pop-up behind third base in foul territory. Little Charlie Grobmann back-pedaled and tripped over his feet, while left fielder Joel Pollacheck lost the ball in the sun. Robert was given a new life at bat, which in turn induced his dad to shout: "Hey, Big Buck, hit the ball out of the park."

"Must you use those words?" asked Walker-Beefer. "There are women in the stands."

Mr. Buck did not respond, but Barbara Wilson proceeded to answer Mrs. Grobmann and Mrs. Martin. "You have to consider different building requirements such as local construction codes; space requirements; average temperature and insulation factors; building design such as open air or enclosed, horizontal or vertical, one floor or multiple floors; construction materials such as brick or cinder block, plastic or wood cabinets and furniture, hardwood floors or carpet; and big ticket items such as the number of elevators, size of the parking lot, and number and size of the windows and doors."

Buck commented: "A downtown New York, Chicago, or Los Angeles attorney charges $250 to $400 an hour compared to $125 to $200 in Savannah, New Orleans, or San Antonio. A union carpenter costs more than $50 an hour in the Northeast and Midwest urban areas; it cost half price in the South, and in rural America it is even cheaper—about $12 to $15. The cost of land can be twice to ten times as high in one city (New York, Chicago, or Los Angeles) compared to another city (Milwaukee, Tampa, or Little Rock). The cost of a school building can run approximately $100 to $150 per square foot in rural, southern areas and $200 to $400 per square foot in major cities and their adjacent suburbs."

By now the count was three balls and two strikes, and you could hear the Lion parents quietly encouraging the pitcher to strike out Buck, and Bison parents politely rooting for Buck to blast the ball.

"Strike three," bellowed the umpire, as the ball whizzed by Buck, who just stood there in some trance, for the second out.

"Strike! Are you kidding?" gasped Yaeger, "The ball was outside and low!"

Mrs. Walker-Beefer then turned to Yaeger and in a whisper said: "That's what happens when you hire kids to umpire the games. We should be hiring college students or high school umpires. The park district is controlled by the hockey parents. That's where most of the money for sports is earmarked. Gary, you should run for the park district board next year. Perhaps then we would have better umpires."

It was now up to Rudy Dietz. With two outs and three men on base, the Bisons were still trailing by four runs.

McFrey, who had been talking about his golf game to Fred Dietz, Rudy's dad, then commented: "You know there are other factors to consider in determining school costs, that is, square footage and function. High schools need about fifty percent more square feet per student than do elementary schools, to adequately serve their clientele. The reasons are related to specialization and additional facilities for older students—larger auditoriums, pools, theaters, cafeterias, indoor gyms, outdoor ball fields, science labs, art rooms, and student parking lots. Also schools in cold climates cannot use outdoor areas as effectively as schools in warm climates. A typical high school serving a thousand students might comprise fifty square feet per student (at $100 per square foot) in the rural South. Another high school serving the same number of students might comprise seventy-five square feet per student (at $400 per square foot) in the urban Northeast or Midwest. The school's total cost in the Northeast or Midwest can run three to four times as high as in rural America. One high school costs $5,000 (50 sq. ft. × $100) per student and the other costs $15,000 (75 sq. ft. × $200) per student."

Dietz didn't respond to these figures, and only wanted to talk about his golf game, that his lessons with the golf pro were paying off, and that he broke eighty last week.

Yaeger grunted to Dietz and spoke about the Cuban cigars he loved but had overpaid for—$20 apiece. Then, someone asked how he knew whether the cigars were really from Cuba.

One of the parents asked McFrey and Buck how they knew so much about costs of building schools. McFrey answered the *Wall Street Journal* and *Forbes*. Buck referred to the *Reader's Digest* and *Ladies' Home Journal*—that almost everyone in America, including politicians and pedestrians on the street, had an opinion about schooling and the cost of education.

But Rudy then hit the ball into the gap between center and right field, easily scoring the runners on second and third. When the dust cleared, Rudy was on second with a double, and Jason was perched on third base. Mr. and Mrs. Dietz and the Bison fans politely applauded. The tying run was on second, and Darrell Phillips was coming up to bat.

"Come on, Darrell," yelled his mother. His dad Brad, who was sitting next to his wife, nervously sighed. "He has been in a hitting slump. We should have sent him to batting school."

Sandra and Heather then changed the conversation to *Sex in the City*, about how one of the main characters, Cathy, "did it" in the bathtub with some nameless guy she picked up in a bar, and that one of the other girls just met a guy in the park who comes from Bismarck and shoots bears with bows and arrows. "Boy, could I use that guy, in more ways than one," said Heather.

One of the ladies thought she was a nerd of some sort because she was not familiar with the program, but Sandra assured her that it would have no bearing on her popularity. She sighed a breath of relief and began thinking about switching to digital cable in order to expand her television knowledge base.

Talk quickly flipped to *Harry Potter and the Chamber of Secrets*. According to Catherine Phillips, young Darrell really liked it, although some of the ladies in the stands, particularly Mrs. McFrey, thought one or two of the local librarians objected to it "because it was about wizards and witches, just plain silly and unrealistic." Finally, this conversation drifted to the safer tones and safer sex themes in *Ladies' Home Journal*: "Ten Tips to Stir Up Your Husband's Adrenaline" and "Clothes Don't Make the Women."

The conversation then turned back to the cost of schools, and Martin asked: "If school costs are so high, then why do we have to build a new school? Why not add a wing to one or two of the schools?"

"The north side of town is growing rapidly," stated Wilson. "According to some professor, this person named Ornstein from New York City, public school investment in new schools, compared to other public sectors, has been minimal in the last fifteen years because of taxpayer resistance. Nationwide, sixty percent of the schools were constructed in the 1950s and 1960s, when student enrollments were increasing, and only eight percent were built between 1980 and 1995. More than twenty percent are over fifty years old, and the percentage is growing each year. Our four elementary schools fall into the latter category."

Wilson continued: "Schools in cities suffer the greatest need of repair because they are the oldest and most decayed and suffer from the most vandalism. Nearly thirty-five percent of the schools in the older industrial cities of the Northeast and Midwest were built before 1930, and a large number were constructed before 1900. For example, forty-five percent of Chicago's 595 school buildings were built before 1930, and as many as 75 schools still in existence in 1995 were built before 1900. In Akron, Buffalo, Houston, Kansas City (Missouri), and Portland, half or more of the schools were built before 1930."

"So what if the schools are old? They were built better than most new schools," declared Buck.

"Get with it," asserted Brad Phillips, "This is Yankee Heights, not Akron or Buffalo."

"Strike one," declared the umpire.

"A school building has five stages to its life. It has lived its normal life the first twenty years, especially in the Sun Belt where construction is cheaper," commented McFrey. "When it is twenty to thirty years old, frequent replacement of equipment is needed. When it is thirty to forty years old, most of the original equipment and materials need to be replaced, especially roofs, heating equipment, and asphalt parking areas," so the conversation continued until McFrey was talking about sixty- to seventy-five-year-old buildings that had to be abandoned or replaced.

"Strike two," yelled the umpire.

"Oh gosh! I hope he doesn't strike out," sighed Mr. Dietz.

"Just pretend you're playing golf with your friends—keep your negative thoughts to yourself," asserted Grobmann.

Darrell hit the next pitch through the infield, but since the outfielders were playing shallow, only one run scored and the coach held Rudy at third. The fans sighed; why had the coach held the tying run at third base? Phillips was more vocal: "What's wrong with the coach? It would have taken a perfect throw to get the runner out at the plate. Doesn't the coach want to win?"

"It's only a game," commented Martin. "The idea is for the children to have fun."

"Well, it's more fun to win than lose," responded Phillips.

Kathy Elliot agreed with Phillips. "I think the coach is strange. I hear that last year he had the second-grade players pick numbers from a hat to determine the batting order for each game."

"It sounds like he wants all the children to enjoy the game," said Martin.

"Well, you can't win when your best hitter is batting last or next to last," snapped back Phillips.

"This coach's attitude is better than the coach's attitude that my son had to deal with last year," asserted Yen. "You know my son is not the best player. The coach told us the wrong time for the playoff game. We arrived two hours late, during the next to last inning. The coach claimed we misunderstood him."

"Come on, no one in Yankee Heights would do that—just to win," snapped Martin.

Again, the conversation turned to the cost of schools. "According to the professor," said Smith, "the nation's school infrastructure is in a state of critical repair. By infrastructure, he means the basic physical facilities that underpin the school plant—plumbing, sewer, heat, electric, roof, masonry, carpentry, etcetera. Schools seem to be deteriorating at a faster rate than they can be repaired, and faster than most other public facilities. Plumbing, electrical wiring, and heating systems in many schools are dangerously out of date, roofing is below code, window panes need to be replaced with improved insulation ratings, and exterior construction such as brickwork, stone, and wood is chipped or cracked."

Rudy's mother, Joyce Dietz, then spoke up. "Do you know, I read in *USA Today*, or was it *Education News*, that the accumulated cost to repair the nation's public schools, according to knowledgeable sources, is conservatively placed at $10 to $15 billion? The cost for repairs and replacement run about $10 per square foot for schools over twenty-five years old and as high as $20 per square foot for schools over fifty years old."

"What makes repairs so expensive?" asked Martin.

Smith responded, "A nationwide survey by that New York professor of the largest one hundred school districts identified in rank order the top three repair items on which schools are spending money: (1) roofs, averaging $21,555 per school and $29 per student; (2) heating and air conditioning at $17,652 per school and $24 per student; and (3) painting at $15,101 per school and $22 per student. Other costly repair items, in descending order, were plumbing and sewer repairs, electric repairs, carpentry, brick and mortar, carpet, and tile."

Phillips was fired up. "What does he know, that professor? He comes from New York. Those people think they know everything. Most of them have never crossed the Hudson, and think everything beyond the river is cow country!"

"Come on, Brad. Some New Yorkers are okay. I have a brother living fifteen miles outside of New York, and he likes it just fine."

"I know, they have the best bagels, the best pizza, the best steakhouses, the best newspaper, the best fashions, the newest art and music, the biggest buildings—the best and biggest of everything," responded Phillips.

"I get the point," asserted Grobmann. "But why are the schools in such a poor state of repair? How is it that Heather is such an expert?"

McFrey stated that every taxpayer who reads the newspapers is an "expert" on schooling; the media is full of juicy information about school costs, test scores, and state standards. He then proceeded to answer Grobmann's original question about school repairs.

"School budgets are constantly trimmed at the local level," commented McFrey. "Whenever there is a chance of funding a new program, buying new textbooks, or replacing the heating system, the special interest groups opt for the new program or textbooks. In addition, the operating budget devoted to increased energy costs and energy-saving devices has robbed schools of money for repairs and maintenance. Many states have enacted tax limitations that have also resulted in sharp cuts in structural maintenance and capital outlays for repairs and replacement."

Wilson then commented about the weather and the barbecue she was having next week for the Brownies in her daughter's class.

"You know, those cream puffs you served last week at your Sunday brunch were delightful," declared Grobmann. Actually, she was about to ask what was wrong with cookies or donuts, but then realized she was now living in Yankee Heights.

Wilson continued. "Thank you! I'm so glad you enjoyed them. Gosh, I hope the weather is as nice for next weekend as it is today."

"That reminds me," responded Grobmann, "the weather is severe in certain parts of the country. Here in Yankee Heights, there are 100 to 120 degree annual temperature ranges that I bet causes considerable contraction and expansion of school buildings, roofs, and pavement."

McFrey then spoke about how the intense cold made the water and sewer system, as well as exterior brick, vulnerable to cracks and leaks. "In addition, acid rain, common in industrialized or dense areas, causes deterioration of all structural surfaces. All of these problems affect school buildings."

Phillips then interrupted the discussion. "The public seems unaware of the time bomb that is ticking in U.S. schools. What catches our attention is student test scores and the need to upgrade the curriculum. Operating efficiencies and school repairs are not on the minds of the public unless there is a call for new taxes."

"I'll go one step farther," said McFrey. "Most school officials are aware of the problem, but since the public is rarely concerned about structural problems it has left it for the next generation of schoolpeople and taxpayers to deal with it. Ignoring the problem will not make it go away; inadequate school facilities will potentially lead to inadequate schools. The longer we wait, the greater the cost for future educational services and the more difficult it becomes to sustain long-term educational growth and financial solvency among school districts."

Smith then commented, "Either we devote, today, a greater share of local and state revenues for the repair and renovations of our schools or we burden our children and grandchildren with crippling educational expenses."

"I wouldn't be so gloomy," said Martin. "Student output correlates with the student input—not new schools or smaller class sizes. It's not how much money we spend on education that counts, rather it comes down to family and community influence. Reformers and media freaks don't want to talk about this issue, and I personally feel we don't need a new school if it means higher taxes. I think we will do just fine, here at Yankee Heights."

The conversation was interrupted as Ken Lopatka walked on four pitches to load up the bases. The tying run was still on third, the winning run now on second—and Zack Nagler was coming to the plate.

"Politics is not the issue," replied McFrey. "We cannot continue to repair schools. Eventually we have to build new ones, especially when existing ones become too old and too crowded. We have made enrollment projections for the next five years, and we are in need of a school."

"Strike one," the umpire hollered.

"What kind of school do you envision?" asked Wilson.

Zack's dad, Steven Nagler, an architect, answered, "Schools in the future will cost more than current prices because the designs will be more complex and built for varied functions using more sophisticated components and materials."

"Strike two," said the umpire.

At this point, Nagler's voice was quivering, because his son was down to the last strike.

"Ball one," the fans heard the umpire say. Then, Zack fouled the next two pitches, and his dad continued. "There will probably be more technological equipment such as computers, videos, and satellite dishes; school laboratories; aerobic equipment and weights; places for small-group and independent study; flexible spaces, module classrooms, and adaptable walls and furniture; contrasting or great spaces such as common rooms, atriums, and open courtyards; innovative spaces and materials such as underground structures, decks with chairs and tables, and new plastic and prefabricated materials."

Catherine Phillips then joined the conversation. "That reminds me. I love your home, Barbara; it is so modern, so airy and full of so many windows. Where did you get that beautiful green chair and matching ottoman?"

In the meantime Nagler continued his conversation with Barbara Wilson. "Today's boxy classrooms and rectangular buildings will increasingly be replaced by flexible spaces and a variety of exterior designs."

However, Barbara responded to Catherine. "Do you really like my chair and ottoman? Do you know I searched for the right match in so many magazines and department stores. I'm so glad you like the match."

Zack hit the next pitch—a line drive to second base. It was caught and the game was over. In a flash, the Bison fans were demoralized. "Why did the coach hold up the runner at third?" was frequently asked as the parents filed out of the stands.

Yaeger commented, "Hey, Steven. Your son hit the ball well. Too bad it was caught. We could have used the win."

"What place are we in now?" asked Martin.

"Fourth or fifth," stated Wilson.

"That's frustrating," said one of the mothers. "We need to win more games; it's good training for the future."

"It's only a game," said Martin.

Steven Nagler then commented, "I think I'll enroll Zack in batting school twice a week for the rest of the summer."

Questions to Consider

1. In general, how would you describe the parents' behavior at the ball game?

2. How typical are these suburban parents? How would you describe the tolerance level of these parents?

3. Given the fact that the conversation on school repair is based on real research information, how would you describe the condition of American schools?

4. What factors are considered in determining school costs?

5. How do you envision the future design of schools? In ten years from now? Twenty years from now?

6. Who is your favorite character or parent? Why?

7. Call or write the public information officer of your state's department of education to determine how it allocates to each school district an adequate level of dollars to recognize the cost of effective programs and the various needs of its student body. Does the state's system of finance agree with your views about school finance and equality funding?

Recommended Readings

Kern Alexander, *Proposals for the Elimination of Wealth-Based Disparities in Public Education* (Columbus, OH: Ohio Department of Public Education, 1995).

Percy E. Burrup, Vern Brimley, and Rulon Garfield, *Financing Education in a Climate of Change*, 7th ed. (Needham Heights, MA: Allyn & Bacon, 1999).

Paul Hill, Lawrence Pierce, and James Guthrie, *Reinventing Public Education* (Chicago: University of Chicago Press, 1997).

Allan Odden and Lawrence O. Picus, *School Finance: A Policy Perspective*, 2nd ed. (Boston: McGraw-Hill, 2000).

William G. Spady, *Paradigm Lost: Reclaiming America's Educational Future* (Arlington, VA: American Association of School Administrators, 1998).

21

Preparing for Suburban School Desegregation

Much of the support for desegregation stems from the 1950s *Brown v. Board of Education* decision. This case, involving students from five different states and including reports by several prominent social scientists (spearheaded by Kenneth Clark, a black psychologist from the City College of New York), indicated that segregation made black children aware that whites considered them inferior and thus their learning was impaired. The outcome: Racially segregated schools were considered inherently inferior.

As argued by the NAACP, the crucial question was: "Does segregation of children in public schools solely on the basis of race, even though the physical facilities and other 'tangible' factors may be equal, deprive children of the minority group of equal educational opportunity? We believe it does." It has been pointed out that the reports of the social scientists were based on inadequate or questionable data from a methodological point of view, and what accounted for the decision was recognition that "separate but equal" was against the spirit of the U.S. Constitution. Since it was impossible to have segregation and full equality, *de jure* segregation, that is, segregation imposed by law, was ruled illegal.

Schools and communities in the North–South border states responded positively and with "all deliberate speed," as required. Attempts to desegregate the schools in the South was not easy or quick, and resulted in violence and the need for federal troops to protect black students. It was not until the mid-1960s that school desegregation was a reality in the Deep South.

As the northern and western cities experienced migration of blacks in the 1950s and 1960s, *de facto* desegregation, based on patterns of residential segregation, became apparent. Concern mounted to alleviate school segregation in the North, and the New York City Board of Education took the lead in a 1954 statement of objectives to implement the *Brown* decision. Attendance boundaries were modified, and free transportation was given to students who wished to transfer to other schools. The total effect was limited, however.

The Cleveland and Detroit schools followed with similar statements and efforts, also with limited results, in the late 1950s. For the greater part, the official policy in the schools outside the South was "color-blind." Several court cases in the North were brought by black plaintiffs to force school boards to take active steps to reduce segregation, or "racial imbalance," as it was called, and many decisions of the lower courts in the early 1960s ordered school systems to abandon segregated education.

By 1975, the once all-segregated schools of the eleven southern states were more integrated than the rest of the country; government statistics, printed by the U.S. Commission on Civil Rights, showed that 38 percent of black students in the South were attending integrated schools (50 percent or more white), compared to 27 percent in the North and West. This gap had steadily increased after 1965, and despite 208 court cases across the country, *de jure* segregation (based on the law) had in the South been offset by increasing *de facto* segregation in the North and West.

What reformers and the courts had not recognized was the growing "white flight" from the big cities to surrounding suburbs, making it nearly impossible to integrate city schools by themselves. This pattern of white flight trickled down from large northern cities to smaller cities and southern cities. By the 1970s, it was apparent that the only way to desegregate many city schools was to cross boundaries of city districts with a predominance of minority students to include adjacent and predominantly white suburbs.

In *Bradley v. Milliken* (1975), the concept of metropolitan busing in the Detroit area was rejected, but the following year in the *Newburg* decision the Louisville schools were merged with the surrounding Jefferson County suburban schools for purposes of school integration, and in *Evans v. Buchanan*, the Wilmington, Delaware, schools were desegregated in conjunction with surrounding suburbs. In both Louisville and Wilmington, the cases hinged on the fact that black suburban students had been required to cross district lines before 1954 to attend schools in the respective cities. The *Bradley* decision in Detroit, followed by the *Brinkman* decision in Dayton, Ohio, in 1977 set the tone for the courts in the 1980s, which was to determine whether any action by a suburban or county school system was intended to or did, in fact, discriminate against minority students or teachers. If such violations were found, the lower courts have ruled in favor of metropolitan busing and a system-wide remedy that assigns city students to surrounding suburban schools.

The problem is that the U.S. Supreme Court during the 1990s has dramatically reversed school desegregation plans ordered by lower courts, thus reducing much of the pressure to desegregate schools. To be sure, the appointees of Nixon, Reagan, and Bush had a dramatic effect on the Court's composition and political slant. Even Clarence Thomas, the one black judge on the bench appointed by Bush, has taken the majority view that school districts can be released from the lower court desegregation decisions if the districts have made good faith efforts and have eliminated, to the extent possible, vestiges of segregated facilities or practices.

The case study below is representative of a situation that is unlikely to happen on a large scale with the Supreme Court's composition, at least not until the ideology of the Court changes. However, it is bound to occur on a smaller scale, and in various parts of the country, depending on historical circumstance, state and local politics, and changing racial patterns in the suburbs. The community residents in the case study live in a cocoon, and are trying to hold on to a way of life that is slowly disappearing from the American landscape—as the nation and its suburbs become increasingly multiethnic and diverse.

ISSUES

As part of the state school integration plan that goes into effect next September, the Big-City School District in Ohio will be integrated with the adjacent suburban schools. As many as 23,500 students, black and Hispanic, will be bused no more than forty-five minutes one way to one of twenty-five public schools and four school districts within a twenty-mile radius from all sides of the city.

John Dewey Junior High School is one of the suburban schools affected; it consists of 750 students and is currently 96 percent white, 3 percent Asian American, and 1 percent black. The community consists of 5,200 families and 14,400 people; the mean family income is $118,000 and there are more than 100 millionaires living in the community. The teacher turnover at Dewey School is nil (what some might call a graying teaching staff), since the pay scale is extremely high and the school is considered one of the best in academics within the state.

Next fall, seventy-five students, representing a 10 percent increase in enrollments, will be bused into the school; the following year another 5 percent will be bused into the school. The community is not looking forward to the change that is about to take place, but they are resigned to the fact that a controversial court order will be implemented. Five proposals, along with objections or disadvantages, are being considered by a special school–community committee, consisting of representative students, parents, teachers, and administrators. The proposals are listed below.

1. *Proposal.* All teachers are to enroll in a human relations course at a nearby university to be taught by a sociologist who has expertise in race relations. The school district will pay for the course.

Objection. Some teachers reject this idea since there is a presumed assumption of wrongdoing, poor human relation skills, or incompetence on the part of the teachers.

2. *Proposal.* All students, black, Hispanic, and white, are to be required to take a human relations course for one year; the course shall be developed by the English and social studies departments. The course is to consist of black and Hispanic history and culture, as well as a list of recommended books to read.

Objection. Some parents feel the course will put their children, that is, the white students, on the defense in terms of their own culture, ethnicity, and self-concept. Other parents feel the course will be "soft" at best and a "rap" session at worst, which in turn will detract from the academic rigor of the school.

3. *Proposal.* A Black Heritage Club and a Hispanic Heritage Club, for anyone who wishes to join, will be formed and meet twice a week after 3:00 p.m. (The school has fifteen clubs that meet after school, such as debating, golf, chess, and French club.)

Objection. Some parents and teachers feel the club will covertly discriminate against white students. Moreover, they feel the club is potentially racist, since a White Heritage Club would be branded as racist or neofacist.

4. *Proposal.* As many as seventy-five families will be asked to volunteer to "adopt" one of the inner-city students and invite them into their home for a weekend in August to get to know their child who attends the school, as well as the

community. The family will serve as a future support system, and the children involved will become "buddies." A picnic on Sunday afternoon will serve as the culminating activity.

Objection. Some parents feel the difference in wealth will unintentionally create more problems than it will resolve. There is acceptance of a picnic and "buddy" system to be developed by the school without the weekend live-in situation.

5. *Proposal.* Within the first month of school, a series of welcome procedures will include (1) a special assembly for the student body that stresses American ethnic songs and diversity, (2) a Friday night dance that stresses the theme of brotherhood and invites a black or Hispanic band and white band to play at the dance, and (3) a guest speaker from the minority community, one of five planned for the year, to speak to the faculty after school hours.

Objection. Some people feel the idea of these special events is overkill and only makes parents and students feel a problem exists. Those who object contend it is best to go slow, and introduce procedures or activities as needed. Employing a scatter-gun approach will not resolve individual problems, and only drain the time, effort, and resources of the school.

The community was divided over the proposed options and asked the administration to hire a desegregation expert. Robert Von Goldenhoff from Harvard appeared at a roundtable meeting the next month. Instead of giving advice, he asked the community to make its own decisions, solve its own problems, in context with its own needs and attitudes. He would help in providing an overview of the desegregation movement within the last fifty years.

"First, let me start with some projections, to wake you up to reality. The U.S. Census predicts that by 2050 race in America will be turned upside down. The number of minorities will increase to the point where they will become the majority and whites the minority. Today's school enrollments exemplify the future; it is the most racial mix of students this country has ever experienced. Its members are nearly fifty percent nonwhite—either black, Hispanic, Asian, or Native American; and the white students have grown up with much more exposure to people of all races and ethnic flavors than their moms and dads, through athletic, school, and social activities, including dating, and the media.

"Today, cities like New York, Houston, Miami, and Los Angeles are already 'majority minority.' If you want to shield your son or daughter from the future, then you need to move to the Dakotas or Wyoming, which is still more than ninety-five percent white, and eliminate TV from your household.

"We have some decisions to make today. Instead of thinking about how you are going to help the poor or disenfranchised, perhaps you need to ask how your children's exposure to minority students will help them cope with their own attitudes— discomfort, fear, acceptance—and become better adjusted and better prepared to function in the larger society, away from this cocoon. As parents, most of you will not be around in the year 2050, but your children will be living in a country where they will be in a minority.

"You have some hard decisions, some pondering to do. Let me help you come to grips on a philosophical level; this may help modify your thinking.

"Most Americans buy into Martin Luther King's vision, which seeks some common ground, some common heritage—both political and moral—between blacks and whites. King's struggle for integration was based on fair treatment and social justice for all Americans. It was rooted in the Supreme Court's 1954 ruling in *Brown v. Board of Education,* which holds that school segregation harms—and school desegregation benefits—the self-esteem and achievement of black students. It was further supported by civil rights legislation, which grew out of the Kennedy–Johnson administration. However, King understood that laws alone would not suffice; people needed the proper attitude and commitment for desegregation to work in which people would treat each other as equal, based on the content of their character not their skin color.

"King's ideal," Von Goldenhoff continued, "is still vigorously promoted by the NAACP; nonetheless, among most black Americans there is the feeling that school desegregation is futile, that much energy and effort have been put into it with laws and policies, without much results. White America has been so resistant to desegregation that blacks, today, feel they are banging their heads against the wall. The current feeling is one of demoralization, and many ex-desegregationists now opt for basic education reforms in black schools such as compensatory funding, teacher accountability, school choice, and vouchers.

"It would be nice if we could get beyond color, but since we cannot, a great number of blacks have kissed off desegregation and subscribe to Malcolm X's view. It is a separationist perspective, what some might call self-segregationist," remarked Von Goldenhoff. "Malcolm's vision is rooted in the ideas of Marcus Garvey, an early twentieth-century militant, who justified black anger and black rage and called for black separation. His vision was also bolstered by the black power movement of the 1960s, with college poster bearers such as H. Rap Brown, Eldridge Cleaver, and Stokley Carmichael, who encouraged black violence and black control of their own institutions—and by liberal wisdom illustrated in the 1968 Kerner Commission report that promoted black identity, labeled white America as racist, and legitimized black rioting in the cities as a legitimate reaction to social circumstances.

"To this end, Malcolm preached that blacks and whites were fundamentally different and blacks should glorify their differences and not hide or deny them; it was essential to defy the white world—compromise or integration was a sellout. Why work with the white man who was fundamentally a racist, actually the devil?

"The emphasis on differences and separation crops up today in many ways: when discussion focuses on black identity, black language, and black culture; when someone sports a sweatshirt that says, 'It's a black thing. You wouldn't understand'; when blacks remind us they are Afro-Americans; when corporations provide special sensitivity or diversity training; when schools and colleges promote black clubs, under the guise of diversity or multiculturalism, or segregated, self-imposed dorms, or celebrate Black History Week. It's not only our laws which make us conscious of racial categories, but also far worse is this new national credo which highlights our differences, under the guise of diversity, not what we share or have in common. To question this new credo is to appear to be a flag-waving neoconservative, or worse."

Von Goldenhoff continued. "Malcolm's view seems to be winning the hearts and minds of Americans. The big-city schools are more segregated, not less, especially in the North and West, than prior to the *Brown* decision. The majority of us, fifty-eight percent blacks and fifty-four percent whites, according to a 1998 Gallup Poll, feel race relations between the two races will always be a problem. If the preaching of Malcolm X is embraced, then a permanent sense of grievance and rage will prevail. Hence, it becomes impossible to work with each other in an honest and trusting way; it becomes impossible to desegregate our schools and communities. If racial identity shapes our lives, if it is the driving force in social relationships, then we will never have harmony, we will never adopt King's dream—to think of each other as brothers, or at least as equals on a legal and moral basis."

"This is a very interesting theory," asserted one parent. "The question is: Do black students achieve more in desegregated schools or in predominantly black schools? Given the black student gains in reading achievement in the last twenty years, what is the contributing factor?"

"To be truthful," asserted Von Goldenhoff, "depending on the research document we read, a case for both positions can be made. In fact, there is a more important factor which correlates today with black achievement: the educational levels of black parents. This corresponds with the classic Coleman report, *Equality of Educational Opportunity,* published in 1966 and at that time the largest statistical educational study involving 625,000 children and 4,000 schools. For black and white students, achievement was related to the parents' education and socioeconomic status; the schools did almost nothing to close the gap between the rich and poor, disadvantaged and advantaged learners."

He went on to say that most reformers are uncomfortable with the Coleman data, because it threatens the notion of reform, blames the victim, and gets teachers and the schools off the hook. "A great deal of criticism, therefore, has been leveled against the report, including that achievement is almost exclusively a measure of verbal abilities, which are more likely to be a product of the child's home than his school experience; and it is difficult to find circumstances where we can measure and account for all of the factors that result in student achievement. Finally, there were numerous statistical problems recognized by Coleman himself; for this reason, he permitted a low correlation of two to represent the level of acceptance whereas most studies would require a higher correlation."

"All this is mumbo jumbo to me," said one of the parents.

"The problem is," answered Von Goldenhoff, "there are many other large-scale reports that confirm the Coleman data. Of course, there are other studies that seem to contradict it or raise more hope. I refer to the 'more effective school' literature which purports that strong principal leadership, a clear school mission, an orderly climate, higher expectations among the staff, high time-on-task and student engagement in planning activities, among other factors, result in high-performing poor schools and inner-city schools."

"Are you saying that it doesn't really matter if schools are desegregated or not?" asked Renée Goulet, a divorced mother. "Or are you saying there is no need to desegregate because we have not found the right formula for improving achievement in predominantly poor and minority schools?"

Von Goldenhoff was about to respond to Goulet's questions, when Phil McKinnley, a parent and part-time news reporter for the local *Villager* paper, rose from his seat in the audience: "Your theories are interesting and provide food for thought. But how do you respond to the conservative ideas of John McWhorter, a black social scientist from the West Coast?"

"What do you want me to say? What he says is interesting and provocative."

"Do you know what he claims?"

"Yes. Many black students are haunted by the stereotype of black mental inferiority and anti-intellectualism, and that the problem is amplified in testing situations that build stress and self-doubt to the point where they just give up. The problem will not easily go away because it is traceable less to present-day racism than to the legacy of past racism."

"How do you deal with this problem in an integrated school?" asked McKinnley. "Doesn't the situation become aggravated when blacks are placed in a predominantly white school setting?"

"Well, it's an issue. But this inferiority complex you talk about is compounded by the dominant culture, the stereotypes promulgated in the American novel and mass media, and in the publication about IQ, heredity, and scholastic achievement, which date back to Arthur Jensen and more recently to Herrnstein and Murray's *The Bell Curve*."

"Actually, your history is clouded," snapped McKinnley. "I would go back to Spencer and Darwin, and their ideas of survival of the fittest."

"I don't think I need a history lesson, and I don't think blacks want to hear or deal with these subtleties. Although I cannot speak for blacks, I assume they would conclude that McWhorter does not serve black interests and that the goal of racists is merely to find excuses and to keep black people at the bottom of the totem pole arbitrarily, as they have done for centuries. This is Malcolm's point of view, and my point of view."

"Well, your kind of rhetoric is designed to maintain pressure on the political system, and it is part of a new black strategy for demanding reparations. Listen, black Africans were involved in the slave trade traffic, thousands of black Americans were slave owners, and my ancestors immigrated to America after slavery was abolished."

"Your attitude, sir, is common and illustrates the mental and physical barriers imposed by white society," responded Von Goldenhoff. "I can talk about black pride and the strengths of black families. But, now, we need to talk about communication and school integration for the good of the community and country."

"That's public talk, not real talk."

"Then stay in your closet, if you feel that way, and keep your head buried in the sand. Jim Crow is dead, the Klan is dead, and your views are old hat."

"Are Malcolm X's views dead? Are the Black Panthers dead? Is the Nation of Islam dead?" remarked McKinnley. "Their views are more extreme and influence the media and black community."

"I think we need to get back to the original question about school desegregation, and avoid this kind of rhetoric. Let me try to respond to Ms. Goulet's concerns about and reasons for desegregation. You desegregate for moral reasons, because you believe it's right and because of your inner attitudes. This basically would correspond with King's position and the NAACP. Let me also point out that the increased education of black parents may not be the direct cause of student achievement gains. Rather, the family's educational status probably leads to specific family behaviors and attitudes such as motivation, expectations, child-rearing practices, longer, more formal dialogue, and so on—all of which translate into academic improvement. This all corresponds with the socioeconomic improvement of black families in the last twenty years."

One of the parents responded in a way that surprised the Harvard consultant. "Most intellectuals like you fail to grasp that you no longer have clout with the educational Establishment—school board members, policy makers, or government officials. Big business and government interests are dictating to the schools, both directly and indirectly, with their money, jobs, and legislation. Other than a few intellectuals who write best sellers or get on talk shows, no one really cares what the likes of you have to say, especially since the children of businesspeople and government officials, as well as most of the middle class, perform well in school."

The parent continued: "The Kennedy era and Camelot is over, that is, the last period when the best and brightest influenced policy makers and power brokers. You can count on your fingers how many people in this audience know who is the president of Harvard or Yale, or the name of any intellectual or professor that speaks to Bush on a regular basis. High-tech stockbrokers and analysts on CNN or Fox News have much more influence in our country, and on voters in general, than do intellectuals. For every person who watches *Meet the Press* or *Crossfire,* there are probably ten times more checking their retirement portfolio on CNBC's morning *Squawk Box,* afternoon *Closing Bell,* and evening *Business Center.*

"I get my news from TV's Hall of Fame anchormen—Tom, Peter, and Dan," said McKinnley. "Do you know that Dan is over 70 years old?"

"Seems like you are fixated on father figures—even worse, omniscient white men decreeing 'the way it is,'" asserted Goulet.

"Give me a break. Soon you will be comparing my thinking to some 'oldie-goldie' like the Weavers or Peter, Paul, and Mary."

"I think you mean 'golden oldies,' and I was thinking more like *The Three Stooges.* In our education consultant's world, it might be Dewey, Piaget, and Skinner."

Von Goldenhoff spoke. "Does this mean we should forget about or dismiss them for better preserved, wired, antiestablishment sources?"

McKinnley was well versed in education matters and frequently reported on education news. He responded. "Depending on how you get your news, or how techno you are, Tom, Peter, and Dan are either icons or dinosaurs. Depending on your education philosophy and how you view school reform, you can argue that Dewey, Piaget, and Skinner are world-renowned pioneers or old hat and irrelevant, as ideal sources of pedagogical knowledge whose theories have stood the test of time, or as WASP educators who never really considered race or ethnicity, class, gender, and sexual orientation. Despite all the hype, your colleagues from Harvard and other academic institutions might refer to Dewey, Piaget, and Skinner as the vanguard and basis of reform for teaching and learning or as relics, like *The Three Mouseketeers,* part of an old paradigm, superseded by Internet sources and postmodern narratives, biographies, and reflective practices."

"How would you define the three news anchormen?" asked Goulet.

"More like *The Three Musketeers,* once considered suave and debonaire, with their wide collars and power capes, but now out of sync with the in-crowd who scores a ten on Left Bank news and Soho or MTV news and out of step with youth standards of cool. Let's face it, the typical fan of Dan and Dewey or Pete and Piaget is ready for Nexium and Ditropan."

"Where are you going with this?" asked Von Goldenhoff. "What does this have to do with the issue at hand?"

"Listen, people like you fail to grasp that my generation and the younger generation, what I call the guppies and yuppies and what you social scientists call the baby boom and X generation, came of age and succeeded on the basis of the SATs, by studying and perspiring, by being self-made and high achieving. We people see affirmative action as a means of keeping good people out, and not as a tool to give good people the benefit of the doubt or to bring them into the system. Too many people do not want to work, rather they want a free ride. I see intellectuals and consultants like you, people espousing social science theories, as the crux of the problem—perverting the ideas of equality and mobility, as well as the notion of hard work and achievement. It's the 'preppie people,' the 'silent majority,' and everyday 'hard-working people' who put Bush over the top, many who in a former period would have voted Democrat and would have been more inclined in the past to listen to intellectuals, or even professors."

"It is an interesting point of view that you express, and it sounds more like something I would hear on *Hardball* or the *O'Reilly Factor,* but the problem is not going to go away by drawing lines in the sand or digging trenches around our homes and communities to protect our white picket fences. That's a bygone era which blames the victim and ignores growing diversity in this country."

"What about the point of constructing a pluralistic society where individuals are valued and respected for their differences and their commonality? Can this be achieved? Can we push and pull in opposite directions—differences and commonality?" asked Mary Maslak, a parent and local bank branch manager.

"Race and ethnicity cannot be changed," said Von Goldenhoff. "But it is possible for schools to bring people into a common heritage or common culture in which people share core values, the same language, and similar beliefs with regard to country and possibly family upbringing. To be sure, some of us still accept the notion of assimilation of various racial and ethnic groups and some the concept of plurality. Assimilationists argue that the role of schools has always been to socialize the young generation, to teach the common values and language, and that nurturing racial and ethnic differences is faulty logic, even dangerous, because it will highlight our tribal differences and balkanize the nation.

Others argue that the melting pot is a myth, that it didn't work for blacks, it leads to identity problems among all minority groups and, even worse, the homogenization of the majority group over the minority groups. We are a 'salad bowl' society—all in the same salad, but with unique features. These differences need to be maintained and respected by others, not for political or separatist reasons, but for the social and psychological welfare of the individual and group."

Tom Harding, a school board member, claimed that "at home on the weekends, in church and in the neighborhood, we all have a right to assert our racial, ethnic, and religious identities. There is no reason why blacks or Hispanics should be any different or considered separationist for what Poles, Italians, and Jews do or what I do as an Irish Catholic. Nor do our cultural and linguistic differences undermine our national purpose. We have always found a balance between ethnicity and patriotism. My father loved to dance the Irish jig and he died in the Korean War. An overwhelming percentage of black and Hispanic soldiers died in Korea and Vietnam. My only concern is that if race shapes our thinking or dominates the social or economic outcomes of life, if one group is discriminated against or given preferences, that will continue to promote hostilities and we will never live as brothers. We will always be paralyzed.

"Your point, Mr. Harding, corresponds with my view."

"So, as a board member, I would like to know what policy makes the most sense? What do you recommend?"

"Implement what you are comfortable in doing, what you feel is right and what you can live with and accept," asserted Von Goldenhoff. "Follow the law, consider moral, cultural, and civic issues. I cannot tell you what to do. I think this is what is wrong with the present law involving race. It attempts to dictate against the real attitudes of the majority. Each community, and the various racial and ethnic groups— within the community, must find the common ground and balance the needs of the majority with minority groups—otherwise, we will continue to remain apart."

"Given your expertise, you must have some preferences," asserted Maslak.

"I can only say that the discrepancy between the ideal and the reality of the situation for black and white people in this country was the subject of what Gunnar Myrdal called *An American Dilemma,* in his classic study in 1944. He indicated the race problem would never go away; it would always haunt us. One's judgment of to what extent the discrepancy remains today in the wake of civil rights legislation, compensatory funding, minority college scholarships, and affirmative action, and to what extent the problem applies among other minority groups, is based as much as anything on one's own political beliefs and personal biases. I can produce hundreds of reports about single-parent households, family size, reading scores, delinquency, and housing. After a while, it's all a blur. Reality is how you want to perceive it.

"For example, what I say in print or to you, today, or in class with my students can vary dramatically and depend on my personal experiences and agenda. When King gave his speech that defined the dreams of black Americans in 1963, there were 300 black public officials and three percent of black Americans held college degrees. In 1999, 8,800 black Americans held public office and thirteen percent (coinciding with the black population) had college degrees.

"I could also say that nearly one hundred fifty years after the Emancipation Proclamation, racism is still alive. There are no 'whites only, blacks only' signs; we have eliminated legal discrimination. But we will never eliminate racism from the social fabric of our society. In places like New York, Houston, and LA, there are more black and Hispanic males in prison than in college. You don't have to be a rocket scientist or social scientist to understand that injustice played a role in some of these convictions. It happened simply because some of the defendants were colored and poor.

"Now, my first perspective provides hope and is acceptable to white America; the second connotes pessimism, a view from the bottom, and is designed to make white America think, to put them on the defensive.

"Now here is a third perspective: From the 1960s to the present, blacks as a group made significant educational and economic progress in terms of lower dropout rates and narrowing of reading and test scores, lower unemployment, and a narrowing of the income gap. Within the black community, however, there is a deepening schism between the able and less able, between the better educated and those with few skills. Drugs, violence, single-parent households, and illegitimacy are disturbing and growing behaviors within the black underclass that the larger black community must resolve. Hence, this schism makes it appear that much less progress has been made and results in the ploy that whites must be at fault and more must be done in terms of compensation, quotas and reparations. This third perspective could be construed as neoconservative and unacceptable to many members of the black community. Ironically, this perspective dates back to the 1970s and the views of Andrew Brimmer, a black economist, and has been reintroduced, today, by black educators such as Bart Landry, Thomas Sowell, and William Wilson.

"All of you, in this community, must consider your own personal and political views and do what you feel is right, what you know is right. There are five proposals for consideration. As you consider the various proposals, remember the issue is moral, not educational," continued Von Goldenhoff. "As for the legal issue, it is in the background. It is not critical, however; it is almost nil, given the overall conservative outlook of the Supreme Court and its view that federal legislation should not interfere with state rights or the day-to-day operation of the local schools. Let your heart and spirit guide you, not facts or statistics. To what extent we fight one another for the economic pie or work together to help all Americans, and to what extent we consider morality, justice, and equity to guide our beliefs and values will be a factor.

"Believe me," as his voice faded, "I have helped you much more than you might realize. I hope it all sinks in. Good luck in deciding on your proposals. It's time to close the session and have the wine and cheese I was promised."

Questions to Consider

1. To what extent do you agree or disagree with the first proposal to require all teachers to attend a human relations course at the nearby university?

2. To what extent do you agree or disagree with the second proposal, which requires all students to take a human relations course, and which highlights black and Hispanic history and culture?

3. What are your feelings about a Black Heritage Club for a junior high school that is to become integrated? What are your feelings about a White Heritage Club, given the same circumstances?

4. The weekend visitation proposal caused some dissent from the parents. Do you feel there is more potential benefit or harm in the idea? Why or why not? Do you accept or reject the other parts of the proposal, that is, the buddy system and picnic?

5. Should the school preplan a number of welcome events within the first thirty days of school? Do you agree or disagree with the three welcome events being proposed? Should any one be omitted or modified?

6. Which theory do you prefer—King's vision or Malcolm's vision? Which vision best describes America today?

7. Interview a local school district administrator or use the Internet to find out what a particular suburban school district is doing to promote school integration.

Recommended Readings

Kenneth B. Clark, *Prejudice and Your Child,* 2nd ed. (Boston: Beacon Press, 1963).

James S. Coleman, et al., *Equality of Educational Opportunity* (Washington, DC: U.S. Government Printing Office, 1966).

John McWhorter, *Losing the Race* (New York: Simon & Schuster, 2001).

Gary Orfield and Susan Eaton, *Dismantling Desegregation: The Quiet Reversal of Brown v. Board of Education* (New York: New Press, 1996).

Thomas Sowell, *Race and Culture: A World View* (New York: Basic Books, 1994).

V

Multicultural and International Education

Race and
School Reform

Different levels of action flow from prejudice, from a mild ethnic slur to the most overt act, extermination. Five levels are noted. The first is a verbal expression of prejudice such as: "I don't like blacks" or "All Jews are aggressive," or "Women belong in the kitchen." At the next level, the prejudiced person avoids members of the group he or she dislikes; this does no direct harm to the disliked person. The flight of whites from the city to the suburbs because of black in-migration in a neighborhood or an increase of black students in the local school illustrates this kind of avoidance. The third level of action resulting from prejudice is discrimination; this does direct harm to members of the disliked group by excluding them from certain types of jobs, housing, and education. At the fourth level there is physical abuse; members of the disliked group are beaten in the streets, as in the Jewish pogroms of Eastern Europe or attacks on Japanese-Americans in Los Angeles during World War II. The fifth and most extreme level is death or extermination, such as the massacre of Native Americans in the United States or the lynching of blacks after the Civil War and Chinese workers in the Far West before the turn of the twentieth century. Of course, the Holocaust stands out as the most horrific example of extermination, and the ethnic cleansing that took place in Sarajevo and Kosova represents the most recent example of extermination of an ethnic group.

Many people think of prejudice and discrimination as one and the same process; they are not. In many instances people who are prejudiced are unable or unwilling to act on their beliefs and attitudes. For most of us, values, laws, and customs intervene between our individual attitudes and our capacity to act accordingly. We usually do not act on our own personal prejudices although our dinner table conversation may reflect these prejudices. For the most part, we are constrained in our behavior by the social situation and social policy.

Discrimination is a socially learned behavior of majority group members that is designed to support and justify their prejudices and rationalizations of continued dominance. This discrimination is built into the very structure and form of society and affects the people in it. If members of a society have been socialized to believe that certain minorities are just "dumb," "lazy," or "violent," it is natural for them to formulate social policy and build institutions that discriminate against those minorities. And, once discrimination is institutionalized by a society, it is difficult to change individual behavior.

The racial divide between whites and blacks is rooted in 350 years of history. Highly skeptical about race relations, often described in terms of the domination and subdivision of people, whites are accused of not fully understanding black suffering and black ideology, nor experiencing as a subordinate class the dominant power structure. Although today the dominant power structure no longer relies on using police dogs and burning crosses and churches, it has still hardened black suspicion and resistance. Every time a black person gets pulled over by a white police officer in a predominantly white suburb, or is denied access to a predominantly white church or community, black distrust of whites is reinforced.

For blacks there is the dilemma of people trying to live a normal life but always feeling under attack or potential attack. Once in a while, and only for a while, an "outsider" is allowed privileged and intimate entry into the lives of black people. Charles Dunlap and William Johnson, in the case study below, come close to achieving this relationship. They seem to be very blunt about their personal views. Both Dunlap and Johnson exhibit mutual respect and honesty about how they perceive the "truth" and their social world.

Most whites don't fully understand black history or black culture, since they have not been touched by the same events in the same way. White America has the luxury of examining black–white relations as a "racial" or "moral" dilemma (not as oppressive deeds) and in a sociological context (not in dominant–subordinate terms). Most Americans have the distance by birth (being white) and geography (living on the other side of the tracks) to examine the facts in a cool and objective manner. But, in this country, black–white differences, in historical and cultural perspective, spill over in nearly all institutions, including inner-city classrooms and schools: White teachers are sometimes told they will never be fully qualified to teach black children, for they can never fully appreciate "blackness" and "black rights-consciousness." Of course, this has little to do with professional or academic qualifications; it deals with the mind, the heart, the soul—the differences in feelings and attitudes, the differences in history and culture.

By the same token, a different type of "race card" has surfaced that enables liberal and minority groups to automatically accept the need for black teachers in black schools, and to ignore academic qualifications of minority teachers. In a way, it is like claiming you have to be French to teach French, Chinese to teach Far Eastern history, or Indian to teach about the Hindu religion. It also suggests that a man cannot teach women's studies, and a white English teacher is on very thin ice teaching about Richard Wright, Gwendolyn Brooks, or Toni Morrison.

In the 1960s, when the civil rights movement surfaced, black writers such as James Baldwin and Ralph Ellison and black political leaders such as Martin Luther King, Bayard Rustin, and Whitney Young sought to eliminate color consciousness from the law, to make it color blind. As the integrationist movement transformed to Black Power in the 1960s and 1970s, the racial divide increased. By the mid-1970s, pressure had increased to opt for black community control of schools and to consider race in the law and in making decisions about who gets into what college or gets what job.

The notion of blackness, black conscience, and black culture is a splinter theme. Based on the original strategy of racial equality and integration, many blacks are now blaming whites for the persistence of black problems and are continually raising the issue of victimization, the need for affirmative action, and a double standard—one for whites, one for blacks. The outcome of this dilemma is that no matter what statistics are used to show steady improvement (i.e., narrowing economic differences) or persistent gaps (i.e., standardized test scores), a critical mass of blacks will not be satisfied with the reasons and will point to white society as the culprit. On the other hand, most whites feel they are being blamed or penalized for nothing they did, and they see themselves or their ancestors as immigrants who have had to overcome their own ethnic, religious, and economic difficulties. Many of these issues surface as background issues in the dialogue below between the white and black educators. Their different life experiences and perspectives create much of the divide in the case study, the same divide that shapes society.

ISSUES

Mr. Charles Dunlap, a white teacher, had been teaching history for twenty-three years, including fifteen years at Jefferson Junior High School, an inner-city school that is 80 percent black, 15 percent Hispanic, 3 percent white, and 2 percent "others." He did not want to attend next week's faculty meeting at 3 p.m. whereby he would have to listen to the recommendations of a recent report on how to improve schooling in the inner cities. The report was published by the State Commission on Human Relations, and he had read his share of similar reports on school reform during his teaching career.

Most of the reports were the same: Schools and teachers are usually at fault; the majority of teachers are white and they do not understand the culture of inner-city students, nor their basic needs and interests. Teachers are usually considered prejudicial and bigoted in their views or as having lowered expectations for minority students. The textbooks, tests, counselors, and curriculum are considered biased. Dunlap did not want to hear some consultant tell him he was part of the problem—with little or no mention of individual, family, or community responsibility.

For Dunlap, the people who wrote these reports were politically naive or merely advancing their own brand of politics at the expense of the majority of teachers, and in the face of common sense and traditional values. Anyone who questioned these reports in public was usually labeled as racist or mean spirited. So why listen to another report? Why raise questions? The best thing, in Dunlap's view, was to excuse himself from the meeting.

When he told his principal, Mr. Jones, that he would not be attending the forthcoming teacher meeting, when the human relations report would be discussed, Jones, who is black, suggested that he did not fully understand the problem of being black or Hispanic in America, nor did he fully understand his students. Attending the meeting would be helpful, and he would be expected to attend the meeting unless he had a doctor's note describing his illness.

"What exists in public schools," Jones said to Dunlap, "is a system that primarily supports the language, traditions, and values of white, middle-class American society. It is monocultural and culturally restrictive. The curriculum, the tests, and the majority of teachers do not reflect or appreciate the diverse cultural, racial, or ethnic groups of America." Jones continued with an increasingly assertive voice. "Your own attitude illustrates what is wrong with schools in urban America. You are not dedicated to teaching these kids. You are being paid to teach these kids and, therefore, you are accountable to them—short and simple. You are merely marking time, waiting for your pension to kick in. You, and many of your colleagues in this school, need to gain insight into your own attitudes and behaviors. You need a more positive outlook: That with the right efforts to improve schools, something can be done to reverse the increasing number of at-risk students who either drop out or graduate as functional illiterates. If society fails to do something about this problem, then we will all eventually go down with the ship—so Dunlap, you need to personally shape up or ship out."

Dunlap was tired of hearing this party line, and he felt protected by tenure. He politely said, "Listen, I don't want to listen to this story. I have as much or more dedication as the next teacher, white or black, and I teach as good or better than the vast majority of my colleagues, white or black. My supervisory evaluations are excellent, so stop telling me how inadequate I am or that my attitude needs to be improved."

Dunlap continued: "I really don't need to hear the report tomorrow. I really don't want to hear about melting-pot theories, tossed-salad theories, or diversity theories. I don't need to listen to another report about school reform; those types of reports are rarely anything more than old wine bottled under a new label. Most of these reports don't make sense, and they are written by people who never taught in the inner-city schools. And, by saying this, please don't brand me as a racist or defeatist. To be honest, Mr. Jones, I really don't want to hear how I'm to blame for the problems of others. It boils down to individual responsibility and hard work, family pride, and values. You don't want to hear the other side. In fact, your side feels the word *individual* is a red flag for racism and that *group* privileges should prevail. You don't want to hear about student or parental responsibility. You would rather just point to schools and society."

The next day Mr. Dunlap did not attend school. He took a personal day off which he had saved (two personal days/year), and called in early before school started to report that he was not going to be there. When he returned the following day there was a memo, written by the school principal, in his mailbox. The memo accused him of being "racially and culturally insensitive" with his students; consequently, he would have to attend a series of six special human relations workshops after school that were designed to sensitize teachers to the needs of minority students. If he refused to attend these workshops, he would be recommended for three days' suspension without pay (which was feasible according to a strict interpretation of the teachers' contract). Furthermore, his principal pointed out in the same memo, there was a report in his file, about five years old, from a black student who had appealed a "C" grade. During the appeal, the student in writing had accused Mr. Dunlap of racism, based on the way he graded the student's essay test.

After a day of reflection, Mr. Dunlap wrote back to the principal: He was going to contact the union and file a grievance against the principal. He ended his memo: "I'm not going to be bullied by you or be accused of being 'racially insensitive' after fifteen years of teaching in this school. In my years at this school, I have taught more than 2,500 minority students about American history, and I am not going to allow you to set me up with the claim by one student who didn't like his grade or because I took a personal day off."

Two days later, Dunlap was chatting with his friend and colleague, William Johnson, who was also a history teacher and veteran, like Dunlap. Johnson chastised Dunlap for pushing Jones's buttons and failing to play the game. "All this discussion—concerning racial disparities in IQ and achievement scores, grade point averages, dropout and graduation rates, delinquency behaviors, income—really boils down to language. Jones uses the words *affirmative action, racial insensitivity*, and *equality* to describe what you call *quotas, racially driven*, and *excellence*. He would hire a qualified black teacher, and you would prefer the most qualified teacher. In assessing student achievement, he puts the blame on the biases of tests, teachers, schools, and the system. You tend to focus on educational achievement differences in terms of family, personal, and peer expectations and behavior; that gets you and other teachers off the hook. However, I admit, in the black community, youth who aim for high achievement are often put down for acting 'white.'"

"Personally, I don't want to hear about this racial nonsense; it's overkill. Our beloved principal is hanging the entire episode on racial accusations. I've heard this story many times, too many times. I'm bored by it; it has little effect on me. In fact, all I do is shut down, close my ears, and say 'ho hum.'"

Johnson responded. "Jones and I see the world in a different light, and in different colors, because of history, because of our life experiences. You have to understand that Jones is always looking over his shoulder, and so am I."

"It's your problem and his problem. It distorts your reality," said Dunlap.

"Jones understands the situation better than you do, and so do I, because we are both black and have lived these experiences on a regular basis. He is forced to play by a different set of rules than you do. He has to push hard because white America is slow to change when it comes to racial tolerance. He sometimes plays the race card, talks about racism, and sometimes uses racial terms in public to put whites on the defensive. Eventually, all of us in this country are going to have to come to terms with our sentiments about race and racial differences."

Dunlap had a different slant on race relations. "I realize that much of the debate over race, and now even gender, deals with emotions, biases, and assumptions. One's views on the subject are more a matter of faith, not facts; more a matter of political rhetoric, not social science data. But the effort to make excuses for gaps in test scores, preferences in college admissions or jobs, or to defend deviant social behavior merely diverts attention away from the real problem. How long are you going to say 'It's the white man's fault'? When are you going to take responsibility for your own behavior?"

"Let me tell you a story involving history. Most black artists, novelists, and poets have lived in the shadow of their own melancholy, trying to free themselves from the constraints of white society and their own turbulent lives, and confronting their oppressors—sometimes obliquely and sometimes with rage—retelling episodes and events from their lives and community in their own halftones and undertones. For some it was a fine line between realism and absurdity, not because of a personal flaw, but because of the inescapable harsh conditions imposed on blacks."

"For centuries," Johnson continued, "my people had to wear masks and disguises, dance to someone else's tune, and often become tricksters, jive artists, informers, and hustlers in order to survive. Given the context of the times, Amos and Andy were only trying to survive, and Eldridge Cleaver and Malcolm X were basically reacting and acting out their resentment and hostility toward white America, which they saw as the oppressor and dominant force. In the same context, repeatedly O.J. Simpson was considered a hero by the black community because he beat the white system that for centuries had beaten down blacks."

"Listen," said Dunlap. "When the Irish or Italians came to this country, they didn't have it easy. When the Chinese came to the West Coast, they didn't have it easy. American history books, the media, and all the people who read the *New Republic* or *Atlantic Monthly* don't want to hear or discuss this part of American society. It's glossed over or never discussed. Go see *Snow Falls on Cedars* and learn how the Japanese were treated during World War II. Go see *Sunshine* and learn the Jewish story of discrimination and nonacceptance, despite their willingness to play by the rules of the dominant Christian society and even convert. Go look at a John Wayne film and try to understand how white America robbed and exploited Native Americans. Other immigrants, because of their color or religion, have had it tough. Enough is enough with your stories of racism."

"You're missing the point, and that's why Jones came down on you. It's nearly impossible for whites to fully understand the grinding effects of racism, condoned by centuries of law, how it affects the mind and body and how it builds resentment, frustration, and anger. Race is a very powerful factor all over the world. Here in the United States it now enables blacks to require whites to prove themselves by passing a litmus test for enlightenment, sensitivity, and sometimes ideological responsibility. And you failed the test, by Jones's standard," responded Johnson.

"That's a lot of bull; these are all excuses. It's a play for sympathy and a free ride. Let me tell you, I don't know any country where there is free lunch. If you want free lunch, then there are trade-offs and consequences. Frankly, you need to stop using race as an excuse to curtail frank discussion, to hold back or put a person on the defensive, or to hire, promote, or fire others."

"You are living in 'la la land,' hiding behind a white picket fence and rose-colored lenses. People like you can't face facts filtered by centuries of racism." Johnson then pointed out that never in our history have we had such a diverse student population in our schools as now. Never have educators been more challenged to rid themselves of past racist attitudes that track black students into second-rate programs or to try to homogenize students of different backgrounds into one average group. "The schools can no longer continue to mirror the inequities of society," he claimed. "Too many teachers and schools have marginalized the less fortunate, especially those who have colored skins."

Johnson continued: "You often use black–white differences to keep us down. You use merit as a yardstick, which is nothing more than a pen-and-pencil skill, and then rationalize unequal outcomes. You put down black language and elevate formal English as the proper form of communication. You ignore black culture, except during Black History Week or Martin Luther King's birthday, and formulate schools around white, middle-class values. All of these actions, Charles, suggest the domination of one group and subordination of another group. Jones knows all this. But as a black principal, he is not aiming at peaceful coexistence between the races, as most people do; he is trying to go beyond the coexistence model to reach mutual understanding and respect. He was merely seeking your understanding and respect on the issues. He wanted your cooperation, and you blew him off."

"I don't have an attitude problem, and I'm not a bigot. I'm a damn good teacher, and I resent having to defend my competency. The principal may have good intentions, but he overstepped his authority. People like him too often use words such as *racist* or *bigoted* to put whites on the defense. By resorting to racially loaded terms, you can suppress ideas that run counter to your orthodoxy or, even worse, do what Jones is trying to do to me—put me on the defensive and possibly go after my job. His view about my attitude and behavior has less to do with my teaching ability than with his own personal struggles with race. The issue over race reform is complex and sensitive, but the solution is not in another report that puts down whites. This is a dead-end strategy, based on 1960s and 1970s conventional wisdom, that leads to dishonesty and hostility.

"What we need is genuine dialogue. But just try to raise questions or have an honest discussion in public on the issues; it is impossible given the labels, name calling, and politically correct dictums that follow," asserted Dunlap. "Schools and colleges persist in trying to control the expression of ideas that may be considered counter to the liberal-minority dogma. Try to introduce a level playing field, or a balanced viewpoint, one that criticizes politically correct dogma, and the roof caves in."

"If you feel that uncomfortable, you can always seek another teacher or course."

"Look schools and colleges loudly promote the rhetoric of pluralism, diversity, and equality, yet they practice strict intellectual conformity, a party line that promulgates attacks on Western civilization and white America. The idea that a classroom should be converted to ideological purposes is a perversion of critical thought."

Johnson responded. "Certain groups that define themselves as minorities, whether they are women, blacks, Hispanics, homosexuals, the physically disabled, or even overweight people, are seeking their own self-determination."

"That sounds peachy-keen. However, when I went to school, we had a habit of inquiry that was not stifled by ulterior, political, or correct considerations about ideas. Anyone today who doesn't subscribe to the multicultural or multisexual party line is immediately attacked in most classrooms. My political view is different from Jones's, but that doesn't give him the right to tell me I need to attend human relations or sensitivity training sessions. As a white, straight, male with a 34-belt size, I feel I'm fair game, a target, for every person who feels discriminated against in some way."

Dunlap continued, "Our history department has $1,000 this year for guest speakers. The diversity club has $10,000 for its budget, and that disparity is common in most schools and colleges. Try to raise questions about budget equity and you're either ignored or put down as a racist. Jones came after me, not because I blew him off, but because I was expressing my independence from politically correct dogma, his view of what is right and just. I have only one question: How much did that human relations or diversity consultant, for one day of service, cost the school? $3,000? $5,000? This thing about diversity is a racket. If I was black, I bet I could charge a big fee for a two-hour speech on human relations or cultural pluralism."

"That's a terrible remark," said Johnson, visibly angry. "That was not called for. What you are illustrating is the desire to confine those with no power and to perpetuate their powerlessness. Black educators need to address the problems and issues involving the education of black children, and if we are paid more money for our 'black expertise,' so be it. Consider it a part of the reparations cost of the past economic colonialization of black people, victims of greed, cruelty, and guilt of their former masters. Like it or not, that is how many black people think."

"Well, I think there should be a 'majority' or 'white' club and it should also have $10,000 for its budget. You face those facts."

"Your problem is, the consultant was black and you think he was ripping off the system," Johnson retorted. "It's a matter of prejudice, resentment, and competitiveness—and these feelings are widespread among white teachers. It is easier to deal with overt hatred, like a teacher referring to her students as 'niggers' or 'jungle bunnies.' The jury can quickly get rid of that teacher. It is much more difficult to build racial harmony when people don't realize or admit to their racism. It's like fighting the same battle over and over, and making no progress."

"This is racist rhetoric. The point I was making is that there is a payoff because someone like the consultant is a minority person and relies on ethnic politics, reverse discrimination, the threat of litigation, or uses ploys—like you are doing—to curtail criticism or frank discussion. Just try to fire a black person who is incompetent, and see how the roof falls in, given the politics of race and reverse discrimination."

"Perish the thought that you might have racist tendencies. Jones and I have experienced a chronicle of racial injustices, and thus we see the world much different than you do. Jones was reacting to the way he perceived you, and in context with history."

Dunlap answered, "Don't try to lump all whites or most whites together as racists or assume that most white teachers harbor deep-seated prejudices and resentment. Your own political leaders, from Jesse to Julius, admit that black people must stop blaming whites for all black problems, that you have your own legacy of self-hatred, violence, and oppression among each other. Jackson and Bond also point out that black youth need to sweat a little more in school, and less on the basketball court."

"That was mean spirited," said Johnson. "Black parents don't have the same pocketbooks as whites, and are forced to rely on the public schools, whereas the majority of whites can pull their kids out and send them to private or parochial schools. Black parents have to worry about teachers' low expectations, particularly if the child is a boy. The feelings you express are the reasons why blacks find it hard to trust white teachers, and why Jones is on your back."

"If black politicians can talk about lack of achievement and lack of hard work among black students, why can't white educators who are in the classrooms?"

"Because it has different sounds and different implications. Because the ghetto's invisible walls were erected by white society; because the inhabitants are subject people and white teachers are part of white society."

Dunlap reacted. "That's old style race baiting. The difference between black achievement and lack of achievement has more to do with solid academic preparation, hard work, a sense of confidence, and not turning one's mind inward or looking to blame others. One's own attitude, expectations, and motivation count. I'm not saying that history and social and political nuances are irrelevant. Rather, self-concept, self-identification, and self-determination have more to do with personal motivation and personal achievement than social and racial factors. Bill, I'll put it bluntly: The black community needs to shift responsibility to the individual, and not always refer to the problems of society or the cry of victimization and racism. The quicker blacks and other minorities stop internalizing their entitlement attitude, the better off they will be and the less resentment among white students who feel they are not part of the problem and who have to sweat and study because they have no entitlements. 'Just do it,' and stop making excuses over and over."

"Most blacks do not want to hear or deal with these subtleties," asserted Johnson, "and merely conclude that the goal of racists is not merely exclusion on the basis of race, but to keep blacks at the bottom of the heap, powerless and penniless, as they have done for centuries. Blacks do not want to hear they are ill-served by racial quotas, because quotas encourage special treatment, or that as a group they cannot academically compete with whites. Similarly, they don't want to hear your shit about black self-concept or black responsibility; that's all white jive to keep them into an Aunt Jemima or Amos and Andy zone. Jones would prefer not to have to deal with your attitude, and he can't help but see your ancestors, and if not your ancestors, then your contemporaries' ancestors who kept the yoke of oppression on blacks with slavery, and then Jim Crow laws and segregation patterns. That's what comes to Jones's mind when you speak your mind to him."

"Let's face it. There is a double standard that permits guys like you and Jones to say things and do things that I can't say and neither can other whites say, at least not in public without getting grief from someone. Jones is able to push the envelope because he is black, and your view of psychology and sociology is nothing but excuses for blacks who are looking to play by different rules."

"Jones was right. You have an attitude problem," responded Johnson.

"Again," said Dunlap, "you are using the race card to defend Jones; he used the same card to put me on the defense and to ignore fifteen years of excellent teacher evaluations."

"Look, let me just tell you there is an invisible wall, erected by white society, by those in power, to limit those who have no power and to perpetuate their powerlessness. Jones and I refer to this as 'institutional racism.' Sometimes we are forced to use what you call the race card to try to break down this wall, this form of racism."

"I understand more than you realize," responded Dunlap. "When you enter most stores, you feel black, but I don't feel white. When I enter this school, even though there is a majority of black students, I don't feel white. I feel like a teacher who has a job to do, and I'm pretty good at it. When Jones enters the school, I believe he feels like a black principal who has to shape up the white teachers. Now you tell me who is racist."

"How can you speak for Jones?"

"The way he behaves, the way you told me he integrates his life experiences with present experiences," Dunlap continued. "Race is not the major issue as you claim. The real issue is economics. Living in Scarsdale or Winnetka is not a white thing, but a money thing. Eating fried chicken has more to do with money than color."

Johnson answered, "The most important thing I've learned is the relationship between time and race relations. We've come a long way, since we were kids in school. Charlie, you and I can be honest with each other. It has something to do with mutual respect and collegiality, but it also has something to do with racial progress."

"Bill, this might be hard for you to accept. I know it's impossible for Jones to accept. A white person can be just as sensitive about race as a black person."

"Charlie, I don't want to continue to argue with you. But you and I have very different life experiences. You cannot be as sensitive about race or race issues as Jones or myself. Jones and I have to live with race on a daily basis. We cannot escape from it. Even when we are home and we want to relax, say, read a magazine or watch television, we are bombarded by different pictures and myths. The discrepancy between reality and the dream burns into our mind."

Johnson continued, "I'll just say that the schools are where the pressures of racial harmony and economic mobility are the greatest, because this is where youth come together under one roof, and this is where the formal education process takes place for the next generation. School is also the place where racial harmony and mobility can break from the seams—over issues involving desegregation, community control, hiring and promoting personnel, test scores, and tracking."

"Bill, you're a hundred percent right. But I need to introduce a joker. In all the schools and colleges I've been to, when you visit the cafeteria I see black students socializing with blacks and white students with whites. There is very little mixing or melting of races. The saddest experience is when I see educated adults, black teachers conjugating with blacks, and whites with whites, in the cafeteria or teacher's lounge. The irony is, we are supposed to be teaching about breaking down segregationist and prejudiced patterns."

"No question, actions speak louder than words," asserted Johnson. "Now let me tell you about Jones. He's my man; he's got the right moves. His IQ as a principal is equivalent to Einstein's IQ in physics. In six months on the job, he got us to break down those barriers in the cafeteria. No other principal took the time or had the ability to do that."

"You have a good point. Maybe I'll make an appointment tomorrow with Jones. You know, play the bureaucratic game and apologize."

"Do it today. I think Jones would like it. I also think he knows you're a good teacher."

"You know, Bill, even when we agree, we are still disagreeing. For my ego, I'll wait that one day. Try to understand."

"I understand, Charlie. Believe me I do."

"I think we both understand, sometimes more than others may realize. I think it has more to do with age than time—or maybe it's a little bit of both," said Dunlap.

"You're my man, Charlie. You got the right stuff. By the way, did you see the recent pictures of my kids? I have to show you how much James, Jesse, and Deborah have grown."

Questions to Consider

1. To what extent do you agree with Dunlap? Was there no need for him to listen to another report on school reform, especially if he thinks it will be critical of teachers?

2. To what extent do you agree with Jones? Is Mr. Dunlap's attitude the real problem? and is it a common attitude exhibited by many inner-city teachers?

3. To what extent is Dunlap correct? Instead of pointing the finger of responsibility toward teachers, is it time to point the other way—at students and the family?

4. To what extent is Jones correct that as professionals all of us need to explore or reflect on our own attitudes and behaviors? Those who are not for school reform need to be reeducated or reassigned (Jones's words were "shipped out").

5. Did Dunlap do the right thing by calling the school early to say he was taking a personal day off? Should he have attended the meeting, given his conversation with Jones? Was Jones correct in writing the memo? In calling him racially insensitive? In recommending special workshops or possible suspension? In mentioning a past incident with another student? Was Dunlap correct in filing a grievance? Was there a middle course of action or compromise that might have been viable? If so, what is it?

6. How do you view Johnson's point that whites continue to try to put down blacks? That pen-and-pencil tests are irrelevant? That it's appropriate for blacks to use the race card to put whites on the defense?

7. If you were Jones, or one of Dunlap's colleagues, what advice would you have given to Dunlap? Share your ideas with the class.

Recommended Readings

Gordon Allport, *The Nature of Prejudice* (New York: Doubleday, 1958).

Nathan Glazer, *We Are All Multiculturalists Now* (Cambridge, MA: Harvard University Press, 1997).

Christopher Jencks and Meredith Phillips, *The Black–White Test Score Gap* (Washington, DC: Brookings Institution Press, 1998).

Susan E. Mayer and Paul E. Peterson, *Earning and Learning: How Schools Matter* (Washington, DC: Brookings Institution Press, 1999).

Kwame Ture and Charles V. Hamilton, *Black Power*, 2nd ed. (New York: Random House, 1992).

23

A New Form
of
Bilingualism

As early as 1782, the American farmer St. John de Crevecoeur commented that the colonists were being "melted into a 'new race' of men." Israel Zangwill's 1908 play *The Melting Pot* popularized this term and called attention to the challenge of "Americanizing" large streams of immigrants who were entering the United States at the turn of the century. In educating diverse groups of immigrants, the public school system focused on socializing immigrant students, a euphemism for developing an American identity. Immigrant students learned how "Americans" were supposed to talk, look, and behave in class and school.

In class, a formal and planned curriculum was presented with emphasis on American history, civic education, and English instruction. Outside of class, an informal and unplanned curriculum also socialized children; in fact, peer pressure was sometimes more powerful than the influence of classroom teachers.

Beginning in the 1950s and 1960s, scholars began to point out that the melting pot had not assimilated all ethnic groups. Glazer and Moynihan's *Beyond the Melting Pot* in 1963 revealed that the newest immigrants in New York City, particularly blacks from the South and Hispanics from Puerto Rico, had not fully assimilated. Their population continued to grow and they continued to retain their identity because of their rural backgrounds, limited education and skill levels, and color. A similar thesis was presented in Michael Novak's *The Unmeltable Ethnics*, ten years later, regarding European and Catholic immigrants from Eastern and Southern Europe. The reason for this group retaining its identity was linked to religion, language, and folk culture, and the fact that their working-class skills did not match the postindustrial skills required in the information and technological society.

In the 1960s, as leaders of the civil rights movement fought to reduce the exclusion of minority groups, emphasis shifted (in some interpretations) from a stress on assimilation to a stress on diversity and cultural pluralism. In place of the metaphor of the melting pot, the concept of *cultural pluralism* introduced new metaphors, such as a "tossed salad" or a "mosaic," that allow for distinctive group characteristics within a larger whole. To endorse multicultural education and cultural pluralism is to accept the notion that there is no one model American. With this viewpoint, differences among people and groups are considered positive.

Our bilingual efforts in education are representative of the shift from assimilation to diversity, from the melting pot theme to cultural pluralism. Bilingualism is characterized by increased funding for Hispanic, Asian-American, and Native American students; by the Bilingual Act in 1968, which expanded bilingual programs in American schools; and by the 1974 U.S. Supreme Court ruling in *Lau v. Nicholas*, which stated that schools must take steps to help students who "are certain to find their classroom experiences wholly incomprehensible" because they do not understand English. The courts, as well as policy makers and educators, have taken an active role in providing educational opportunities for limited-English-speaking (LES) and non-English-speaking (NES) students. According to the *Digest of Education Statistics*, congressional appropriations for bilingual education increased from $6.1 million in 1970 to $169 million in 1980. In 1990, appropriations were $203 million, and in 2000 it was $225 million, illustrating that these funds have now leveled off.

Although the federal and state governments fund bilingual projects for more than sixty language groups speaking various Asian, Indo-European, and Native American languages, the majority (about 70 percent) of children in these projects are Hispanic. Although this country continues to attract hundreds of thousands of immigrants from around the world each year, Hispanics represent the fastest growing ethnic population in the country. In 1980, 15 million was the legal Hispanic population. Based on current immigration and fertility trends, the Hispanic population reached 30 million in the year 2000 (10.8 percent of the total population) and should reach 47 million in 2020 (14.7 percent), surpassing the U.S. black population (14 percent) as the largest minority group. Because of concentration, Hispanics have a very strong sense of empowerment and political clout in many states such as California, Texas, and New Mexico, and in some cities like New York City, Miami, and San Diego, which turns the concept of minority status upside down and inside out.

On the heels of the Hispanic population is the Asian group—the next fastest growing minority group. According to census data, the Asian population totaled 12 million in 2000 (4.3 percent) and will be 20 million in 2020 (6.3 percent) compared to 4 million (2 percent) in 1980. It is clear from these numbers that the composition of the United States is undergoing considerable ethnic change—largely because of immigration trends—and the federal government is responding in the schools by requiring that the states and local educational agencies meet the needs of these minority children.

Controversies over bilingual education have become somewhat embittered as federal and state actions have led to the establishment of various bilingual programs. There are arguments between those who would "immerse" children in the English-language environment and those who believe initial instruction will be more effective in the native language. On one side are those who favor maintenance because they believe this would help build a constructive sense of identity, and on the other are those who believe that cultural maintenance is harmful because it separates groups from one another or discourages students from mastering English well enough to function successfully in the larger society.

Adherents and opponents of bilingual education also differ on the related issues of whether bilingual programs are designed to provide teaching jobs for native-language speakers and whether individuals who fill these jobs are competent in English. Observers who favor bilingual and bicultural maintenance believe that the schools need many more adults who can teach LES or NES students in their own language, whereas observers who favor transitional programs feel that very few native-language or bilingual speakers are required to staff a legitimate program.

ISSUES

A new bilingual program entered unexpectedly into the lives of the parents of one of the larger elementary school districts in southern Texas, somewhere between Lubbock and Pecos, sometimes called Kmart country. The program is to be funded by the federal government for six years, at a cost of $115 million per year, and requires all children—Hispanic and non-Hispanic—in first grade through sixth, to be taught in small classrooms (fifteen or fewer students), 50 percent in Spanish and 50 percent in English.

The first obvious question is this: Why should non-Hispanic children be taught 50 percent in Spanish? The next question is: How did the bilingual movement reach the point where it requires nonimmigrant and English-speaking children to learn in the language of immigrant and non-English-speaking children? These two questions became the crux of a heated discussion among parents and teachers of the school district that was about to implement the program.

Assistant Program Director José Florez was first to speak. He pointed out that a dual-language precedent had already been established in many European, Asian, and Latin countries. "The ministry of education in these countries insists that all students learn the mother tongue and usually English, although in some countries, as in the old East European bloc, the second language was Russian. In our school district, forty-five percent of the students are Latino, and within five years it will be about fifty-five to sixty percent. By sharing language and culture, Hispanic and non-Hispanic children will develop more empathy, understanding, and respect for one another."

"I don't see it that way," commented Robert Flax, one of the parents in the audience. "English is turning into the primary language in Europe and many parts of Asia and Latin America; it is also the official language of the world wide web. I'm sure the French will recover from this blow. I hope the bilingual advocates can recover from California's Proposition 227, which puts an end to the public schools offering instruction mainly in native languages. I have heard the voters of Arizona also eliminated bilingual programs, passing the measure by an even wider margin than in California. Arizona's children under ten years are to be taught almost exclusively in English."

Greta Flossengruber, a parent of a prekindergarten child, was quick to raise her hand. "Empathy and understanding are nice words, but they do not help my child compete in a technological and information-based society in which English is spoken. There is no reason why my child has to waste time in her formative years—when learning and developmental growth is at a maximum potential. She needs to learn the 'three Rs' and she needs to master English—not Spanish."

Flax was just as vocal in his opinion. "I want my sons to read and write English, like other Americans, and not to learn someone else's language and customs which they do not share. This is the United States. Hispanic kids have to learn English, and the more English the better. American kids don't have to learn Spanish. English is the international language. Educated people around the world today speak English—not Spanish, not even French or German."

The Hispanic parents were silent, but one of the Mexican-American teachers, Mrs. Gloria Martiñez, spoke up: "The main idea of the program is to establish Spanish as a school district language on an equal level with English. Like Canada, our school district will become bilingual and set a precedent for the rest of the state as well as many other states in the Southwest. Our schools are paving the way for the future. We will become a demonstration school district, and federal funding should dramatically increase. This is a great opportunity, and we need to give the program a chance to succeed. In the end, all of the children will benefit by fluently speaking two languages."

Then Martiñez stated: "Spanish should no longer be recognized as a foreign language, or a language taught only to limited-English-speaking Hispanics, rather it should be a second language as French is in certain parts of Canada. Since the 1980s, nearly half of our annual immigrant population has been Hispanic. The fastest growing nationwide minority population, nearly fifteen percent by 2015, is also Hispanic, soon to outpace the black population in the United States. Ignoring the needs of our Spanish-speaking population, or thinking that Mexican and other Latin American borders will be shut down, is as silly as the 1950s Cold War policy, which tried to ignore and isolate mainland China, which comprises one-fifth of the world population."

"I don't want to alarm my white colleagues," said Luis Pescada, a sixth-grade teacher. "I read one of Harold Hodgkinson's articles; he points out that by 2010, and we all know that's around the corner, whites will account for only nine percent of the world's population, compared to seventeen percent in 1997—making them the world's smallest ethnic minority. While twenty-six percent of all Americans are nonwhite, among school children it is thirty-seven percent nonwhite and it will be fifty percent by 2050. I think all of you need to get used to communicating and cooperating with minorities, unless, of course you want to hang out in Montana or Wyoming."

"Does it really matter?" asked Martiñez. "I recall a *Newsweek* piece about Latino America. The Hispanic population grew thirty-eight percent between 1900 and 2000—to thirty-one million—while the overall population grew just nine percent. Based on immigration and fertility trends, by 2050 the Hispanic population is projected to hit ninety-six million. Hispanics are clustered in large states, those with a total of 217 out of 270 electoral college votes needed for the presidency. Face the future. Anyone running for president, and who expects to win, better speak Spanish. There is no reason why all children should not speak Spanish, too."

"Your remarks, Gloria, are a little inflammatory and send our white neighbors into the trenches," said Florez. "Let me put it in positive terms. Hispanics are hip, hot, and making history. We are changing the way the United States looks, feels, and thinks. Our food, music, dance, and language are changing American culture. Our votes count. Florida put Bush into the White House, and the Hispanic vote was crucial."

"I agree," chimed in Richard Sinatra, a parent and insurance agent. "Hispanics are shaping pop culture, population projections, and presidential elections. The Latin American wave is changing the shape of this country. There are places in Houston, Miami, New York, Los Angeles, and San Diego with sights and sounds that remind me of a foreign country, like little Havana or Tijuana or sunny downtown San Juan."

Sinatra continued. "Let's face it, demographic upheaval is shaping the country and changing our student enrollments. Regardless of backlash against immigrants and blue-collar nervousness, the Hispanic population keeps growing in our large cities and states that decide national elections."

"I prefer you use the term *Spanish*," said Pescada. "*Hispanic* is a term used by American educators and policy makers to describe people from South and Central

America, Mexico, and Puerto Rico. In Florida, the term is *Latino*. *Chicano* is used in California."

"Did you know that three-fourths of the Hispanics own their own homes in Southern Florida?" asserted Martínez.

"That's neat," said Flax, "but it doesn't mean anything to me—at least not in Texas. Gee, come to think of it, Hispanics must be smarter than I thought."

"That's a terrible statement," Martínez responded.

"In Bushland, we keep things simple. In our post-9/11 world, either you are part of the civilized world or a terrorist. You're either with us, or against us. You're either smart or dumb. There are no shades of gray, no sitting on the fence."

"I think we are mixing politics with education," asserted Flax. "The problem with bilingual education, and the reason why it was recently rejected by California and Arizona voters, is that it fell under the sway of political activists like you who linked the program to minority rights and group rights. By the late 1970s the federal government insisted that school districts offer bilingual education, with emphasis on native language instruction in school, or be cut off from federal funds. How can anyone learn English in school when they speak Spanish all day (or eighty to ninety percent) in class, and then go home and speak Spanish all day at home?"

"That's an unfair generalization and a racist remark," responded Pescada. "There are many different language programs for teaching English to immigrants. Bilingual education or the *traditional* program is only one: where ninety percent of the instruction is in the students' native language. There are *maintenance* and *transitional* programs designed to move students quickly to English, as well as *dual immersion* which is fifty percent native language and fifty percent English and *English as a second language,* which is primarily English."

Sinatra commented: "In two recent government surveys, Hispanic parents overwhelmingly maintained that their children should be taught English as soon as possible. In one study, published by the Center for Equal Opportunity, sixty-three percent said English should be taught first and only seventeen percent said their children should learn Spanish first. In the second survey, published by the Department of Education, eighty percent of parents whose children were enrolled in special language programs opposed teaching language-minority children a non-English language if it meant less time for teaching them English. The problem is that most minority parents, especially immigrant parents, are intimidated by the system and afraid to speak up against minority activists in public. But no matter how you slice it, their kids are stuck. Like other immigrants, those who want to preserve their language or culture should do so in their own homes, churches, and communities. This is America—where English is the common language and where English should be spoken in school for the kids' own good."

Flax interrupted, "The education bureaucrats are not innocent. Most prefer the budget-rich bilingual programs paid by state and federal grants, so they have decided that Spanish-speaking kids cannot learn to read until they become fluent in English. What a great excuse for why there is a Hispanic–white student achievement gap. Anyone with half a wit knows the same basic reading methods are used regardless of whether kids are learning in their native language or a second language."

"That's debatable, but instructional methodology is not the issue," insisted Florez. "The schools have been experimenting with bilingual programs for some thirty-five years, or ten years more than I've been alive, for its immigrant children, but it has never fully embraced it, nor the concept of multiculturalism. Rather than help immigrant children retain their native language and customs, most bilingual programs have tried to wean them away from their language and culture. Even students who enroll in high school foreign language programs do so for practical reasons related to college admission."

"Listen," instisted Flax, "the grievance industry can get private and public money and preferences without ever having to show progress. This is why Hispanics and blacks don't aspire in the educational arena. Why work hard or sweat when you can make demands with no accountability. It doesn't matter what education or social program we implement; in fact, the idea is to keep on dreaming up new programs and new excuses. At least California has taken a stand against affirmative action, against preferences, and against bilingualism."

Flax continued, "Where I come from, near the Chattahoochee River, along with a host of others from Arizona and California, there is nothing wrong with controlling immigration, ending affirmative action, or dismantling bilingual programs."

"I'd rather not hear your list of grievances or moral platitudes. The truth is, your statements are silly and insensitive."

"Well, no one in his right mind declares himself to be an apostle of racism or injustice, therefore, I take issue with your assessment."

"The truth is," declared Pescada, "Robert could be Peter Pan, Batman, Spiderman, or anyone else, and he would be the same and say the same things. He is being honest, whereas many others use code words or are more dishonest in public."

"Well, that doesn't excuse his racist ideas," declared Florez. "He should really clean up his act."

"The problem is, Robert sometimes resorts to double meanings to make a point that is too clever, or cute, for some of us to understand," asserted Pescada, "It's his way of dealing with superficiality."

"Let's get with it," responded Sinatra. "We all know that special programs can be used to create and support myths and to bolster whatever message you wish to push on the public. You can also call anyone a racist—and put the person on the defense and stifle speech. Some people used to call Al Shanker a racist because he advocated school integration and opposed community control and ethnic hiring of teachers and administrators. People used to call James Conant a racist because he urged vocational education for low-achieving students from slum areas. In some revisionary circles, John Dewey was considered a racist, because he felt the school's role was to assimilate and Americanize immigrant children."

"The problem is, whether you are a traditional rationalist or a postmodern relativist, both deny it is possible to identify the truth. Anyone can be a moral giant or a racist—depending on what side of the fence someone is sitting on," declared Sinatra.

"How would you identify or classify those educators?" asked Martínez.

"The better course is to think of these men as bearers of rationality whose ideas you accept because they coincide with your social lens and view of reality or you reject because they don't fit your perspective of the world or you view them as a threat to your goals and strategies—and leave it at that."

"The bottom line," noted Pescada, "is that twenty-nine percent of Hispanic students drop out of high school, according to the *Digest of Education Statistics,* compared to thirteen percent of black students and seven percent of whites. That's not a soothing statistic, given demographic trends in this country. American productivity is at stake."

"That may be partially true," said Flossengruber, "but how do you explain the data that suggest the overwhelming majority of Hispanic parents want their children taught English as quickly as possible, and their feelings are shared by nearly everyone else in America, including privately most teachers and Hispanic politicians. It's vocal groups, civil rights groups, bilingual educators, and wimpy professors who are divorced from reality and screw up policy that advocate these bilingual programs."

"There is nothing wrong with Anglos learning Spanish, given the huge numbers of Hispanics in the community and nation. You can't appreciate our Latino culture by eating tacos, dancing salsa, or listening to Ricky Martin and Jennifer Lopez. Whites need to move beyond stereotypes that pigeonhole us as landscapers, entertainers, or illegals," asserted Pescada.

"My kids know the lyrics of *Livin' la Vida Loca*," said Flax. "I also know that Sammy Sosa comes from the Dominican Republic and that Jose Canseco is Cuban-American. I think Jennifer Lopez has all the right moves. If she ran for political office, I might even vote for her. I understand and appreciate diversity."

"Bob is being cute and missing the real issue," said Sinatra. "I'm afraid of corrupting our language with new reading books that ask students to 'see Spot run multiculturally.' The stories of basal readers that my kids come home with, instead of having excerpts of good literature, emphasize multicultural themes, and are full of non-English words that my children will never use. They don't need to know the Iriquois word for *beaver*, or how it is pronounced or spelled, and they don't need to know some Nigerian or Kenyan folktale. This is all pseudo-literature, to placate progressive educators."

"Don't you understand the moral and social reasons for their selections?" asked Florez. "I'm not stupid. I don't accept the belief that students have to hold hands to respect each other's ethnic identity or learn inspirational tales they will never use."

Sinatra responded. "Do all these new multicultural texts have to ignore or criticize our European heritage? My concern is that we are lowering reading standards, ignoring the mastery of vocabulary and grammar to validate the identity of different words and dialects. I'm tired of these new literacy and language methods. What happened to the English language?"

Flossengruber asserted that the discussion had digressed: "It's not a proven fact that the English-speaking children will become fluent in Spanish. There is no extrinsic need for them to learn the language, as there is for Spanish-speaking children to learn English. My guess is that many Anglo children don't want to learn Spanish. This program may be politically correct, and coincides with the 'in' themes of cultural diversity and minority rights, but you are forcing my children and many others to become guinea pigs. The pressure and extra time to learn two languages will detract from learning essential knowledge. The extra few hundred dollars per child derived from funding will not compensate for the learning gaps that might result because of the time wasted in teaching Spanish to my children."

Flax added to the dissent. "If the school board adopts this program and forces my children to participate, then we need to elect a new board which better represents the community. We have the votes, I believe, to get rid of this board and the program."

The assistant principal, Prithi Marwah, pointed out that every parent had the right to opt out of the program; the school district had made provisions to bus children to the neighboring district. But this only further angered the critics, who made it clear they were taxpayers who expected their children to be educated in neighbor-hood schools.

Sinatra then asserted that the original idea of bilingualism was to create "transi-tional" programs so that immigrant children could eventually be mainstreamed into English-speaking classes. Then, as time went on, some bilingual advocates envi-sioned a way of expanding the life of the programs and related jobs by imposing "maintenance" programs and using the schools to enforce ethnic and cultural soli-darity. He then commented: "What started out in 1968 as a $5 million budget snowballed now into a $225 million per year bonanza for bilingual advocates, with no clear evidence that these programs work or achieve their academic goals."

Marwah, who was known for her sometimes outspoken views, remarked: "As an indication of how powerful bilingual groups have become, now some wish to force nonimmigrant children to learn a second language—and thus create more bilingual jobs and bureaucracy. Spanish-speaking children have become pawns for Spanish-speaking educators. But I refuse to allow our children to become pawns, too. We need more common sense and fewer fads. There is no reason for any school to buy into this new form of bilingualism."

"This is not some lilly white suburb," declared Pescada, "where the taxpayer is often unwilling to pay extra for bilingual programs, which benefit low-income immi-grants. This is Texas, the home of Sam Houston, Lyndon Johnson, and the Dallas Cowboys—and where immigrant students outnumber American-born students. It could also be one of ten other major states like California, Florida, or New York. Let's call an enchilada an enchilada. Immersion, maintenance, and transition approaches, or whatever spin we select, is a political decision first and a pedagogical one second. A little dose of political reality might help educators better understand the messages voiced by the advocates and critics of bilingualism, as well as cultural pluralism."

"Did you ever hear of the cold-turkey approach? No bilingualism at all! Complete elimination!" stated Flax.

"Not really, but I can distinguish between an enchilada, a blintz, and an egg roll," said Flossengruber. "The point is, we should no longer colonize Spanish-speaking children with English only or Gap jeans or John Wayne movies."

Marwah spoke. "Look, there are many theories and instructional programs, all with their own advocates. The same is true with other programs like cooperative learning, mastery learning, whole-language instruction, and so on. It's academic mumbo jumbo. You can advocate any approach, including the pasta marinara, chop suey, or taco loco approach—whatever soothes your taste buds. It's no different when academics use tech-nical language such as normal curve equivalents, standard error of measurements, or other esoteric research procedures to evaluate the result of some bilingual programs—or any education program."

One of the non-Hispanic teachers appealed to the audience. "Let's get down to real-ity. The continued existence of racial and ethnic barriers in this country makes this program morally and socially imperative. We need to rid ourselves of cultural igno-rance, European ethnocentrism, and prejudice toward all minorities. We live in a growing multicultural, multilinguistic society. This whole discussion tries to stop the clock; it is outdated, mean spirited, and repugnant. No language, no culture is supe-rior to another one. If we felt that Spanish was on a par with English, we would not be hearing this criticism toward the program—at least not without even trying it. If we were fair-minded or open, we would have looked at the merits of the program—smaller classrooms, increased federal funding, and a chance for Anglo children to become fluent in Spanish and better understand their neighbors."

One of the older teachers then said, "Listen, I don't understand all this fuss. It reminds me a little of 'Elvis the Pelvis' and the emotions and outrage caused by his hair and hips. If you want to implement this new program, and you give parents the option to say no, then go do it. But make sure the program is staffed by professionals who can speak formal English and who can be understood by all the students. This is a criticism of many of today's bilingual problems."

"Elvis wasn't Hispanic!" cried Martiñez.

"Forget it. You wouldn't know him if he sat in your lap. Just do it! Go implement the program. Passivity is often the culprit of reform."

But Flossengruber responded. "This is liberal crap. Both of you teachers are relying on the politics and language of the 1960s. The point is, many of you have no children in this school district, and it is easy for you to voice your progressive opinions. We don't need you to dangle millions of dollars at us or to talk about learning a foreign language or culture at the expense of displacing or reducing instruction in what our children need to learn to get ahead. There are people who will always try to revise the curriculum. But the idea of forcing American students to take Spanish, or having the option to vacate the schools, is preposterous; educators like you who accuse others of racism and ethnocentrism play word games and stir up storms of protest."

Said Pescada: "I'm not going to respond to those personal charges, other than saying I'm sorry for you and all the children who are affected by people like you. You and your friends fail to see the worth of the program and need to bolster racial and ethnic harmony in our country and beyond our borders. As the leader of the free world, as the nation with such awesome power like ours, there are many moral issues that our country needs to face, and people like you will never understand these issues unless they are standing in front of your nose."

Questions to Consider

1. In general, does the new bilingual program have more advantages or disadvantages?
2. Would you encourage your own children to participate in this new bilingual program?
3. The non-Hispanic parents were overwhelmingly against the program. What might the school board have done prior to planning and implementing the program to improve the community view of the program?
4. California and Arizona have curtailed bilingual education for all non-English-speaking students. Do you feel the rest of the nation should or should not limit bilingual education?
5. Both Sinatra and Flax hinted that almost all bilingual programs were failures and that the original idea had grown into a huge funding and job agency. Do you agree or disagree with this viewpoint?

6. One non-Hispanic teacher argued that the parental criticism of the program reflected racist and ethnocentric attitudes toward minorities. Do you agree or disagree with her viewpoint?

7. Ask a Hispanic educator to talk to the class about special social and cultural problems Hispanic students have in school. What can you learn from this person that might be useful with your own teaching?

Recommended Readings

James A. Banks, *Teaching Strategies for Ethnic Studies*, 7th ed. (Boston: Allyn & Bacon, 2001).

Linda Chavez, *Out of the Barrio* (New York: Basic Books, 1991).

Geneva Gay, *Culturally Responsive Teaching* (New York: Teachers College Press, Columbia University, 2000).

Daniel P. Liston and Kenneth M. Zeichner, *Culture and Teaching* (Mahwah, NJ: Erlbaum, 1996).

Lucy Tse, *Why Don't They Learn English?* (New York: Teachers College Press, Columbia University, 2001).

24

Inclusion:
How Far
Should It Go?

Prior to the implementation of the Education for All Handicapped Children Act (PL 94-142) of 1975, which was expanded by the Americans with Disabilities Act (ADA) in 1990 and Individuals with Disabilities Education Act (IDEA) in 1990 and reauthorization of IDEA in 1997, most students with disabilities were placed in special education schools or segregated in special education classes. Today, the law clearly states that children with disabilities (the old word was *handicapped*) are to be educated in the "least restrictive environment." Students with disabilities must also be provided with related services designed to meet their needs at public expense under public supervision and direction. Broadly interpreted, this includes medical services and supplies, elevators, bus lifts, and so forth. Schools must also establish a standard of care for all children enrolled in their schools, and they have to ensure that all teachers and school personnel exercise prudence and professional judgment in dealing with children with disabilities to ensure they are not discriminated against or harmed through acts of omission or policy while in school.

Unlike prior legislation, which generally mandated that states receiving federal funds maintain a policy of educating children with disabilities, the current law (IDEA) requires that states have "an approved plan meeting certain specified guidelines assuring all disabled children education benefits and prepare them for employment and independent living." Schools must identify who might be eligible for special education services, including preschool, elementary, and secondary schooling. Schools must not only adopt policies that serve all students with disabilities, but they must also conduct searches to locate such students as well.

Much of the movement to expand the education services of children with disabilities and to protect their rights is based on civil rights legislation, particularly *Brown v. Board of Education* in 1954 and the special education research community at the college and university level. The movement's success, with its stress on mainstreaming, means that you are going to work with a broad range of students of varied abilities, personalities, and behaviors.

You will probably be attending special workshops and seminars on issues involving students with disabilities, proper procedures for working with and teaching these children, liability issues, and related policy issues. As a teacher, you will be expected to write, or participate in writing as a member of a team, Individualized Education Plans (IEPs) for each child identified as a special education student, including the child's present level of educational performance, how his or her disability affects classroom involvement, measurable goals or objectives to meet the needs of the child and enable the child to progress in the mainstream, and the progress being made by the child.

The law also requires that you identify the needs of the child, and not the child's disability category, that you include the child in the "regular" classroom or "general curriculum" whenever possible, and not be quick to recommend or remove the child from the "normal" or "regular" setting, "except when the nature of the problem is so severe that education in a regular classroom cannot be achieved satisfactorily." It is when student removal takes place that much of the litigation surfaces.

Children with disabilities are not expected to achieve on par with children who don't have disabilities. Academic success is not the only purpose of inclusion; allowing the child to socialize with children who don't have disabilities and to fully function as well as possible in the larger society are major purposes since they obviously benefit the children with disabilities and even their nondisabled peers.

ISSUES

Superintendent Peter Dumbo of the Peekskill Elementary School District, in a local newspaper article, urged a moratorium on placing all children with disabilities in a regular classroom in order to cut costs. As might be expected, the superintendent's recommendation drew a flood of responses ranging all sides of the spectrum.

Some parents were relieved to know that finally someone with common sense and guts was willing to question the policy that all children, regardless of their mental or physical condition, should be placed in regular classrooms. One parent wrote: "My child has not learned anything this year in school. There are two emotionally disturbed kids in his classroom which the teacher cannot control. They frequently blurt out noises, wander around the room, and play with toys or the radio when the teacher is talking or the students are reciting. The principal refuses to move my child to another class, since other parents would want the same for their children."

Another parent asked: "Why do so many students have to be labeled and set aside in a special category to receive special services, or to be entitled to special consideration? Most of these special programs have produced very few benefits."

Then there were letters which advised the superintendent that there was no point to starting a debate about inclusion. "All children with disabilities have a legal right to placement in a regular classroom," wrote one parent. "Moreover, a good teacher should be able to meet the abilities and needs of each child in the classroom by altering the situation—for example, utilizing diagnostic tests to assess individual learning problems; varying the amount of time allowed for different students to learn each skill or subject; employing visual and concrete materials to facilitate understanding; grouping students according to needs, interests, and tasks; assigning student helpers or tutors to children who need assistance; adjusting tasks and assignments to coincide with different learning styles, aptitudes, and learning problems; using mastery learning techniques; and evaluating students' work by relying on authentic tests and portfolios."

Wrote one educator, Steve Soll, "It is true that the Education for All Handicapped Children Act gave youngsters with disabilities the right to a 'free and appropriate public education in the least restrictive environment.' But this doesn't tell us whether the 'least restrictive environment' that is 'appropriate' for a particular child is a special education class or a regular classroom."

"What if placement doesn't work out?" continued Soll. "Suppose the boy or girl's disability involves violent behavior that regularly turns the class upside down? What are the legal procedures for removing the youngster from the class? What protection does the law offer the teachers and the other students in the meantime?

"According to the courts, the student cannot be suspended for more than ten days a year, though if the school district petitions the court a temporary restraining order could be granted. But few school districts go to such trouble, since it involves several meetings, hearings, and appeals. Otherwise, the kid is back in the classroom, no matter what he did or will do. This includes hitting other students or the teacher or bringing a knife to class."

One educator, Chen Kazantev, had a different version to support. "The courts now take an active role in protecting the rights and improving education opportunities for students with special disabilities; furthermore, an increasing number of students are being identified as handicapped. The U.S. government reports that approximately thirteen percent of the public school enrollments are considered handicapped, compared to five percent in 1975, the year handicapped legislation first went into effect. Why the dramatic increase in numbers? Before the law required action, and before federal money was made available, the schools were unwilling to provide full services to disabled children."

Another educator defended the schools and argued that many students in the past "fell through the cracks, because their test scores were not quite low enough or their behavior was not disruptive enough to qualify for additional help that only a label can bring. The recent labels—learning disabled (LD), behaviorally disabled (BD), and cognitively disabled (CD)—now help millions of students receive meaningful services that once did not."

One of the teachers, Sandra Berlin, wrote a highly charged response. "I have problems with all these disability and special education laws, imposed by well-intentioned people who don't teach. As a teacher, I watch helplessly as my colleagues try to cope with students who must be placed in the 'least restrictive environment.' Too many of these students fly off the handle, disrupt the entire class, and receive most of the teacher's attention. They receive civil rights protection but cannot be disciplined in a normal or routine way for causing a host of difficulties."

"When we say *handicapped*," she continued, "what image comes to mind? Blind, deaf, autistic, epileptic, speech impaired? Well, in the last ten years I have walked hundreds of hallway miles in my school watching these so-called handicapped children deface property, bang on classroom windows, shout obscenities, and even dance on desks. They know they are a protected class and have to be coddled by teachers and school officials. The students I'm talking about are not blind, deaf, mute, or walking on crutches or sitting in wheelchairs. They are what Section 504 of the Rehabilitation Act, extended by the Americans with Disabilities Act (ADA), loosely calls *behaviorally disabled*. Even worse, parental advocacy groups and education pressure groups, supported by attorneys, are quick to sue and blame the schools when the children misbehave or are removed from mainstream classrooms. Three cheers for the superintendent."

A parent of a hyperactive child wrote a sidebar response to the Berlin piece, exhibiting even more anger. "Why don't we just label all difficult to teach kids as 'freaks,' 'weirdos,' or simply 'disturbed,' or whatever label sounds more politically correct, and put them all together in one school, away from so-called 'normal' and 'regular' students. Afterwards, we can start separating all the Jewish students, homophobic students, or obese students—and put them in separate classrooms or schools. Then we can separate all students whose last names end with a vowel or who have an uncle named Vinnie or Muhammad. Perhaps we can even extend separate facilities for bald-headed educators, those with big bellies or hips, or those who have visual or hearing loss—and put them in separate offices, separate floors, or separate schools."

But William Woods III, a local lawyer from a white-shoe firm, was quick to bring things into perspective and point out in print that "the law obligates schools to educate every student with a disability in the least restrictive environment; students with disabilities can be placed in alternative settings so long as the alternative represents a setting from the least restrictive continuum, not the most restrictive side. The district's efforts cannot be token, and the school cannot abdicate its responsibility to save money. The law needs to protect these children, because we cannot depend on the good nature and goodwill of people who have the vote."

Viola Ashutosh, a parent, wrote: "My big concern is that a disproportionate number of minority students are classified as disabled, especially mentally retarded or emotionally disturbed, and segregated into special classes. To the extent I am right, we have made little progress since the *Brown* decision, which outlawed school segregation in 1954. I'm afraid some special education programs have become dumping grounds for minority students, as well as for other students considered different or troublesome for school personnel."

Another parent criticized school authorities for being too quick to sort and classify students as learning disabled or generally disabled. "Since 1975, the number classified into this group has more than tripled and totals 2.7 million. Should the likes of Tom Sawyer, Huckleberry Finn, or Holden Caulfield be considered disabled? Too many borderline students are sorted into special education categories and too many parents insist their children act 'normal' and take a daily Ritalin pill."

Said a school administrator, "The schools respond very differently to students with disabilities. Some are quick to label and remove kids from regular classrooms. Some move slowly and consider various alternatives and a range of services. Still others dump kids into regular classrooms in the name of inclusion, even though minimal services are available. There is no agreed-on policy, and the schools are subject to criticism regardless of the policies they implement."

Another educator, Jim Beane, had firm convictions about making schools inclusive. "We need to set a deadline for federal legislation to eliminate separate schooling for all students, especially the culturally diverse and special education student. We must reduce all forms of 'set asides' in what I call school segregation; reduce suspensions and expulsions of students; and place the burden of proof on those people who continue to obstruct mainstreaming. By segregating students because of their behavior or learning problems, we only further alienate and isolate them from their peers, teachers, schools, and community, which in turn causes other social, psychological, and learning problems."

One parent from a nearby town, Gupta Hrynszyn, had a similar view. "We should not have to defend inclusion. Those who advocate exclusion should have to defend their views. It is important for all students to learn in a school setting that represents the kind of world they have to live in now and after school. We live in a diverse world in terms of race, class, religion, gender, and disabilities. We must start with the assumption that all children, including those with disabilities, need to be educated in a regular classroom or integrated setting."

But another parent had the opposite view. "Some parents of special needs children support inclusion and others feel just the opposite. Many parents, and some advocates of special education, actually prefer their children in a special class, even if it means segregation, to ensure they receive adequate services. They actually fear the schools will reduce costs and services for their children in a regular classroom. Inclusion, without proper resources and teacher training, will not work. Also, most students with severe disabilities prefer a special class or school because of fear of peer rejection and feelings of inadequacy."

"That may be true," responded a teacher. "But I never knew a parent of a disabled child who did not want that child someday to function in the larger community with people who were not also blind or with people who were not also physically handicapped. Inclusion must be the ultimate object of schools and society."

Still another reader defended exclusion under certain circumstances. "We need different kinds of teachers and likewise different kinds of instruction for deaf and blind students, as well as emotionally disturbed and mentally retarded students—an environment that a regular classroom cannot possibly provide because of the larger number of students and lack of training among regularly certified teachers. We must be willing to admit that some children will perform better in an exclusive setting than in an alternative setup."

"Better in what?" wrote one parent in response. "Better in reading? Better in making friends with regular children? Better in being part of the school and community? Better prepared to function in a normal society? What we really need is a host of services in conjunction with regular, integrated classrooms. The law of the land, the concept of the least restrictive environment, means that we make serious attempts to meet the needs of all students in a regular classroom, whenever possible and without segregating them."

But another parent, Karl Oldham, pointed out, "There are wide differences in children's needs and the best environment that can address these different needs. I don't believe we should accuse the schools of segregating students, something that is illegal and harmful when it is forced on a particular group. Sometimes implementing special programs, with small numbers of students who have the same disability, is the best practice. As long as decisions are made on an individual basis and not a group basis, with input from the parent and possibly the child's physician, it is wrong to use the word *segregation*."

Said one school administrator: "There isn't anything illegal or educationally unsound in meeting the needs of students outside the regular classroom. In fact, the law requires we consider both options, including an approach along a continuum of alternatives. What we need is a variety of options and special services in context with providing the least restrictive environment."

Ulsa Liefaard, another teacher, tended to agree with Oldham and the administrator. "In the past, special education teachers and their students bore the brunt of inappropriate placements; however, these teachers were trained for their assignments and classroom size was very small. If total inclusion becomes the norm and the regular classroom becomes the standard placement for all children with disabilities, more classes will be disrupted. Teachers who have little or no extra help in dealing with special needs children will be trying to cope with unfamiliar problems, and in much larger classrooms than the special education classrooms."

Liefaard continued: "We can expect very little learning to go on in these classrooms. Students and teachers will be forced to tolerate disruptive students who are required by law to stay put until the school follows a host of legal procedures to change the placement. I am not saying that all students with disabilities should be denied placement in regular classrooms or that they create enormous problems. But it is just as senseless to think that all students with disabilities have a right to be placed in a regular classroom because some will benefit there. School authorities need room to exercise professional judgment the way other professionals do who run other institutions. Children with disabilities are individuals, not a bureaucratic category, and their placements need to be done on a case-by-case basis."

Commented another teacher, "Instead of labeling, grouping, and segregating children because they are handicapped or disabled, we should concentrate on more effective instruction for all low-achieving students, as part of regular classroom instruction. If we could pool compensatory funding, Title 1 funding, special education resources, and other budget line items for improving instruction with regular pupil funding, then the handicapped student should be assigned to and can benefit from the regular classroom. In short, there should be no retreat for mainstreaming handicapped children. They may have special needs and need special attention, but they are not morons or idiots—and we should not treat them as if they have the plague. The real problem is that old methods don't die easily. People would rather not break from tradition unless it directly benefits them."

An elementary school teacher, Anna Lowe, put it this way. "There is no separate knowledge base for teaching mildly retarded, mildly emotionally disturbed, or mildly disruptive students like there is for students who are severely retarded, emotionally disturbed, or disruptive or who are blind or deaf. In many schools, children who consistently score low on standardized reading tests and IQ tests or who are chronic nuisances in class are given some label and shipped into a special program or enrichment class. It makes life easier for teachers and schools to take the simple approach, that is, to label and get the student out of the mainstream class."

A sixth-grade teacher wrote: "Most teachers are unable to reach and teach twenty-five to thirty students who have wide ranges in reading ability, say, five or six grade levels, and major differences in emotional behavior (students who are severely depressed, disruptive, or hostile). They were not trained for this assignment, and it is doubtful if more than a handful of teachers in each school have the long-term motivation and ability to do so. This is not a teacher attitude or competency problem. It is an *inclusion* problem when we try to integrate severely disabled students into regular classrooms, without proper teacher training and support services, to satisfy what critics or the courts say is the right thing to do.

"It is a simple matter of statistics," the teacher continued. "In the name of inclusion, we put kids into regular classrooms, some who are bound to be highly disruptive, hostile, or violent. Then we cannot expedite their removal because of the law. Not until we provide the mechanism for quick removal of students who need to be removed from the regular classroom will I support inclusion."

Judy Litz, another teacher, disagreed. "I am aware of the research that warns full inclusion hinders the educational outcomes of regular students, and regular teachers often receive little help in dealing with disabled students. I have been teaching for twenty years. Inclusion works with regular teachers who know how to teach and manage students. Good teaching works with all kinds of students—abled as well as disabled. Poor teaching doesn't work well with any group of students. Let's stop making excuses for professionals who are paid to teach and professors who are paid to train teachers."

One of the parents, Loya Eñriquez, made a related remark: "The issue of educational overburden needs to be considered. There is a greater proportion of special needs students—namely, low-achieving, poor, minority, bilingual, and handicapped students—in the city schools than in suburban or rural schools. These students require remedial programs and services and more money per student than the average student. Moreover, the need for additional services and money tends to increase geometrically with high concentrations of special needs students (i.e., smaller classes, special programs, more remedial services, and special personnel), just as it does in highly populated poor areas of cities (higher vandalism costs, higher maintenance costs, higher insurance costs, more security personnel, more specialists, more social-welfare programs). Where is all this money going to come from, given the fact that most taxpayers already feel overtaxed, most state budgets are at deficit or near deficit levels, and the federal government continuously talks about streamlining the budget?"

Raymond Herbert, a retirement home director and volunteer fireman, wrote, "I'm concerned about my high-school daughter who is only searching for a level playing field. She is a solid, mainstreamed student, normal, and even above average in academic ability. Her SAT scores are 1250. She has no education disabilities, education advocates, no special preferences, and no minority status since she is white and bright and middle class. The only scholarship money she qualifies for is $500 for belonging to the Girls 6 Feet Plus Club. Because she is not a valedictorian or star tennis player, sentimental favorites for college admission personnel, she has no chance to get into her first-choice colleges. She is considered boring by the admissions people and her mother and I have no special alumni relationship with any elite college. We need to pay more attention to our bright students who have no special labels, no special handicaps, no special status, before they become troubled, depressed, or doubt their abilities and settle for second best."

Said another parent, Linda Tafel, in the same news article, "The two-story elementary school in my neighborhood is financially pinched. But the school insisted that an elevator be built to serve the second floor at a cost of $75,000 to benefit one student in a wheelchair. The child's classes could have been held on the main floor, so no elevator would be required. We could have rehired two of the teachers who were fired, and thus reduced the average classroom size from 25:1 to 24:1. Why should the needs of one student prevail over the needs of three hundred other students in the school, under the guise that the law is the law. It is these federal requirements that cause resentment and feed the growing conservative movement which seeks to curtail silly spending."

Wrote Stacey Belle, a professor from a nearby state university: "Education subsidies for special education amount to nearly three times the spending for regular students. In some big-city districts which have a high proportionate number of disabled students, forty to fifty percent of the budget goes for fifteen to twenty percent of the students classified in need of special services. In some suburban school districts, $25,000 to 50,000 per year is spent on one child with severe disabilities, which may include transportation, a full-time nurse, special equipment, and extra tutoring. These kids get plenty of help, at the expense of others, and the issues of equity and intrinsic payoff can be raised. No one wants to raise these issues because it would be considered insensitive and politically incorrect. But just think—if we spent similar sums on average and above average learners, consider the benefits for society."

Professor Belle commented that in 1975, when the law was first passed to help educate students with disabilities, the federal government agreed to pick up about forty percent of the cost, and most states picked up another thirty to forty percent. Twenty-five years later, the feds are funding no more than twelve percent of the cost and in some recent years less than ten percent. "The pressure on local school districts is enormous, and some school administrators would rather not remove kids from regular classrooms because money is not available for special classes and special teachers."

Another teacher tried to sum up the situation, "I really don't worry about special education students or students who are classified with disabilities, since they have many advocate groups who promote their needs. There is a whole group of teachers, professors, and state education officials trained in special education who continuously put pressure on the system. The influence of these groups is illustrated by increased laws and court rulings that protect these students and provide increased school district and state services and funding: more than double and in some cases triple the expenditures for the average pupil. What I worry about is the balancing of the rights and needs of all students—and that as we continue to increase the monies for special education, we must make sure we do not rob Peter, that is, reduce the budget for 'regular' education, to pay Paul."

As a result of the flood of responses to the superintendent's original statement, a local reporter called for a follow-up comment: "Dr. Dumbo, do you have anything else to say about the issue of inclusion? Do you have any other words of wisdom?"

"Off the record, I could say that from now on before I make a public statement I will consult with Ann Landers or Dr. Joyce Brothers. I could tell you 'no comment' or that the issues will be studied at the next executive council meeting. None of the above, if I may be candid.

"For the record, the issues can only be discussed objectively by those who have no stake in the outcomes, rather who have lofty platonic motives. To say that those who express their discontent have good or bad motives is not to deny that some of the statements are based on sound judgment and others on hypocritical reasons. For every individual who feels compelled to criticize teachers and schools for sincere reasons, there are an equal number—possibly more—who do so for power, prestige, or some hidden agenda. The point is, it is fashionable to champion students and scold teachers and principals. Whether motives are altruistic or selfish, smart or silly, motives they are, so that when one claims that schools are good or bad, or a particular school program is good or bad, you must ask good for what and bad for whom?"

"Sir, what are you trying to say?"

"I will let you figure it out."

"Can I quote your last statement?"

"No. But you can say that I welcome the opinions of the people as representative of the democratic process on which this nation is founded. The voices of the people will be considered, but these voices are based on biases and personal opinions. Of course, biases and opinions are nothing to be embarrassed about. They are what they are, nothing more, nothing less. Honorable and reasonable people, despite their views, when given the facts, can compromise and reach agreement on policy."

"Sir, have you gone over the line? What are you saying? What does all this have to do with inclusion?"

"I have already commented. You wrote about it."

"But what about all those responses that were printed in the paper?"

"Well, you can report that three or four parents from the community were opposed to my decision to place a moratorium on inclusion. Off the record, once more, much of this controversy is fruitless. The superintendent is responsible for making school-wide decisions, and you have already printed that decision."

Dumbo continued. "You may think I'm poking fun or dissing you. No, I'm making a point. It boils down to common sense. There are certain principles worth defending and certain ones worth overlooking or ignoring.

"Remember, we are still off the record. Education is a strange phenomenon; the issues are never resolved. They lure us back into an arena that Cicero would relish. Education is socialization. Since society is always changing, the issues in education change. Those of us in education cannot escape from the issues; they will always be knocking at our front door. But this issue is not a perennial issue. It will come and pass, like so many other issues in education."

"Sir, what shall I report to the public?"

"Let me give you a tip. But, first, do you know that my critics call me the 'old fart' and 'Pinhead Peter'? Do you think that is proper or polite?"

"Enough of this chatter. Please, Dr. Dumbo."

"Tell the readers the district-wide reading scores on the state exam for the fourth grade are up from the 88th percentile to 92.3, and the eighth-grade scores rose six points and are now at the 94th percentile. Young man, I have to end our meeting. Off the record, I hope you never lose your sense of wonder and faith in people."

"Sir, what is your point?"

"The reading scores, young man. That's all that counts! Now, I have to attend a social for the newcomers club. Do you know fifty-five new elementary school parents have moved into town since the summer? That's fifty-five potential votes for the coming school bond referendum. I have to review my welcome speech. I'm introducing Sid, the school board president. Now, off the record, he is a navy man, like me, and a fine golfer. We play regularly on Saturdays. We have a foursome at Eisenhower Park. He broke eighty last week and made three birdies. I bet there will be several golfers in the audience. I think I'll make a reference to his game when I introduce him to the newcomers."

"What does all this have to do with inclusion?"

"Almost everything, young man, next to the reading scores, just about everything."

"But, what, what does this mean?"

"It means I'm the superintendent—now and in the future."

Questions to Consider

1. Why is special education an important national issue?

2. What are the teaching–learning issues involved with mainstreaming special education students?

3. What can teachers in regular classrooms do to help special education students who are assigned to their classrooms?

4. Why do you feel more students are being labeled as having a disability and being in need of special education?

5. Why do you believe arguments concerning inclusion have surfaced among school administrators, parents, and advocates of special education students?

6. What is your view of the superintendent? Now, remember to consider your own biases. For example, are you an advocate of exclusion or inclusion? Are you an advocate of straight talk or oblique talk for superintendents? Are you a potential recruit for the Old Boys' club? Do you believe school business should be conducted on the golf course?

7. Use the Internet to find out what school districts are doing to mainstream students. Does mainstreaming seem to work? What changes regarding inclusion have taken place during the past few years?

Recommended Readings

Tom Billington, *Separating, Losing, and Excluding Children* (New York: Routledge, 2000).

Jean B. Crockett and James M. Kauffman, *The Least Restrictive Environment* (Mahwah, NJ: Erlbaum, 2000).

Samuel A. Kirk, James Gallagher, and Nicholas Anastasiow, *Educating Exceptional Children*, 9th ed. (Boston: Houghton Mifflin, 2000).

Janet Lerner, *Learning Disabilities*, 8th ed. (Boston: Houghton Mifflin, 2000).

Tom Savage, *Teaching Self-Control Through Management and Discipline*, 2nd ed. (Needham Heights, MA: Allyn & Bacon, 1999).

25

Programs
for
Gifted Students

Concern for the education of gifted and talented students reached a high point during the 1950s and 1960s, coinciding with the post-*Sputnik* and Cold War era, and then began to decline throughout the closing years of the century. The commitment to educating the gifted and talented for the last several decades has been slight compared to efforts directed at the disadvantaged and other special populations, such as bilingual students or those with learning disabilities. Twenty-five years ago, two authorities (Passow and Tannenbaum) pointed out that only "a very small percentage of the gifted and talented population [was] being serviced by existing programs [about] 4 percent of the 1.5 to 2.5 million children." A similar statement (even worse) was made in 2001 by the president of the American Educational Research Association's "SIG Research on Gifted and Talented Students."

The breakdown of the federal budget and obligations for specially funded programs at the elementary and secondary levels, listed annually in the *Digest of Education Statistics*, does not even include gifted and talented students (even though it lists just about every other imaginable special student group you can think of), because the expenditures are next to zero; it has no impact on the budget. Similarly, there is absolutely no federal legislation concerning the gifted and talented among the 150 federal acts, amendments, and programs enacted between 1960 and 2000. There may be a program at a school that you know about, but federal inaction says much more than one isolated story.

A low funding priority and lack of trained personnel, coupled with few pressure groups for the gifted and talented, result in a scarcity of money and programs for these children—a complete about-face from the post-*Sputnik* and Cold War era, highlighted by the concerns of Arthur Bestor, Jerome Bruner, James Conant, John Gardner, and Admiral Hyman Rickover. Too many educators and policy makers today think these types of students are smart enough to get by on their own, and they don't need extra recognition, extra "strokes," or extra support. But it is a travesty to overlook and ignore these students. At all levels of government, these students may be the real disadvantaged students—in terms of low education priority, program development, and funding. This group has no politician, no educator of influence, no political or social group speaking for them.

Almost everyone seems to say that these students can make it on their own, which is false, since 15 to 20 percent of gifted and talented students have traditionally dropped out of high school—some largely because of boredom, some because of personal baggage, and some because of pregnancy. Yet these are the same children and youth who have the most potential to shape our future world, especially in areas of science, medicine, and technology. The political, social, and business sectors need these youth; they represent a large portion of the future leadership for society, and they should be nurtured at the school level.

The final issue or question, which the case study revolves around, is this: Can we afford and should we be concerned with the gifted and talented at the elementary school levels? The high schools seem to have many more programs for these students. Why? Does this reflect political and social priorities, the academic curriculum, or the fact that there are many more subject-based teachers?

ISSUES

Tully Elementary School is located in an upper-middle-class suburb of a large Midwestern city. It is one of five elementary schools in the school district, and it is a small school consisting of 440 students. The village population is 94 percent white, 5 percent Asian, and 1 percent black. All of the parents in the community are professionals or businesspeople, and nearly 90 percent—wives and husbands alike—have at least a bachelor's degree. Property taxes are becoming an issue, however, since taxes have more than doubled in the last eight years.

Poverty, crime, and drugs are not issues in the school or community. The favorite topic of discussion among the parents is where they are vacationing for Christmas or spring break. Summer camp for their children ranks second, and what college or university the older brothers and sisters are applying to or attending runs a close third.

This year the big controversy in the school is whether there should be special enrichment classes in math and science, starting at the third grade and extending to the sixth grade. Most extra program resources, in the past as well as now, have been earmarked for both advanced and remedial reading programs. The advanced and talented readers are exposed to the Junior Great Books program; depending on their grade level, students read fifteen to thirty books of their choice throughout the year. Remedial reading programs comprise student–teacher ratios of ten to one and are supplemented three times a week with one-to-one tutoring by parent volunteers and teacher aides.

National assessment scores at Tully Elementary School reflect where time, effort, and money are being spent. Reading scores for the school are at the 93rd percentile nationwide; in mathematics they are at the 67th percentile; in science they fall in the 74th percentile. The teachers and parents are meeting now, at an afternoon open forum with coffee and cake, to discuss the merits of a special enrichment mathematics program. Parents and teachers have mixed feelings on the issue and are about evenly divided. Parents whose children might qualify for the math program support it. Teachers tend to be divided on the issue according to progressive and essentialist philosophical views; the so-called progressives view the program as unnecessary, elitist, or putting too much pressure on the children who qualify. So-called essentialists feel it's an important program; it helps beef up the curriculum, and it is good for the children, school, and community.

One of the parents, John Suderland, notes the following: "Our math and science achievement scores should be higher, given the type of students and community. We need to tap our talented math and science students for their own potential and the good of society. We may be losing future mathematicians or scientists because of our lax attitude."

Yu Shuq Liu, a fourth-grade teacher, whose own teacher training emphasized reading and writing methodology and minimal math, put it this way: "Why this sudden urge for enrichment math programs? There is no Cold War. School success is based on reading. If you can't read, then you can't succeed. If you can't solve math programs, then you only do poorly in one subject."

Miroslaw Barraza, a sixth-grade teacher, had a different view and raised two points. Although there was no threat of war, he pointed out: "This country is affected by economic competition on a global level. Much new technology and knowledge is based on science and math." The discussion then diverted to the trends that suggest many scientific, mathematical, and computer-based jobs in the United States were being filled by foreign-born professionals, and without this brain-drain from other countries, the United States would be unable to fulfill its scientific and technological needs. "Do you really believe any society can afford to ignore its gifted students, not to nurture math and science talent among its youth?"

"I think that we need to nurture all our youth, otherwise this nation will decline. Our gifted students will manage once they reach high school and college," said Joyce Fine, a parent whose three sons were not gifted. "There are plenty of honors and advanced placement programs at the high school level, and many big-city school districts and metropolitan areas have special math and science high schools for gifted and bright students. Do we really need these kind of programs at the elementary level? Do kids need this type of pressure?"

Barraza responded, "Advanced classes and gifted programs should not only be offered at the secondary school level, but also at the elementary level. The problem is that there are no advocate groups for the gifted making this demand."

"Somehow the vast majority of gifted and bright students find the fast track, the Ivy League colleges, and the corporate board rooms," said Fine. "I really feel the gifted do not merit special consideration."

"What we need to do is broaden the definitions of gifted and talented, and not only single out those with analytical and verbal abilities," remarked Liu. "Those who are creative, artistic, and have people skills and who are in the middle and low end of the academic continuum might appear to be gifted, at least much brighter than we originally thought."

"But the schools already do this. We have gifted music and art programs and sports scholarships," said Suderland, a parent whose child was one of the top readers in his class. "What Ms. Liu is suggesting is that we mask or water down programs for the gifted and brighter student."

"Not really," responded Liu. "I'm trying to go beyond one-size-fits-all thinking. I recall Howard Gardner's theory of multiple intelligences and Robert Sternberg's method of identifying the gifted in areas of analysis, creativity, and practical or social leadership skills. Once we go beyond traditional verbal and numerical areas of cognition, a more diverse group of students from ethnic and socioeconomic levels, is identified as gifted."

"I still feel that once we get into novel ways of describing gifted and highly intelligent students," mentioned Barraza, "we enter into the arena of politics and we ignore the importance of verbal and analytical abilities. We start rewarding soft subjects, soft teaching methods, and soft standards under the guise of serving disadvantaged and diverse populations. Most federal and compensatory programs are already earmarked for these students."

Barraza then struck a sensitive chord. "I believe many of us who teach at Tully are well versed in reading principles and children's literature, but feel uncomfortable teaching math or science concepts because our professional training did not prepare us, and still others feel uncomfortable teaching highly talented students because they represent a challenge for us."

Hoto Keiji, teacher and advocate of gifted children, stated: "If you read the research on what gifted students think about their education, more than half report they are not challenged in their schoolwork. That is a national tragedy—a waste of brain power and human capital. We cannot depend on the average teacher, untrained in working with the gifted or talented, to provide a relevant, interesting, and worthwhile curriculum for these students, especially in a heterogeneous class of twenty-five or more students."

Barraza noted, "The biggest enemy is time—extra academic time needed for low-achieving and average students to absorb the basic knowledge and skills of the subject; consequently, there is minimal time remaining to be concerned with discovery, inquiry, and problem solving."

"Shouldn't all students have the opportunity to learn relevant, interesting, and worthwhile subject matter?" asked Suderland. "Why can't teachers stress high-order thinking for all students?"

Liu responded, "Of course, all students should be provided with a challenging curriculum that requires their full intellectual abilities. But it is not that simple. Teachers are often unsure of their ability to teach very bright students—especially because they often become withdrawn or disruptive when confronted with practice and drill, or repetitive work, making them easy to confuse with those of average or low ability."

"I don't want to sound like some wild-eyed doofus," said Barraza, "but the vast majority of teachers prefer to teach linear thinkers and right-answer-oriented students who are willing to listen and please their teachers, copy by rote from the blackboard, and regurgitate the textbook—all of which coincide with sequential models of teaching. Sounds boring, low-level, and robotic—you bet! Teachers prefer straight-arrow students who will give them minimal trouble, ask few questions, speak in black and white and not speak in shades of gray, and not waste time. Remember, most teachers are content driven, time driven, and test driven. We have a certain amount of content to teach in a certain amount of time and then to be tested, as part of outcome-based and standard-based education. Few teachers have the self-confidence to teach creative and divergent thinkers."

"The basic characteristic of the gifted is that they learn material in much less time than other students, and remember more and have a larger knowledge base," asserted Liu, "making the spiral curriculum or the need to reinforce previous learning irrelevant and boring for them. They also process ideas and concepts at a more abstract and complex way than their classmates. Teachers need to provide alternative activities and enriching curricula without it turning into busy work or extra credit for content they have already mastered. Few teachers have been trained to recognize and teach these students."

Keiji then pointed to a related problem. "Other teachers may feel unconcerned about giving special attention to kids who are quick to understand the work while so many are struggling. This attitude of indifference is reinforced by the lack of an agreed-on definition of who is gifted and talented and the lack of legal or federal requirements to educate these students to their maximum potential. In general, schools receive very little or no extra funding for these students, no extra books or materials, no pressure from government agencies. So why bother?"

"Is there any data on this lack of funding?" asked one of the parents.

"You bet," answered Keiji. "I was skimming the *NASSP Bulletin* in the principal's office last week. Since the 1970s, only two cents of every hundred government dollars for education has been spent on the gifted. I read elsewhere that federal spending for the gifted is so miniscule that its *Digest of Education Statistics* doesn't even include this area of spending, despite all the other special education programs it lists."

"My real concern is that there is a growing trend among educators and politicians to dismantle special programs for the gifted in the name of egalitarianism and diversity," said another parent whose child was eligible for the special gifted program.

"Actually, identification of gifted science and especially math students is not easy," commented Liu. "Many may not be achieving at their potential level, may not show unusual interest, effort, or motivation during instruction; many may not even score unusually high on standardized tests because the content measures mastery of facts and methods and low-level associations. Gifted students think at different and higher levels than those measured by these tests."

Barraza nodded in agreement and then stated: "The vast majority of elementary teachers have difficulty identifying and teaching these students. Elementary teachers are too busy focusing on basic math and science, and have little time to note the different thinking processes of bright and talented kids. Most teachers prefer docile students who give us right answers, not unusual answers that make us ponder or slow us down in class discussion. With all of these new state testing standards, the idea is to teach facts, to prepare students to answer a particular knowledge base—not to encourage independent and complex thought."

"How can we identify these students?" asked one of the parents.

"What makes these students different," said Keiji, "is the way they internalize, modify, and reshape problems; the strategies they use are sometimes unusual or unconventional. They are willing to play with ideas, see things in different ways, and have a high tolerance for working out problems for a long period of time—considering different paths and methods of arriving at solutions. Teachers who feel a student is gifted in math or science need to observe and discuss with students how they are processing information, how they arrive at solutions, and the different array of levels on which they think—whether they are intuitive, multiple, abstract, three-dimensional, and so on. This is no easy task for a teacher who is content driven or concerned about practice and drill or whether the students in class are learning the basics. Gifted students, once identified, need to be regrouped and exposed to more challenging work."

Then Fine, who felt one of her children was having trouble in math, asked, "What about the kids who need special tutoring in math?" She continued, "I'm against all these enriched or elitist programs. A few children receive most of the attention at the expense of others. These programs create a few winners and lots of losers. The bright children will succeed without these programs."

Liu, who was one of the more progressive teachers, then pointed out, "Average children receive little attention and many fall into the cracks throughout school. It's the high-end and low-end children that receive most of our attention and resources, and there is little need for another program that recognizes bright and talented children."

Henrick Ullman, a fifth-grade teacher who believed in the old notion of meritocracy, replied: "Your points are important. But we already have a math tutoring program for the slower students who wish to come in early before classes begin, and we have many after-school classes, activities, and clubs for all students, including what you call average students."

One of the other parents, whose gifted child was often late for class in the morning and sometimes in trouble with his teacher, got up and responded with emotion. "I'm not sure if the school meets the needs or interests of all of our students, especially those who are very creative, much smarter, or a little different than the others. A number of students feel bored with school, and others feel isolated or different from their peers. My child is made to feel like a nerd and is often ridiculed by his classmates. The schools have so many special tests and labels; it is so easy to mislabel children who are different, including some very talented or creative students who don't fit into the norm."

"I know exactly what you're talking about," said Trudy Fuzuki, a parent and attorney. "My older child was several years ahead of his classmates in math and often miserable in school because he was forced to learn in the same way and at the same rate as his classmates. Not until he reached middle school was he put into an advanced class. During his whole elementary experience, he felt different, isolated, and alone. He only had one other friend who was in the same boat with him."

"The real problem is," commented Suderland, "that there is pressure in the schools to detrack and degroup and only allow heterogeneous classes—disregarding gifted students like your son. Gifted students are asked to learn about democracy and socialization through heterogeneous grouping and cooperative learning groups. The mixed-ability groupings benefit average and low-ability students, according to conventional research, but gifted and highly able students need to be grouped together by ability or achievement levels for the majority of the school day in *all* academic case subjects, and provided with acceleration opportunities."

"I know that all too well," responded Fuzuki. "This is why I'm thinking of a private school or charter school for my little girl, who is bright like my older son. The results of this meeting determine what my husband and I decide to do. We even thought about home schooling, but our jobs prevent it. However, I understand why home schooling is gaining in popularity."

"Under the guise of school improvement and democracy, there is a new reform model to integrate advanced learning and high-order thinking programs into the general curriculum," noted Ullman. "What originated as special programs for gifted and talented students is being prescribed for all students in many schools. The ideas of Howard Gardner and Robert Sternberg, and now Joseph Renzulli, have been adapted to include multiple aptitudes and potentials so that all students can be included in programs for the gifted. The new reform models reflect democratic ideas that accommodate a wider range of individual differences in the general student population, at the expense of focusing on students with high intelligence and other cognitive abilities."

"I guess if you are progressive, liberal, or a proponent of diversity, you support the idea," noted Keiji. "What happens if you believe in high academic standards, test scores and grades—and reject subjective criteria and view background and experience as a proxy for race or eliminating academic standards. Am I to be labeled as morally corrupt, an irrelevant technocrat, some elitist or racist—and then dismissed?"

Keiji continued: "Asking less of underachievers perpetuates underachievement. Twisting the concept of gifted and talented so everyone feels they have some special gift or talent blurs or even eliminates standards. It's wonderful to talk about excellent plumbers or waiters, but it's more important for society to produce excellent engineers and physicians."

Fred Lunenburg, the vice principal of the school, then commented, "I would prefer to think that the school does an excellent job meeting the needs of the vast majority of students. This is not a perfect system, and I guess a few children do fall into the cracks. The point is, however, a math or science enrichment program means we need to hire another experienced teacher. This amounts to $40,000 to $60,000 plus benefits." He then said that only ten to fifteen students per grade level would benefit, and he wasn't sure whether all grade levels K–6 would have the program. "If Tully School gets another math teacher, then the other schools in the district might want one." Given the mood of the community regarding property taxes, and the general reform opinion promoting mixed-ability grouping, he wasn't sure whether the superintendent or school board would recommend the new gifted program for such a small number of students.

Obviously, Barraza, Keiji, and Fuzuki were for the special program, but another parent asked what other schools in the state were doing for their gifted—to get an idea or benchmark before voting.

The vice principal spoke up. "Policies for educating the gifted vary among the states, and really depend on the prevailing attitude of individual schools and local administrators. The vast majority of elementary schools favor pull-out programs, but they are often limited to once or twice a week and are not too effective, and high schools favor academic tracks and special classes such as honors and advanced placement. A few school counselors encourage their gifted to attend special summer programs at colleges, and large cities such as New York, Chicago, and Los Angeles have special high schools devoted to science, math, and technology."

Fine, whose children ranged from average to slightly above average readers, asked: "Why do we have to put these students into a special group, given mixed research on whether homogeneous grouping is beneficial for high ability or gifted students? Don't we risk ghettoizing these students? Why does some parent have to worry about his or her child who is in the top five percent of his or her class? The worst case scenario is the kid will not go to Harvard; he will get admitted into Vanderbilt or Vassar."

"You raise several good points," said Ullman. "First, in heterogeneous groups, and especially cooperative learning groups, gifted and talented students are frequently mistreated and used. I realize there are some strong advocates of heterogeneous grouping who say otherwise. But very bright and gifted students often assume the role of teacher or tutor, seldom the role of learner. Second, placing gifted or talented students in a special group, according to the research I read, has a positive effect on their achievement levels and self-esteem. These students are usually bored and tune out in heterogeneous groups, unless the teacher is exceptional and able to meet their special needs and interests."

"We have very bright and gifted students competing for top rankings in their high school graduating classes," said Suderland, "because the colleges look at the academic ranking. In the high school where my oldest son attends, there are students who refuse to take nonhonor courses like music or art, because they are worth less in the ranking system. These students have figured out the system by junior high school, and their parents have figured it out when the kids were in the womb."

"I know a parent who sued a nearby school district because his son had to share valedictorian honors with two others who took fewer honor classes," declared Keiji. "I know someone else who sued another district because the advisor failed to tell his daughter she was eligible for another honor class and wound up in second place with a 104.7 average next to someone with a 104.8 average."

Another parent spoke. "I really can't feel sorry for all those overachievers or gifted and talented students who wind up at these so-called second best places."

Fuzuki joined in, arguing that a lot of jealousy and resentment is directed at gifted and talented students, and that the conversation was teetering in that direction. "It is wrong to take the attitude that these kids have it all or are spoiled. Many of these kids have their own mental health and personal problems. They cannot find other class-mates who fully understand them or want to socialize with them. These kids need spe-cial programs to challenge them, to help them make friends, so they better enjoy school. They have rights, too."

Fine remarked: "This sounds like the 'Rich Parents School Reform Movement' or the 'Gifted Society of Education.' I'll cut to the chase. Educators need to be a little less concerned with identifying or teaching students who feel they are better than others and more concerned about helping all students. This is not a fascist society, where all the trains must run on time, rather it is a democratic society where majority needs are respected. I don't think the programs you talk about do anything to improve schools overall. Only a few elite students will benefit. If we want to raise math and science scores in our school, we should think about all the students, especially those who need additional help in their studies."

Fine continued. "I'm curious, however. Exactly, what type of program do you advo-cate for our gifted students?"

The vice principal responded. "I'm against the typical pull-out program at the ele-mentary level. We need advanced classes, similar to the ones offered at the middle and high school levels. In many cases, if the elementary school is too small and its resources limited or it has very few gifted math or science students, then the students should join other elementary students within the district at the neighborhood middle school. Similarly, those in middle schools might have to take courses at the high school level, and so on. Some small, rural school districts might have to collaborate and bring gifted students together for weekly or monthly classes, so they can be taught by teachers who are specialists in their subjects."

"I'm a believer in cable TV, computerized courses, on-line and Internet courses, and virtual classrooms serving as a vehicle for expanding geographical boundaries and increasing student participation," said Ullman. "We don't lack resources. If we did, however, I would tell school officials to bang on the doors of local and regional computer firms, engineering firms, and scientific, medical, and research companies for grants and donations, instructional hardware, and specialized personnel."

The vice principal interrupted. "As for the exact program, I urge a pull-out program five days a week in math and science for grades one through four. From grade five on, I urge placing a cluster or special group of the top students into an accelerated class. Finally, schools need to hire teachers who are highly competent in subject areas and have a strong professional and academic commitment toward their subjects. This does not mean we preclude methodology, but I find too many elementary teachers more knowledgable in pedagogical principles than in content areas, more knowledgable in teaching reading and literacy than math or science."

"I notice you didn't address the issue of race or class," commented Ullman. "Are you advocating a new or modified form of segregation, with code words such as gifted or ability to mask the outcomes?"

Lunenburg answered: "I am fully aware that this criticism has infected the educational landscape in the last ten years or so. I reject the idea that gifted education is elitist or racist because few minorities, except for Asian-Americans, enroll in these programs. If you want to use race and diversity as a yardstick or as a criterion to qualify a program, then what about school orchestras? School theater? Basketball? The chess or math teams? More girls than boys participate in school orchestras. The percentage of homosexuals performing in school plays exceeds the national student percentage. Basketball has become a black sport: just watch the typical college or pro game. Chess and math at the local high school level is forty to fifty percent Asian-American, but the student population is less than five percent Asian-American. Where do we draw the line? Just because some program is overwhelmingly white or middle class, do we eliminate it? Do high schools eliminate golf, tennis, lacrosse, volleyball, and swimming also, because there are more white athletes than minority athletes, more middle-class than lower-class students? Maybe we should also eliminate Latin, French, and German since few minorities enroll in these foreign language courses."

Questions to Consider

1. To what extent do you agree with Ms. Liu's comment: "School success is based on reading. If you can't read, then you can't succeed in school." How do international factors, such as threat of war or economic competition, affect the curriculum?

2. We have more average students ("C" and "B" students) than exceptional students. Given that we have limited resources, where should the emphasis be? Do too many average students fall through the cracks? How do we balance the needs of all students: talented, average, and slow students?

3. To what extent do you feel talented and gifted students, especially the creative ones, are bored with school? Mislabeled in school? Receive too much attention in school?

4. The vice principal was unsure about support for a special math teacher to meet the needs of a small group of children. What are the issues in this community? Do you feel that elementary schools—rich and poor alike—need enriched math programs? Why or why not?

5. Whose teacher views (Barraza, Keiji, Liu, or Ullman) do you favor? Why?

6. Whose parental views (Fine, Fuzuki, or Suderland) do you favor? Why?

7. Interview teachers in a nearby school to determine their views about gifted programs. To what extent do these views coincide with your views? Report to the class.

Recommended Readings

Benjamin S. Bloom, *Developing Talent in Young People* (New York: Ballentine, 1985).

Howard Gardner, *Multiple Intelligences* (New York: Basic Books, 1993).

George F. Madaus, *The Influence of Testing on Teaching Math and Science in Grades 4–12* (Chestnut Hill, MA: Boston College, 1992).

David Perkins, *Smart Schools: Better Thinking and Learning for Every Child* (New York: Free Press, 1992).

Robert J. Sternberg, *Successful Intelligence* (New York: Plume, 1997).

26

Part I: Diversity and the Global Village*

Since the publication of *A Nation at Risk* in 1983, there has been a slight average increase in science and mathematics course work among graduating high school students, about 3/10 of one year (for example, 2.5 to 2.8 years). But the data are not impressive when comparisons are made with high school seniors in other advanced, technological countries. Japanese, South Korean, and Hong Kong school students, for example, average 1¼ science courses per year and 1½ math courses per year, including calculus and statistics.

One result is that Japanese, South Korean, and Hong Kong students consistently outperform American students on international tests in science and mathematics, and the gaps increase in the higher grades in part because of the cumulative effects of more courses and more hours in science and math. Put differently, in the last thirty years there have been three international mathematics and science studies (TIMSS) comparing industrialized countries in grades 4, 8, and 12. The conclusion for all three studies is clear: The longer American students stay in school, the farther they fall behind their counterparts in most industrialized nations. In the last TIMSS report, U.S. fourth-grade students in math ranked eighth out of eighteen industrialized countries that participated, and in science they tied for third place. In the eighth grade, U.S. students ranked below twenty-three out of thirty-eight industrialized countries in math and ranked below fourteen in science. In the twelfth grade, twenty industrialized countries were tested. U.S. students ranked last in math. Eighteen industrialized countries were tested in science, and U.S. students ranked below sixteen countries. While the international average math/science scores were 500, the U.S. average in math was 461 and in science 480.

The picture of comparisons worsens when education spending is compared on an international level. Because it is unreasonable to make comparisons with Third World or developing nations, most of the U.S. government comparisons are made with countries similar to ours. The United States spends 4.8 percent of its gross domestic product on education; we ranked tenth among the twenty countries listed in the *Digest of Education Statistics*. But our expenditures per student are higher—second only to Switzerland.

One way to view these patterns is to conclude that the United States makes an average effort to finance education. Because its capacity for funding education is high, an average effort is insufficient. In America we also have very high academic expendi-

---

*Chapters 26 and 27 are interrelated.

tures. Our nation devotes resources to many different public areas, especially social
security, health, and medicine; therefore, the argument can be made that we are actually doing very well in our overall social and education funding patterns.

When we look at what we spend and what we produce, we learn sadly that our output, as measured in the form of international achievement test scores, is very low compared to that of other industrialized nations. Even worse, countries like Japan, South
Korea, and Singapore rank low in education spending, yet they have the highest math and
science scores, while we have near the lowest in the eighth and twelfth grades. The inference here is that U.S. school expenditures do not correlate with academic output; other
variables are more important.

Among the common reasons or excuses given for the consistently low scores of
American students are these:

1. American twelfth-grade students average almost one year younger (18.0 compared to 18.7) than their international counterparts.
2. About 25 percent of the test items in math and science reflect topics that are not
   studied by American test takers.
3. About 20 to 33 percent of American middle school and high school science and
   math teachers are teaching out of license; furthermore, nearly half of those certified to teach science and math are not qualified to teach the courses they teach.
   For example, a science teacher may not be qualified to teach physics (only biology
   and chemistry) and a math teacher may not be qualified to teach calculus (only
   algebra and geometry).
4. A larger proportion of American teachers quit the profession, especially in the first
   five years (about 50 percent in inner-city schools), so that teachers in other industrialized nations are on the average considerably more experienced than American
   teachers. In addition, teachers in Europe and Asia are afforded much more prestige than in the United States and, in fact, many of the politicians and foreign ministers abroad were former teachers and professors.
5. American science and math textbooks are numerous—some above average, some
   below average in quality—whereas textbooks in other countries are approved by
   the ministry of education so there is consistency of coverage. Our textbooks
   emphasize breadth of topics, to please a wide audience (15,000 different school
   districts) at the expense of depth of topics. The outcome is that American textbooks (and teachers who rely on these textbooks) foster superficial learning of a
   large body of information, while students of other countries with a ministry of education have more time to think about procedures, to frame hypotheses, make predictions, and acquire skills to conduct experiments and contrast ideas and findings.
6. American students have less homework (23 percent of eleventh graders report no
   assigned homework, 14 percent do not do their homework, and 26 percent do
   less than one hour per day of homework) and engage in more social and out-of-
   school activities than their international counterparts.
7. American students average 3.5 hours per day of TV viewing, not to mention computer time, and we know there is an inverse relationship between TV viewing and
   student achievement, especially after the second grade since the positive effects of
   watching *Sesame Street* and other language skill programs are irrelevant after age 7.

8. European and Asian students have a longer school day and school year with European countries averaging about 200 days and Asian countries averaging about 220 days, compared to the United States, which has about a 180-day school calendar.

9. Student poverty among American students is the highest, about 21 to 25 percent. It is nearly 50 percent higher than any other industrialized country; next comes Australia with 14 percent and Canada with 13.5 percent. Moreover, we know that poverty clearly correlates in an inverse relationship with student achievement. In addition, we have among the highest or highest student rates of drug addiction, student violence, gang activity, and teenage pregnancy among industrialized nations.

10. Finally, the breakdown of the American family is well documented; more than 50 percent of American students live with a single head of household; this number approaches 75 percent in our big cities where student achievement is the lowest compared to other parts of the country.

ISSUES

We will always be at war; today, it is an economic war with Western Europe and Asia and a terrorist war with Middle Eastern groups. If our schools and colleges don't upgrade standards by testing and tracking students, demanding more homework, beefing up the curriculum, insisting on tougher teacher certification requirements, and holding teachers accountable, then we will lose the war—slowly but surely—first by our decline in human capital and then by our decline in economic capital.

History is strewn with visions of new eras and new civilizations that in the end have fallen to the wayside. Our children's future and their children's future is at stake. If we are to maintain our international stature, then we will need to improve our human capital by reforming our schools. If not, we will eventually decline or become second rate—like every great civilization, since the Persians, Egyptians, Greeks, and Romans to the Aztecs, Incas, and Mayans; like every great empire, from Charlemagne, the Hapsburgs, and Romanovs to the Arabics, Ottomans, and Mongols; or like every great colonial superpower before the United States—from the shrinkage of the Spanish, Portuguese, English, and French empires to second- and third-rate status, to the complete demise of the Third Reich and the Soviet Union. The rise and fall of civilizations and superpowers is inevitable, similar to the rise and fall of plant species, animal species, and people. Everything that grows must die.

What should our teachers and schools do to help change the course of events? This was the question asked of teachers sitting in a small college seminar on American education, with their professor and a guest speaker.

Jorge Rosanvallon, a science teacher at an inner-city school, was the first to comment: "I've heard similar predictions for the last twenty years, that is, since I started to teach. More than seventy-five percent of students in my school are unable to read at grade level, much less grasp the basic concepts of science or math. My school consists of 2,400 students, including 525 high school seniors. We have one physics class this year, enrolling seventeen students. A couple of years ago I recommended that the school offer an advanced placement course in chemistry and biology for college credit. My colleagues laughed at me. When I told my colleagues that Japanese and Korean high school students take an equivalent of twenty-five percent more math and science courses than their American counterparts, they told me I should wake up to reality: that the educational issues in our school deal with reading, writing, classroom management, and drugs."

"Jorge is merely touching the surface. I teach in a big-city junior high school where the kids are at an age in which they lack maturity and inner controls; they readily fly off the handle and engage in disruptive behavior," said Jason Bentley, a language arts teacher. "Because many of these children have learning disabled and special education labels, we cannot suspend or expel them easily; there are even legal restrictions when we try to enforce discipline. We cannot even get substitute teachers on a regular basis for our school, and the ones that are recruited often refuse to come back the next day—or worse, get sick and walk out in the middle of the day. Last year, 21,500 sub requests went unfilled in the Chicago schools; in L.A. the number was nearly 40,000. I don't think it's much different in the sunny parts of Houston or Miami. Many of my colleagues can't cope with the social and psychological problems the kids bring with them to school, so academic problems rarely get addressed."

Bentley continued, "I read recently in *Phi Delta Kappan* for one of my other graduate courses that the teacher turnover in the twenty-five largest city school systems ranges between ten and fifteen percent per year and teacher absentees—largely for purposes of 'R and R'—averages 12.5 days per year or three hundred percent higher than suburban schools. The remaining teachers give up and mark time. Why? Those in power to change the system already have. Believe me—indifference and despair are contagious."

Rosanvallon, who was flipping through the *U.S. Digest of Education Statistics*, spoke up. "Government officials, businesspeople, and academics, since the days of 'Camelot' and the Great Society have explored solutions to inner-city schools to no avail. A six-year-old in the inner city has a twelve percent chance of learning to read and write at the ninth-grade level or higher by the time he is seventeen years old. Nearly fifty percent of these youth drop out of school by age sixteen. Nationwide, 160,000 students miss school daily—more than half because of drugs, gangs, intimidation, or fear. Add that to the two hundred teachers who are attacked each day in school and you better understand the phrases *war zone, battle fatigue*, and *teacher turnover*. Internationally, the learning gap is dramatic, and the math and science wars are being lost in our inner-city schools, not in our factories or with our battleships."

"I was attending New York University when Frank Riessman, who was teaching there in 1962, popularized the term *culturally deprived*. In the following year, Harry Passow, at Columbia University, used the terms *depressed areas* and *disadvantaged children*," said Professor Anatoly Kirpichenko. "In 1950, the number of deprived or disadvantaged students in our twenty-five largest cities was one out of ten. In 1960, the number was one out of three; in 1970, it was one out of two. By 1990 the figure was ninety percent and in the year 2000 it exceeded ninety-five percent. I guess a lot of these demographic changes have something to do with immigration trends, minority birth rates, and white flight. Eventually, schools in depressed areas, what we now call the inner city, are burdened by the weight of poverty; they drain our educational budgets, and many of their products drain our social and welfare programs. Most important, their students depress our international test scores and depress our human capital."

Prakash Srinivasa is a foreign language teacher in a suburban high school. His school offers up to four years of German, French, and Spanish; there is also a three-year sequence in Latin. Colleagues in his department feel that he is too idealistic. Why? "I suggested a foreign language sequence in Mandarin. High school educators will soon wake up and realize that the Japanese are no longer at our door steps, rather it will be the Chinese. More people in the world speak Mandarin as a first language than English, and the future economic market with the most potential is in China, not Japan and not Western Europe.

"American businesspeople and government representatives don't know the language, customs, or culture of China—and are at a disadvantage in understanding and dealing with them. We have ignored this sleeping giant for too long. Is it old-fashioned stupidity or ethnocentrism that causes us to ignore 1.2 billion people or twenty percent of the world's population? Of course, some people feel the Chinese live in some far off place and are still preoccupied with fish-grabbing and gathering rice in muddy waters. Others are preoccupied with 9/11 and see terrorists at every airport. My colleagues also remark that English is the international language, and we need not be concerned about whether we speak Japanese or Chinese; the world's educated populace speaks English; the international business populace speaks English. I think my colleagues, and other educators, are living in the past by offering only German, French, Spanish, and Latin."

"Prakash's point is interesting, but I think the biggest problem is the mind-set of progressive critics and reformers," said Shakil Hjalmar, a junior high school math teacher. "Consider all the interest and academic time spent on sex education, ranging from classroom demonstrations of proper condom use, lessons on gender bias, alternative lifestyles, and AIDS prevention; consider the new emphasis on social skills training—what to say if your friend wants to play PlayStation and you prefer chess, how to make friends in school or what fork to use for salads, and how posture and facial expressions influence people; consider the emphasis on diversity, whether it really matters that northwestern Montana is a highly diverse area, almost like Houston and Miami, according to a multicultural map I'm required to display in my room. Does it really matter that whites are now Anglos, blacks are now African-Americans, and Spanish-Americans are now called Hispanics?"

"With all these fads in the curriculum," remarked Srinivasa, "it is not hard to see why reading, math, and science scores don't improve much, or why if you ask American eighth-grade students on national or international tests where Indonesia or Pakistan is, a goodly number will tell you it is a city in Europe or in Africa. A substantial percentage of students living in Boston cannot even name the six New England states. We have had ambitious national reform programs—lots of hoopla from post-*Sputnik* to the present national standards movement—but progress has been minimal."

Professor Kirpichenko spoke. "Allow me to provide a brief historical overview of the *Sputnik* and Cold War era, since you mention it. I recall the works of Bestor, Conant, Koerner, and Rickover. We would label these educators as essentialist philosophers. They all sought to improve the education of college-bound, gifted, and talented students, and to increase and improve science, math, and foreign language courses, in order to beat the Soviets and to ensure the safety of our skies and oceans. Similarly, they blamed progressive educators, especially John Dewey, for watering down the curriculum and betraying academic excellence.

"During this period I recall Wernher Von Braun, the German-educated missile expert, reminiscing about his own education and the superiority of the European education system before the U.S. Senate Committee in 1958. Let me read from a passage:

> I do not remember that I ever attended any classes in Europe on 'family life' or 'human relations,' or subjects like boy–girl relations. We just learned reading, writing, and arithmetic in the lower schools. Later on they taught us technical and scientific subjects, but nothing else.

"Von Braun's friend and president of the California Institute of Technology, Lee DuBridge, also testified on the same day. He argued that a student's right to an education is a right which persists as far as his intellectual capacities and ambitions should take him. Unfortunately, the senators did not ask Von Braun or DuBridge what schools or society should do with the intellectually less able student, those secondary students who cannot add three-digit numbers or write a coherent sentence. But some would argue that had we listened to the advice of Von Braun and DuBridge, we would not be in such a mess now—worrying that high school students today are posting lower SAT scores than during the post-*Sputnik* era, despite the fact that we have quadrupled our spending per student (after inflation) since Von Braun and DuBridge testified before the Senate."

"Are you one of those conservative educators who continue to blame Progressives for a soft and watered-down curriculum?" asked Srinivasa. "Are you advocating that we reduce education spending? Or are you saying we should emphasize academic tracking and the 'survival of the fittest' or smartest?"

"Of course not. The political pendulum has swung too far to the left on college campuses to advocate a Darwinist philosophy. My colleagues overwhelmingly voted blue and would ostracize me, and my department head would hand me my early retirement papers."

The professor's guest speaker, L.L. Fusarelli from Plainsville University, spoke up. "In the 1950s, you might recall, there were many more viable job options for high school graduates, even dropouts. We were growing economically, and other industrialized nations were still in shambles because of the big war. Brawny and slow-witted young men could work in factories, steel mills, and shipyards, build roads and bridges, cut down trees and work in paper mills, mine our coal, and drill for oil. But now our industrial society has just about disappeared, except for a few thousand factories that are still north of the Rio. The $25/hour union worker has been replaced by the $8/hour hamburger helper and telemarketing operator."

"Where did women place in the job equation?" asked Rosanvallon.

"As underpaid semiprofessionals, such as teachers, nurses, or social workers, or as nonpaid housewives and mothers," remarked Fusarelli. "I guess the Betty Crocker image prevailed among most married women."

"Thank goodness for Betty Friedan and Gloria Steinem."

"Unquestionably they helped, but the real breakthrough was the transformation from an industrialized society to an information society, which reduced the importance of muscle power," said Kirpichenko.

Bentley, who has been teaching in the junior high school for nearly twenty-five years, interrupted the conversation. "I've heard these voices of doom and gloom since the Cold War era. Ivan could read and calculate better than Johnny. The military fear of the USSR has been replaced today by terrorists and the economic competition with the Japanese, Koreans, and Germans. These are homogeneous nations that do not have ethnic and racial problems which spill over in their schools or society. We are a nation of many nations, but our immigrant population is driven to succeed and provides the basis for our future mathematicians, scientists, and computer wizards. Thank goodness for brain-drain from other nations to this one. It only takes a handful of talented and motivated people, with innovative and creative ideas to make a major impact on society."

"Jason has an interesting point," remarked Rosanvallon. "If we had to rely on American kids for our nation's future, we would be in deep shit. I've read all of the reasons why our students score low on international tests. Put bluntly, American students are slackers. They're too fat, too lazy, and too consumed with themselves; they have been spoiled by their parents and don't want to work hard in school. It's mainly immigrants kids with very few material assets who are willing to work hard in school."

"I have a different perspective on immigration," said Srinivasa. "As a nation, we are importing terrorism and poverty by permitting an increasing number of immigrants from non-Western and undeveloped countries. Annually about 800,000 immigrants are legally permitted, and about 300,000 to 500,000 illegals arrive. Immigration numbers represent a threefold increase from 1970, when the immigrant population (first generation) represented five percent of the total population. Today, it represents nine percent. Moreover, the new immigrants come from different countries than the old. In the 1950s, two-thirds of a much smaller number came from Europe and Canada. Since the 1980s, nearly fifty percent have come from Mexico, other parts of Latin America, and the Caribbean; nearly forty percent from Asia and the Middle East; five percent from Africa; and five percent from Europe and Canada."

"Would you adopt E. D. Hirsch's idea of cultural literacy?" asked Bentley, "That there is a base or set of 'essential names, phrases, dates, and concepts,' some five thousand in total, that 'every American needs to know.' Given the growing diversity that exists in the country, do you think our education should embrace background knowledge that promotes a national form of communication, a national curriculum, and a Western perspective since our history and culture is Western? If you follow Hirsch to the letter, about eighty percent of his recommended list of items are pre-1900, rooted in the Western classics, or what some kids refer to as 'paleolithic' life."

Rosanvallon responded. "I'm not concerned about the theories of assimilation or diversity. I'm more concerned about reducing ethnic enclaves. Hirsch's idea of cultural literacy enables kids to communicate with grandparents, southerners with northerners, and blacks, whites, and Asians."

"My concern is that Hirsch, either overtly or covertly, is promoting a set of myths and facts, based on a monolithic culture—middle class, white, and Western," asserted Bentley. "Furthermore, who is Hirsch or anyone else to say that an educated or culturally literate person is someone who knows about Brutus, *Catch-22*, and El Cid, and not 98 Degrees, U2, and 401K? My concern is that there are a host of school districts that buy into Hirsch's view of cultural literacy—these are the same school districts that were still using McGuffey readers fifty years after the book was first published."

"Hirsch's ideas cannot be out of step with reality," remarked Rosanvallon. "Barnes and Nobles and Borders Books sell his books, like McDonald's sells hamburgers. Hirsch is now telling us what first graders, second graders—all the way to twelfth graders—should know."

"It sounds like he is the 'Pied Piper of Pedagogy' or the 'Big Cheese' of all the cheese heads in Wisconsin," remarked Bentley.

"As far as I'm concerned, Hirsch and a few others like Mortimer Adler, William Bennett, and Diane Ravitch, are only trying to upgrade academic standards, what the old essentialists during the post-*Sputnik* era tried to do," explained Professor Kirpichenko.

"Most new immigrants are poor, uneducated, don't speak English, and are unable to prosper in an information society that de-emphasizes manual labor," said Hjalmar. "Put simply, many of the new immigrants worsen our poverty indicators. For example, between 1970 and 2000 the number of people identified as poor by the U.S. government rose six million and totaled thirty-five million—as if American social policy was regressive. Of the total, forty percent were Hispanics. The recent immigrants allow critics to step up political rhetoric, claiming so-called racism and government failure."

"The problem is," said Professor Kirpichenko, "the government is spending $200 billion per year on social and welfare programs, and it has spent over $2 trillion since the beginning of the War on Poverty in the 1960s. That is enough money to purchase nearly half of the *Fortune 500* companies, or to repair the infrastructure of every road, bridge, tunnel, and sewer system in the country. Not only does this investment in welfare cost hundreds of billions per year in lost revenue, but it has also helped to replace the work ethic with dependence. By rewarding dysfunctional behavior, the welfare system has contributed to a permanent underclass exemplified by a host of social and educational problems; it produces future generations robbed of self-esteem, productivity, and hope."

"Professor, if I didn't know better, I would swear you and Shakil were old-fashioned rednecks, driving a pickup truck down some dusty road or drinking in some neighborhood tavern, and speaking with Archie Bunker or Al Bundy," asserted Rosanvallon.

"Look," asserted Kirpichenko, "the War on Poverty began in my generation, under the Johnson administration. Forty years ago, twenty to twenty-five percent of American students lived in poverty. We put great faith in American schools to enhance social mobility and equality. Today, the same percentage of American students lives in poverty, and it's as if all the money we've spent on education for the last forty years has had no effect. Who do we blame? The poor, the welfare system, teachers like you? We need some accountability linked to this spending!"

Once more Rosanvallon responded. "I'm a believer that immigrants built this society, and it is their sweat, toil, and brains that made this country great. Social policy is controversial, and there are no silver bullets to save us, but I do believe that those who live on the downside of advantage are more destined to remain at the bottom of the heap. If you need a culprit, then look at the capitalistic system. The rich get richer, and the poor remain poor except for a few individuals who manage to become modern-day gladiators or super-duper entertainers. The more fronts capitalism breeds, the more it proliferates, and the more it crushes the weak and poor."

"You must know," the professor responded, "I would not qualify for ACLU membership or be considered part of the Woodstock crowd, even though I was a part of that generation, if I may say so. But you sound like a typical neo-Marxist who feels that when capitalists proliferate they cannibalize the poor. The truth is, I advocate curtailing public money for educating children of illegal immigrants who comprise about four to five percent of the nation's public school enrollment. I might even round up all the illegals and ship them back to their countries. But I also feel we need to address our failing schools, and determine what we are getting for all the money we spend before we give out more and more money, for more and more special programs. This doesn't make me a redneck or a leatherneck, an elephant or a donkey."

"You have to be kidding. The immigrant parents of the children would not go back to where they came from. It would only make the next generation of immigrants even poorer," said Bentley. "And, if we reduce our education spending, the inner-city schools which have the greatest needs, will suffer the most."

"You mean the next generation of illegal immigrants or welfare recipients," asserted Kirpichenko. "Listen, there is no international threat today from a military or economic standpoint. Although terrorism and rogue nations with nuclear missiles are a reality, the Cold War has ended. America stands alone as the only superpower in the world. The problem that exists is domestic. All I'm saying is we need to slow down immigration and implement some restrictions so we don't become a dumping ground for the Third World."

"That sounds like an old Know-Nothing or Ku Klux Klan statement to me," responded Bentley. "Your view on immigration and interpretation of history does little to prepare students to work in an urban or diverse school setting."

"But the previous statements about rednecks and now the KKK have a trendy ring which I call liberal baiting," said the professor. "In academic circles, we have all types of liberal, conservative, and postmodernist categories and labels. But the arguments are often just as nasty and controversial."

"My concern is that your conservative views," indicated Rosanvallon, "seem directed at minority and ethnic groups; they reflect the old rhapsodies of McCarthyists in the 1950s who preferred being dead than red, and also the Know-Nothings of the 1850s who hated immigrants and wanted to restrict immigration. We have enough hate groups today, existing under various Aryan and far right names, currently advancing their fascist slogans and literature on the Internet. There is little difference between the old Klan, the Nazi S.S., and today's right-wing fringe groups. All of these organizations recruit good family men and churchgoers; their members are not deviants, delinquents, drug addicts, or womanizers; they are just plain dangerous and dislike all forms of diversity."

Professor Fusarelli, who was dozing during the heated conversation, raised his head and introduced some positive sound bytes into the discussion. "Until the early 1990s America had seen its national self-confidence eroded by a series of international problems, real and imagined. The old military and economic threats have withered. Although technology can be leveraged to kill thousands of people, cripple worldwide companies, and close down airports throughout the country, we are in a new age of prosperity. The USSR is in shambles, reduced to a third-rate power and run by an unsavory group of red and brown (communist-fascist) shirts."

Fusarelli continued: "We now know that Iraq is a paper tiger and Saddam has a few screws missing. We also understand that the Japanese are not ten feet tall or super-smart. The Japanese confidence—or arrogance—has dwindled under the heat of a meltdown of its financial markets. 'At the rate things are going, we are all going to wind up working for the Japanese,' predicted Lester Thurow, the Harvard economics guru, a few years ago. Mr. Thurow was one of thousands of pessimists who sang in the American-doomed and mournful choir. Thank the Lord for Mr. Alan Greenspan, who understood the international market better than Mr. Thurow."

Fusarelli, now sipping some herbal tea, raised his voice. "The only thing left for critics and pessimists to worry about is the growing protectionism of Europe, Islamic fanaticism, and whether China will continue to peacefully coexist with its neighbors. China is buying and spying its way to superpower status and its nuclear arsenal is growing. At the very least, it would like to restore its nation to the traditional Middle Kingdom status as Asia's dominant power, thus threatening the entire Pacific Rim."

"Of course, if you belong to Greenpeace or the Sierra Club, there is still panic that the whole world is going to be poorer, even collapse, because of unchecked population growth and the eventual exhaustion of natural resources, food, and drinking water. Paul Ehrlich's time-bomb predictions of overpopulation, written in 1974, are still with us, just like the Pepsi Generation is alive and well—although they now have some gray hair and wrinkles. Then, of course, there are increasing levels of carbon dioxide and other greenhouse gases, which are affecting the world's ozone layer, climate, and ecosystems."

Hjalmar, who had been teaching math for five years, felt that parents and teachers put too much emphasis on academics. "Personal, social, and moral development are just as important as cognitive development in determining the outcomes of life." He is also a strong believer of luck and timing, and that luck counts more than good grades in determining the outcomes of life. "Luck and timing, that is, being in the right place at the right time, and not grades, determine who we marry. Having good physical and mental health is crucial—and has more to do with good genes, or what I call luck, and common sense about exercise and diet than a good education. I know a great many educated people who are unhealthy or unhappy. Being a good sex partner is important, too, and that has nothing to do with a good education. Being a good person, a moral person, has little to do with cognition. I know a number of highly educated people who are angry and unethical; some are outright thieves or political tyrants. I think there are many more successful bankers, lawyers, and salespeople who are more socially adept than academically adept. Personality, which includes social skills, moti-vation, and tenacity, has more to do with economic success than getting A's in school. In fact, a good number of A students wind up working for C students. Education has been oversold as a middle-class panacea, as the only road to success."

Professor Fusarelli then inserted his opinions. "Complicated answers are devised to mask the truth. It all boils down to human capital, not economic capital. Brains create knowledge and wealth, and there are four ingredients in developing human capital: families, communities, teachers, and schools. All share in the responsibility of educat-ing children and youth. Parents and communities cannot do it without good teachers and schools, and teachers and schools cannot do it without support from parents and communities. Instead of trying to determine who is to blame for the reason why

Johnny can't read or compete on international achievement tests, we need to work together so our children and the nation as a whole can prosper."

At this point, the class was given a ten-minute break.

Questions to Consider

1. Do you believe in the rise and fall of civilizations? (Hegel, Toynbee, and Spengler did.) If so, what economic and social predictions would you make about our country for the next ten years? For the remaining century?

2. Less than 0.3 percent of the U.S. high schools offers Mandarin as a foreign language to study. To what extent would you like to see Mandarin courses offered in large high schools that could hire qualified personnel?

3. One teacher (Rosanvallon) argued that it was impractical to offer advanced courses in math and science, since his students had trouble learning the basics. Another teacher (Hjalmar) insisted that the culprit was progressive thought—too much emphasis on elective subjects, social skills, and curriculum fads. The professor felt it was our failure to heed the words of essentialist philosophers, some fifty years ago, who urged beefing up the curriculum. In your opinion, why are schools failing?

4. Two opposing views on immigration were voiced. Which view do you support?

5. The argument was made that Japan is no longer a threat to the American economy, and the long-run threat to America is mainland China. What is your opinion?

6. One teacher (Srinivasa) expressed the need to slow down immigration, while another teacher (Bentley) seemed to favor immigration. Another teacher (Hjalmar) contended that all the fuss about test scores is silly, since luck and personality are the major determinants in life. What is your opinion? Still another teacher wanted to increase the teaching of Mandarin because of the size of China and its potential marketplace in the world economy. What is your opinion?

7. Are citizens in other countries more or less satisfied with their schools than in the United States? Use Internet resources to find the answer. *Hint:* Check out the *Comparative Education Review*, the International Association for the Evaluation of Educational Achievement, and international education books published by Brookings Institution, Phi Delta Kappa, and Routledge/Falmer Press.

Recommended Readings

Jerome Bruner, *The Culture of Education* (Cambridge, MA: Harvard University Press, 1996).

Adrian Karatnycky, *Freedom in the World* (Piscataway, NJ: Transaction Publishers, 2002).

Jane Roland Martin, *Cultural Miseducation* (New York: Teachers College Press, Columbia University, 2002).

Allan C. Ornstein, *Teaching and Schooling in America: Pre and Post September 11* (Boston: Allyn & Bacon, 2003).

N. Ken Shimahara et al., *Ethnicity, Race, and Nationality in Education* (Mahwah, NJ: Erlbaum, 2001).

27

Part II: International Test Comparisons

When the students returned, the discussion became more technical, factual, and focused on international test scores and learning gaps between American and international students.

"To tell you the truth," maintained Professor Kirpichenko, "I'm tired of hearing how poorly American students test compared to students of other industrialized nations. At first, in the mid-1960s and early 1970s, the discussion was limited to scholarly journals. Little attention was paid to curriculum reform or policy implications. The focus was on the test methodology of conducting large-scale international tests.

"The warning signals started in 1977, when the College Board pointed out a steady decline in SAT scores for fifteen consecutive years, followed by the publication of *A Nation at Risk* in 1983, which indicated enrollment declines in high school math and science courses and growing scientific and technological illiteracy among our students. The warning signals stimulated media attention, which today is full blown. Each international test and American students' ranking are reported as a major sporting event with headlines showing how poor Americans place."

"How bad is bad?" asked one of the students.

"Since the mid-1960s and on nineteen international tests," commented the professor, Americans never scored first or second, only once third, but placed last or next to last more than ten times, mostly in math and science. The implications are clear: the low performance of American schools and poor quality of American schools.

"The analysis of the situation is worse if we stop and consider that the Asian school systems—China, Hong Kong, Korea, Singapore, Japan, and Taiwan—spend twenty-five to forty percent less money per student than we do, and their classroom sizes average thirty or more students, while ours average eighteen. Obviously, resources are not the issue. No wonder some people resent more education spending."

"That may be true," commented Harry Wang, a high school music teacher. "And no one mentions that Asian students average eight hours per day compared to five and a half hours in the United States. The Asian school year is about 220 days, including a halfday on Saturday, whereas the U.S. school year averages 180 days. If you consider the eight-hour Asian school day, multiply it by 180, and add four hours times an additional forty Saturdays, then Asian schools average 1,600 hours per year compared to our 990 hours. That translates to sixty percent more schooling. If the extra 610 hours per year are multiplied over twelve years, from grades one through twelve, this equates

279

to 7,320 extra hours or 7.4 more years of schooling in Asia than in the United States. That explains much of the difference in international test scores, especially in the latter grades as the additional hours accumulate."

"Since we don't live in Timbuktu or Tahiti, I guess we need to be worried," remarked Srinivasa. "Perhaps we need to modify the American school calendar—more hours or more days."

Wang answered. "Let me give you more bad news. According to *The Condition of Education*, as many as twenty-one percent of our nine-year-olds and eleven percent of our fourteen-year-olds watch five or more hours of television each day. American students average approximately three and a half hours of TV viewing per day, after school when mom and dad are often working, while Asian students are attending private and group tutoring sessions for about two hours a day after school. Asian students honor the family by studying, obtaining good grades, scoring high on tests, and attending college. Our students average slightly less than one hour of homework a day compared to three hours for Asian students. It is not that our students are stupid; it is that they don't work hard."

"Don't you think kids should have fun?" asserted Srinivasa.

"If you believe in A. S. Neill's *Summerhill*, the answer is yes," remarked Kirpichenko.

"What happens if you believe in child psychology or the whole child?" asked Bentley.

"Then we are not going to place high on international tests."

"Do you think the emphasis on progressive and humanistic education—the notion of relevancy, cooperative learning, social promotion, and grade inflation—has something to do with our poor showing on international tests?" asked Fusarelli.

"There is another factor which deals with honor and hard work," said Wang. "Students in Asia are well disciplined and taught by parents, teachers, and tutors to conform to rules. Asian students are expected to respect teachers, to behave in school, and to study. From early in the child's life, morality, hard work, honor, and uprightness are taught in the Asian home and transferred to the school setting; moreover, the subject of morality, based on traditional values, is taught in school from the early grades on."

"In contrast," Wang continued, "American students exhibit much less respect for their teachers, for studying and learning in general. Morality is left for the home and church. Whatever the reason, whether the problem is the home, peer group, or television, or lack of spiritual guidance, our students do not readily conform to rules. Many U.S. schools are plagued by student behavior problems that interfere with education purposes. According to the NEA, 'discipline problems/negative attitudes' of American students is ranked the second most serious problem that burdens the teacher's ability to teach, and it is the most serious problem in big-city schools. In many cases, students have more rights in American schools than do the teachers."

"Yes. But there are many technical or testing factors to consider," responded Kirpichenko. "First, there is the problem of constructing measures of educational achievement which produce comparable results across countries; test items do not have the same difficulty across countries because of different emphasis on content."

"Second, much of the difference in scores is attributable to three social factors: number of parents in the home, parental educational level, and family income level. All of these social factors are cumulative and influence school achievement. As social deprivation mounts, the longer American students stay in school, the further behind they fall compared to their counterparts in other industrialized nations."

"Talking about social factors," observed Fusarelli, "once we start carving out class and ethnic factors, some discernible trends become apparent. If we single out advantaged school districts, characterized by high spending and low student poverty, they place second in the last TIMSS math and science tests, just below Japan. Also, we learn that Asian-American students outscored all nations and students, and students in the states of Iowa and North Dakota tied for third place. Of course, someone might ask how many students take the tests in suburban America or Iowa and North Dakota, and I would say enough to show a pattern based on social class and ethnicity."

Fusarelli continued. "Scores among countries are tightly bunched in the middle, so that small differences in raw scores produce large differences in ranks. For example, in the last international math test, had U.S. eighth graders scored seventy-two percent correct instead of sixty-seven, they would have finished fifth instead of thirteenth. The same pattern existed for the international reading tests. Again, the scores were tightly bunched so that second-place France and eighth-place America were only fourteen points apart on a six-hundred-point scale. Of course, when these scores were released, the fact that American fourteen-year-olds scored eighth out of thirty-one nations was viewed as bad news."

"All of this test information and facts are difficult to follow. What are you trying to say? Are you and our professor providing excuses why American students score low?" asked one of the students.

Professor Kirpichenko then pointed out, "Two well-known researchers, Berliner and Biddle, have gone so far as to claim the international test crisis is a hoax, and they published a book called *The Manufactured Crisis* to explain their views."

"You put a lot of blame on a lot of people. Who stands out as the most disingenuous or ideological?" asked Bentley.

"I'm not sure," said Fusarelli, "but I feel many researchers and professors who should know better, or do know better, are swayed by the herd. There are too many wimpy professors. By remaining silent or refusing to defend the schools, they add fuel to the crisis by permitting the public and politicians free reign to criticize schools."

"So what else is new? The critics have been criticizing America's schools for the last fifty years, since *Sputnik*," asserted Bentley. "In fact, some people since the Neolithic era have made a career of criticizing teachers and schools; they rely on the same words and phrases, and exhibit the same angry personality, repeatedly."

"In the end," Fusarelli continued, "the teachers are singled out, and the people turn to solutions that attempt to get the teacher under the guise of high-stakes testing and accountability."

"Are you saying that the nation's schools are not as bad as the popular press and critics claim and as most of us think?" asked Bentley.

"I believe the news media has created a crisis that doesn't exist," said Professor Fusarelli, "putting emphasis on the negative and ignoring the more positive test comparisons. The headlines talk about our students coming in dead last or next to last in subjects like math and science or that American schools rate an F. The public reads the newspapers and magazines and formulates a negative opinion. In addition, some business and political groups approach the situation from a political perspective that assumes the worst, and some researchers who have staked their professional reputation and grant money on results also assume the worst."

"How, then, do you respond to the dismal results of our eighth-and twelfth-grade students on the international tests? To be blunt, the American taxpayer has spent billions for failure."

Hjalmar threw in his two cents: "No question. It matters little if we talk about the first, second, or third international tests. American students rank in the cellar, or next to the cellar, among the industrialized nations on almost every math and science test, and they certainly cannot compete with twelfth-grade students from Japan, Taiwan, Korea, and Hong Kong."

"In the old days," said Srinivasa, "during *Sputnik*, we were told American students could not compete with the Soviets. You know the outcome of that contest. Now we are told we cannot academically compete with most of the industrialized world. That would be a concern if we were in economic or military decline, and we are not. Why can't we just ease up and smell the roses?"

"That is a misleading analysis," maintained Bentley. "Students at this grade level have no reason to perform well on a test which has no relevance to them. Their college applications have already been filled out, and then they mentally go into cruise control and coast the rest of the year; moreover, the students and teachers never learn the results of the test so why should they knock themselves out? In addition, because of tracking at the high school level, and the different content internationally, the twelfth-grade curriculum varies among countries. Of forty-five calculus questions on the last test, twenty-four were taught in Japan before the twelfth grade and only four in the United States. What we need to do is change the curriculum or test content. We emphasize too much repetition, what Jerome Bruner and others call the 'spiral curriculum,' and we don't encourage our students to take rigorous math and science courses. Part of the problem also deals with the value we assign math and science. In Japan, twenty-two percent of all college degrees are in engineering compared to seven percent in the United States. Only four industrialized countries have a smaller percentage of degrees in engineering than in the United States."

"How do you know all this information?" asked Hjalmar.

"I read."

"This notion about different curricula is overplayed," remarked Wang. "One of the best kept secrets why Asian students outperform American students is that in addition to a much longer school year, their learning is continuous. School vacations are shorter and spaced throughout the year. During vacation time, Asian students receive homework assignments from their teachers and attend tutoring sessions. Learning doesn't stop; it is rooted in the Asian culture and value system. In contrast, American students often need to relearn in September and October what they learned the previous year. I guess you can say Asian kids are on the fast track, while American kids are on the slow track or summer track."

"When do these fast-track kids have time to eat?" asked Bentley.

"If you have to know, during school, after school, and before tutoring."

"Doesn't that lead to a little overstress?"

"More middle-class American high school kids cheat on tests than Asian kids and the suicide ratios are about equal," said Rosanvallon. "Educators in most countries just don't want to talk about the academic pressure they impose on children and youth. Teachers seem caught up in the business of testing, grading, and evaluating students. They spend about thirty percent of their professional time preparing, administering, and grading tests. How dull!"

"How can kids who study all day have fun? You are only young once," asked Stacey Edmonson, a fourth-grade teacher.

Professor Fusarelli responded. "It's a matter of what you consider to be fun. Most American youth have nothing better to do with their free time than watch TV, surf the Internet, and finish off a bag of potato chips or peanuts. Others take to the streets and get into trouble."

"Well," remarked Edmonson, "our kids can beat the kids from Taiwan and Japan in Little League baseball, so all of our kids can't be couch potatoes."

"Are you on pills?" remarked Rosanvallon. "What does baseball have to do with academics? What does hitting a baseball have to do with the quality of instruction, the need to improve teacher preparation, or to hire more science and math teachers?"

"All I'm saying is that kids should also have fun," said Edmonson. "Anyway, it's all a bunch of mixed messages. It's like asking who's on first and what's on second. If you ask ten people on the street how to improve schools, you would get ten different answers. Pick up the *Wall Street Journal*, *USA Today*, or *Newsweek*, or listen to CNN and Fox News, and you get the flavor of how diversified are the criticisms and solutions regarding American education."

"I would simply focus on the school calendar as the major reason for the differences in test scores among our twelfth-grade students and their industrialized counterparts. Even the European school year averages close to two hundred days per year. The differences in the amount of schooling have a cumulative effect. Try to learn tennis or golf without sufficient practice," stated Professor Kirpichenko. "Compare two readers—one who practices about one-fifth less time and what effect that has on both readers over twelve years."

"Part of the problem is that many junior high school math and science teachers prefer teaching at the high school level. Their attitude affects their teaching, which, in turn, affects student learning. Then, if they manage to transfer out, they create a temporary vacuum and teachers out of license initially fill in and teach math and science. Our junior high school math and science instruction is at best second rate," said Wang. "Of course, if you go by international test rankings, it is much worse."

"Another factor is that American schools provide too many remedial and typical classes in math and science, and not enough advanced courses," maintained Rosanvallon. Students in our country are not expected to perspire when they learn. By the twelfth grade, Asian students are required to take extra courses in science and math (including courses in calculus and statistics) than American students. Only about fifty percent of our high school students take three years of math and science, and only twenty-five percent take physics—even though most of our technological advances are rooted in physics concepts.

"There is sufficient agreement among researchers that students learn what they are taught and expected to learn, and students in countries with more demanding curriculum learn more and perform better. Asian students have greater academic time and opportunity to learn and are expected to learn by their parents and teachers. However, American parents and teachers feel that ability counts more than effort—resulting in lowered expectations and lower performance among lower-class students in our country. American educators have a fancy term for describing this attitude and behavior; they call it the *self-fulfilling prophecy.*"

Bentley pointed out that because of tracking, there were greater differences among American students than Asian students in terms of quantity and quality of content, even with courses of the same title. "In the absence of uniform state requirements and national or state testing for promotion, social class factors produce major differences in course enrollments. U.S. children of better educated parents are more likely to take more math and science courses and more advanced courses than the majority of American students. The gap is too difficult to close at high school; the basis of achievement and curriculum reform is rooted in the elementary schools, starting with the first grade."

"What is your suggestion?" asked Hjalmar.

"To raise standards for all students, not just for the college-bound or talented student, as in the *Sputnik* era. To insist on a common academic core for all students, to achieve equity and excellence at the same time. It goes back to the reform ideas of Mortimer Adler, E. D. Hirsch, John Goodlad, and Ted Sizer, who want a common curriculum for all students."

"That sounds like pie in the sky—ignoring the fact that because of social and economic circumstances, many students have difficulty learning the basics," asserted Srinivasa. "Even worse, the reform ideas that you speak about suggest a national curriculum and national testing movement that many people oppose."

"In the long run," insisted Professor Kirpichenko, "things have a way of working out in America. We are blessed with Yankee ingenuity and resources."

"We live in a different world today," announced Rosanvallon. "A push of a button brings us instant televised news from Africa, instant computerized information from the World Wide Web, and instant cash from almost any banking source around the globe. It takes split seconds to launch missiles or emit chemical pollutants from a factory in some desert, which then travels across geographical borders and oceans. We know all too well about the tragedy at the World Trade Center. We are a global village and we are a nation of many nations, more diverse than in the past, so that the term *Yankee* is no longer relevant."

"We live in a far more complex and technologically advanced society which requires higher levels of education than in the past for all its citizens," declared Professor Fusarelli. "In fact, we are living in an age where scientific, technological, and electronic changes are so rapid that the world around us is changing at exponential rates. Every fifteen years or so our scientific and technical knowledge doubles. It can be affirmed unequivocally that the amount of scientific and technological knowledge available at the end of one's life (seventy-five years) will be one hundred times what it was when he or she was born. In fact, ninety percent of scientists and engineers who ever lived are alive today."

"Listen," said Hjalmar, "Just about everyone in the United States seems to be an education expert, and just about everyone—including educators, politicians, and businesspeople—seem alarmed by our international achievement rankings. I guess that results in healthy debate and subsequent school improvement."

"If you really want to know," asserted Kirpichenko, "all this concern about international assessment and educational progress among American students has created a cottage industry among researchers and critics: analyzing and reanalyzing, comparing and contrasting the data from these tests for the next century like it was a World Series or Super Bowl event. We even award special plaques and certificates for schools that rank high on international tests. Based on these test results, as well as other high-stakes tests, we debate curriculum reform and educational policy until we are blue in the face."

"I think the whole debate on curriculum really comes down to the old question, 'What knowledge is of most worth?' which was raised by Herbert Spencer in 1860," asserted Fusarelli. "Spencer argued that science was the most practical subject for the survival of the individual and society, yet it occupied minimal space in the curriculum because impractical traditions prevailed. What Spencer said yesterday seems relevant today."

"I think Alvin Toffler, in *Future Shock*, was on target when he argued that 'nothing should be included in the required curriculum unless it can be strongly justified in terms of the future.' If this means scrapping a substantial part of the curriculum, Toffler would say 'so be it,'" said Wang. "The need for constantly revising and pruning the curriculum is apparent, and that is our job as professionals."

"I suspect we will eventually come to some agreement on what should be taught in American schools," said Edmonson. "Once content standards are agreed on, we will move to a state or national test to measure performance."

"All this talk about standards and reform is blown out of proportion by education critics who hammer away in professional journals, and now the news media, that Americans finish last or near the bottom on international tests. Just add more hours and more days to the school calendar. Assuming no change in the *quality* of instruction, the change in *quantity* of instruction will result in major improvement in our international rankings," said Professor Kirpichenko.

"Time out, peace.... When I went to school," said Rosanvallon, "we could finish our homework during lunch time or on the school bus. I spent plenty of time trading baseball cards, watching *Gilligan's Island*, and just hanging out with the guys. Today's middle-class kids are saddled down with guitar or piano lessons, art workshops, karate, and skating or tennis practice. Some of these kids today are so wound up, there isn't enough time in the day for them to unwind. They are either sleep deprived or popping Ritalin."

"It's a matter of priorities. While our kids are on the soccer field on Saturday, pumped up by screaming parents, most kids in Asia are attending school for half a day. I don't think children and youth in Taiwan, Korea, or Japan are more frazzled or sleep deprived, even though they have more homework and school time," remarked Edmonson.

"I beg to differ. I think most Asian students are highly competitive and driven to succeed in school. If they don't succeed, they lose face and experience a great deal of anxiety and frustration," responded Srinivasa.

"Part of the problem is there are so many more college scholarships for athletics than for academics," claimed Wang. "Middle- and upper-middle-class parents go crazy and push their kids to succeed on the athletic field. They spend much more money on private instruction for sports, about $50 an hour, than for academic tutoring. Some of these kids have had private tennis, golf, and lacrosse lessons since they were eight or nine years old. These parents even complain that the school gives too much homework, because it interferes with their children's sports activities and practice. The parents I'm talking about are not only reliving their youth through their children's performance on the athletic field, but also don't like to see other kids perform well— despite their polite conversation—because it might damage their children's playing time or chances to receive sufficient recognition and rewards, or possibly an athletic scholarship for college."

"I see the same type of sports competitiveness in *Fortune 500* corporate boards. To some extent, this aggressive personality is formed on the playing field—the desire to win, even if it means knocking out your opponent or sending him to the sidelines with an injury. I feel Harry is right. Sports priorities have taken control over academic priorities in many American households, and it's pumped up by the media and the $50 million, five-year contracts for professional athletes," asserted Bentley.

"The real problem is," said Rosanvallon, "American kids go home after school to a one-parent home where mom has little time for them or a dual working parent home where there is minimal parental supervision and less time available for assisting kids with homework. Asian children are greeted by mom, who is considered the second teacher, with responsibility for tutoring and helping with homework."

"Do you think your remarks are either gender biased or chauvinist?" asserted Bentley. "Your statements seem out of place; even worse, you seem stuck in a time warp— say, the pre-1960s. Let me ask, what's wrong with a one-parent household? Do you really expect women with professional careers to stay at home washing dishes and diapers?"

"I can no longer use the word *hysterical*, but I'm reminded of General McCall who said 'nuts' to his german counterpart."

"Why can't you just use the word *irrational* instead of *nuts*? And who is this McCall character? Isn't that some kind of women's magazine?"

"You need to know your history. I'll let you figure it out."

"What about television? A University of Michigan study found that while nine- and eleven-year-olds spend three and a half hours a week on homework, they spend thirteen and a half hours watching TV. If you add e-mail time and time for gabbing on the phone, the same kids waste another seven to eight hours a week. The only kids in America who are stressed out in large numbers are those high school kids trying to get into Ivy League colleges and who need all A's," said Bentley.

"I know many of their parents," remarked Rosanvallon, "since I grew up in Great Neck, New York, and also lived in Highland Park, Illinois. When these kids were two years old, their parents gave them an alphabet book, starting with apples and apricots, to help them pronounce and memorize words. When they entered first grade, for their birthday or some special occasion, they were given a book of world maps in color to learn the continents and oceans. These kids, now, have three hours or more of homework a day, but there are three to four city kids for every one of these suburban kids who do zero homework because they have other responsibilities or because it's such a low priority that many no longer carry notebooks home, much less a textbook or backpack to school. Did you know more than twenty percent of the teachers in Boston's and Buffalo's public high schools don't even assign homework, because only a handful of their students will do it? How can these students pass state exams or compete on international tests?"

"Let's face it," said Isador Ishkabibble, a speech therapist and special education teacher, "practice makes perfect, and practice comes after school hours. In Asian countries, tutoring sessions and homework are less problematic because family and school priorities are in sync about the need to study, adult authority is evident, and children are expected to please parents and teachers and excel."

"I think it's a matter of expectations," continued Rosanvallon. "As a nation, we don't have the same high expectations as Asian parents do for their children. Progressive schooling is often considered the culprit, but I think we are operating in a much less traditional society, with fewer adult controls. When you are king of the mountain or queen of the manor for a long period, you begin to lose some of your motivation and drive. First-generation immigrants in America work harder and longer hours than the second generation, and much harder than suburban homogenized Americans, many who come from the Give Me generation."

"Aren't you generalizing?" asked Professor Fusarelli.

"I'm trying to counteract some of the professor's remarks he made about immigration, which I thought were racist."

"Well, all these statements about smart Asian students who work harder in school could be considered racist today," responded Wang. "We shouldn't be making generalizations about any ethnic group."

"I hope we are not going to drift back to the thought police," declared Srinivasa. "Soon we'll be debating who has the right to lead the Scouts or whether the Scout oath, which talks about 'duty to God and . . . country,' should be banned or modified."

"I think the message is clear. Education is not just what happens in school," remarked Ishkabibble. "It must be considered in a social context. It takes place at home or on the street, with the scouts or street gangs, in church or at local malls, in front of the television or computer, and with other mass media and communication systems."

"Why is it that none of the education experts ever mention those points?" asked Bentley.

"Because they are part of the new academic industry that reports on international comparisons. They would not be able to talk about the poor condition of American education, American learning gaps, or the D's and F's in international competition," commented Professor Fusarelli. "Just think of all the professors, researchers, and critics who would have to tone down their polemics on American education. Even though the Cold War is over, and the Red Menace has disappeared, we are still living in the shadow of Admiral Rickover and Arthur Bestor."

"Are these educators from paleolithic times?" said Ishkabibble. "Does that mean we don't have to beef up the curriculum? Are the national reform movement, the standards movement, the voucher and charter movements unnecessary or overkill?"

Professor Fusarelli was now unwrapping a crunchy granola bar. "Americans love to debate and dissect their own schools and society. It is the cornerstone of a democracy and rooted in the thinking and teaching of Socrates. Only in a democracy can we criticize the system without fear of reprisal or worse."

"Coming from a closed society in which public debate was limited," remarked Kirpichenko, "I can appreciate how the free exchange of ideas results in a healthy, invigorating, and improved society. American students tend to take democracy for granted. Recent immigrants do not. If American educators could not compare and criticize international achievement levels, they would find something else to debate and dissect. That's healthy and that leads to school improvement. As for all of these reform movements . . . who really knows? Who can really say for sure what works under what conditions, when the variables are so numerous and complex?"

"As for Rickover and Bestor," Professor Kirpichenko continued, "I mentioned them earlier in my discussion. Perhaps Mr. Ishkabibble, you were doodling or gazing out the window. Recall they were conservative critics of American education, some fifty years ago, who attacked progressive education as soft education. Although they relied on the pencil technology to make their point, their ideas still seem to have a relevant ring to many politicians and businesspeople today who wish to beef up the curriculum. And, now that the session and term is just about over, let me say fairwell.

"Ah, I just had a senior moment. Allow me to add, actually paraphrase, from a king-sized memo I just received from an old friend and professor, the author, who also studied at New York University when he was an inch taller and three inches thinner. It helps explain his logic and statements."

It's been a blast. I hope you had fun reading the book, trying to decipher when I was serious or mirth-making. If you wish to register a pithy statement, as a friend or critic, don't e-mail me. I'm still immersed in pen-and-pencil technology. Just write to me. Now, I know some of you have not read the introduction and are thinking or asking, 'Where?' I suggest you return to the preface, and mend your ways.

If some of the names sound familiar or closely resemble some person you know, please remember all the characters and episodes are fictitious, and so are the descriptions of the people. If some of you disagree with some of my engaging thoughts, please don't act like a spoiled child and throw a temper tantrum, or jump up and down, because the dialogue did not go your way. There is nothing in the book that can be verified by the scientific observer or postmodern relativist. In fact, since scientific theories and postmodern logic extrapolate beyond the data, it can be argued that very little can ever be verified or derived as truth.

If you think I went off the deep end once too often, please consider my age and the cumulative effect of all the (1) pollution I've inhaled, (2) wine I've consumed and tap water I drank thinking it was bottled spring water, (3) cigars I've smoked, (4) nuts I've eaten, (5) pesticide spray I've swallowed thinking I was eating healthy, and (6) politically correct workshops I never attended because I didn't read my e-mail. I take minimal responsibility for upsetting you, rather suggest you work on improving your own personality and sense of humor.

If you thought my statements were clever or witty, however, and if you were amused here and there, then let me invoke a few intellectual attributes and folklore: Two cheers to all the (1) books I've read and truths I never believed, (2) myths and isms I understood but rejected, and (3) heroes and gods I never worshipped. I have relied on the collective wisdom of our culture and my understanding of life, and then filtered that through my personality and biases, and added my own magic to the mix.

The outcome is an education medicine that is older than chicken soup, and like your mom once said, 'It can't hurt but might possibly help.' Thus, we have a new complex phenomenon, a new theory, called *chicken soup education*. I hope you have enjoyed my brand of chicken soup—my special terminology, my special dialogue, my special ideas, my way of breaking the mold, a so-called sensible alternative to a textbook. As a final disclaimer, I do admit that very few of you will find my medicine to be logical, scientific, respectful, or scholarly. So what! I'm not ashamed. I'm too old to be scolded, and I have tenure. So I won't be invited to your next cocktail party, or be asked to speak at your next school or university summer institute.

Now, I've got a long list of reasons for what I've said and done. There are no regrets and nothing I can't explain. Maybe I didn't say everything I should have said and maybe there were things I shouldn't have said. Perhaps there was too much storytelling, too many engaging characters (not to mention a host of funny-sounding foreign names), too many imaginary quotations, and too much posturing. Perhaps the language was peculiar, and the words textured, in a few places; however, that was part of the satire. Anyway there is nothing I can say now or do about it. I cannot take away those words or phrases, make some changes, so you feel better or believe that the author is really a good sort of guy—just getting old and ugly, tired and worn out, going through his stages, until he reaches some whimsical land.

Nonetheless, I don't think I ever crossed the line or degenerated into a lack of civility or decency. Perhaps you can accuse me of incorporating pop culture and provocative speech into the text, instilling some vim and vigor into the academic arena, and discussing strongly held opinions on highly charged topics, often verboten in print and college classrooms. Maybe, you can also accuse me of not making it clear when I was serious or spoofing, blinking or winking—or say that some double-meaning words were too clever or cute. Light-hearted jests were interweaved with serious ideas, not an easy task for someone to write or read (and appreciate) who has been marooned too long in the world of education speak. The point is that there are hundreds of textbooks with simple sentences, where words are sanitized and emotions are anesthetized, so that the reader becomes numb without Novocain. That was not the book I wrote; the idea was to excite and provoke the reader and to combat dry rot of the mind.

Questions to Consider

1. How much concern do you have about our international test rankings? Do you feel the media has been fair in presenting the international test rankings to the American public?

2. The school day and school calendar were widely discussed topics. Do you believe American students should have an extended school day or school year? How much longer? For what school level or age group?

3. Television time and homework time are hotly debated issues. What are your views about curtailing TV time and increasing homework time among American children and youth? How practical or realistic are your views?

4. Several testing and social-class factors were mentioned to explain our international rankings. Do you feel these factors mask or explain our test scores? Do you feel they are valid or invalid, politically objective or biased?

5. The issues of shorter school vacations and continuous learning, as well as tutoring sessions and family values, were discussed in context with the learning gap between American and Asian students. How important is each of these factors in determining educational outcomes? Which one is most important? Why?

6. Bentley, Edmonson, Rosanvallon, Srinivasa, and Wang had different views for improving the curriculum. Of this group, which two characters or teachers had views similar to your views? In what way?

7. Use the Internet to find recent rankings of U.S. students on international tests. Has the American position improved or declined?

Recommended Readings

Gerald W. Bracey, *Bail Me Out* (Bloomington, IN: Phi Delta Kappan, 2000).

Stanley Elam, *How America Views Its Schools* (Bloomington, IN: Phi Delta Kappan, 1995).

Gary Orfield and Mindy Kornhaber, eds. *Raising Standards or Raising Barriers?* (Washington, DC: Brookings Institution, 2001).

Thomas Popkewitz, *Cultural History and Education* (New York: Routledge, 2001).

David Reynolds, *World Class Schools* (New York: Routledge, 2001).

Bibliography

A Nation at Risk (Washington, DC: National Commission on Excellence in Education, 1983).
Beginning with this government report, attention has turned to a host of policy reports for the last twenty years concerning the need for higher academic standards for all students, to hold teachers and principals accountable, and to increase federal aid for education of at-risk children. (8, 27)*

Adler, Mortimer J. *The Paideia Proposal: An Educational Syllabus* (New York: Macmillan, 1984).
A revival of *perennialism* and the *great books* idea, Adler recommended three teaching/learning experiences: (1) *organized knowledge* to be taught by didactic instruction, (2) development of *basic learning skills* by coaching, and (3) understanding of *ideas and values* to be taught by the Socratic method; these three areas of concentration are the same, previously outlined by John Dewey in *Democracy and Education*. (26, 27)

Apple, Michael. *Teachers and Texts* (New York: Routledge & Kegan Paul, 1986).
In a technological society, schools become distributors of cultural capital, which in turn leads to power for one group and domination of subordinate groups who lack this cultural capital (or knowledge). Although some educators label Apple as a neo-Marxist, he considers himself a *critical pedagogist*. (2)

Bennett, William. *The Broken Hearth: Reversing the Moral Collapse of the American Family* (New York: Doubleday, 2001).
Bennett writes and speaks about traditional values and virtues that characterize and rely on the nuclear family, church, and school, as well as such ideas as honesty, thrift, hard work, responsibility, patriotism, and heroism. (2, 26)

Berliner, David, and Bruce Biddle. *The Manufactured Crisis: Myths, Fraud, and the Attack on America's Public Schools* (Reading, MA: Addison-Wesley-Longman, 1995).
The critics have manipulated the media and professional journals in making it appear that teachers and schools are failing to educate most of their clientele, but this image contradicts reality; none of the new "reform" ideas such as vouchers, charter schools, or accountability schemes are likely to improve student international achievement scores, given the massive amount of child poverty in our country. (27)

Bestor, Arthur E. *The Restoration of Learning* (New York: Knopf, 1955).
An *essentialist* educator, Bestor argued that a good education should provide "sound training in fundamental ways of thinking" represented by the liberal arts and other disciplines that enhance "cultural understanding and intellectual power." (2, 26, 27)

Bloom, Benjamin S. *Stability and Change in Human Characteristics* (New York: Wiley, 1964).
This classic text rejected the position that intelligence is based mainly on genetic factors. Stressing the importance of early childhood *environment*, Bloom's research helped lead to the compensatory education and Head Start movements which are still with us today. (9)

Bloom, Benjamin S. *All Our Children Learning* (New York: McGraw-Hill, 1981).
Bloom distinguishes between time needed to learn and time available for learning; high-achieving students need less time than low-achieving students to learn the same material. The need is to vary instructional time for different individuals or groups of students for purpose of mastery instruction. (15)

---

*At the end of each reference, the numbers in parentheses indicate the corresponding chapters.

Bode, Boyd Henry. *Progressive Education at the Crossroads* (New York: Newson, 1938).
A *progressive* educator, Boyd warned that progressivism would fall to the wayside if it continued to focus on the child at the expense of content. (2)

Brameld, Theodore. *Patterns of Educational Philosophy* (New York: World, 1950).
An early *reconstructionist* philosopher, Brameld urged that teachers stand up for what is right, become change agents and encourage their students to do the same, and subsequently improve society. (2)

Brimmer, Andrew. "The Deepening Schism." Paper presented at Tuskegee University, Nashville, TN, April 1970.
Although blacks have made significant education and economic progress in terms of reducing achievement and income gaps between blacks and whites, beneath these overall improvements is a deepening *schism* within the black community between the able and less able, between the well prepared and the unprepared. (21)

Broudy, Harry S. *The Real World of the Public Schools* (New York: Harcourt, Brace, 1972).
"Everybody wants to talk about education, but virtually nobody has anything good to say about it." The basic solution is to improve school quality by raising standards and resisting reforms of political activists and political groups driven by their own agendas. (3)

Brown, H. Rap. *Die Nigger Die!* (New York: Dial Press, 1969).
A black nationalist who argued "violence is as American as cherry pie," "violence is a necessary part of revolutionary struggle," and "power comes from the barrel of a gun." (21)

Bruner, Jerome S. *The Process of Education* (Cambridge, MA: Harvard University Press, 1960).
Largely influenced by *Piagetian and environmental theory*, Bruner is most noted for the idea "that any subject can be taught in some intellectually honest form to any child at any stage of development," and that disciplines or subject matter should be taught in progressively more complex forms—implying the state of readiness, maturation, and cognitive growth development. (8, 13, 27)

Carmichael, Stokely and Charles V. Hamilton. *Black Power: The Politics of Liberation* (New York: Random House, 1967).
The black–white situation is based on colonialism and imperialism whereby blacks are subordinated and oppressed by the white power structure; blacks are urged to gain control of their own community institutions, including schools. (21)

Cleaver, Eldridge. *Soul on Ice* (New York: McGraw-Hill, 1968).
The head of the black nationalist movement called the Black Panthers, Cleaver outlined a militant black perspective regarding political ideology, propaganda, and community and institutional relations; the "struggle" rejected integration, promoted black political power, and called on nonwhites of the world to unite in their "struggle" against their white "oppressors." (21)

Coleman, Jerome S. *Equality of Educational Opportunity* (Washington, DC: U.S. Government Printing Office, 1966).
The most important *variables related to student achievement* are the child's family background, peer group, and social class of the school and community. School and teacher variables play a minor role; moreover, hard-to-change variables such as the teachers' experience and verbal scores on standardized tests correlate more with student achievement compared to easy-to-change variables such as teacher turnover or teacher absences. (9, 15, 21)

Comenius, John Amos. *The Visible World in Pictures*, rev. ed. (Syracuse, NY: Bordeen, 1887).
Generally considered the greatest education theorist of the seventeenth century, this Czech educator believed in the natural development of the child (which influenced Rousseau's thinking); he stressed natural and permissive methods of instruction, based on child growth and development, which still embody *progressive* teaching theory. (2)

Conant, James B. *The American High School Today* (New York: McGraw-Hill, 1959).
After visiting fifty-five high schools, Conant set down some twenty-one recommendations for improving high schools. As an *essentialist* educator, his major emphasis of reform was related to ability grouping and serving the needs of the highly gifted (top 3 percent of the student population) and academically talented (next 20 percent) in terms of scholastic aptitude. (7, 13, 26)

Conant, James B. *The Education of American Teachers* (New York: McGraw-Hill, 1964).
As a moderate critic of teachers and schools and as president of Harvard University, Conant outlined twenty-six recommendations for improving the education and performance of American teachers by recruiting teachers from the top 30 percent of the high-school graduating class, increasing their liberal arts studies, ensuring they student teach, having the foundations courses taught by professors of liberal arts, and assigning them to teaching duties they were specifically prepared to teach. (13, 26)

Counts, George S. *Dare the School Build a New Social Order?* (New York: John Day, 1932).
Counts criticized progressive educators for emphasizing child-centered, play schools at the expense of ignoring major social issues and for not developing a comprehensive theory of social welfare. An early *reconstructionist* educator, many of his reform ideas were later adopted by critical pedagogists and educational neo-Marxists. (2)

Darwin, Charles. *Origin of the Species* (London: John Murray, 1859).
The book that shook the foundation of the church's view of the universe and the notion of creationism. Darwin outlined a theory of biological evolutionary process and *survival of the fittest* to explain how animals and human societies evolve to more complex forms, characterized by intelligence and a variety of specialized tasks. His ideas influenced Herrnstein and Spencer (see separate entries). (26)

Dewey, John. *How We Think* (Lexington, MA: Heath, 1910).
The chief function of teaching and learning is to enhance rational thinking, problem solving and scientific inquiry and thus improve the child's reasoning process. (2)

Dewey, John. *Democracy and Education* (New York: Macmillan, 1916).
Dewey is the best known *progressive* educator and probably the most influential educator of the twentieth century; in this text, he examines the purposes of education in a democracy and sees education as a form of socialization and vehicle for improving society. (1, 2, 10, 26)

Dewey, John. *Experience and Education* (New York: Macmillan, 1938).
One of his latest books before his death, Dewey summed up his philosophy and tried to balance traditional and progressive philosophy and the idea of subject matter with the needs and interests of students. He warned against extreme philosophical positions or "isms." (2, 11, 26)

DuBridge, Lee.
Testifying before a U.S. Senate Committee in 1958 (at the height of the *Sputnik*/Cold War era) and in his role as president of the California Institute of Technology, he urged that science and mathematics be "singled out for federal support," scholarship money be provided for "unusually gifted and ambitious students," and that a student's education coincide with his intellectual abilities in terms of tracking and admission to college. (26)

Ehrlich, Paul. *The Population Bomb* (New York: Ballantine, 1968).
An eye-opening book written nearly thirty-five years ago, Ehrlich pointed out that the worldwide ecosystem and food supply was in jeopardy and could no longer support the growing population. Sometime in the twenty-first century, we can expect large portions of vegetation, topsoil, natural resources, and animal life (*Homosapiens* included) to be in short supply or threatened by global conditions. (26)

Freire, Paulo. *Pedagogy of the Oppressed* (New York: Herder & Herder, 1970).
Freire's best known book examines the relationship among culture, poverty, power, and politics of education; the need is for the oppressed to take action and overcome their oppression. He describes how oppressed people can move through different stages to ultimately take action and seize power. (2)

Freire, Paulo. *Pedagogy of Freedom: Ethics, Democracy and Civic Courage* (Boulder, CO: Rowman & Littlefield, 2000).
As a *neo-Marxist educator*, Freire urges teachers to help students examine major social and political issues on a domestic and global level. He outlines a curriculum that is less institutionalized, formal, and discriminatory for purposes of "emancipation." (1)

Froebel, Friedrich. *The Education of Man* (New York: Appleton, 1889).
A nineteenth-century German educator, Froebel is best known for his development of the *kindergarten*, what he called the "child's garden." He believed that three- and four-year-old children should attend school, and it should be organized around play and individual and group interests and activities. Froebel's kindergarten was first transplanted in the United States in Watertown, Wisconsin, in 1955 by Margaret Schurz. (2)

Gardner, Howard. *Frames of Mind: The Theory of Multiple Intelligences* (New York: Basic Books, 1983).
Gardner's well-known paradigm is this: Intelligence is not a monolithic concept but can be represented by one of eight different domains or talents including verbal, musical, spatial, personal/social, bodily kinesthetic, etc. Different children exhibit different domains or talents which should be nurtured by teachers and schools. (7, 15, 25)

Gardner, John W. *Excellence: Can We Be Equal and Excellent Too?*, rev. ed. (New York: W. W. Norton, 1995).
Gardner seeks to balance the notion of *excellence and equality*, suggesting that American schools and society can work to achieve both ends—and it must for their own social health and vitality. (1)

Giroux, Henry. *Teachers as Intellectuals: Toward a Critical Pedagogy of Learning* (Westport, CT: Bergin and Garvey, 1988).
Incorporating principles of *critical pedagogy* (analyzing, critiquing, and evaluating social and political issues), Giroux believes that the teacher must act as an intellectual and help transform and improve society. Teachers need to help students develop language literacy and theoretical skills to validate and critically engage others in different cultural milieu. (2)

Goleman, Daniel. *Emotional Intelligence* (New York: Bantam, 1995).
Ignoring the emotional aspects of humans is shortsighted. By neglecting the emotional thinking of students, we do them more disservice than if we shortchanged the development of their cognitive thinking. Both emotional and rational aspects of students (and adults) are crucial for complete living. (15)

Good, Thomas L., and Jere E. Brophy. *Looking in Classrooms*, 8th ed. (Reading, MA: Addison-Wesley-Longman, 2000).
A comprehensive book delineating generic methods of effective teaching; the focus is on *teacher products* (not processes) or student outcomes. (2)

Goodlad, John I. *A Place Called School: Prospects for the Future* (New York: McGraw-Hill, 1984). Probably his best known book, Goodlad points out that classrooms are places where emotions and feelings are kept "flat" or "neutral," where the focus is on "control," and where "enthusiasm" and "joy" are kept to a minimum—de-emphasized because of fear of losing control. (11, 27)

Goodlad, John I. *Teachers for Our Nation's Schools* (San Francisco: Jossey-Bass, 1990). Possibly the most influential *teacher-educator* of the last third of the twentieth century, Goodlad feels it is essential to build professional self-worth among future teachers, a sense of innovation and accountability, and a concern for moral issues for teaching in a democracy. (13)

Herrnstein, Richard, and Charles Murray. *The Bell Curve* (New York, Free Press, 1994). A highly controversial book which argues that genetic differences among groups produce differences in IQ, learning patterns, and abilities; the connection between IQ, meritocracy, and social position is purported. Critics respond that environmental factors, particularly family and schooling, influence IQ and school achievement, and success or failure and status differences. (21)

Hirsch, E. D. *Cultural Literacy: What Every American Needs to Know* (Boston: Houghton Mifflin, 1987). A national best-selling book, Hirsch (a modern-day *essentialist*) focuses on background knowledge necessary for cultural (he calls it "functional") literacy and effective communication for our nation's students; the book includes some five thousand names, phrases and concepts every literate American should know. (1, 2, 11, 13, 26, 27)

Hutchins, Robert M. *The Higher Learning in America* (New Haven, CT: Yale University Press, 1962). Hutchins was president of the University of Chicago, a *perennialist theorist*, and recommended the *great books* of Western civilization as the crux of the curriculum. Whereas most educators describe the ideal education in terms of subject matter, he described it as "one that develops intellectual power" and is "calculated to develop the mind." (1)

Illich, Ivan. *Deschooling Society* (New York: Harper & Row, 1971). An early *neo-Marxist* education book, the author wants to end the schools' monopoly over education and replace schools with informal community networks, taught by friends, peers, and skilled adults. (2)

Jencks, Christopher. *Inequality: A Reassessment of the Effect of Family and Schooling in America* (New York: Basic Books, 1972). School achievement depends largely on a single factor, namely, family characteristics of the students; all other factors are secondary or irrelevant. This is little evidence that school reform or special programs can substantially influence student outcomes or reduce inequality among students. (9)

Jensen, Arthur R. "How Much Can We Boost IQ and Scholastic Achievement?" *Harvard Educational Review* (Winter 1969), pp. 1–123. This article sparked a major controversy about the role of heredity in determining intelligence and the differences in cognitive skills and achievement tests between blacks and whites. It also sparked a host of rebuttals, centering around racial prejudice and the biases of standardized tests. Thirty years later, this controversy has not disappeared. (21)

Jersild, Arthur. *When Teachers Face Themselves* (New York: Teachers College Press, Columbia University, 1955). A classic text about the concerns, anxieties, and feelings of teachers; the search for the meaning of teaching; and the need to face and be comfortable with one's self on a personal and professional level. (16)

Kilpatrick, William H. *Foundations of Method* (New York: Macmillan, 1925).
The progressive education movement has consisted of many groups, and among the most influential in the early twentieth century was the *activity-centered curriculum* spearheaded by Kilpatrick. Both Kilpatrick and Dewey were colleagues at Columbia University when Kilpatrick published the book. (1, 2)

King, Martin Luther, Jr. *Where Do We Go From Here?: Chaos or Community* (New York: Harper & Row, 1967).
King outlines his philosophy of nonviolence and protest strategy against segregation; opposition to civil rights demonstrations are also described. (21)

Koerner, James D. *The Miseducation of American Teachers* (Boston: Houghton Mifflin, 1963).
A highly critical book about the educational Establishment, especially teacher preparation institutions. Koerner saw a need to reduce education courses and beef up the remaining ones. (13, 26)

Kohn, Alfie. *The Schools Our Children Deserve* (Boston: Houghton Mifflin, 1999).
Kohn is anti-tracking, anti-testing, and anti-standards-based education. All of these popular reform measures (tracking, testing, and standards-based education), he argues, go hand-in-hand with a shallow approach to teaching and learning. (7)

Landry, Bart. *The New Black Middle Class* (Berkeley: University of California Press, 1987).
Between 1950 and 1980 the number of black families earning $50,000 or more nearly quadrupled; however, many black Americans still live in poverty, indicating a *split* between a growing middle-class segment and a larger segment residing in urban squalor and exhibiting socially dysfunctional behavior—crime, delinquency, drug abuse, etc. (21)

Lortie, Dan C. *Schoolteacher: A Sociological Study* (Chicago: University of Chicago Press, 1975).
A classic text about the teaching profession. Teaching ranks in between occupations characterized by "casual" entry and those that place difficult demands on potential members; reasons for entering the profession are internalized during childhood and triggered in adulthood. (12)

Malcolm X. *Malcolm X Speaks* (New York: Merit, 1965).
Although Malcolm's views continuously evolved and became more tolerant over the years, he rejected Western civilization and white society as evil, decadent, corrupt, and oppressive; the law protected the "enemy" or power structure because it was devised by them, and there was an appeal to followers as bearers of racial pride and power. (21)

Mann, Horace. *The Republic and the School*, rev. ed. (New York Teachers College Press, Columbia University, 1957).
Mann was a leading proponent of the *common school movement*. As a Massachusetts legislator and later as the first Massachusetts commissioner of education, he convinced taxpayers that it was in their best interests to support public schools. (1)

Mayer, Martin. *The Schools* (New York: Harper & Brothers, 1961).
A freelance writer, *moderate critic*, and New York City school board member, Mayer described what is taught and learned in schools, how human daily events shape classrooms and schools, and how routine and rules shape the culture of teaching and teacher–student relationships. (16)

McLaren, Peter. *Revolutionary Multiculturalism* (Boulder, CO: Westview Press, 1997).
A *radical educator*, sometimes called a *neo-Marxist*, McLaren seeks to reconceptualize and reconstitute social relations, cultural formations, and institutional arrangements so that the exploited and oppressed can be emancipated from the ruling and dominant groups. (2)

McWhorter, John H. *Losing the Race: Self-Sabotage in Black America* (New York: Simon and Schuster, 2001).
   If anyone is looking to stir up controversy about black and white achievement gaps, and use the "race card" as a strategy, then McWhorter's book will do it. His basic premise is that the "cult of anti-intellectualism" and "cult of victimology" have gripped black America and is the major reason why blacks lag behind whites in the academic arena, not prejudice on poor schools. (21)

Montessori, Maria. *The Discovery of the Child*, rev. ed. (New York: Ballentine, 1972).
   A *progressive educator* who worked in the slums of Italy at the turn of the twentieth century. Her teaching principles mixed play with cognitive activities—what she called "practical, sensory, and formal skills." (2)

Moynihan, Pat. *The Negro Family: The Case for National Action* (Washington, DC: U.S. Government Printing Offices, 1965).
   This report created a major controversy because of its implications that the illegitimacy rates and family structure of blacks were the major cause of blacks remaining in a lower-class status. Jesse Jackson was to make a similar point twenty-five years later without subsequent controversy. (9)

Myrdal, Gunnar. *An American Dilemma* (New York: Harper & Row, 1944).
   Considered a classic text on race relations, the discrepancies between the ideal and reality of the situation for black and white people in this country was the subject of what Myrdal called the *American dilemma*. (21)

Neill, A. S. *Summerhill: A Radical Approach to Child Rearing* (New York: Hart, 1960).
   A *romantic progressivist*, Neill operated a private school, Summerhill, in Suffolk, England, for more than forty years. He incorporated a school philosophy based on the innate goodness of the child (the views of Rousseau, Pestalozzi, and Froebel), and the replacement of authority for freedom which Dewey warned. Neill claimed that the "child is innately wise and realistic." (27)

Oakes, Jeannie, et al. *Becoming Good American Schools* (San Francisco: Jossey-Bass, 2000).
   American society embraces democratic ends and equal opportunity for its schools but resists such ends and opportunity by ability grouping and tracking students. How do educators make sense of contradictions like these which are inherent in the school reform literature? (7)

Passow, A. Harry. *Education in Depressed Areas* (New York: Teachers College Press, Columbia University, 1963).
   As an outgrowth of a Columbia University workshop, Passow published one of the first books on the inner-city child (described as the "deprived," "disadvantaged," or "underprivileged" child during the early period of research on the subject). He brought together several psychologists and teaching/learning specialists who examined the roots and causes of social, cultural, and psychological differences between lower-class and middle-class students. (26)

Perrone, Vito. *Teacher with a Heart* (New York: Teachers College Press, Columbia University, 1998).
   The teacher who makes a difference understands that teaching is about personal relationships, sensitivity, and caring about the lives of students. (16)

Pestalozzi, Johann. *How Gertrude Teaches Her Children* (Syracuse, NY: Bordeen, 1900).
A Swiss *progressive educator* of the nineteenth century, he insisted that the young child learn through his senses rather than with written words; his educational principles were based on Rousseau's theories. He developed the "general" and "special" method of teaching young children. The general method provided emotional security, trust, and affection for the children; the special method considered the auditory and visual senses of children in the teaching process (2).

Piaget, Jean. *The Psychology of Intelligence* (London: Broadway, 1950).
The leading *cognitive psychologist* of the twentieth century, Piaget was instrumental in showing that the child's thinking process corresponds with stages of growth or maturation, and by approximately age fifteen youth can formally reason as adults. (2)

Ravitch, Diane. *Left Back: A Century of Failed School Reforms* (New York: Simon and Schuster, 2000).
A highly controversial book, blaming progressive education for poor academic standards and permissive methods of teaching; somewhat like the books written by *essentialists* during the *Sputnik* era. (13, 16, 26)

Resnick, Lauren. *Education and Learning to Think* (Washington, DC: National Academy Press, 1987).
A cognitive psychologist with a *constructionist* view of learning, Resnick believes that students learn through a process of making connections between new information and prior information; constructionists stress the need to relate new content to knowledge and experiences students already possess. (13)

Rickover, Hyman. *Education and Freedom* (New York: E. P. Dutton, 1959).
An *essentialist* thinker along the lines of Bestor, Rickover maintained that the school curriculum should emphasize reading, writing, arithmetic, and research skills at the elementary level and science, mathematics, history, English, and foreign languages at the high school level. Education involves perspiration—and not play or social activities. (2, 26, 27)

Riessman, Frank. *The Culturally Deprived Child* (New York: Harper & Row, 1962).
Riessman was one of the first educators to describe inner-city children as having a number of positive characteristics that were overlooked by people (teachers, social workers, etc.) who worked with them: exceptional physical orientation, hidden verbal ability, creative potential, group cohesiveness, informality, sense of humor, frankness, and ability to manipulate others. He argued the "deprived" child had his or her own culture and that this culture was in conflict in middle-class schools. (26)

Rosenshine, Barak, and Carla Meister. "Reciprocal Teaching: A Review of the Research," *Review of Educational Research* (October 1994), pp. 479–530.
A direct instructional approach to teaching and learning which incorporates practice, drill, explanations, feedback, assessment, review, and further testing; a popular method of teaching low-achieving students. (2)

Rousseau, Jean Jacques. *Emile*, rev. ed. (New York: Teachers College Press, Columbia University, 1962). (Originally published in Amsterdam, 1762.)
Rousseau's fundamental theory is "Everything is good if it comes from the hand of ... Nature; but everything degenerates in the hand of man." Education should emphasize the natural instincts and interests of the child. (2)

Rugg, Harold, and Ann Shumaker. *The Child-Centered School* (New York: World Book, 1928).
In an era in which progressive educators stressed the need for student input in planning the curriculum, Rugg, who was a *reconstructionist* and *radical educator*, advocated that curriculum specialists and teachers should develop curriculum. (2)

Sarason, Seymour. *Teaching as a Performing Art* (New York: Teachers College Press, Columbia University, 1999).
The teacher is described as a performing artist, a person who instructs and connects with his or her audience (students) as an actor; the art of teaching involves both thinking and feeling, both knowing and valuing. (16)

Shulman, Lee S. "Knowledge and Teaching: Foundations of the New Reform," *Harvard Educational Review* (February 1987), pp. 1–22.
As with Resnick, Shulman is a *constructivist* who believes that new knowledge is built on old knowledge structures; students must elaborate, question, and examine new content in relation to familiar content, thus the process of reflecting and reasoning is enhanced. (13)

Sizer, Theodore R. *Horace's Compromise* (Boston: Houghton Mifflin, 1984).
Sizer writes clearly and simply, reminding us that the basis of school reform should come from our teachers; he asks us to think about changing the curriculum to promote moral character and ethics, as well as intellectual thought and communication (mainly through spoken language, visual expression, and writing). (16, 27)

Sowell, Thomas. *Black Education: Myths and Tragedies* (New York: McKay, 1972).
Among his many books on race, education, and economics, this is one of Sowell's earliest ones to examine the relationship between *black academic achievement*, hard work and studying, and making no excuses for black students who do not meet academic standards. (15, 21)

Spencer, Herbert. *Education: Intellectual, Moral and Physical* (New York: Appleton, 1860).
Because of the *laws of nature*, only intelligent and productive populations adapt to environmental changes—and exhibit social, economic, and scientific progress. Less intelligent, weak, or lazy people fail intellectually, morally, and/or physically and either become second-class groups or slowly disappear. (27)

Sternberg, Robert. *Metaphors of Mind: Conceptions of the Nature of Intelligence* (New York: Cambridge University Press, 1990).
Sternberg distinguishes between *critical and creative thinking* and among different forms of critical thinking (higher order, performance based, and knowledge based) and creative thinking (artistic, musical, scientific, manual, and so on). Whereas critical thinking often suggests problem solving and convergent behaviors, creative thinking often suggests novel responses and divergent behaviors. (7, 25)

Toffler, Alvin. *Future Shock* (New York: Random House, 1970).
A well-known *futurist*, Toffler noted over thirty years ago that we were entering a period of "future shock." We have too many goods and services from which to choose, and our ability to choose wisely from all of these options is becoming increasingly limited because of human overload (for example, try choosing the best long-distance phone company or cell phone). (27)

Tyler, Ralph W. *Basic Principles of Curriculum and Instruction* (Chicago: University of Chicago Press, 1949).
Originally written as a course syllabus for his students at the University of Chicago, the book was published in 1949 and has gone through over 40 printings. In 128 pages, Tyler covers the basic components of planning and developing a curriculum. (8)

Von Braun, Wernher.
A German-educated missile expert (who once was in charge of the Nazi rocket project) and head of the U.S. *Apollo* moon-landing mission, Von Braun appeared before the same U.S. Senate Committee as DuBridge, in 1958, and urged ending "family life," "life adjustment," and "human relations" subjects and adopting the European system of education, which emphasized *technical and scientific subjects*, tracking, and academic excellence. (26)

Wilson, William J. *The Truly Disadvantaged* (Chicago: University of Chicago Press, 1987).
Many blacks still live in neighborhoods with households headed by a single woman and where rates of crime, delinquency, drug abuse, and teenage pregnancy are very high; poverty schools in big cities are overloaded with social and educational problems that call for highly competent and educated teachers. (15, 21)

Wright, Benjamin, and Shirley A. Tuska. "From a Dream to Life in the Psychology of Becoming a Teacher," *School Review* (September 1968), pp. 259–293.
The authors' research shows that teaching is rooted in the expressions of early yearnings and fantasies of childhood and adolescence, especially among many female teachers. (12)